Learning to Read Biblical Hebrew

Learning to Read Biblical Hebrew: An Introductory Grammar

Robert Ray Ellis

Baylor University Press
Waco, Texas USA

Cover Design by Joan Osth

Ellis, Robert Ray.
Learning to read biblical Hebrew : an introductory grammar / Robert Ray Ellis.
p. cm.
Includes index.
ISBN-13: 978-1-932792-56-0
1. Hebrew language—Grammar. 2. Hebrew language—Grammar—Problems, exercises, etc. I. Title.

PJ4567.3.E45 2006
492.4'82421—dc22

2006019302

Printed in the United States of America on acid-free paper with a minimum of 30% pcw recycled content.

Dedicated to
Teresa, Katherine, and Laura,
who are שִׂמְחַת גִּילִי

Table of Contents

Acknowledgments

I am grateful to my family for making this book possible. My parents taught me to love language, and my father planted the seed for this grammar when he taught Greek to me from the textbook he wrote. My wife and daughters, who are God's greatest gifts to me, have sacrificially given time for me to work on the project. Teresa unfailingly loves and encourages me with her deep wisdom. Katherine and Laura inspire me with their joy for life and goodness.

Harry Hunt, my Hebrew teacher and mentor, taught me to love this remarkable language and to cultivate compassionate excellence. Southwestern Baptist Theological Seminary provided a sabbatical to begin this project, and then several years later Hardin-Simmons University and Logsdon School of Theology provided a sabbatical that allowed for its completion. Many graduate student assistants have painstakingly helped with this grammar through the years – most recently, Jason Patrick, Nathan Maxwell, Meredith Stone, Cory Murman, Walt Henson, and Amanda Cutbirth. Finally, I am grateful to all my students who year by year teach and inspire me with their hunger to read the ancient sacred words of the Hebrew Bible.

לֹא לָנוּ יְהוָה לֹא לָנוּ כִּי־לְשִׁמְךָ תֵּן כָּבוֹד
Psalm 115:1

Robert R. Ellis
Logsdon Seminary
Hardin-Simmons University
Abilene, Texas

Note: For free online helps related to this Hebrew grammar go to www.hsutx.edu/hebrewgrammar.

Abbreviations and Symbols

Ab	absolute
act	active
adj	adjective
adv	adverb
art	article
BDB	Brown, Driver, and Briggs
BHS	*Biblia Hebraica Stuttgatensia*
cohort	cohortative
conj	conjunction
Cs	construct
dem adj	demonstrative adjective
Du	dual
Eng	English
F	feminine
FP	feminine, plural
FS	feminine, singular
G/N	gender and number
hif	hifil
hit	hitpael
hof	hofal
impf	imperfect
impv	imperative
inf	infinitive
juss	jussive
M	masculine
Mm	*Masora magna*
MP	masculine, plural
Mp	*Masora parva*
MS	masculine, singular
MT	Masoretic text
N	noun
NFP	noun, feminine, plural
NFS	noun, feminine, singular
nif	nifal
NMP	noun, masculine, plural
NMS	noun, masculine, singular
P	plural
part	participle
pass	passive
perf	perfect
P/G/N	person, gender, and number
prep	preposition
pron	pronoun
PS	pronominal suffix
S	singular
V	verb
vav conj	*vav* conjunction
vav cons	*vav* consecutive
1CP	first, common, plural
1CS	first, common, singular
2FP	second, feminine, plural
2FS	second, feminine, singular
2MP	second, masculine, plural
2MS	second, masculine, singular
3CP	third, common, plural
3FP	third, feminine, plural
3FS	third, feminine, singular
3MP	third, masculine, plural
3MS	third, masculine, singular

<table>
<tr><td>▸</td><td>Indicates that an example follows</td></tr>
<tr><td>✓</td><td>Indicates that a special note follows</td></tr>
<tr><td>|</td><td>Stands between Hebrew words that are not syntactically connected</td></tr>
<tr><td>></td><td>Indicates that a Hebrew verb root follows</td></tr>
<tr><td>□</td><td>Stands for an unspecified Hebrew consonant</td></tr>
<tr><td>◁</td><td>Stands for an unspecified Hebrew imperfect verb prefix</td></tr>
<tr><td>▷</td><td>Stands for an unspecified Hebrew suffix</td></tr>
<tr><td>└──┘</td><td>Stands for a Hebrew word of unspecified length</td></tr>
<tr><td>└─</td><td>Stands for the end of a Hebrew word of unspecified length</td></tr>
<tr><td>/</td><td>Marks division between syllables in transliteration</td></tr>
<tr><td>˂</td><td>Major accent on a Hebrew word (placed above a consonant)</td></tr>
<tr><td>´</td><td>Major accent in transliteration (placed above a vowel)</td></tr>
</table>

Lesson 1

Consonants

1A Consonants

1. Introduction

a. The only true letters in the Hebrew alphabet are consonants. In biblical Hebrew vowels are indicated by a system of markings, called "pointings," which appear in connection with consonants. Vowel pointings will be discussed in the next lesson.

b. In Hebrew the consonants which form words, and the words which form sentences, are read from right to left, instead of left to right as in English. In the history of writing the Hebrew language various scripts have been used. This Grammar employs the square script that appears in contemporary Hebrew Bibles.

c. On the following page is a chart which presents the consonants of the Hebrew alphabet, giving their names, forms, transliteration (or phonetic value), and pronunciation.

(1) The names of the consonants – like other grammatical terms throughout this Grammar – are written in English with simplified spellings to make them easier for beginning students to remember. The names of the consonants in Hebrew appear in Appendix 1, section 1.

(2) The following consonant chart provides a pronunciation system based on modern Hebrew. Traditional or classical pronunciation is also indicated where it varies from modern Hebrew.

2. Consonant chart

Name	Form	Trans-literation	Pronunciation	
			Modern	Traditional
Alef [*Aleph*][1]	א	ʾ	{silent}	
Bet	בּ ב	b ḇ [bh, v]	*b* as in *boy* *v* as in *vine*	
Gimel	גּ ג	g ḡ [gh]	*g* as in *girl*	*g* as in *girl* *g* as in *leg*
Dalet	דּ ד	d ḏ [dh]	*d* as in *door*	*d* as in *door* *th* as in *thin*
He	ה	h	*h* as in *hat*	
Vav [*Waw*]	ו	v [w]	*v* as in *vine*[2]	*w* as in *well*
Zayin	ז	z	*z* as in *zeal*	
Het	ח	ḥ [ch]	*ch* as in *Bach*	
Tet	ט	ṭ	*t* as in *time*	*t* as in *cut*
Yod	י	y	*y* as in *yes*[2]	
Kaf [*Kaph*]	כּ כ ך[3]	k ḵ [kh]	*k* as in *king* *ch* as in *Bach*	
Lamed	ל	l	*l* as in *let*	
Mem	מ ם	m	*m* as in *met*	
Nun	נ ן	n	*n* as in *net*	
Samek	ס	s	*s* as in *set*	
Ayin	ע	ʿ	{silent}	
Pe	פּ פ ף	p p̄ [ph, f]	*p* as in *pet* *f* as in *fun*	
Sade	צ ץ	ṣ	*ts* as in *nets*	
Qof [*Qoph*]	ק	q [ḳ]	*k* as in *king*	*k* as in *bark*
Resh	ר	r	*r* as in *rich*	
Sin	שׂ	ś	*s* as in *set*	
Shin	שׁ	š [sh]	*sh* as in *shoe*	
Tav [*Taw*]	תּ ת	t ṯ [th]	*t* as in *time*	*t* as in *time* *th* as in *thin*

[1] Brackets indicate alternatives that may be found in other Hebrew resources.

[2] The pronunciation of ו and י may vary when combined with vowels. See the next lesson.

[3] When two forms appear on a line, the second is a "final form."

3. Characteristics of certain consonants

a. Final forms

Most consonants have the same form whether they appear at the beginning, middle, or end of a word. However, five consonants – *kaf*, *mem*, *nun*, *pe*, and *sade* – have different forms, depending upon where the consonant appears in a word. For these five consonants the "medial forms" of כ, מ, נ, פ and צ are used when the consonants appear at the beginning or in the middle of a word. The "final forms" of ך, ם, ן, ף, and ץ are used if the consonant appears at the end of a word. The following words illustrate the use of the medial and final forms.

- כמוך ("like you") has medial and final *kaf*s and a medial *mem*.
- מכם ("from you") has medial and final *mem*s and a medial *kaf*.
- נתן ("give") has medial and final *nun*s.
- צרף ("refine") has a medial *sade* and a final *pe*.
- פרץ ("break through") has a medial *pe* and a final *sade*.

b. *Begadkefat* consonants

(1) The six consonants בּ, גּ, דּ, כּ, פּ, and תּ may appear with a dot in the center (as just written), or without the dot as ב, ג, ד, כ, פ, and ת. The dot is a *dagesh-lene* whose nature will be discussed later. A popular mnemonic device for remembering these six consonants is *begadkefat*, which employs the first letter in the name of each consonant.

(2) Two of the *begadkefat* consonants also have final forms: *kaf* and *pe*. The final ך and ף cannot take the dot which is a *dagesh-lene*.

c. Guttural consonants

Four consonants are known as gutturals, since originally they were pronounced primarily in the throat. They are א, ה, ח, and ע. As gutturals they have some unique features which will be discussed in future lessons. The consonant ר sometimes acts in the same manner as a guttural.

d. Labial consonants

Three consonants are known as labials, since they are pronounced primarily with the lips. They are בּ, מ, and פּ.

e. Quiescent consonants

(1) א, ה, ו, and י are called quiescent consonants because they sometimes quiesce

or become silent, losing their consonantal properties. For example, while consonants at the beginning or in the middle of a word normally have vowel pointings, in some situations the quiescents lose their ability to receive a vowel. This and other characteristics of quiescents will be discussed in future lessons.

(2) When ה appears at the end of a word it can have a dot, called a *mappiq* (מַפִּיק = "pronounced"), which strengthens the ה so that it retains its consonantal character rather than quiescing.

- לָהּ ("to her") has a *mappiq* in the הּ, which means it does not quiesce.

f. Sibilant consonants

Five consonants are known as sibilants because their pronunciation involves an *s* sound. They are ז, ס, צ, שׂ and שׁ.

4. Writing the forms of the consonants

When learning the write the forms of the consonants, the student must take care to distinguish between certain forms which might easily be confused with one another. Note the distinctions in the following pairs.

(1) ג ב	(6) ר ד	(11) ן ו	(16) ם מ
(2) כ ב	(7) ח ה	(12) ר ו	(17) ס מ
(3) נ ג	(8) ת ח	(13) מ ט	(18) ס ם
(4) ז ד	(9) ז ו	(14) נ כ	(19) צ ע
(5) ך ד	(10) י ו	(15) ן ך	(20) שׁ שׂ

5. Transliteration

a. Knowing the transliteration of Hebrew has several advantages. It allows one to comprehend Hebrew that is written only in transliterated form. It also permits the easy comparison of transliterated Hebrew with transliterated words from other Semitic languages (that is, other ancient-Near-Eastern languages in the same family as Hebrew). For the beginning student transliteration can be an aid in learning the correct pronunciation of words; however, the student must come to the point of being able to pronounce Hebrew without the help of transliteration.

b. While Hebrew is read from right to left, transliteration is read from left to right (in the normal English manner), as the following examples illustrate. These Hebrew words are spelled with consonants only. Transliterations appear to the right, as well as translations in parentheses.

(1)	אכל	ʾk̲l	("eat")	(16)	גּדול	gd̲vl	("great")
(2)	גּם	gm	("also")	(17)	מעשׂה	mʿśh	("work")
(3)	שׂדה	śd̲h	("field")	(18)	חסד	ḥsd̲	("steadfast love")
(4)	דּבר	db̲r	("word")	(19)	אלף	ʾlp̄	("thousand")
(5)	הלך	hlk̲	("go")	(20)	נגשׁ	ng̲š	("approach")
(6)	תּחת	tḥt	("beneath")	(21)	קטן	qṭn	("small")
(7)	נפשׁ	np̄š	("living being")	(22)	זהב	zhb̲	("gold")
(8)	טוב	ṭvb̲	("good")	(23)	דּרך	drk̲	("way")
(9)	כּהן	khn	("priest")	(24)	שׂים	śym	("set")
(10)	סור	svr	("turn aside")	(25)	חלץ	ḥlṣ	("withdraw")
(11)	נפל	np̄l	("fall")	(26)	אנכי	ʾnk̲y	("I")
(12)	צבא	ṣb̲ʾ	("army")	(27)	כּסף	ksp̄	("silver")
(13)	תּוך	tvk̲	("midst")	(28)	צדיק	ṣd̲yq	("righteous")
(14)	בּגד	bg̲d̲	("garment")	(29)	פּלשׁתּי	plšt̲y	("Philistine")
(15)	פּנים	pnym	("face")	(30)	מזבּח	mzbḥ	("altar")

6. Pronunciation

a. Some Hebrew consonants have sounds which are very difficult for English-speaking persons to reproduce. The **א** and **ע** are glottal stops (producing guttural sounds) that are especially challenging. They may be imitated by a slight stopping of the breath. However, for the sake of simplicity they are treated in this Grammar as if they are silent letters.

b. Theoretically, the *begadkefat* consonants have harder or sharper sounds when the dot or *dagesh-lene* is present, and softer or duller sounds when the *dagesh-lene* is absent. However, this softening of the *begadkefat*s when they lack the *dagesh-lene* actually occurs with only three of these consonants in modern Hebrew pronunciation. These three are *bet*, *kaf*, and *pe*:

בּ	=	*b* (as in *boy*)	ב	=	*v* (as in *vine*)
כּ	=	*k* (as in *king*)	כ	=	*ch* (as in *Bach*)
פּ	=	*p* (as in *pet*)	פ	=	*f* (as in *fun*)

The presence or absence of the *dagesh-lene* does not change the pronunciation of the other three *begadkefat* consonants:

גּ or ג	=	*g* (as in *girl*)
דּ or ד	=	*d* (as in *door*)
תּ or ת	=	*t* (as in *time*)

c. The pronunciation of ח and כ involve a hard *ch* sound which is spoken low in the throat, like the German *ch*, as in *Bach*.

d. The pronunciation of צ involves the eliding of two consonantal sounds: *t* followed immediately by *s*, as in the word *nets*.

Lesson 1: Exercises

a. Repeatedly write and pronounce the Hebrew consonants until their forms and sounds become familiar.

b. Section 1A.4 lists pairs of consonants that might easily be confused with one another. Write each pair three times, making sure to form the letters distinctly. While writing them, note how the pairs of letters may be distinguished from one another through such features as curved or pointed corners, or the presence or absence of "tittles" (or "tabs").

c. Reproduce from memory the consonant chart in section 1A.2, with the exception of the traditional pronunciation and items in brackets.

d. From memory list the consonants in the following categories.

(1) Gutturals	(3) Quiescents
(2) Labials	(4) Sibilants

e. Practice transliterating the Hebrew words in section 1A.5b. While doing this exercise, cover the transliterations that appear beside the words. When finished check the work against the answers in the book.

f. The following words from the Hebrew Bible are written with consonants only; the spelling of some is modified to make them appropriate for this lesson. Rewrite the words in Hebrew and then transliterate them, noting their resemblance to familiar biblical names or terms. A scripture reference for each word appears in parentheses.

(1)	אלהים	(Ge 1:1)	(21)	זרבבל	(Ezr 2:2)
(2)	יהוה	(Ge 2:4)	(22)	גּשׁן	(Ge 45:10)
(3)	תּרח	(Ge 11:24)	(23)	סיני	(Ex 19:1)
(4)	אברם	(Ge 11:26)	(24)	כּנען	(Jos 5:12)
(5)	שׂרי[1]	(Ge 12:5)	(25)	ארץ	(1Sa 13:19)
(6)	לוט	(Ge 12:5)	(26)	ישׂראל	(1Sa 13:19)
(7)	מלכּיצדק	(Ge 14:18)	(27)	ירדן[2]	(Nu 26:3)
(8)	הגר	(Ge 16:1)	(28)	ערבה	(Dt 1:7)
(9)	ישׁמעאל	(Ge 16:11)	(29)	שׁפלה	(Dt 1:7)
(10)	אברהם	(Ge 17:5)	(30)	נגב	(Dt 1:7)
(11)	שׂרה	(Ge 17:15)	(31)	לבנון	(Dt 3:25)
(12)	יצחק	(Ge 17:19)	(32)	שׁכם	(Ge 12:6)
(13)	אבימלך	(Ge 20:2)	(33)	בּיתאל	(Ge 12:8)
(14)	רבקה	(Ge 22:23)	(34)	חברון	(Ge 13:18)
(15)	גּדעון	(Jdg 6:11)	(35)	מגדדּו	(Jos 12:21)
(16)	נתן	(2Sa 5:14)	(36)	גּרזים	(Jdg 9:7)
(17)	אסתּר	(Est 2:7)	(37)	ירושׁלם	(2Sa 5:5)
(18)	מרדּכי	(Est 2:7)	(38)	שׁבבּת	(Ex 20:8)
(19)	המן	(Est 3:1)	(39)	שׂרפים	(Isa 6:2)
(20)	דּניאל	(Da 1:6)	(40)	שׁלום	(Nu 6:26)

g. Find in a Hebrew Bible words (21) to (40) from the preceding exercise. Note that from the perspective of English-speaking persons, the Hebrew Bible is read from back to front. If one is using the *Biblia Hebraica Stuttgartensia* (*BHS*) – the standard edition for academic purposes, a table of contents appears at the end of the prolegomena (after page LV). Although this table employs Latin and Hebrew terms, most of the names of biblical books can be easily deciphered. While finding the words listed above in *BHS*, ignore for now the markings around the consonants (most

[1] Note that in this word and several others a *yod* or *vav* sometimes seems to represent a vowel rather than a consonant (with *yod* = *e* or *i* and *vav* = *o* or *u*). The following lesson will explain how these two consonants sometimes function to represent vowels. In this exercise simply give their consonantal transliteration.

[2] Notice that the traditional English transliteration of Hebrew names sometimes renders a י as *j* rather than *y*. Use the technically correct *y* for the purposes of this exercise.

of which are vowel pointings). Also note that *BHS* occasionally alters the spelling of the words, sometimes adding prefixed letters or omitting doubled consonants. The significance of these differences will be explained in future lessons.

h. Sometimes poetic texts in the Hebrew Bible employ an acrostic as a literary device, with the result that successive stichs (or lines) of poetry begin with successive consonants of the Hebrew alphabet.

   (1) Notice the use of an acrostic in Psalm 34 by looking in a Hebrew Bible. In *BHS* the pattern is emphasized by listing the successive letters of the Hebrew alphabet in the margin. Observe that the Psalm 34 acrostic does not have separate lines for *sin* and *shin*, a typical feature of Hebrew acrostics (since the two letters would appear the same in an unpointed [pre-Masoretic] text). Besides the *sin* and *shin*, one other letter is missing from the acrostic in Psalm 34. Identify which consonant is missing.

   (2) Find at least one other Psalm which employs an acrostic and observe whether or not the consonantal pattern is complete.

Lesson 2

VOWELS

2A VOWELS

1. Introduction

a. Originally biblical Hebrew was written only with consonants; no vowels appeared in the text. When reading one had to supply the vowels from one's knowledge of the language. Later in the development of Hebrew a few of the consonants were used to indicate the presence of certain vowels. Around AD 500-1000 a group of Jewish scholars called Masoretes (from *massorah* [מַסּוֹרָה] = "tradition") introduced an ingenious system for indicating all of the vowels in the Hebrew Bible. Their system designates vowels by means of pointings or marks (mostly dots and dashes) which are placed around the consonants in such a way that the consonantal text itself is not altered. The resulting pointed Hebrew Bible is known as the Masoretic text (*MT*).

b. The chart on the following page groups Hebrew vowels in two broad classifications: full vowels and half vowels. Full vowels are further divided into three subgroups: short, long and naturally-long. Half vowels are divided into two subgroups: simple *sheva* and composite *shevas*.

c. The chart also presents the name,[1] form, transliteration, and approximate pronunciation of each vowel. The location of the vowels in relation to consonants is indicated by use of the symbol □ which stands for a consonant.

[1] The names of the consonants in Hebrew appear in Appendix 1, section 1.

2. Vowel chart

a. Full Vowels

(1) Short

Name	Form	Trans-literation	Pronunciation: Modern	Pronunciation: Traditional
Patah	□ַ	a	*a* as in *father*	*a* as in *had*
Segol	□ֶ	e	*e* as in *bed*	
Hireq	□ִ	i	*i* as in *machine*	*i* as in *hit*
Qames-hatuf	□ָ	o	*o* as in *row*	*o* as in *top*
Qibbus	□ֻ	u	*u* as in *rule*	*u* as in *nut*

(2) Long

Name	Form	Trans-literation	Pronunciation: Modern	Pronunciation: Traditional
Qames	□ָ	ā	*a* as in *father*	
Sere	□ֵ	ē	*e* as in *bed*	*e* as in *they*
Holem	□ֹ	ō	*o* as in *row*	

(3) Naturally-long

Name	Form	Trans-literation	Pronunciation: Modern	Pronunciation: Traditional
Sere-yod	□ֵי	ê	*e* as in *they*	
Hireq-yod	□ִי	î	*i* as in *machine*	
Holem-vav [*-waw*][1]	□וֹ	ô	*o* as in *row*	
Shureq	□וּ	û	*u* as in *rule*	

b. Half vowels

(1) Simple *sheva*

Name	Form	Trans-literation	Pronunciation: Modern	Pronunciation: Traditional
Sheva [*Shewa*]	□ְ	^{e}[2]	*e* as in *below*[3]	

(2) Composite *shevas* Reduced

Name	Form	Trans-literation	Pronunciation: Modern	Pronunciation: Traditional
Hatef-patah	□ֲ	^{ă}	*a* as in *father*	*a* as in *had*
Hatef-segol	□ֱ	^{ĕ}	*e* as in *bed*	
Hatef-qames	□ֳ	^{ŏ}	*o* as in *row*	*o* as in *top*

[1] The brackets indicate alternative spellings.

[2] Note that the transliteration for each of the half vowels is a superscript letter.

[3] A simple *sheva* is not always pronounced. See Lesson 3C.

3. Full vowels

a. The classification of full vowels in the preceding chart as short, long, and naturally-long is more useful for grammatical purposes than for the sake of pronunciation. These distinctions in vowel length are usually not expressed in the pronunciation of contemporary Hebrew – a matter that is discussed later. (See section 2A.6)

b. Naturally-long vowels

(1) It was mentioned previously that even before the Masoretes introduced their system of vowel pointings some consonants – namely, the quiescents – could serve as "vowel letters," indicating the presence of a vowel in the Hebrew text.[1] When these consonants represented vowels, the Masoretes simply created special vowel forms which were the combination of the consonants and particular vowel pointings or dots.[2]

(2) Two of the quiescents, ו and י, occur frequently as vowel forms. They are treated in this Grammar as "naturally-long vowels," so termed because they are long vowels that are naturally represented in the consonantal text. The vowel forms which combine ו and י with certain short vowels and other pointings are as follows.

Yod + *sere* = ◌ֵי (*sere-yod*)[3]

Yod + *hireq* = ◌ִי (*hireq-yod*)

Vav + *holem* = ◌וֹ (*holem-vav*)

Vav + a dot = ◌וּ (*shureq*)

c. *Qames* and *qames-hatuf*

Qames, a long vowel, and *qames-hatuf*, a short vowel, are represented by the same symbol: ◌ָ. The way to determine which vowel is intended by this symbol will be discussed in Lesson 3D.

[1] The classical term used for the quiescents when they represent vowels is *matres lectionis*, which means "mothers of reading."

[2] To illustrate the Masoretes' approach, if the consonantal text had הי in a situation where the *yod* represented a long *i* vowel, the Masoretes simply added a *hireq* before the *yod* to indicate the long vowel by means of the combination of the *hireq* and the *yod*. The result would be הִי.

[3] ◌ֶי (*segol-yod*) sometimes serves as the naturally-long "e" vowel instead of *sere-yod.*

4. Half Vowels

a. The English language has nothing equivalent to the half vowels (the simple *sheva* and the composite *sheva*s). They are unique in that, as their name suggests, they are weaker than full vowels. This weakness is obvious in two ways.

(1) Half vowels (along with consonants) cannot serve to form a syllable, while full vowels can. (See Lesson 3B.1).

(2) In pronunciation the half vowels receive a more abbreviated sound than the full vowels. This situation is indicated by the names of the composite *sheva*s, for the word *hatef* means "hurried." Thus a *hatef-patah* is a "hurried," or abbreviated, *patah*; a *hatef-segol* is a rapidly spoken *segol*; and a *hatef-qames* sounds like an abbreviated *qames-hatuf.*

b. The simple *sheva* may be either vocalized or silent. When vocalized it usually sounds like the rapidly spoken *e* in *below*. The circumstances in which the simple *sheva* is vocalized or silent will be discussed in Lesson 3C.

c. The composite *sheva*s have the following characteristics.

(1) They are always vocalized, never silent.

(2) They occur only with the gutturals (א, ה, ח, and ע), which prefer composite *sheva*s to the simple *sheva.*

(3) They occur only with a guttural that stands at the beginning of a syllable, as the following words illustrate. In each case the composite *sheva* occurs at the beginning of the word and therefore at the beginning of a syllable.

- חֲמִישִׁי = ḥămîšî ("fifth")
- אֱלֹהִים = ʾĕlōhîm ("God")
- עֳנִי = ʿŏnî ("poverty")

5. Placement of vowels with consonants

a. The naturally-long vowels are placed following a consonant and read after that consonant, as the following illustrate.

בֵּי = bê	בּוֹ = bô
בִּי = bî	בּוּ = bû

b. Most of the other vowels (those which are not naturally-long) are placed directly beneath a consonant and read after that consonant, as the following illustrate.

בָּ = bā or bo[1]	בֻּ = bu
בֵּ = bē	בְּ = b^e^
בַּ = ba	הֲ = hă
בֶּ = be	הֱ = hĕ
בִּ = bi	הֳ = hŏ

c. The *holem* is an exception to this pattern of placing the vowel beneath a consonant, in that it appears above the left-hand corner of a consonant.

- בֹּ = bō

  ✓ In some Hebrew scripts, such as the one used in this Grammar, when a *holem* appears above a *sin*, the *holem* and the dot above the left side of the *sin* fall on top of one another, so that only one dot is visible. For example, in the word שֹׂבַע = śōḇaᶜ ("plenty") the dot above the first consonant serves both to identify the letter as a *sin* (in contrast to a *shin*) and to indicate that the *sin* has a *holem* above it. Since every non-quiescent consonant at the beginning or in the middle of a word must have a vowel, and since the *sin* in שׂבַע has no other vowel marked, one can assume that its vowel is a *holem*.

d. Every consonant in a word is normally accompanied by a vowel, except for the last consonant, which may or may not have a vowel.

(1) A final *kaf* usually has either a *qames* or a simple *sheva* within it, so that it appears as ךָ or ךְ, as in the words אַתְּךָ ("you" *M*) and אִתָּךְ ("you" *F*)

(2) As discussed above, in some situations the quiescent consonants (א, ה, ו, and י) are not accompanied by a vowel, even when they occur in the middle of a word. In such a situation the quiescent consonant has lost its consonantal character – that is, it has lost its ability to support a vowel.

- אֱלֹהִים ("God") begins with the quiescent א, which has the vowel *hatef-segol*. When the preposition לְ ("to") is attached to the front of this word it is spelled לֵאלֹהִים ("to God"). Note that the quiescent א loses its vowel in this situation. (See Lesson 6A.2.)

(3) While ו and י can lose their consonantal status and represent naturally-long vowels (◌ִי, ◌ֵי, ◌וֹ, or ◌וּ), they can also stand as normal consonants which

[1] See section 3D.

support vowel pointings. The following clues describe how to distinguish between the functioning of ו and י as vowel letters and as typical consonants.

(a) When ו has a *holem* above it (וֹ), the ו normally represents a *holem-vav* and not a consonant, as in the word בּוֹשׁ = bôš ("to be ashamed").[1]

(b) However, when ו is accompanied by any vowel pointing other than a *holem*, it functions as a normal consonant with a vowel, as in the word מָוֶת = māveṯ ("death").

(c) When ו has a dot (וּ) and no other pointing, it represents a *shureq* and not a consonant, as in the word מוּת = mûṯ ("to die").

(d) When י is preceded by a *sere* or *hireq* (◌ֵי or ◌ִי), the י can have no vowel pointing (beneath, above, or after it), and the י is part of either a *sere-yod* or a *hireq-yod*, as in בֵּית = bêṯ ("house of") or הִיא = hîʾ ("she").

(e) However, when י has vowel pointing (beneath, above, or after it), it does not form a naturally-long vowel but stands as a consonant with a vowel, as in בַּיִת = bayiṯ ("house").

e. Furtive *patah*

(1) While most vowels are placed beneath a consonant and read after that consonant, the vowel *patah* forms an exception to this principle in one special circumstance. When the gutturals ה, ח, or ע occur at the end of a word, they sometimes take a unique *patah* called a furtive ("stealthy") *patah*.[2] The furtive *patah* is placed beneath a guttural but pronounced before that guttural. This furtive *patah* is like the half vowels in that it is hurried in pronunciation and cannot form a separate syllable. (See Lesson 3B.1b(2).) The occurrence of a furtive *patah* before a guttural is due to the

[1] An exception occurs when וֹ is preceded by a vowel rather than a consonant. To illustrate, in עָוֹן ("sin") the וֹ is the consonant *vav* with a *holem* rather the vowel *holem-vaw* because the וֹ is preceded by a *qames*. Two vowels cannot occur without an intervening consonant (except in the case of a furtive *patah*).

[2] The furtive *patah* may occur when ה, ח, or ע appear at the end of a word and they are preceded by a naturally-long or long *e*, *i*, *o*, or *u* vowel (that is, any naturally-long or any long vowel except *qames*). See Malcom J.A. Horsnell, *A Review and Reference Grammar for Biblical Hebrew*, rev. ed. (Hamilton, Ontario: McMaster University Press, 1999), 28.

fact that the gutturals prefer an *a* vowel before them. Anytime a *patah* appears below ה, ח, or ע at then end of a word, one can assume that it is a furtive *patah*.

(2) The following words illustrate that a furtive *patah* is transliterated and pronounced before the final consonant.

- גָּבֹהַּ[1] = gāḇōah ("proud")
- אֹרֵחַ = ʾōrēaḥ ("wandering")
- רֵעַ = rēaʿ ("friend")

6. Pronunciation of vowels and vowel classes

a. Hebrew grammars reflect a great deal of variety in the systems of vowel pronunciation that they recommend.[2] Since it is impossible to reconstruct with confidence the manner in which Hebrew was pronounced in antiquity, this Grammar opts for a pronunciation system based on modern Hebrew. Modern pronunciation generally does not distinguish between long and short vowel sounds, except in the case of the *e* vowels (*sere-yod, sere, segol,* and *hatef-segol*).

b. The system of pronunciation represented in this Grammar assigns one sound to each vowel for the sake of simplicity; however, in actual practice the sounds of vowels may not be static, for their pronunciation can be affected by accompanying consonants and vowels.

c. Besides being classified according to length, as in the chart of section 2A.2, vowels may also be grouped in classes of sound – that is, A, E, I, O, or U classes, as the following chart indicates. Note that in each class the vowels are organized to indicate a shortening (reduction) of sound as one moves from left to right in the chart, so that the column of half vowels indicates the shortest (most reduced) sound in each class. A column summarizing vowel pronunciation also accompanies the chart.

---

[1] While the script used in this Grammar places a furtive *patah* beneath the center of a final consonant, some other Hebrew scripts (such as the one used in *BHS*) place it beneath the right side of a final guttural, emphasizing the fact that it is pronounced before the guttural.

[2] For discussion and bibliography regarding the pronunciation of vowels, see Horsnell, 11-19.

	Naturally-long	Long	Short	Half vowels[1]	Pronunciation
A class:	[2]	□ָ (*Qames*)	□ַ (*Patah*)	□ֲ (*Hatef-patah*)	*a* as in *father*
E class:	□ֵי (*Sere-yod*)	••			*e* as in *they*
		□ֵ (*Sere*)	□ֶ (*Segol*)	□ֱ (*Hatef-segol*)	*e* as in *bed*
I class:	□ִי (*Hireq-yod*)		□ִ (*Hireq*)	[3]	*i* as in *machine*
O class:	□וֹ (*Holem-vav*)	□ֹ (*Holem*)	□ָ (*Qames-hatuf*)	□ֳ (*Hatef-qames*)	*o* as in *row*
U class:	□וּ (*Shureq*)		□ֻ (*Qibbus*)	[4]	*u* as in *rule*
Simple *sheva*				□ְ (*Sheva*)	*e* as in *below*

d. The following chart depicts some situations where the consonants ו and י occur at the end of words in combination with one another and certain vowels. The chart indicates how to pronunciation these unusual constructions.[5]

---

[1] Only the gutturals take composite *sheva*s, which are the half vowels that can be classified by sound. Non-guttural consonants take a simple *sheva* as the most reduced (shortest) vowel in each class. The simple *sheva* is placed in a separate category in this chart since it does not belong to a particular class (A, E, I, O, or U) and appears with non-gutturals in all vowel classes.

[2] Some grammars identify □ָה at the end of a word as a naturally-long "A class" vowel, transliterated as â.

[3] Since this vowel class lacks a composite *sheva*, *hatef-segol* can serve in the "I class" as a half vowel with gutturals.

[4] Since this vowel class lacks a composite *sheva*, *hatef-qames* can serve in the "U class" as a half vowel with gutturals.

[5] See Horsnell, 13; Thomas O. Lambdin, *Introduction to Biblical Hebrew* (New York: Scribner's, 1971), XVII; and James D. Martin, *Davidson's Introductory Hebrew Grammar*, 27th ed. (Edinburgh: T&T Clark, 1993), 18.

Ending with *vav*	Pronunciation
□ַו = av	
□ָו = āv	*av* as in *Java*
□ָיו = āyv[1]	
□ֵו = ēv	*av* as in *cave*
□ֵיו = êv	
□ִו = iv	*ev* as in *eve*
□ִיו = îv	

Ending with *yod*	Pronunciation
□ַי = ay	*ay* as in *aye*
□ָי = āy	
□ֶי = ey	*ey* as in *they*
וֹי = ôy	*oi* as in *boil*
□ֹי = ōy	
וּי = ûy	*ouie* as in *Louie*

7. Transliteration

a. The naturally-long vowels are transliterated with the symbol ˆ above them: ê (*sere-yod*), î (*hireq-yod*), ô (*holem-vav*), and û (*shureq*).

b. The long vowels are transliterated with the symbol ˉ above them: ā (*qames*), ē (*sere*), and ō (*holem*).

c. The short vowels are transliterated with no symbol above them: a (*patah*), e (*segol*), i (*hireq*), o (*qames-hatuf*), and u (*qibbus*).

d. The half vowels are transliterated with superscript letters. In addition, the composite *sheva*s have the mark ˘ above them. Thus, in transliteration, the half vowels are ᵉ (*sheva*), ᵃ̆ (*hatef-patah*), ᵉ̆ (*hatef-segol*), and ᵒ̆ (*hatef-qames*).

c. The following words from the Hebrew Bible illustrate the manner in which vowels and consonants are transliterated. In each case the symbol □ָ always stands for a *qames*, with the exception of word number (14), where it is a *qames-hatuf*, as the note indicates.

(1)	עֵץ	ʿēṣ	("tree")
(2)	חַי	ḥay	("alive")
(3)	אָדוֹן	ʾāḏôn	("lord")
(4)	זֶרַע	zeraʿ	("seed")
(5)	פִּיו	pîv	("his mouth")
(6)	גּוֹי	gôy	("nation")
(7)	מַיִם	mayim	("water")

[1] In this chart where *vav* follows *yod*, the *yod* has quiesced so that it cannot support a vowel.

(8)	אֲשֶׁר	ʾăšer	(“who”)
(9)	קֹדֶשׁ	qōḏeš	(“holiness”)
(10)	שְׁנֵי	šᵉnê	(“two of”)
(11)	לֶאֱכֹל	leʾĕḵōl	(“to eat”)
(12)	אַחֲרָיו	ʾaḥărāyv	(“after him”)
(13)	גְּבוּל	gᵉḇûl	(“border”)
(14)	אָהֳלִי[1]	ʾohŏlî	(“my tent”)
(15)	נְאֻם	nᵉʾum	(“utterance”)
(16)	הֶעֱלָה	heʿĕlāh	(“he brought”)
(17)	בֹּקֶר	bōqer	(“morning”)
(18)	גָּלוּי	gālûy	(“being uncovered”)
(19)	עִם	ʿim	(“with”)
(20)	לְהֵיטִיב	lᵉhêṭîḇ	(“to be good”)
(21)	רוּחַ	rûaḥ	(“spirit”)
(22)	חֻצוֹת	ḥuṣôṯ	(“streets”)
(23)	אֱמֻנִים	ʾĕmunîm	(“faithfulness”)
(24)	עֲלֵיהֶן	ʿălêhen	(“upon them”)
(25)	שָׁלֹשׁ[2]	šālōš	(“three”)
(26)	חֳדָשִׁים	ḥŏḏāšîm	(“months”)
(27)	פְּקָדוּךָ	pᵉqāḏûḵā	(“they sought you”)
(28)	חֳלִי	ḥŏlî	(“sickness”)
(29)	וְיֵבֹשׁוּ	vᵉyēḇōšûv	(“and they were ashamed”)
(30)	טִירוֹתֵיהֶם	ṭîrôṯêhem	(“their encampments”)

Lesson 2: Exercises

a. Repeatedly write and pronounce the Hebrew vowels until their forms and sounds become familiar.

b. Reproduce from memory the vowel chart in section 2A.2, with the exception of the traditional pronunciation and the items in brackets.

[1] The first vowel in this word is a *qames-hatuf*. The reason why is explained in the next lesson.

[2] Note that the dot above the final *shin* in this word also serves to indicate the vowel *holem*.

c. Practice transliterating the Hebrew words in section 2A.7e. While doing this exercise, cover the transliterations that appear beside the words. When finished check the work against the answers in the book.

d. The following names come from the Hebrew Bible – some are well known; others are not so familiar. At times the spelling of the names is slightly altered to meet the purpose of this lesson. Rewrite the names in Hebrew and then transliterate them. Also pronounce each name and note when the transliteration and pronunciation are similar to or divergent from the typical English rendering of these names. In this exercise the symbol ◌ָ always stands for a *qames,* instead of a *qames-hatuf.*

(1)	אָדָם	(Ge 4:25)	(21)	דָּן	(Ge 35:25)
(2)	קַיִן	(Ge 4:2)	(22)	נַפְתָּלִי	(Ge 35:25)
(3)	הָבֶל	(Ge 4:2)	(23)	גָּד	(Ge 35:26)
(4)	שֵׁת	(Ge 5:6)	(24)	אָשֵׁר	(Ge 35:26)
(5)	אֱנוֹשׁ	(Ge 5:6)	(25)	מֹשֶׁה	(Ex 4:14)
(6)	קֵינָן	(Ge 5:12)	(26)	אַהֲרֹן	(Ex 4:14)
(7)	מְתוּשֶׁלַח	(Ge 5:25)	(27)	מִרְיָם	(Ex 15:20)
(8)	נֹחַ	(Ge 5:32)	(28)	יְהוֹשֻׁעַ	(Ex 17:9)
(9)	עֵשָׂו	(Ge 25:25)	(29)	דָּוִד	(1Sa 16:13)
(10)	יַעֲקֹב	(Ge 25:26)	(30)	שְׁלֹמֹה	(2Sa 5:14)
(11)	לֵאָה	(Ge 29:31)	(31)	אֱלִיפַז	(Job 2:11)
(12)	רָחֵל	(Ge 29:31)	(32)	תֵּימָנִי	(Job 2:11)
(13)	רְאוּבֵן	(Ge 35:23)	(33)	בִּלְדַּד	(Job 2:11)
(14)	שִׁמְעוֹן	(Ge 35:23)	(34)	שׁוּחִי	(Job 2:11)
(15)	לֵוִי	(Ge 35:23)	(35)	צוֹפַר	(Job 2:11)
(16)	יְהוּדָה	(Ge 35:23)	(36)	נַעֲמָתִי	(Job 2:11)
(17)	יִשְׂשָׂכָר[1]	(Ge 35:23)	(37)	יִרְמְיָהוּ	(Jer 1:1)
(18)	זְבוּלֻן	(Ge 35:23)	(38)	חַגַּי	(Hag 1:1)
(19)	יוֹסֵף	(Ge 35:24)	(39)	נְחֶמְיָה	(Ne 1:1)
(20)	בִּנְיָמִן	(Ge 35:24)	(40)	חֳבַיְיָה	(Ne 7:63)

[1] Note that this word and several others in the exercise seem to have a *sheva* that is silent rather than vocalized. This function of the *sheva* is discussed in the next lesson.

e. Practice the pronunciation of the following Hebrew words. Attempt to say them without transliterating them. In this exercise the symbol ◌ָ always stands for a *qames*, with the exception of word number (25), where it is a *qames-hatuf*, as the note indicates.

(1) רַב ("many")
(2) יָד ("hand")
(3) זֶה ("this")
(4) לֵב ("heart")
(5) בֵּין ("between")
(6) מִן ("from")
(7) עִיר ("city")
(8) כֹּל ("all")
(9) יוֹם ("day")
(10) עֻגָה ("bread-cake")
(11) קוּם ("to rise")
(12) מְאֹד ("very")
(13) אֲנִי ("I")
(14) אֱמֶת ("truth")
(15) חַיִל ("power")
(16) כֹּחַ ("strength")
(17) אֵם ("mother")
(18) הוֹי ("woe")
(19) אָוֶן ("trouble")
(20) שָׂרָיו ("his officials")
(21) חֻשִׁים ("hastening")
(22) עֲצֵי ("trees of")
(23) גֵּו ("back")
(24) אוּלַי ("perhaps")
(25) מָחֳרָת[1] ("next day")
(26) שׁוּב ("to return")
(27) אֱנוֹשׁ ("men")
(28) כְּלִי ("vessel")
(29) מָשִׁיחַ ("anointed one")
(30) חֳרָשִׁים ("wooded hills")

[1] The first vowel in this word is a *qames-hatuf*.

Lesson 3

Accenting, Syllables, Simple *Sheva*, *Qames-Hatuf*, Transliteration

3A Accenting

1. Major accent for a word

a. The Masoretes developed a highly specialized system of accenting for sentences in the Hebrew Bible. At this point the student needs only to be concerned with the primary accenting of individual words. The syllable which receives the major accent in a word is called the tone (or tonic) syllable; it is stressed in reading. When it is necessary to mark the tone syllable, this Grammar uses the symbol ◌֫ in Hebrew script to indicate the accent. In transliteration the symbol ´ denotes an accented syllable.

b. Most words receive their major accent on the last syllable.[1] When the last syllable is accented, typically no special mark appears in this Grammar to indicate that fact, although such a mark may occasionally appear for the purpose of clarity or illustration.

- אָדָם ("man") has two syllables. The first is אָ (ʾā) and the second is דָם (ḏām). Since no accent mark appears with the word, one can assume that the second (or last) syllable is accented. If the accent mark were shown, it would appear as אָדָ֫ם.

c. Some words receive their major accent on the next to last, or penultimate, syllable.[2] When this is the case the accented syllable is marked. The major accent in a word never comes before the penultimate syllable.

- שַׁ֫עַר ("gate") has two syllables, which are שַׁ֫ (šá) and עַר (ʿar). The first, or penultimate, syllable is accented as the symbol ◌֫ indicates.

---

[1] The Hebrew term for an accent on the last syllable is *milra*.

[2] The Hebrew term for an accent on the penultimate syllable is *milel*.

2. *Meteg*

a. In addition to a major accent, some words have a secondary accent which is known as a *meteg* (מֶ֫תֶג = "bridle"). It appears as a vertical stroke beneath a consonant. Typically, it is placed to left of vowels, as illustrated by בָֽ, בֵֽ, and בַֽ. However, the *meteg* can appear to the right of a vowel, as in בַֽ. In the case of a consonant which does not have a vowel beneath it, the *meteg* appears by itself under that consonant, as in הֽ and הֽוֹ.

b. Practically speaking, the *meteg* causes a speaker to pause in pronunciation.[1]

- In לָֽרָקִיעַ ("to the expanse") a *meteg* occurs to the left of the first *qames*. It causes a speaker to pause after לָֽ (lā), the first syllable of the word. This pause means that לָֽ receives a secondary stress. Since no major accent appears on the word, one assumes that the last syllable, קִיעַ (qîaʿ), is accented and thereby receives the major stress in pronunciation.

3B Syllables

1. Characteristics of syllables

a. A syllable normally begins with a consonant.[2]

b. Along with a consonant, every syllable also has one full vowel (that is, a naturally-long, long, or short vowel). However, a syllable never has more than one full vowel (except in the case of a furtive *patah*, as discussed below). Consequently, a word typically has as many syllables as it has full vowels.

- הַר = har ("mountain") has one syllable, since it has only one vowel, a *patah*.
- שָׁמַר = šā/mar[3] ("he kept") has two vowels (*qames* and *patah*) and therefore has two syllables: שָׁ (šā) and מַר (mar).

(1) As mentioned earlier, a half vowel (that is, a simple or a composite *sheva*) along with a consonant cannot form a separate syllable.

---

[1] There are a number of situations in which a *meteg* may occur; for discussion see Paul Joüon, *A Grammar of Biblical Hebrew*, trans. T. Muraoka (Rome: Pontifical Biblical Institute, 1996), §14; and E. Kautzsch, ed., *Gesenius' Hebrew Grammar*, 2d English ed., A. E. Cowley, ed. (Oxford: Clarendon Press, 1910), §16c-i. In this Grammar the circumstance in which a *meteg* consistently appears is with a *qames* before a vocal *sheva* (□ָֽ□ְ). See section 3D.1c.

[2] An exception to this rule may occur when the *vav* conjunction is prefixed to the beginning of a word. In some cases the *vav* conjunction becomes the vowel *shureq*. See Lesson 6B.2b(2).

[3] The symbol / in transliteration designates a division between syllables.

- בְּרִית = b^e^rîṯ ("covenant") has only one syllable since it has only one full vowel, a *hireq-yod*. Even though בְּ (b^e^) may sound as though it forms a syllable, it cannot because the *sheva* is a half vowel.[1]
- אֲדָמָה = ʾădā/māh ("land") has two syllables since it has two full vowels (two *qameses*). The first syllable is אֲדָ (ʾădā) and the second syllable is מָה (māh). אֲ (ʾă) cannot form a separate syllable since it has a half vowel.

(2) The one exception to the rule that no syllable has more than one full vowel occurs in the case of the furtive *patah.* (See Lesson 2A.5e.) When a furtive *patah* occurs at the end of a word, it does not mark the beginning of a separate syllable.

- רוּחַ = rûaḥ ("spirit") has only one syllable because the second vowel is a furtive *patah*, which cannot form a separate syllable.

2. Open syllables

a. Syllables may be of two types: open and closed.

b. An open syllable is distinguished by two basic features.

(1) First, an open syllable ends with a full vowel.

(a) The basic pattern for an open syllable is CONSONANT + FULL VOWEL [CV].

- כִּי = kî ("that") forms one syllable which is open; it follows the CV pattern.
- נָתַן = nā/ṯan ("he gave") has two syllables. The first, נָ (nā), is open; it follows the CV pattern.

(b) The pattern of an open syllable may be affected by the following.

[1] If a simple or composite *sheva* occurs under the first consonant of an open syllable, then the resulting pattern is CONSONANT (with a *sheva*) + CONSONANT + FULL VOWEL [CCV].

- בְּנֵי = b^e^nê ("sons of") and אֲחֵי = ʾăḥê ("brothers of") each has only one open syllable because each has only one full vowel. The consonants with *shevas* cannot form separate syllables.

[2] The quiescents א and ה never close a syllable at the end of a word. In

---

[1] The point that a consonant with a *sheva* cannot form a syllable is emphasized by the tendency in modern Hebrew sometimes to omit the vocal *sheva* in pronunciation, so that בְּרִית sounds like brîṯ.

addition, א cannot close a syllable in the middle of a word. Therefore, any syllable ending with א forms an open syllable [CVʾ]. Any final syllable (that is, last syllable of a word) ending with ה creates an open syllable [CVh]. An exception occurs if ה at the end of a word has a *mappiq* (הּ); in that case הּ does close the syllable. (See Lesson 1A.3e(2).)

- בּוֹא = ḇôʾ ("to come") and כֹּה = kōh ("thus") each has one open syllable since neither א nor ה can close the final syllable of a word.
- The second syllable of קָרָאתָ = qā/rāʾ/ṯā ("you called") is open since א cannot close a syllable in the middle of a word.
- בָּהּ = bāh ("in her"), however, does not form an open syllable because the ה at the end has a *mappiq*. This word forms a closed syllable, which is discussed in the next section.

(2) The second basic feature of an open syllable is that its vowel is usually long (or naturally-long) unless the syllable is accented, then the vowel may be either long or short.[1]

- מָלַךְ = mā/laḵ ("he was king") has two syllables. The first syllable is open, has a long vowel, and is not accented.
- In לֶ֫חֶם = lé/ḥem ("bread") the first syllable is open and accented; it has a short vowel.
- In סֵ֫פֶר = sḗ/p̄er ("writing") the first syllable is open and accented, but this time the open syllable has a long vowel.
- מִי = mî ("who") has only one syllable, consequently that syllable is accented. It is an open syllable with a naturally-long vowel.
- Both syllables in תּוֹרָה (tô/rāh) are open (since ה cannot close the final syllable). The first syllable has a naturally-long vowel and is unaccented; the second is accented with a long vowel.

✓ Since a *meteg* is a secondary accent that causes the reader to pause in pronunciation, it always marks an open syllable whether the vowel with

[1] There are some exceptions to this rule which will be noted in future lessons. See Lesson 5B.4b; Lesson 6A.2b(4) and 6B.2b(4).

the *meteg* is long or short.

- In רָֽבְתָה = rā/ḇᵉṯāh ("she was great") and וַֽיְהִי = va/yᵉhî ("and he was") a *meteg* makes the first syllable of each word open. In one case the open syllable has a long vowel; in the other the vowel is short.

3. Closed syllables

A closed syllable is distinguished by two basic features.

a. First, a closed syllable ends with a consonant instead of a full vowel.

(1) The typical pattern for a closed syllable is CONSONANT + FULL VOWEL + CONSONANT [CVC].

- עַם = ʿam ("people") has one syllable which is closed; it follows the CVC pattern.
- The second syllable of חֶ֫רֶב = ḥé/reḇ ("sword") is a closed syllable; it also follows the CVC pattern.

(2) The pattern of a closed syllable may be affected by the following.

[a] If a simple or composite *sheva* occurs under the first consonant of a closed syllable, then the resulting pattern is CONSONANT (with a *sheva*) + CONSONANT + FULL VOWEL + CONSONANT [CCVC].

- בְּנוֹת = bᵉṯôṯ ("daughters of") and אֲרוֹן = ʾărôn ("ark") each has one closed syllable, following the pattern of CCVC. The consonants with *sheva*s cannot form separate syllables.

[b] As discussed earlier, א may quiesce (that is, lose its consonantal status), meaning that it can neither support a vowel nor close a syllable. This quiescent א may appear in a middle of a closed syllable [CVʾC].

- רֹאשׁ = rōʾš ("head") has only one vowel and therefore only one closed syllable, following a CVʾC pattern.

b. The second basic feature of a closed syllable is that its vowel is usually short, unless accented, then the vowel may be short or long (including naturally-long).

- The second syllable of שֶׁ֫בַע = šé/ḇaʿ ("seven") is closed and unaccented; it has a short vowel.
- The second syllable of לָקַט = lā/qaṭ ("he picked up") is closed and accented; it has a short vowel. (One assumes the second syllable is accented since no accent appears above the first syllable.)

- The second syllable of גָּדוֹל = gā/ḏôl (“great”) is closed and accented; it has a naturally-long vowel.

3C Simple *Sheva*

1. As mentioned in lesson 2, the simple *sheva* functions in two ways: it may either be vocalized or silent. These two functions may be identified as follows.
   a. A simple *sheva* is vocalized only when it occurs at the beginning (that is, under the first consonant) of a syllable. The appearance of a vocal *sheva* at the beginning of a syllable typically occurs in four situations.
      (1) A *sheva* at the beginning of a word is always vocal, since it occurs at the beginning of a syllable.
         - נְאֻם = n^{e}ʾum (“utterance”) has a vocal *sheva*.

      (2) A *sheva* which occurs after a long vowel is typically vocal. To say the same thing another way, a *sheva* after an open syllable is a vocal *sheva* since it is also occurring at the beginning of a syllable.
         - כּוֹכְבֵי = kô/ḵ^{e}ḇê (“stars of”) has two open syllables since it has two long vowels. The *sheva* under the second כ is vocal because it comes after a long vowel or after an open syllable.

      (3) A *sheva* which occurs after a *meteg* is vocal, since it is also occurring at the beginning of a syllable.
         - In מָֽשְׁלָה = mā/š^{e}lāh (“she ruled”) the *meteg* indicates that the first syllable is מָֽ. Consequently, שְׁ begins a new syllable with a vocal *sheva*.

      (4) When two *shevas* occur together (that is, under two consecutive consonants) in the middle of a word, the second *sheva* is vocal because it is occurring at the beginning of syllable. This situation is more fully discussed later in this section.

   b. A simple *sheva* is silent when it occurs at the end of syllable – that is, under a consonant which closes a syllable. In such a case the *sheva* appears after a short vowel and functions like a syllable divider. To say it another way, a silent *sheva* can occur only at the end of a closed syllable; it cannot occur at the end of an open syllable.
      - In יִשְׂרָאֵל = yiś/rā/ʾēl (“Israel”) the *sheva* occurs after the short vowel

hireq and therefore comes at the end of a closed syllable. Since the *sheva* is silent and functioning as a syllable divider, it does not appear in the transliteration.

- ✓ It may be helpful, however, in the beginning for the student to first transliterate all the *shevas* in a word and then to mark a syllable division through the ones which are silent, indicating they are syllable dividers.

- ▸ The *sheva* in the final *kaf* ךְ מֶ֫לֶךְ mé/leḵ ("king") appears at the end of a closed syllable; it is therefore silent and omitted from transliteration.

2. If two *shevas* occur together (that is, under two consecutive consonants) in the middle of a word, the first one is silent, and the second one is vocal. Such is the case because the first *sheva* will occur after a short vowel and will stand at the end of a closed syllable. The second *sheva* will occur at the beginning of a new syllable.
   - ▸ נִכְרְתָה = nik/reṯāh ("she was cut off") has two consecutive *shevas*. Since the first (under the כ) occurs after a short vowel (a *hireq*), it is silent and functions to close the first syllable. The second *sheva* is vocal, standing at the beginning (under the first consonant) of the second syllable.

3D *Qames-Hatuf*

1. As discussed above, the symbol ָ can stand for two different vowels: either the long vowel *qames* (ā) or the short vowel *qames-hatuf* (o). The following are basic guidelines for distinguishing between them.
   a. Since *qames-hatuf* is a short vowel, it typically appears in a closed, unaccented syllable. It cannot occur in an open, accented syllable.[1]
      - ▸ In וַיְיָ֫מָת[2] = vay/yā́/moṯ ("and he died") the second syllable, rather than the last, is accented. Therefore, the vowel in the second syllable, יָ֫ (yā), is a *qames*. Since the last syllable, מָת (moṯ), is closed and unaccented, it has the short vowel *qames-hatuf*.

   b. The vowel ָ is always a *qames* if it is accented. It is usually a *qames* in an

---

[1] Future lessons will explain that a *qames-hatuf* can appear in an open, unaccented syllable when followed by a *hatef-qames*. See Lesson 6A.2b(4) and 6B.2b(4).

[2] This word would normally be written as וַיָּ֫מָת with a *dagesh-forte* in the *yod*. See Lesson 4B.2.

open syllable or when it appears with a *meteg*. (At this stage of learning the language, one can assume that whenever ◌ָ appears in an open syllable or with a *meteg* it is a *qames*.)

- In דָבָר = dā/ḇār ("word") each of the two syllables has the long vowel *qames*, since the first syllable is open and the second syllable is accented.
- In שָֽׁמְרָה = šā/mᵉrāh ("preserve") the first vowel is a *qames* in an open syllable, as indicated by the *meteg*.

✓ Since א cannot close a syllable, any syllable which ends with ◌ָא is an open syllable and the vowel before the א is a *qames*. Similarly, since ה (without a *mappiq*) cannot close the final syllable of a word, any word which ends with ◌ָה has a final syllable that is open, and the vowel before the ה has to be a *qames*.

  - The last vowel in מָצָא = mā/ṣāʾ ("he found") is *qames* because the last syllable is open.
  - Likewise, מֵאָה = mē/ʾāh ("hundred") ends with an open syllable whose vowel is *qames*.

c. If an unaccented ◌ָ is followed by a silent *sheva*, it is a *qames-hatuf*. However, if ◌ָ (whether accented or not) is followed by a vocal *sheva*, it is a *qames*. In this Grammar a *meteg* aids in making this distinction:

◌ָ◌ְ (without an accent) = *qames-hatuf* followed by silent *sheva*

◌ָֽ◌ְ = *qames* followed by vocal *sheva*.[1]

- In הָחְתֵּל = hoḥ/tēl ("to be wrapped") the vowel ◌ָ (which is followed by a *sheva*) has no accent marked above it; therefore, the ◌ָ is a *qames-hatuf* and the *sheva* which follows is a syllable divider. The result is that the first syllable of the word is the closed syllable הָחְ (hoḥ), which has a short vowel. To say it another way, this word is not transliterated as hā/ḥᵉtēl (beginning with an open syllable that has a long vowel), because the vowel ◌ָ is not accented and is followed by a *sheva*.

[1] Other resources do not always use the *meteg* in this manner. For example, where this Grammar has מָֽשְׁלָה = mā/šᵉlāh ("she ruled"), another resource may omit the *meteg*, as in מָשְׁלָה = mā/šᵉlāh ("she ruled"). By the time such cases are encountered in translation, the student's understanding of verb forms will guide the identification of *qames* and *qames-hatuf*.

- The first syllable of חָכְמָה = ḥoḵ/māh ("wisdom") is the closed syllable חָכְ (ḥoḵ) with the short vowel *qames-hatuf*. This vowel has no *meteg*, is unaccented, and is followed by a *sheva*. The second syllable, מָה (māh), has the long vowel *qames*, since it is accented and the ה leaves the syllable open.
- In יָכָלְתָּ = yā/ḵol/tā ("you will be able") the first syllable is open, so it has the long vowel *qames*. Since a *sheva* follows the unaccented vowel ◌ָ in the second syllable, the vowel is a *qames-hatuf* and the syllable is closed. The vowel in the last syllable is a *qames* because the syllable is open as well as accented.
- In רָאָֽתְךָ = rā/ʾā/t^{e}ḵā ("he saw you") all the full vowels are *qames*es. Each appears in an open syllable. In addition, the second *qames* has a *meteg*, which means that it is followed by a vocal *sheva*.

3E Transliteration

The words below illustrate the transliteration of accents, syllable division, simple *sheva*, and *qames-hatuf*

(1)	מָקוֹם	mā/qôm	("place")
(2)	עֶ֫רֶב	ʿé/reḇ	("evening")
(3)	אֲרָם	ʾ^{ă}rām	("Aram")
(4)	יֹדְעֵי	yō/ḏ^{e}ʿê	("knowing of")
(5)	מִשְׂגָּב	miś/gāḇ	("refuge")
(6)	וְאֹתָהּ	v^{e}ʾō/ṯāh	("and her")
(7)	כָּֽבְדוּ	kā/ḇ^{e}ḏû	("they were heavy")
(8)	זֹאת	zōʾṯ	("this")
(9)	לְמִינָהּ	l^{e}mî/nāh	("according to its kind")
(10)	אֱזָר	ʾ^{ĕ}zār	("put on")
(11)	וְנִפְקְחוּ	v^{e}nip̄/q^{e}ḥû	("and they will be opened")
(12)	בֵּינְךָ	bê/n^{e}ḵā	("between you")
(13)	הָבְקְעָה	hoḇ/q^{e}ʿāh	("she was broken into")
(14)	רֵאשִׁית	rēʾ/šîṯ	("first")
(15)	פָּֽשְׁעוּ	pā/š^{e}ʿû	("they rebelled")
(16)	גְּחֹנְךָ	g^{e}ḥō/n^{e}ḵā	("your stomach")
(17)	מַזְרִיעַ	maz/rîaʿ	("yielding seed")

(18)	יֹאמַר	yō^{ɔ}/mar	(“he will say”)
(19)	יַהַרְגֵנִי	ya/har/ḡē/nî	(“he will kill me”)
(20)	לְמוֹעֲדִים	l^{e}mô/^{c}^{ă}d̲îm	(“for seasons”)
(21)	בְּטֶרֶם	b^{e}ṭé/rem	(“before”)
(22)	אֲכָלְךָ	ɔ^{ă}k̲ol/k̲ā	(“your eating”)
(23)	קָדְקֳדוֹ	qod̲/q^{ŏ}d̲ô	(“his head”)
(24)	פִּרְיָהּ	pir/yāh	(“her fruit”)
(25)	נְעוּרַיִם	n^{e}^{c}û/rá/yim	(“youth”)
(26)	וָאַשְׂבִּעַ	vā/ɔaś/bia^{c}	(“and I satisfied”)
(27)	מְלַאכְתּוֹ[1]	m^{e}laɔk̲/tô	(“his work”)
(28)	אַרְמְנוֹתֶיהָ	ɔar/m^{e}nô/t̲éy/hā[2]	(“her palaces”)
(29)	מְשֻׁבוֹתַיִךְ	m^{e}šu/b̲ô/t̲á/yik̲	(“your turning back”)
(30)	וְנִבְרְכוּ	v^{e}nib̲/r^{e}k̲û	(“and they will be blessed”)

Lesson 3: Exercises

a. Pronounce these Hebrew words and identify whether their syllables are open or closed.

(1) אֵת (“with”)
(2) בּוֹ (“in him”)
(3) נָא (“please”)
(4) מָה (“what?”)
(5) דָּם (“blood”)
(6) אֲנִי (“I”)
(7) לָהּ (“for her”)
(8) פֶּה (“mouth”)
(9) הִיא (“she”)
(10) בְּרִיחַ (“gate bar ”)

b. The seven words of Genesis 1:1 appear below (with slightly modified spelling). Indicate how many syllables there are in each Hebrew word, then pronounce each word.

(1) בְּרֵאשִׁית (“in beginning”)
(2) בָּרָא (“he created”)
(3) אֱלֹהִים (“God”)
(4) אֵת [3]
(5) הַשָּׁמַיִם (“the heavens”)
(6) וְאֵת (“and”)
(7) הָאָרֶץ (“the earth”)

---

[1] The quiescent א cannot close a syllable. The first syllable, however, is not מְלַא, since it would form an open syllable with a short vowel. Instead the first syllable is closed: מְלַאכְ.

[2] The transliteration of the syllable תֶי treats the *yod* as a quiescent. The vowel may also be understood as an alternate spelling of *sere-yod* (see footnote 3 of Lesson 2A.3b(2)), whereby the transliteration would be t̲ê.

[3] This word has no translation; it simply indicates that the next word is an object of the main verb in the clause. Note that this word appears again later in the verse with the conjunction “and” prefixed to it.

c. Practice transliterating the Hebrew words in section 3E. While doing this exercise, cover the transliterations that appear beside the words. When finished check the work against the answers in the book. Then pronounce each word.

✓ Appendix 1 contains an abbreviated summary of grammatical principles, including guidelines for recognizing syllables and for transliteration. Item 4 of the guidelines provides a summary which is relevant for the exercises in this lesson.

d. Transliterate the following words. While doing so, be sure to indicate syllable division and mark an accented syllable, if an accent mark appears on the Hebrew word. Then pronounce each word.

(1) אוּלַי ("perhaps")
(2) עֶ֫צֶם ("bone")
(3) לְקוֹל ("for a voice")
(4) רְשָׁעָה ("wicked")
(5) מִשְׁפָּט ("justice")
(6) אֵיךְ ("how?")
(7) גָּבֹהַּ ("high")
(8) קָדְשִׁי ("my holiness")
(9) צֵאתְךָ ("your going out")
(10) חֹ֫שֶׁךְ ("darkness")
(11) עֲמָלֵ֫נוּ ("our trouble")
(12) לֵאוֹר ("to be lighted")
(13) כָּמוֹךָ ("like your")
(14) פַּרְעֹה ("Pharaoh")
(15) אֹיְבֶ֫יךָ ("your enemies")
(16) בְּאָזְנֵי ("in ears of")
(17) עָ֫וֶל ("injustice")
(18) בִּיהוּדָה ("in Judah")
(19) אֱהָבֶ֫הָ ("love her")
(20) חָקְךָ ("your statute")
(21) תֹּאחֵז ("she will grasp")
(22) עֲבָדִים ("servants")
(23) מִלְחֶ֫מֶת ("battle of")
(24) נִדְמֵיתִי ("I am ruined")
(25) מִשְׁתָּיו ("his feasts")
(26) נֹטְעִים ("planting")
(27) הִקְדַּשְׁתִּ֫יךָ ("I made you holy")
(28) אַרְצָהּ ("her land")
(29) שֹׁמַ֫עַת ("listening")
(30) לֻֽקֳחָה ("she was taken")
(31) לָעֵינַ֫יִם ("to the eyes")
(32) וִהְיִיתֶם ("and you will be")
(33) לְהַשְׁלִיחַ ("to cause to send")
(34) מִשְׁפְּחֹת ("families")
(35) טֵאטֵאתִיהָ ("I will sweep it")
(36) בַּֽנְחֻשְׁתַּ֫יִם ("in chains")
(37) וָאֶטְמְנֵ֫הוּ ("and I hid it")
(38) בְּצַחְצָחוֹת ("in parched lands")
(39) וְאַלְמְנֹתֶ֫יךָ ("and your widows")
(40) מַחְשְׁבוֹתֵיכֶם ("your plans")

Lesson 4

Maqqef, *Dagesh*, Vowel Alterations

4A *Maqqef*

1. When two or more words are closely linked together in meaning, they may be joined together by the symbol ־ which is called a *maqqef* (מַקֵּף = "binder").
   - In מֶלֶךְ־יִשְׂרָאֵל ("king of Israel" [1Sa 29:3]) a *maqqef* links two nouns, forming a genitival phrase.[1]
   - In עַל־הָאָ֫רֶץ ("upon the earth" [Ge 1:11]) a *maqqef* links a preposition (עַל = "upon") and a noun (הָאָ֫רֶץ = "the earth"), forming a prepositional phrase.
   - In וַֽיְהִי־בֹ֫קֶר ("and it was morning" [Ge 1:5]) a *maqqef* links a verb (וַֽיְהִי = "and it was") and a predicate noun (בֹּ֫קֶר = "morning"), forming a verb clause.
2. When words are linked by a *maqqef* they are considered to be one word for the purposes of pronunciation and accenting. Thus a word group which is linked by a *maqqef* has a major accent only on the last or next to last syllable of the whole word group, rather than having major accents on each of the words linked by the *maqqef*. This shift of accent to the end of a word group may cause an alteration of vowels in the words that the *maqqef* links together.
   - בֵּן = bēn ("son") and אַבְרָהָם = ʾaḇ/rā/hām ("Abraham") each have a major accent when they stand alone. However, when linked by a *maqqef* in the phrase בֶּן־אַבְרָהָם = ben-ʾaḇ/rā/hām[2] ("son of Abraham" [Ge 25:12]), they are treated as if they are one word. Consequently, only the last syllable of אַבְרָהָם receives a major accent, and בֶּן־ loses its accent. Since בֶּן־ has become a closed, unaccented syllable, its vowel shortens from the long vowel *sere* (בֵּן) to the short vowel *segol* (בֶּן־).
   - When the words כֹּל = kōl ("all") and הָעָם = hā/ʿām ("the people") are linked by a *maqqef* in the phrase כָּל־הָעָם = kol-hā/ʿām ("all of the people"

---

[1] See Lesson 7A.1b.

[2] A hyphen in transliteration represents a *maqqef*.

[Ge 19:4]), only the last syllable (עָם) is accented. Since כָּל־ has become a closed, unaccented syllable, its vowel shortens from a long vowel (*holem*) to a short vowel (*qames-hatuf*).

4B *Dagesh*

The *dagesh* (דָּגֵשׁ) is a dot which occurs in the center of a consonant. There are two types of *dagesh*es, each of which has a special function: the *dagesh-lene* ("soft *dagesh*") and the *dagesh-forte* ("strong *dagesh*").

1. *Dagesh-lene*

a. As discussed above, the *dagesh-lene* occurs only in the *begadkefat* consonants, which are בּ, גּ, דּ, כּ, פּ, and תּ (written here with the *dagesh-lene*). Theoretically, the *dagesh-lene* functions to strengthen these consonants in pronunciation. (See Lesson 1A.6b.)

b. The *dagesh-lene* appears in the *begadkefat* consonants only in a certain circumstance: when the consonants begin a syllable that is not preceded by a full vowel (naturally-long, long, or short).

- In בָּנָה = bā/nāh ("he built") the בּ has a *dagesh-lene* since it begins a syllable and there is no full vowel preceding it.
- In אֶבְנֶה = ʾeḇ/neh ("I will build") the ב cannot have a *dagesh-lene* for two reasons: it occurs at the end rather than at the beginning of a syllable, and it is preceded by a full vowel (*segol*).
- In כָּבוֹד = kā/ḇôḏ ("honor") the כּ has a *dagesh-lene* since it begins a syllable and does not follow a full vowel. The ב also begins a syllable; however, it cannot have a *dagesh-lene* because it is preceded by a full vowel (*qames*). The ד cannot have a *dagesh-lene* because it does not begin a syllable; it is also preceded by a full vowel (*holem-vav*).
- In תִּבְכֶּה = tiḇ/keh ("you will weep") the תּ and כּ both have *dagesh-lene*s because they begin syllables without being preceded by a full vowel. The ב has no *dagesh-lene* because it follows a vowel and closes a syllable.
- In בָּרֲכִי = bā/rᵃḵî ("bless") the בּ has a *dagesh-lene* because it begins a syllable and is not preceded by a full vowel, and the כ lacks a *dagesh-lene* because it does not begin a syllable.

✓ While a *begadkefat* consonant usually has a *dagesh-lene* when it begins a word, the *dagesh-lene* may be omitted if the *begadkefat* consonant follows a word which ends with a vowel. It may also be omitted when following a word which ends with א or ה – quiescent consonants which cannot close final syllables.[1] (See Lesson 3B.2b(1)(b)[2].)

- In כִּי־כֹל = kî-ḵōl ("for all" [1Ch 29:11]) the first *kaf* has a *dagesh-lene* because it begins a syllable and is not preceded by a full vowel. While the second *kaf* begins not only a syllable but also a word, it does not have a *dagesh-lene* because it is preceded by a full vowel (even though that vowel occurs in the previous word). The same would be true if the phrase were written without a *maqqef*: כִּי כֹל.
- In וְהָיָה תַּ֫חַת = vᵉhā/yāh ṯá/ḥaṯ ("and there will be instead" [Is 3:24]) the first ת of תַּ֫חַת does not have a *dagesh-lene* because, while it begins a syllable, it is, for practical purposes, preceded by a full vowel, since the last ה in וְהָיָה is quiescent.

2. *Dagesh-forte*

a. The *dagesh-forte* can appear in all the consonants except the gutturals (א, ה, ח, and ע) and ר. It cannot occur in the first consonant of a word, and it is always preceded by a full vowel.

b. The *dagesh-forte* functions to double a consonant. To illustrate, the word שִׁלַּח ("he sent away") has a *dagesh-forte* in the second consonant; therefore, it is equivalent to the longer spelling שִׁלְלַח. The transliteration of שִׁלַּח indicates the doubled consonant: šil/laḥ. Note that in שִׁלַּח the vowel which appears beneath the לּ (*patah*) is the vowel which accompanies the second ל in the transliteration (as well as in the longer spelling שִׁלְלַח). The first ל is supplied with a simple *sheva* which functions as a syllable divider, and therefore does not appear in transliteration.

- In אַמָּה = ʾam/māh ("cubit") the מּ has a *dagesh-forte*. The word is equivalent to אַמְמָה. The vowel *qames* accompanies the second מ, and the first מ has a silent *sheva* (a syllable divider).
- In עִמְּךָ = ʿim/mᵉḵā ("with you") the מּ has a *dagesh-forte*. The word is

[1] This phenomenon depends upon how closely two words are linked together by accenting. See Joüon, §19.

equivalent to עִמְמְךָ. The first מ has a silent *sheva*, and the second מ has a vocal *sheva*.

- In חָנֵּנִי = ḥon/nḗ/nî ("be gracious to me") the נ has a *dagesh-forte*. The word is equivalent to חָנְנֵנִי. The first נ has a silent *sheva* which marks the end of the first syllable (חָנְ). Since that first syllable is closed and unaccented, its vowel (ָ) is a *qames-hatuf*.
- In וַיִּנָּחֶם = vay/yin/nā/ḥem ("and he was sorry") the י and the נ each have a *dagesh-forte*. The word is equivalent to וַיְיִנְנָחֶם.

c. The two consonants which are used to form naturally-long vowels (ו and י) can, like the other consonants, have a *dagesh-forte*. However, when a ו has a *dagesh-forte* (which appears as וּ), it cannot also be the naturally-long vowel *shureq* (which also appears as וּ). The presence of a vowel with a וּ is the clue that the וּ is a *vav* with a *dagesh-forte* and not a *shureq*, since a *shureq* (being a vowel) cannot have a vowel. Also, a י which is part of a *hireq-yod* can have a *dagesh-forte*.

- In צִוָּה = ṣiv/vāh ("he commanded") the וָּ is a *vav* with a *dagesh-forte*, not a *shureq*, as indicated by the presence of the vowel *qames*. This word is equivalent to צִוְוָה.
- פִּיּוֹת = pî/yôṯ ("mouths") is equivalent to פִּייּוֹת. The first י is part of a *hireq-yod*; the second י begins a new syllable.

3. Distinguishing *dagesh-lene* and *dagesh-forte*

a. Since the *dagesh-lene* and *dagesh-forte* serve different functions, they must be distinguished from one another. The following guidelines indicate how.

(1) A *dagesh* which appears in the interior of a word in any consonant other than a *begadkefat* consonant (בּ, גּ, דּ, כּ, פּ, and תּ) is a *dagesh-forte*.

(2) A *dagesh* in a *begadkefat* consonant which is not preceded by a full vowel is a *dagesh-lene*.

(3) A *dagesh* in a *begadkefat* consonant which is preceded by a full vowel is a *dagesh-forte*.

- In אֵלֶּה = ʾēl/leh ("these") the *dagesh* in the לּ is a *dagesh-forte* rather than a *dagesh-lene* because ל is not a *begadkefat* letter. The לּ is also preceded by a full vowel.
- In גֹּאֵל = gō/ʾēl ("redeemer") the *dagesh* in the גּ is a *dagesh-lene* rather

than a *dagesh-forte* because גּ is a *begadkefat* consonant at the beginning, rather than in the interior, of a word. (A *dagesh-forte* can only occur in the interior of a word.) In addition, the *dagesh* in the גּ cannot be a *dagesh-forte* because the consonant is not preceded by a full vowel.

- In אַרְבַּע = ʾar/baʿ ("four") the *dagesh* in the בּ is a *dagesh-lene* because it occurs in a *begadkefat* consonant at the beginning of a syllable, and the בּ is not preceded by a full vowel.
- In לֻקַּחְתָּ = luq/qāḥ/tā ("you were taken") the *dagesh* in the קּ is a *dagesh-forte* because ק is not a *begadkefat* consonant. The *dagesh* in the תּ is a *dagesh-lene* because תּ is a *begadkefat* consonant and is not preceded by a full vowel.
- In תַּגִּיד = tag̱/gîḏ ("you will declare") the *dagesh* in the תּ is a *dagesh-lene* because תּ is not preceded by a full vowel, and the *dagesh* in the גּ is a *dagesh-forte* because גּ is preceded by a full vowel.

b. When a *dagesh* in a *begadkefat* consonant is a *dagesh-forte*, the second of the doubled consonants will have a *dagesh-lene* (in transliteration), because it will begin a syllable and will not be preceded by a full vowel.

- In דִּבֵּר = diḇ/ber ("he spoke") the דּ has a *dagesh-lene* because it is not preceded by a full vowel, and the בּ has a *dagesh-forte* because it is preceded by a full vowel. A full spelling of דִּבֵּר (that is, without the *dagesh-forte*) would be דִּבְבֵּר. Note that the first ב cannot have a *dagesh-lene* because it is preceded by a full vowel, while the second בּ must have a *dagesh-lene* because it is not preceded by a full vowel.

4. Transliteration

a. The following biblical words provide further illustrations of the transliteration of consonants which have a *dagesh-lene* or a *dagesh-forte*.

(1)	דַּרְכּוֹ	dar/kô	("his way")
(2)	לְבָבְךָ	lᵉḇoḇ/ḵā	("your heart")
(3)	הַיָּם	hay/yām	("the sea")
(4)	הֵ֫נָּה	hḗn/nāh	("they")
(5)	כִּי־כֻלָּם	kî-ḵul/lām	("for all of them")
(6)	רַבָּה	raḇ/bāh	("many")

(7)	מֵחַטָּאתוֹ	mē/ḥaṭ/ṭāʾ/ṯô	("from his sin")
(8)	הַדָּם	haḏ/dām	("the blood")
(9)	מִלְּפָנֶ֫יךָ	mil/l^{e}pā/néy/ḵā	("from before you")
(10)	לְהַצָּלָה	l^{e}haṣ/ṣā/lāh	("to deliver")
(11)	הַדְּבָרִים	haḏ/d^{e}ḇā/rîm	("the words")
(12)	הֱכִינַ֫נִי	h^{ĕ}ḵî/ná/nî	("he established me")
(13)	בַּמְּכוֹנָה	bam/m^{e}ḵô/nāh	("in the stands")
(14)	הַגְּדֹלִים	haḡ/g^{e}ḏō/lîm	("the great ones")
(15)	וַיִּקָּחֻ֫הוּ	vay/yiq/qā/ḥú/hû	("and they took him")
(16)	הָנְחַלְתִּי	hon/ḥal/tî	("I was made to possess")
(17)	הַפַּ֫עַם	hap̄/pá/ʿam	("the occurrence")
(18)	בְּנֵי בְלִיָּ֫עַל	b^{e}nê ḇ^{e}lî/yā/ʿal	("sons of worthlessness")
(19)	וַתִּכְתֹּב	vaṯ/tiḵ/tōḇ	("and she wrote")
(20)	הַמַּבּוּעַ	ham/maḇ/bûaʿ	("the fountain")
(21)	וַיֻּכּוּ	vay/yuḵ/kû	("and they were struck")
(22)	מִקִּרְבָּהּ	miq/qir/bāh	("from her midst")
(23)	וַיִּשְׁתַּ֫חֲווּ	vay/yiš/tá/ḥ^{ă}vû	("and they bowed down")
(24)	הָעַמִּים	hā/ʿam/mîm	("the peoples")
(25)	הָתְפָּקְדוּ	hoṯ/pā/q^{e}ḏû	("they were numbered")
(26)	תִּזָּכַרְנָה	tiz/zā/ḵar/nāh	("she will be remembered")
(27)	הַמַּבּוּל	ham/maḇ/bûl	("the flood")
(28)	וַתִּתֵּן	vaṯ/tiṯ/tēn	("and you gave")
(29)	יִסְּרַתּוּ	yis/s^{e}raṯ/tû	("she taught him")
(30)	הַטִּי־נָא כַדֵּךְ	haṭ/ṭî-nāʾ ḵaḏ/dēḵ	("please extend your jar")

b. The student may find it helpful in the early stages of learning the language to transliterate Hebrew words in order to pronounce them correctly. However, the student will soon learn to pronounce Hebrew words without the crutch of transliteration.

4C Vowel Alterations

1. The vowels of a word may undergo alterations due to changes in the circumstance of a word. Short vowels can lengthen and long vowels can shorten due to such changes as the shifting of an accent or the addition of prefixes or suffixes. The specific patterns by which these vowel alterations occur are quite complex and need not be

learned at this point.[1] It is helpful, however, to have a general understanding of the kind of changes that may occur. An example has already been given in this lesson of the kind of vowel alteration which can occur when there is a change in accenting. As discussed in section 4A.2, when the accent is shifted to the end of a word group which is joined by a *maqqef*, there may be an alteration of vowels, such as the shortening of a vowel in a closed syllable which is no longer accented (בֵּן + *maqqef* + אוֹר = בֶּן־אוֹר). A few other illustrations of vowel alterations follow.

- When a prefixed הָ (a definite article[2]) is added to the word הַר = har ("mountain"), it becomes הָהָר = hā/hār ("the mountain"). The addition of the prefix causes the *patah* in הַר to lengthen to a *qames*.
- When the suffix וּ (a third person, plural verb ending[3]) is added to מָלֵא = mā/lēʾ ("he was full"), it becomes מָֽלְאוּ = mā/leʾû ("they were full"). Note that the *sere* under the ל reduces to a *sheva*. (The *meteg* is added to clarify the fact that the first vowel remains a *qames*; it does not become a *qames-hatuf*.)
- When a particular suffix (first person, pronominal[4]) is added to the word אָחוֹת = ʾā/ḥôṯ ("sister") it becomes אֲחֹתִי = ʾăḥō/ṯî ("my sister"). Note that the *qames* shortens to a *hatef-patah* and the *holem-vav* shortens to a *holem*.
- When the same suffix is added to the word חֹ֫שֶׁךְ = ḥṓ/šeḵ ("darkness"), it becomes חָשְׁכִּי = ḥoš/kî ("my darkness"). Note that the addition of the suffix causes the accent to shift from the first to the last syllable, the *holem* under the ח to shorten to a *qames-hatuf*, and the *segol* under the שׁ to become a *sheva*.

2. Vowel alterations often occur within the classes of vowels. (See Lesson 2A.6.) The examples above illustrate this pattern:

   Within the A class they show *patah* (a) lengthening to *qames* (ā) and also *qames* (ā) shortening to *hatef-patah* (ă)

   Within the E class they show *sere* (ē) and *segol* (e) shortening to *sheva* (e)

   Within the O class they show *holem* (ō) shortening to *qames-hatuf* (o)

---

[1] For a discussion see Joüon, §29.

[2] See Lesson 5B.

[3] See Lesson 12B.2.

[4] See Lesson 9A.

3. However, it is also the case that vowel alterations can occur between vowel classes, especially between E class and I class vowels, and between O class and U class vowels.
   - When a suffix (first person, pronominal) is added to אֵם = ʾēm (“mother”), it becomes אִמִּי = ʾim/mî (“my mother”); and when the same suffix is added to עֹז = ʿōz (“strength”), it becomes עֻזִּי (ʿuz/zî), “my strength.” In the first word the *sere* (ê) shortens to a *hireq* (î), and in the second the *holem* (ō) shortens to a *qibbus* (u).

Lesson 4: Exercises

a. The first part of Genesis 1:2 reads

וְהָאָ֫רֶץ הָיְתָה תֹ֫הוּ וָבֹ֫הוּ

A literal, word-for-word translation is “And-the-earth was formless and-void.” (The hyphens indicate when an English phrase represents a single Hebrew word.) Note that none of the *begadkefat* consonants which appear in these words has a *dagesh-lene*. Explain why the *dagesh-lene* is missing in each case, then pronounce the Hebrew words.

b. Look in a Hebrew Bible at Genesis 1:6. A literal, word-for-word translation of the verse is “And-he-said, God, ‘Let-there-be an-expanse in-the-midst-of the-waters, and-let-there-be a-separating between water from-water.’”

(1) Identify the number of *dagesh-lene*s and *dagesh-forte*s that appear in this verse.

(2) Explain why the eighth word of the verse does not have a *dagesh-lene* in the *bet*.

c. Practice transliterating the Hebrew words in section 4B.4a. While doing this exercise, cover the transliterations that appear beside the words. When finished check the work against the answers in the book. Then pronounce each word.

✓ Remember that Appendix 1 has a convenient summary of guidelines for transliteration.

d. Transliterate the following biblical words. While doing so, be sure to indicate syllable division and mark an accented syllable if an accent mark appears on the Hebrew word. Then pronounce each word.

(1) אִשָּׁה ("woman")
(2) רַגְלַ֫יִם ("feet")
(3) מִדְבָּר ("wilderness")
(4) הַצֹּאן ("the flock")
(5) בָּשָׂר ("flesh")
(6) לֹא־כִי ("not so")
(7) נִפֵּץ ("he shattered")
(8) הַנַּ֫עַר ("the boy")
(9) נִדַּחְתָּ ("you were driven away")
(10) הָשְׁכְּבָה ("be laid to rest")
(11) אַפּוֹ ("his nose")
(12) פִּנָּתָהּ ("corner")
(13) הַשְּׁלִישִׁי ("the third")
(14) הַֽהֹלְכִים ("the ones going")
(15) עֱגֻלּוֹת ("round")
(16) הַמִּזְבֵּחַ ("the altar")
(17) בַּכֹּפֶר ("with the pitch")
(18) אוֹתְכֶם ("you")
(19) רְכֻלָּתֵךְ ("your merchandise")
(20) הֱיוֹת ("to be")
(21) הַמַּטֶּה ("the tribe")
(22) יִשְׁתָּיוּן ("they will drink")
(23) הִתְאַסֵּף ("gathering itself")
(24) הַכְּתֵפֹת ("the supports")
(25) וַיַּצִּ֫בוּ ("and they set up")
(26) בְּצִדָּהּ ("in its side")
(27) לְכֻלָּֽהְנָה ("for the whole")
(28) אֲגַפֶּ֫יךָ ("your armies")
(29) וְהַמַּטִּים ("and the ones turning aside")
(30) כֹּה תֹאמְרוּן ("thus you will say")
(31) תְּאָכְלֵהוּ ("you will eat it")
(32) תַּחְתִּיּוֹת ("lower")
(33) הַֽמְקֻבָּרִים ("the buried ones")
(34) לַכִּיֹּר ("for the washbasin")
(35) בַּשּׁוֹשַׁנִּים ("in the lillies")
(36) קִוִּיתִי ("I will hope")
(37) הַגִּבֹּרִים ("the mighty ones")
(38) מִמֶּ֫נּוּ ("from us")
(39) כָּל־הַקֹּשְׁרִים ("all of the ones conspiring")
(40) נְבוּכַדְרֶאצַּר ("Nebuchadrezzar")

Lesson 5

Nouns, Verbs, and Sentences; Definite Article

5A Nouns, Verbs, and Sentences

The purpose of this section is to provide some fundamental information about nouns, verbs, and sentences, in order to form a basis for the translation of simple sentences.

1. Nouns

a. Gender and number

(1) With regard to gender, every noun is either masculine or feminine; no nouns are neuter.

(2) With regard to number, most nouns have singular and plural forms; a few have dual forms. As the name suggests, the dual form normally indicates a pair of something.

b. Generally, the inflection of a noun (through the occurrence of certain vowels, prefixes, or suffixes) indicates the gender and number of the noun. The means for recognizing inflected nouns will be discussed in a future lesson.

c. The simplest form of a noun is that by which it is listed in a lexicon; hence, it is called the lexical form. The lexical form of a noun is normally the masculine or feminine, singular form. It is this form by which nouns will be presented in the vocabulary lists of lessons.

2. Verbs

a. Indicative verbs (that is, verbs that make statements) occur in two tenses: perfect and imperfect. The nature of these tenses will be discussed in future lessons.

b. Person, gender, and number

(1) Unlike English, a verb in Hebrew indicates whether the subject is first person ("I," "we"), second person ("you"), or third person ("he," "she," "they").

(2) Again unlike English, a verb in Hebrew indicates the gender of the subject – either masculine or feminine.

(3) Like English, a verb in Hebrew is either singular or plural in number.

(4) A Hebrew verb agrees with the subject of a sentence (if one is stated) in person, gender, and number.

c. A verb is inflected by means of prefixes, suffixes, and pointings to indicate its person, gender, and number. The inflection of verbs will be discussed in future lessons. Until that time the vocabulary lists in lessons will indicate the tense, person, gender, and number of verbs by means of the translations which are provided.

- The translation of בָּא as "he came" identifies the verb as perfect tense, third person, singular.

3. Sentences

a. There are two basic kinds of sentences: verb and verbless.

(1) A verb sentence is one which contains a finite verb.

(2) A verbless sentence is one in which no finite verb appears. Such a sentence usually implies a state-of-being verbal idea (such as "is/are" or "was/were").

b. Word order

(1) In a very basic verb sentence the word order often follows this pattern (reading from right to left):

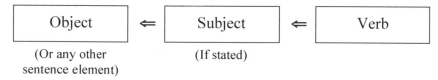

Object	⇐	Subject	⇐	Verb
(Or any other sentence element)		(If stated)		

- The verb clause שָׁלַח דָּוִד מַלְאָכִים (1Sa 25:14), when roughly translated word-for-word, says "He sent, David, messengers." It means "David sent messengers." The first word (שָׁלַח) is a verb; the second word, a proper noun (דָּוִד), is the subject; and the third word, another noun (מַלְאָכִים), is the object of the verb. The verb agrees with the subject with regard to person (third), gender (masculine), and number (singular). To say it another way, the "he" in the translation of the verb "he sent" indicates an agreement of person, gender, and number with the proper noun "David."

(2) In a very basic verbless sentence involving two nouns the word order often follows this pattern (reading from right to left):

Predicate	⇐	Subject

- The verbless sentence יְהוָה מֶלֶךְ (Ps 10:16) is a verbless sentence which may be roughly translated as "the LORD, king." The first word, a proper noun (יְהוָה), is the subject; and the second word, a noun (מֶלֶךְ), is the predicate. No verb appears in the sentence, but a state-of-being verb is implied; therefore, the meaning of the sentence is "the LORD is king."

5B Definite Article

1. Hebrew, unlike English, has no indefinite article ("a" or "an"). However, it may be necessary to supply an indefinite article in an English translation for the sake of clarity.
   - עֹלָה may be translated as "burnt offering" or "a burnt offering," and נַחֲלָה may be translated as "inheritance" or "an inheritance," depending upon the context in which each is used.
2. Hebrew, like English, does have a definite article ("the"). The definite article may be used with a noun, adjective, or participle.
3. The definite article is formed by prefixing the consonant ה to a word. The article never appears alone (that is, not prefixed to a word) and is never separated from a word by a *maqqef.*
4. The definite article is pointed according to the following rules.
   a. Before most consonants (excepting the gutturals and ר) the article is הַ followed by a *dagesh-forte* (placed in the first consonant of the word to which the article is prefixed) (הַּ___).[1]
   - לֵב ("heart") + article = הַלֵּב ("the heart")
   - קוֹל ("voice") + article = הַקּוֹל ("the voice")
   - טוֹב ("good") + article = הַטּוֹב ("the good")

[1] The symbol ___ stands for a word of undetermined length; it is used here to symbolically represent the spelling of the article. Exceptions to rule a. do occur. For example, when the article is attached to a word that begins with יְ or מְ, the article may be הַ with no *dagesh-forte* in the י or the מ. Such exceptions should not cause the student any difficulty in recognizing the presence of the article. See Horsnell, 170; and Joüon, §18m & 35c.

b. Before the "stronger" gutturals ה and ח the definite article is usually הַ (___הַ).[1]
- הֵיכָל ("temple") + article = הַהֵיכָל ("the temple")
- חֻקָּה ("statute") + article = הַחֻקָּה ("the statute")

c. Before the "weaker" gutturals א and ע and before ר the article is usually הָ (___הָ).[2]
- אָב ("father") + article = הָאָב ("the father")
- עִיר ("city") + article = הָעִיר ("the city")
- רֹאשׁ ("head") + article = הָרֹאשׁ ("the head")

d. Before an accented הָ or עָ the article is הָ (___הָ).
- [3]הָר ("mountain") + article = הָהָר ("the mountain")
- עָב ("cloud") + article = הָעָב ("the cloud")

e. Before every חָ and before an unaccented הָ or עָ the article is הֶ (___הֶ).
- חָכָם ("wise") + article = הֶחָכָם ("the wise")
- חָג ("festival") + article = הֶחָג ("the festival")
- הָמוֹן ("sound") + article = הֶהָמוֹן ("the sound")
- עָוֹן ("sin") + article = הֶעָוֹן ("the sin")

✓ Note that rule a. states the usual manner in which the article is pointed (that is, when it is prefixed to a word which begins with a consonant that is not a guttural or ר). Rules b. through e. are exceptions in light of the fact that the gutturals and ר cannot take a *dagesh-forte*.

5. In a few cases the addition of the article to a noun causes minor vowel alterations. Three common words in which alterations occur are as follows.
- אֶ֫רֶץ ("land") + article = הָאָ֫רֶץ ("the land")
- הַר ("mountain") + article = הָהָר ("the mountain")
- עַם ("people") + article = הָעָם ("the people")

---

[1] The student will discover that there are several exceptions to the general rules for syllables described in Lesson 3B. Some exceptions are created by the addition of a prefix to a word, as in this second rule for pointing the article, which creates an open, unaccented syllable with a short vowel (הַ). See Horsnell, 35-6; Joüon, §27c.; and J. Weingreen, *A Practical Grammar for Classical Hebrew*, 2d ed. (Oxford: Clarendon Press, 1959), 24.

[2] Note that the vowel for the ה is lengthened from *patah* to *qames* before the weak gutturals and ר to compensate for the lack of a *dagesh-forte*. The same is also true for the next rule.

[3] A one syllable word is accented. הָר is the spelling for this word when preceded by the article. Without the article it is normally spelled הַר. See section 5B.5.

Lesson 5: Exercises

a. Reproduce from memory the five rules for pointing the definite article.

✓ See Appendix 1 for a convenient summary of these rules.

b. Rewrite the words below with the article and its correct pointing. (The vowels of the words themselves will not change as the article is added.) Also give a translation of the new words. Do the exercise without looking at a list of the rules for pointing the definite article.

▸ *Example:* יָם ("sea") ⇒ *Answer:* הַיָּם ("the sea")

(1)	שֵׁם	("name")	(16)	חֶרֶב	("sword")
(2)	בֶּגֶד	("garment")	(17)	חַיִל	("strength")
(3)	חַי	("living")	(18)	מַיִם	("water")
(4)	אֶבֶן	("stone")	(19)	הָרָה	("pregnant one")
(5)	עֵזֶר	("help")	(20)	עֶבֶד	("servant")
(6)	יוֹם	("day")	(21)	שַׂר	("official")
(7)	רָעָה	("evil")	(22)	עָבִים	("clouds")
(8)	אָח	("brother")	(23)	נֶפֶשׁ	("living being")
(9)	תּוֹרָה	("instruction")	(24)	חָזוֹן	("vision")
(10)	חָגָב	("locust")	(25)	הָרָה[1]	("to a mountain")
(11)	כָּבוֹד	("honor")	(26)	בַּיִת	("house")
(12)	אָדוֹן	("lord")	(27)	עַיִן	("eye")
(13)	מַלְאָךְ	("messenger")	(28)	זָהָב	("gold")
(14)	רוּחַ	("spirit")	(29)	עָמָל	("trouble")
(15)	כֹּהֵן	("priest")	(30)	קֹדֶשׁ	("holiness")

c. Learn to recognize, pronounce, and translate the following vocabulary.

	Word	*Translation*	*Notes*
(1)	אֶל	to, into, toward (*prep*)[2]	

---

[1] When the article is added to this word, the translation is "to the mountain."

[2] When a word can have several translations in English, one must select the translation which best fits the context of the sentence in which the word appears. Grammatical information about vocabulary words is placed in parentheses after the translation. Consult the list of abbreviations at the beginning of this Grammar.

(2)	אֱלֹהִים	God, gods[1] (*NMP*)	
(3)	אֶ֫רֶץ	earth, land (*NFS*)	With *art*: הָאָ֫רֶץ
(4)	בָּא	he came, went, entered (*V*)	Lexical form: בּוֹא[2]
(5)	גּוֹי	nation (*NMS*)	
(6)	הַ___	the (*art*)	Also: הָ or הֶ; prefixed and followed by *dagesh-forte* where possible
(7)	הַר	mountain (*NMS*)	With *art*: הָהָר
(8)	יִשְׂרָאֵל	Israel (*proper N*)	
(9)	מֶ֫לֶךְ	king (*NMS*)	
(10)	עַם	people (*NMS*)	With *art*: הָעָם
(11)	רָאָה	he saw (*V*)	
(12)	רֹאשׁ	head, top (*NMS*)	

d. The following verses from the Hebrew Bible have an "interlinear-style" translation, whereby the English equivalent appears directly beneath each Hebrew word (reading from right to left). The translation of vocabulary words (including the article) and names is omitted. Rewrite the English translation, filling in the blanks with the appropriate vocabulary or transliterated names. When finished, attempt a smoother translation, using the aid of an English version if necessary.

וָיֶ֫פֶת	וְחָם	וְשֵׁם־	נֹחַ	בָּא	הַזֶּה	הַיּוֹם	בְּעֶ֫צֶם	(1)
and ______,	and ______	and[3] ______	______	______	the this,[4]	___ day,	"On (the) same	

[1] The word אֱלֹהִים is a masculine, plural noun. Therefore, it can have the meaning of "gods," as in the phrase אֱלֹהֵי הַנֵּכָר = "(the) gods of the foreigner" (Ge 35:2). (אֱלֹהֵי is an inflected form of אֱלֹהִים which makes the word genitival. See Lesson 7A.1.) However, אֱלֹהִים most often refers to the single deity of Israel, in which case its meaning is "God," as in the phrase אֱלֹהֵי יִשְׂרָאֵל = "(the) God of Israel" (Ex 5:1). The context of a sentence in which the word is used determines its meaning. When the word refers to God, it is treated syntactically as a singular noun – for example, it occurs with singular verbs and singular adjectives.

[2] The lexical form of a word is the form by which it is located in a lexicon; in this case the lexical form is an infinitive.

[3] The *vav* on the front of this name and the next two names is a prefixed conjunction meaning "and."

[4] An adjective, like this demonstrative adjective, follows the noun it modifies and also has the article, because the noun is articular. A smoother translation of the first three words is "On this same day."

בְּנֵי־	נֹחַ	וְאֵשֶׁת	נֹחַ	וּשְׁלֹשֶׁת	נְשֵׁי־	בָנָיו	אִתָּם	אֶל־
sons of	______,	and (the) wife of	______,	and (the) three	wives of	his sons	with them	______

הַתֵּבָה	
___ ark.”	(Ge 7:13)

(2)

מֹשֶׁה	עַבְדִּי	מֵת	וְעַתָּה	קוּם	עֲבֹר	אֶת־	הַיַּרְדֵּן
“______,	my servant,	has died,	so now	arise,	cross over	[1]	______,

הַזֶּה	אַתָּה	וְכָל־	הָעָם	הַזֶּה	אֶל־	הָאָרֶץ	אֲשֶׁר	אָנֹכִי
the this,	you	and all of	______,	the this,	______	______	which	I

נֹתֵן	לָהֶם	לִבְנֵי	יִשְׂרָאֵל	
am giving	to them,	to (the) children of	______.”	(Jos 1:2)

(3)

וַיַּעַל	אֵלָיו	וְהִנֵּה	יֹשֵׁב	עַל־	רֹאשׁ	הָהָר	וַיְדַבֵּר
“And he [a captain] went	to[2] him [Elijah]	and behold	(Elijah was) sitting	on	(the) ______ of	______	and he said

אֵלָיו	אִישׁ	הָאֱלֹהִים	הַמֶּלֶךְ	דִּבֶּר	רֵדָה	
to him [Elijah],	‘Man of	______,	______	says,	“Come down.”””	(2Ki 1:9)

(4)

וַיְחַל	יְהוֹאָחָז	אֶת־פְּנֵי	יְהוָה	וַיִּשְׁמַע	אֵלָיו	יְהוָה	כִּי
“And he entreated,	______,	before	the LORD,	and he listened	to him,	the LORD,	for

רָאָה	אֶת־לַחַץ	יִשְׂרָאֵל	כִּי־לָחַץ	אֹתָם	מֶלֶךְ	אֲרָם	
______	(the) oppres-sion of	______,	that he oppressed	them,	(the) ______ of	______.”	(2Ki 13:4)

[1] אֶת־ is not translatable; it simply indicates that the next word is the object of the verb.

[2] This word is the preposition אֶל with a suffix meaning “him.”

(5)	וַיִּתְהַלְּכוּ	מִגּוֹי	אֶל-	גּוֹי	וּמִמַּמְלָכָה	אֶל-	עַם
	"And (Israel was) wandering	from[1]			and from (one) kingdom		
		______	______	______		______	______,
	אַחֵר						
	another."	(1Ch 16:20)					

e. Pronounce and translate the following words [numbers (1)-(7)] and sentences [numbers (8)-(18)]. Remember that Hebrew is read from right to left. Provide a literal, word-for-word translation. Then attempt a smooth translation which reflects correct word order in English and which supplies the "to be" verb when it is implied in Hebrew.

(1) מֶ֫לֶךְ |[2] הַמֶּ֫לֶךְ (2) אֱלֹהִים | הָאֱלֹהִים (3) רֹאשׁ | הָרֹאשׁ (4) הַר |
הָהָר (5) גּוֹי | הַגּוֹי (6) אֶ֫רֶץ | הָאָ֫רֶץ (7) עַם | הָעָם (8) בָּא אֱלֹהִים אֶל
יִשְׂרָאֵל (9) אֱלֹהִים מֶ֫לֶךְ (10) הָאֱלֹהִים הַמֶּ֫לֶךְ (11) רָאָה הַגּוֹי[3] הָהָר
(12) בָּא מֶ֫לֶךְ אֶל הָעָם (13) רָאָה אֱלֹהִים הָאָ֫רֶץ (14) הַמֶּ֫לֶךְ הָרֹאשׁ[4]
(15) בָּא יִשְׂרָאֵל אֶל הָאֱלֹהִים (16) רָאָה הַמֶּ֫לֶךְ הָהָר (17) בָּא עַם אֶל-
הָאָ֫רֶץ (18) אֱלֹהִים הָרֹאשׁ

---

[1] The *mem* is the preposition "from" which is prefixed to this vocabulary word. It causes a *dagesh-forte* to appear in the first letter of the word.

[2] In exercises the symbol | indicates that the words it separates are not grammatically linked in a sentence; they are to be read as independent words in a series.

[3] הַגּוֹי ("the nation") is a singular, collective noun (that is, its form is singular, but it refers to a collection of people or things). When this noun – or any singular, collective noun (such as יִשְׂרָאֵל = "Israel" or עַם = "people") – is the subject of a verb, that verb may also be singular, agreeing with its subject in number. In a literal, word-for-word English translation the result may appear to be grammatically awkward, such as with sentence (11): "He saw, the nation, the mountain." A smoother translation would be "The nation saw the mountain." It is also possible for collective nouns to take plural verbs. See Lesson 10, Exercise c (15).

[4] רֹאשׁ can mean "head" in the sense of a leader.

Lesson 6

PREPOSITIONS, CONJUNCTIONS, WEAK CONSONANTS

6A PREPOSITIONS

1. Independent prepositions

Most Hebrew prepositions stand as independent words, such as the preposition אֶל ("to, into, toward"), which was introduced in the previous lesson. For example, אֶל stands alone in אֶל־הַכֹּהֵן ("to the priest" [Lv 2:8]). While this prepositional phrase shows a *maqqef* linking the independent preposition to its object, a *maqqef* is not required, as illustrated by אֶל כָּל־הַחַיִּים ("to all of the living" [Ecc 9:4]). Other common independent prepositions will be introduced in this and succeeding lessons.

2. Prefixed prepositions

a. Hebrew has three prepositions which are always prefixed to words. They are בּ ("in, by, with"), כּ ("like, as"), and ל ("to, for, according to").[1] These prefixed prepositions cannot stand alone as independent words.

b. When attached to a word, the prefixed prepositions are pointed according to the following rules.

(1) In most cases the prefixed prepositions take a simple *sheva* (as in ___בְּ).

- שָׁנָה ("a year") + בּ = בְּשָׁנָה ("in[2] a year")
- מַעֲשֶׂה ("a deed") + כּ = כְּמַעֲשֶׂה ("as a deed")
- רֹאשׁ ("a head") + ל = לְרֹאשׁ ("to a head")

---

[1] These prefixed prepositions are evidently derived from three independent prepositions: בְּמוֹ, כְּמוֹ, and לְמוֹ, which occasionally occur in poetic texts in the Hebrew Bible. See Kautzsch, §102c. The translations of the prefixed prepositions given here and in the vocabulary list in the exercises are very common meanings. Other translations are also possible, as lexicons indicate.

[2] Since each of the prefixed prepositions has several possible translations, one must determine which is most appropriate for its context. In the examples in this section various translations are used for the purpose of illustration.

(2) Before a consonant which has a simple *sheva* the prefixed prepositions take a *hireq* (as in בִּ__ְ).

- נְפֹל ("falling") + בּ = בִּנְפֹל ("in falling")
- כְּלִי ("a vessel") + כּ = כִּכְלִי ("as a vessel")
- שְׁמֹעַ ("hear") + ל = לִשְׁמֹעַ ("to hear")

✓ Two *sheva*s cannot appear under successive consonants at the beginning of a word. Consequently, rules (2) through (5) describe what happens when a prefixed preposition is placed before a consonant which has a *sheva*.

(3) Before יְ the prefixed prepositions take a *hireq*, and the *sheva* under the י falls away (as in בִּי__).

- יְשׁוּעָה ("salvation") + בּ = בִּישׁוּעָה ("with salvation")
- יְרוּשָׁלַ͏ִם[1] ("Jerusalem") + כּ = כִּירוּשָׁלַ͏ִם ("like Jerusalem")
- יְהוּדָה ("Judah") + ל = לִיהוּדָה ("to Judah")

✓ The above examples illustrate that the prefixing of the preposition to יְ causes the י to quiesce (that is, lose its capacity to support a vowel) and to merge into a *hireq*-yod, which is the vowel for the preposition.

(4) Before a guttural consonant which has a composite *sheva* the prefixed prepositions usually assume the short vowel which corresponds to the composite *sheva* (as in בַּ__ֲ, בֶּ__ֱ, or בָּ__ֳ).[2]

- אֱנוֹשׁ ("a man") + בּ = בֶּאֱנוֹשׁ ("in a man")
- אֲרִי ("a lion") + כּ = כַּאֲרִי ("like a lion")
- חֳלִי ("sickness") + ל = לָחֳלִי ("for sickness")

✓ As the above examples illustrate, the corresponding short vowel for *hatef-patah* is *patah*; for *hatef-segol* it is *segol*; and for *hatef-qames* it is *qames-hatuf*.

✓ In a few words that begin with אֲ or אֱ the addition of the prefixed preposition causes the א to quiesce, losing its vowel. The following are three common words in which this phenomenon occurs. Note that the preposition has a *patah* in the first case and a *sere* in the last two.

---

[1] See Lesson 7A.2c(3) concerning the spelling of this word.

[2] Note that when the prefixed prepositions take a short vowel they form open, unaccented syllables, creating an exception to the general rule that unaccented, open syllables normally have long vowels.

- ‣ אֲדֹנָי ("[the] Lord") + ב = בַּאדֹנָי ("by [the] Lord")
- ‣ אֱלֹהִים ("God") + כ = כֵּאלֹהִים ("like God")
- ‣ אֱמֹר ("say") + ל = לֵאמֹר ("to say")

(5) Before יְהוָה the prefixed prepositions take a *patah*.[1]

- ‣ יְהוָה ("[the] LORD") + ל = לַיהוָה ("to [the] LORD")

(6) Before an accented syllable the prefixed prepositions frequently take a *qames* (as in בָּ֫___).

- ‣ זֶה ("this") + ב = בָּזֶה ("in this")
- ‣ אֵ֫לֶּה ("these") + כ = כָּאֵ֫לֶּה ("like these")
- ‣ מַ֫יִם ("water") + ל = לָמָ֫יִם[2] ("to water")

(7) When the prefixed prepositions are attached to a word which has the definite article, the ה of the article drops out and the preposition takes the pointing of the article (including the placement of a *dagesh-forte* in the first consonant of the word, should the article require it) (as in הַ_ּ__ + ב = בַ_ּ__).

- ‣ Compare the following pairs of examples, noting how the presence of the article affects the pointing of the prefixed preposition.

שָׁנָה ("a year")	+	ב	=	בְּשָׁנָה ("in a year")
הַשָּׁנָה ("the year")	+	ב	=	בַּשָּׁנָה ("in the year")
מַעֲשֶׂה ("a deed")	+	כ	=	כְּמַעֲשֶׂה ("like a deed")
הַמַּעֲשֶׂה ("the deed")	+	כ	=	כַּמַּעֲשֶׂה ("like the deed")
רֹאשׁ ("a head")	+	ל	=	לְרֹאשׁ ("for a head")
הָרֹאשׁ ("the head")	+	ל	=	לָרֹאשׁ ("for the head")

✓ For most words a simple clue to the presence of the article with the prefixed prepositions is the appearance of a *dagesh-forte* (which usually accompanies the article) in the first consonant of the word, as illustrated by בַּשָּׁנָה ("in the year"). Of course, this clue is not present in the case of

[1] The divine name יְהוָה takes a preposition with a *patah* because the Masoretic pointing of this name (with *sheva* and *qames*) indicates that the reader is to substitute the word אֲדֹנָי ("[the] Lord") for the divine name. Since a prefixed preposition on אֲדֹנָי takes a *patah*, then the preposition on יְהוָה also has a *patah*. See the vocabulary in exercise c.

[2] When the preposition is added to מַ֫יִם, the vowel in the accented syllable lengthens.

words that begin with a guttural or ר, since they cannot take a *dagesh-forte*, as illustrated by לָרֹאשׁ ("for the head"). However, in the case of words beginning with a guttural or ר, the vowel pointing of the preposition usually indicates the presence or absence of the article.

3. Preposition מִן

a. The preposition מִן ("from, out of") commonly occurs as both an independent preposition and as a prefixed preposition. מִן־הָאָרֶץ ("out of the earth" [Ge 2:6]) illustrates its occurrence as an independent preposition.

b. מִן can also be prefixed to a word in an abbreviated form. When prefixed, the ן drops out and the pointing is as follows.

(1) In most cases the preposition is prefixed as מִ, followed by a *dagesh-forte* (placed in the first consonant of the word to which the preposition is prefixed) (מִ ּ__).

- מָקוֹם ("a place") + prefixed מִן = מִמָּקוֹם ("from a place")
- גּוֹי ("a nation") + prefixed מִן = מִגּוֹי ("out of a nation")

✓ The appearance of the *dagesh-forte* after the מ is due to the assimilation of the ן into the first consonant of the word. The *dagesh-forte* compensates for the lost consonant.

(2) Before a guttural or ר the preposition is prefixed as מֵ (מֵ___).

- אֵשׁ ("a fire") + prefixed מִן = מֵאֵשׁ ("out of a fire")
- רֹאשׁ ("a head") + prefixed מִן = מֵרֹאשׁ ("from a head")

✓ The two preceding examples illustrate that the vowel under the מ lengthens from a *hireq* (as described in the first rule) to a *sere* to compensate for the fact that the gutturals and ר cannot take a *dagesh-forte*.

(3) Before יְ the preposition is prefixed as מִ and the *sheva* under the י falls away (מִי__).

- יְהוּדָה ("Judah") + prefixed מִן = מִיהוּדָה ("out of Judah")

(4) When prefixed to a word which has the definite article, the ה remains in place, and the preposition is prefixed as מֵ, according to rule (2) above (הַ ּ__ + מִן = מֵהַ ּ__).

- הַנַּחַל ("the stream") + prefixed מִן = מֵהַנַּחַל ("out of the stream")
- הָעוֹף ("the birds") + prefixed מִן = מֵהָעוֹף ("from the birds")

6B Conjunctions

1. Independent conjunctions

Most Hebrew conjunctions stand as independent words. To illustrate, the independent conjunction כִּי ("that, for, when, because") stands alone in כִּי בָא ("that he came" [Nu 22:36]) and כִּי־רָאָה יְהוָה ("because the LORD saw" [Ge 29:32]). As these phrases indicate, a *maqqef* may or may not appear after an independent conjunction. Several independent conjunctions will be introduced in future vocabulary lists.

2. *Vav* conjunction

a. The most common conjunction in the Hebrew Bible is the *vav* conjunction. It occurs only as a prefix which is attached to words; it cannot stand alone as an independent conjunction. The most common translation for the *vav* conjunction is "and."[1] It can link words, phrases, or clauses.

b. When prefixed to a word, the *vav* conjunction is pointed according to the following rules.

✓ Note that with the exception of number (2) below and the prefixing of the *vav* conjunction to the definite article, these rules are parallel to the rules for pointing the prefixed prepositions.

(1) In most cases the *vav* conjunction takes a *sheva* (וְ___).

- שָׁנָה ("a year") + ו = וְשָׁנָה ("and a year")
- זֶה ("this") + ו = וְזֶה ("and this")
- רֹאשׁ ("a head") + ו = וְרֹאשׁ ("and a head")

(2) Before a consonant which has a simple *sheva* and before the labial consonants (בּ, מ, and פּ) the *vav* conjunction becomes וּ (a shureq) (as in וּ__ְ__ and וּב__).

- שְׁתַּיִם ("two") + ו = וּשְׁתַּיִם ("and two")
- בַּת ("a daughter") + ו = וּבַת ("and a daughter")
- מִשְׁפָּט ("judgment") + ו = וּמִשְׁפָּט ("and judgment")
- פָּנִים ("a face") + ו = וּפָנִים ("and a face")

✓ Note: When the *vav* conjunction occurs as וּ, it forms a syllable which begins with a vowel, rather than a consonant. This feature is the one exception to the rule that a syllable must begin with a consonant.

---

[1] The *vav* conjunction can convey a number of other meanings, depending upon its context, such as, "or, but, also, then, when, since, therefore."

(3) Before יְ the *vav* conjunction takes a *hireq*, and the *sheva* under the י falls away (וִי__).

- יְשׁוּעָה ("salvation") + ו = וִישׁוּעָה ("and salvation")
- יְהוּדָה ("Judah") + ו = וִיהוּדָה ("and Judah")
- יְרוּשָׁלַ͏ִם ("Jerusalem") + ו = וִירוּשָׁלַ͏ִם ("and Jerusalem")

(4) Before a consonant which has a composite *sheva* the *vav* conjunction assumes the short vowel which corresponds to the composite *sheva* (וַ_ֲ_ , וֶ_ֱ_, or וָ_ֳ_).[1]

- עֲבֹדָה ("service") + ו = וַעֲבֹדָה ("and service")
- אֱכֹל ("eat") + ו = וֶאֱכֹל ("and eat")
- חֳלִי ("sickness") + ו = וָחֳלִי ("and sickness")

✓ In two common words which begin with אֲ or אֱ the addition of the *vav* conjunction causes the א to quiesce, losing its vowel. Note that the *vav* has a *patah* in the first case and a *sere* in the second.

- אֲדֹנָי ("[the] Lord") + ו = וַאדֹנָי ("and [the] Lord")
- אֱלֹהִים ("God") + ו = וֵאלֹהִים ("and God")

(5) Before יְהוָה the *vav* conjunction takes a *patah*.[2]

- יְהוָה ("[the] LORD") + ו = וַיהוָה ("and [the] LORD")

(6) Before an accented syllable the *vav* conjunction frequently takes a *qames*. This characteristic is especially prominent when the *vav* conjunction links two nouns which express related ideas (וָ___).[3]

- יוֹם וָלַיְלָה ("day and night")
- זָהָב וָכֶסֶף ("gold and silver")
- רֶכֶב־וָסוּס ("chariot and horse")

c. Prefixing a *vav* conjunction to a word that has a definite article or a prefixed preposition, does not alter either the article or the preposition.

- הָאִשָּׁה ("the woman") + ו = וְהָאִשָּׁה ("and the woman")
- לָאִשָּׁה ("for the woman") + ו = וְלָאִשָּׁה ("and for the woman")

---

[1] As with the prefixed prepositions, so the *vav* conjunction also creates an exception to the general rules of syllabification, since it creates an unaccented, open syllable that has a short vowel.

[2] As noted earlier (in section 6A.2b(5)), a *patah* appears with the divine name because readers substituted אֲדֹנָי ("[the] Lord") for the name, and אֲדֹנָי requires a *patah* with the *vav* conjunction.

[3] See Kautzsch, §104g.

6C Weak Consonants

Some consonants are considered "weak" because they have a greater tendency to cause alterations in the spelling of words than "strong" consonants do. A number of the features of weak consonants have been observed in preceding sections. Below is a summary of the characteristics of these consonants which have been encountered thus far. Other features of weak consonants will appear in succeeding lessons.

1. Guttural consonants (א, ה, ח, ע) and ר
   a. The gutturals normally take a composite *sheva* instead of a simple *sheva.*
   b. The gutturals and ר cannot take a *dagesh-forte*. To compensate for this fact, the vowel before a guttural or ר is sometimes lengthened.
      - While the definite article is normally הַ followed by the *dagesh-forte*, when the article is attached to עֵת ("time") the spelling is הָעֵת ("the time"). Since the ע cannot take a *dagesh-forte*, the preceding vowel is lengthened from *patah* to *qames.*
   c. The gutturals and ר prefer an A-class vowel before and sometimes after them.
      - A furtive *patah* sometimes appears before a guttural at the end of a word, as in רֵעַ ("friend").
2. Quiescent consonants (א, ה, ו, י)
   a. The quiescent consonants may lose their capacity to support a vowel. When this occurs, the vowel preceding the quiescent consonant may be lengthened.
      - When the prefixed preposition לְ is attached to אֱלֹהִים ("God"), it becomes לֵאלֹהִים ("for God"). The vowel under the quiescent א falls away and the preceding vowel under the preposition lengthens from the typical pointing of *sheva* to *sere*.
   b. ו and י can represent naturally-long vowels rather than consonants.
      - When the prefixed preposition בְּ is attached to יְשׁוּעָה ("salvation"), it becomes בִּישׁוּעָה ("with salvation"). The י loses its vowel and becomes part of a *hireq-yod.*
      - When the *vav* conjunction is attached to כְּלִי ("a vessel"), it becomes a *shureq*, as in וּכְלִי ("and a vessel").
   c. א cannot close any syllable, and ה (without a *mappiq*) cannot close the final syllable of a word.

- In כֹּה־דִבֶּר ("thus he spoke" [Ge 24:30]) the ה does not close the syllable, as evidenced by the lack of a *dagesh-lene* in the following consonant.

3. *Nun*

When a נ without a full vowel stands before another consonant, it may be assimilated into that consonant. This assimilation is normally compensated for by a *dagesh-forte* appearing in the consonant after the assimilated נ. Should such compensation not be possible, there may be a lengthening of the vowel before the assimilated נ.

- When the preposition מִן is prefixed to יוֹם ("a day"), it becomes מִיּוֹם ("from a day"). The ן is assimilated into the י, as evidenced by the appearance of a *dagesh-forte*.
- When the preposition מִן is prefixed to הַיּוֹם ("the day"), it becomes מֵהַיּוֹם ("from the day"). Since the ה cannot receive a *dagesh-forte* from the assimilation of the ן, the preceding vowel under the preposition lengthens from the typical pointing of *hireq* to *sere*.

Lesson 6: Exercises

a. Reproduce from memory the rules for pointing the prefixed prepositions.

✓ See Appendix 1 for a convenient summary of these rules.

b. Rewrite the words below with the appropriate prefixed preposition and its correct pointing. Also give a translation of the new words. Do the exercise without looking at a list of the rules for pointing the prefixed preposition.

- *Example:* Prefix בְּ to הַיָּם ("the sea") ⇒ *Answer:* בַּיָּם ("by the sea")

(1) Prefix בְּ to the following:

(a)	שָׁאוּל	("Saul")	(f)	אֵלֶּה	("these")
(b)	קְרֹא	("calling")	(g)	הַשָּׁמַיִם	("the heavens")
(c)	יְמִינִי	("my right hand")	(h)	שְׁלַח	("send")
(d)	הַמִּדְבָּר	("the desert")	(i)	מִצְרַיִם	("Egypt")
(e)	עֳנִי	("affliction")	(j)	אֲדֹנָי	("[the] Lord")

(2) Prefix כְּ to the following:

(a) אֱלֹהִים ("God")
(b) נְשֹׂא ("lifting")
(c) הַפֶּה ("the mouth")
(d) בָּבֶל ("Babylon")
(e) אֲרָזִים ("cedar")
(f) יְקָר ("honor")
(g) הַדָּם ("the blood")
(h) נָחָשׁ ("snake")
(i) הָאִישׁ ("the man")
(j) זֶה ("this")

(3) Prefix לְ to the following:

(a) הַשָּׂדֶה ("the field")
(b) עוֹלָם ("eternity")
(c) שְׁמֹר ("keep")
(d) מַיִם[1] ("water")
(e) יְהוָה ("[the] LORD")
(f) אֲלָפִים ("thousands")
(g) הַנָּבִיא ("the prophet")
(h) יְהוֹשֻׁעַ ("Joshua")
(i) חֲכָמִים ("wise ones")
(j) הַחַטָּאת ("the sin")

c. Learn to recognize, pronounce, and translate the following vocabulary.

	Word	*Translation*	*Notes*
(1)	אָדָם	man, mortal, humankind (*NMS*)	
(2)	בְּ___	in, by, with (*prep*)	Prefixed
(3)	וְ___	and (*conj*)	Prefixed; may link words, phrases, or clauses
(4)	יְהוָה[2]	LORD, the LORD (*proper N*)	
(5)	יָשַׁב	he dwelled, sat (*V*)	
(6)	כְּ___	like, as (*prep*)	Prefixed
(7)	כֹּהֵן	priest (*NMS*)	
(8)	כִּי	that, for, when, because (*conj*)	Introduces a subordinate clause
(9)	לְ___	to, for, according to (*prep*)	Prefixed
(10)	מִן	from, out of (*prep*)	May stand independently or be prefixed

---

[1] See the examples for section 6A.2b(6).

[2] This is the most significant divine name in the Hebrew Bible. As an expression of reverence for this name, ancient Jews began the practice of reading אֲדֹנָי ("[the] Lord"), or in a few cases אֱלֹהִים ("God"), in the place of יהוה. When אֲדֹנָי is to be read, the Masoretes pointed divine name as יְהוָה, and when the reading is to be אֱלֹהִים, the divine name appears as יֱהוִה. This Grammar follows the practice of most English Bibles in translating יְהוָה as "LORD" or "the LORD."

d. An “interlinear-style” translation, which has with some words missing, appears below the Hebrew text of the following verses. Rewrite the English translation, filling in the blanks with a name, vocabulary word, article, prefixed preposition, or conjunction. When finished, provide a smooth translation, consulting an English version as necessary.

בְּצֶלֶם	כִּי	יִשָּׁפֵךְ	דָּמוֹ	בָּאָדָם	הָאָדָם	דַּם	שֹׁפֵךְ	(1)
___ (the) image of	______	will be shed,	his blood	______	______,	blood of	“One who sheds	

	הָאָדָם	אֶת־	עָשָׂה	אֱלֹהִים
(Ge 9:6)	______.”	[1]	he [God] made	______

בְּיוֹם	יְהוָה	מֵאִשֵּׁי	בָּנָיו	וּמִשְׁחַת	אַהֲרֹן	מִשְׁחַת	זֹאת	(2)
___ (the) day (when)	______	___ (the) burnt offerings of	his sons	___ (the) consecrated portion of	______	(the) consecrated portion of	“This is	

	לַיהוָה	לְכַהֵן	אֹתָם	הִקְרִיב
(Lv 7:35)	______.”	___ serve as a priest	them	he presented

לוֹ	הֵנִיחַ־	וַיהוָה	בְּבֵיתוֹ	הַמֶּלֶךְ	יָשַׁב	כִּי־	וַיְהִי[2]	(3)
___ him	gave rest	______	___ his house	______,	______,	______	“___ it happened	

	אֹיְבָיו	מִכָּל־	מִסָּבִיב
(2Sa 7:1)	his enemies.”	___ all of	___ (ones) surrounding,

	כַּאדֹנָיו	כַּעֶבֶד[3]	כַּכֹּהֵן	כָעָם	וְהָיָה	(4)
(Is 24:2)	___ his lord.	___ slave	______	______	“___ it will be	

[1] אֶת־ is not translatable; it simply indicates that the next word is the object of the verb.

[2] The pointing for the *vav* conjunction with this word is governed by a special grammatical feature of the conjunction with imperfect verbs which will be explained in a future lesson.

[3] According to the rules for pointing the definite article, the first *kaf* in this word should have a *qames.*

e. Read aloud and write a translation for the following words [numbers (1)-(7)] and sentences [numbers (8)-(18)].

(1) כֹּהֵן | מִן הַכֹּהֵן | לְכֹהֵן | כְּכֹהֵן | מִכֹּהֵן (2) אָדָם | בְּאָדָם | מֵאָדָם | הָאָדָם | מֵהָאָדָם (3) יְהוָה | וַיהוָה | לַיהוָה | וְלַיהוָה | וּמִן־יְהוָה (4) וּמֶ֫לֶךְ | הַמֶּ֫לֶךְ | כַּמֶּ֫לֶךְ | וְהַמֶּ֫לֶךְ | וּבַמֶּ֫לֶךְ (5) מִן־הַגּוֹי | כְּגוֹי | מֵהַגּוֹי | וְלַגּוֹי | וּבְגוֹי (6) מֵרֹאשׁ | וּמִן־הָרֹאשׁ | לְרֹאשׁ | כָּרֹאשׁ | וּבְרֹאשׁ | וְלָרֹאשׁ (7) בְּעַם | הָעָם | כָּעָם | וּמֵהָעָם | וְלָעָם (8) בָּא הַגּוֹי לְאֶ֫רֶץ (9) יָשַׁב כֹּהֵן בָּהָר (10) בָּא הָאָדָם לַיהוָה (11) וְיָשַׁב הַמֶּ֫לֶךְ בְּיִשְׂרָאֵל (12) רָאָה הָעָם הַר בָּאָ֫רֶץ (13) בָּא הַכֹּהֵן מֵאלֹהִים (14) רָאָה יְהוָה הָעָם כְּגוֹי (15) וּבָא הָעָם אֶל־הָאָ֫רֶץ וְיָשַׁב הָעָם בֵּאלֹהִים בָּאָ֫רֶץ (16) רָאָה יְהוָה כִּי יָשַׁב כֹּהֵן בְּיִשְׂרָאֵל (17) רָאָה אֱלֹהִים כִּי בָא אָדָם כָּרֹאשׁ לַגּוֹי (18) וּבָא הַכֹּהֵן לְיִשְׂרָאֵל וְרָאָה יִשְׂרָאֵל כִּי יְהוָה הָאֱלֹהִים בְּיִשְׂרָאֵל

Lesson 7

NOUNS

7A NOUNS

1. Absolute and construct states

a. Two (or more) nouns can be linked together in a construct relationship. If two nouns are so linked, the first is in a construct state, and the second is in an absolute state. Words in a construct relationship may or may not have a *maqqef.*

- The phrase עַם יִשְׂרָאֵל ("the people of Israel" [2Sa 18:7]) has two nouns in a construct relationship. The first (עַם) is construct, and the second (יִשְׂרָאֵל) is absolute.
- In the phrase כָּל־הַנָּשִׁים ("all of the women" [Ex 15:20]) a *maqqef* links the construct noun (כָּל־) to the absolute noun (הַנָּשִׁים).

b. The construct relationship serves to indicate a genitival idea in the sense that the absolute noun functions as a genitive (or modifier) for the construct noun. This relationship is indicated in English by the insertion of the word "of" after the construct noun.

- In the phrase יוֹם יְהוָה ("the day of the LORD" [Is 13:6]) the absolute word (יְהוָה) functions genitivally by modifying the construct word (יוֹם). To say it another way, the construct word (יוֹם) is dependent upon and limited by the absolute word (יְהוָה), so that יוֹם refers not to all days but to a particular day: "the day of the LORD."

c. As a rule, a construct word cannot take a definite article. However, since definiteness is often implied in a construct relationship, an article may be supplied in translation if the context demands it.[1] The absolute word in a construct relationship can have a definite article.

---

[1] In previous lessons when a construct noun had an implied definite article, the translation of the article appeared in parentheses or brackets as ("the") or ["the"]. Beginning with this lesson the parentheses or brackets will not be used with such implied definite articles, since the student now understands the circumstances in which they may occur.

- In וְרָאוּ בְנֵי־יִשְׂרָאֵל אֶת־פְּנֵי מֹשֶׁה ("And the children of Israel saw the face of Moses" [Ex 34:35]) there are two construct nouns that are definite by implication and therefore require the definite article in English: בְּנֵי = "the children of," and פְּנֵי = "the face of."
- In שִׁמְעוּ דְּבַר־הַמֶּלֶךְ ("Hear the word of the king" or "Hear the king's word" [2Ki 18:28]) the absolute noun has the definite article הַ and the construct noun has an implied definite article.

d. It is possible for two or three construct words to be dependent upon a single absolute word.

- מַטּוֹת בְּנֵי יִשְׂרָאֵל ("the tribes of the children of Israel" [Nu 36:9]) has two construct words followed by an absolute word.
- מִסְפַּר אַנְשֵׁי עַם יִשְׂרָאֵל ("the number of the men of the people of Israel" [Ezr 2:2]) has three construct words followed by an absolute word.

2. Inflection of nouns

a. Nouns are normally inflected with endings which may designate their gender as masculine or feminine; their number as singular, plural, or dual; and their state as absolute or construct.

b. Common endings

(1) The following chart gives the forms of the endings which are used most commonly with nouns.

	SINGULAR		PLURAL	
	Absolute	*Construct*	*Absolute*	*Construct*
M	[none]	[none]	◌ִים	◌ֵי
F	◌ָה	◌ַת	וֹת	וֹת

(2) The following chart illustrates the occurrence of the above endings by use of the words סוּס ("horse" [*M*]) and סוּסָה ("mare" [*F*]).[1]

[1] While the Hebrew examples in this Grammar are normally derived from the Hebrew Bible, it is necessary in some paradigm charts, as with the following one, to include some hypothetical forms for the sake of illustration which are not extant in biblical literature. The masculine form of this word is translated as "horse" rather than "stallion," because it is almost never gender specific in the biblical text, while the feminine form is translated as "mare" since it is always gender specific.

	Singular		Plural	
	Absolute	*Construct*	*Absolute*	*Construct*
M	סוּס ("horse")	סוּס ("horse of")	סוּסִים ("horses")	סוּסֵי ("horses of")
F	סוּסָה ("mare")	סוּסַת ("mare of")	סוּסוֹת ("mares")	סוּסוֹת ("mares of")

✓ Masculine nouns normally have no ending in the singular, whether they are absolute or construct. Consequently, one must determine the absolute or construct state of a masculine, singular noun by the context in which it occurs. The same holds true for feminine, plural nouns which have the same ending in absolute and construct: וֹת.

(3) The preceding chart employs two words, סוּס and סוּסָה, whose spelling does not alter as they are inflected with the common noun endings (except, of course, for the alterations to the endings themselves, such as the changes in the feminine singular from ◌ָה to ◌ַת). To say it another way, as the endings are added to these two nouns the spelling of their "root," סוּס, does not vary. However, most nouns do undergo alterations in spelling as they are inflected with noun endings. They may experience such changes as a shift of accent, a shortening or lengthening of vowels, or the alteration or disappearance of a weak consonant.[1] A future lesson will discuss noun patterns more fully (see Lesson 23B); for now the student simply needs to realize that such changes occur and to be able to recognize nouns in spite of those changes. One aid to recognition is giving special attention to the consonants which make up a noun when learning vocabulary, since most changes in the spelling of inflected nouns involve an alteration of vowels, not consonants.

(4) The following words illustrate the changes which can occur in the spelling of nouns as they are inflected with the common endings. The first column gives the lexical form of the nouns, that is, the form by which they are listed in a lexicon. For most nouns (as for all those below) the lexical form is the

[1] For helpful discussions see Horsnell, 151-165; and Page H. Kelley, *Biblical Hebrew, An Introductory Grammar* (Grand Rapids: William B. Eerdmans, 1992), 58-63.

absolute, singular.[1] The translation of the lexical form and the gender for each noun appears in parentheses in the far right column.

	SINGULAR		PLURAL		
	Absolute	*Construct*	*Absolute*	*Construct*	
(a)	אָדוֹן	אֲדוֹן	אֲדֹנִים	אֲדֹנֵי	("lord" [*M*])
(b)	אֲדָמָה	אַדְמַת	אֲדָמוֹת	אַדְמוֹת	("ground" [*F*])
(c)	דָּבָר	דְּבַר	דְּבָרִים	דִּבְרֵי	("word" [*M*])
(d)	דָּם	דַּם	דָּמִים	דְּמֵי	("blood" [*M*])
(e)	הַר	הַר	הָרִים	הָרֵי	("mountain" [*M*])
(f)	כֹּהֵן	כֹּהֵן	כֹּהֲנִים	כֹּהֲנֵי	("priest" [*M*])
(g)	מֶ֫לֶךְ	מֶ֫לֶךְ	מְלָכִים	מַלְכֵי	("king" [*M*])
(h)	מִנְחָה	מִנְחַת	מִנְחוֹת	מִנְחוֹת	("gift" [*F*])
(i)	מִשְׁפָּחָה	מִשְׁפַּחַת	מִשְׁפָּחוֹת	מִשְׁפְּחוֹת	("clan" [*F*])
(j)	מַעֲשֶׂה	מַעֲשֵׂה	מַעֲשִׂים	מַעֲשֵׂי	("deed" [*M*])
(k)	עַם	עַם	עַמִּים	עַמֵּי	("people" [*M*])

c. Dual endings

(1) A few nouns can take dual endings, which normally indicate two of something. The dual endings, which appear in the chart below, are used for both masculine and feminine nouns.

	DUAL	
	Absolute	*Construct*
M or *F*	◌ַ֫יִם	◌ֵי

✓ Note that the dual, construct ending (◌ֵי) is spelled the same as the construct ending for masculine, plural nouns.

(2) Dual forms typically occur for things found in pairs (such as body parts) or for certain numerals, measurements, and times which involve the number "two" or the concept of duality. Some frequently occurring words with dual forms

[1] A few nouns do not have a singular, absolute form. For example, the lexical form for אֱלֹהִים ("God") is plural, absolute.

appear in the chart below. The translation of the dual, absolute forms appears in parentheses.

	SINGULAR		DUAL		
	Ab	*Cs*	*Ab*	*Cs*	
(a)	אַף	אַף	אַפַּיִם	אַפֵּי	("both nostrils" [*M*])
(b)	אַמָּה	אַמַּת	אַמָּתַיִם	—	("two cubits" [*F*])
(c)	יָד	יַד	יָדַיִם	יְדֵי	("two/both hands" [*F*])
(d)	יוֹם	יוֹם	יוֹמַיִם	יְמֵי	("two days" [*M*])
(e)	עַיִן	עֵין	עֵינַיִם	עֵינֵי	("two/both eyes" [*F*])
(f)	רֶגֶל	רֶגֶל	רַגְלַיִם	רַגְלֵי	("two/both feet" [*F*])
(g)	—	—	שְׁנַיִם	שְׁנֵי	("two" [*M*])
(h)	—	—	שְׁתַּיִם	שְׁתֵּי	("two" [*F*])[1]

(3) A few words which have a dual ending display no known connection with the concept of duality, as the following illustrate.

- יְרוּשָׁלִַם[2] ("Jerusalem")
- מִצְרַיִם ("Egypt")
- מַיִם ("water"[*M*])
- שָׁמַיִם ("heavens"[*M*])

d. Irregular nouns

(1) Some nouns do not employ the common endings listed in the chart above. Illustrations are given below for some of the more frequent exceptions.

(a) Some feminine, singular nouns have no ending. Such often occurs in nouns which refer to that which is naturally feminine or to words which describe paired body parts. However, the lack of an ending occasionally occurs in other feminine, singular nouns.

Singular, Absolute	*Plural, Absolute*
אֵם ("mother" [*F*])	אִמּוֹת ("mothers")
יָד ("hand" [*F*])	יָדוֹת ("hands")

[1] The numerals have both masculine and feminine forms.

[2] In the *MT* the contracted form יְרוּשָׁלִַם is typically used in the place of the full spelling of the word, which is יְרוּשָׁלַיִם.

אֶרֶץ ("land"[*F*])	אֲרָצוֹת ("lands")
נֶפֶשׁ ("living being" [*F*])	נְפָשׁוֹת ("living beings")
רוּחַ ("spirit" [*F*])	רוּחוֹת ("spirits")

(b) Some feminine nouns end with ת in the singular, absolute.

Singular, Absolute	*Plural, Absolute*
בְּרִית ("covenant" [*F*])	—
חַטָּאת ("sin" [*F*])	חַטָּאוֹת ("sins")

(c) A few masculine nouns have the ending וֹת in the plural.

Singular, Absolute	*Plural, Absolute*
אָב ("father" [*M*])	אָבוֹת ("fathers")
מָקוֹם ("place" [*M*])	מְקוֹמוֹת ("places")
קוֹל ("voice" [*M*])	קֹלוֹת ("voices")
שֵׁם ("name" [*M*])	שֵׁמוֹת ("names")

(d) A few feminine nouns have the ending ◌ִים in the plural, absolute.

Singular, Absolute	*Plural, Absolute*
אִשָּׁה ("woman" [*F*])	נָשִׁים ("women")
עִיר ("city" [*F*])	עָרִים ("cities")

(e) A few nouns have both masculine and feminine endings in certain forms.

Singular, Absolute	*Plural, Absolute*
עָב ("cloud" [*F*])	עָבִים (*M*), עָבוֹת (*F*) ("clouds")
שָׁנָה ("year" [*F*])	שָׁנִים (*M*), שְׁנוֹת (*F*) ("years")

(2) The inflection of some irregular nouns involves significant alterations in spelling (beyond an irregular usage of the common endings). Such is the case with the following very common nouns. The translation of their lexical forms and their genders appear in parentheses.[1]

[1] See Horsnell, 164; and Kautzsch, §96.

	Singular		Plural		
	Ab	*Cs*	*Ab*	*Cs*	
(a)	אָב	אֲבִי	אָבוֹת	אֲבוֹת	(“father” [*M*])
(b)	אָח	אֲחִי	אַחִים	אֲחֵי	(“brother” [*M*])
(c)	אִישׁ	אִישׁ	אֲנָשִׁים	אַנְשֵׁי	(“man” [*M*])
(d)	אִשָּׁה	אֵשֶׁת	נָשִׁים	נְשֵׁי	(“woman” [*F*])
(e)	בַּיִת	בֵּית	בָּתִּים	בָּתֵּי	(“house” [*M*])
(f)	בֵּן	בֶּן־ or בִּן־	בָּנִים	בְּנֵי	(“son” [*M*])
(g)	בַּת	בַּת	בָּנוֹת	בְּנוֹת	(“daughter” [*F*])
(h)	יוֹם	יוֹם	יָמִים	יְמֵי	(“day” [*M*])
(i)	כְּלִי	כְּלִי	כֵּלִים	כְּלֵי	(“vessel” [*M*])
(j)	פֶּה	פִּי	פִּיּוֹת פֵּיוֹת	—	(“mouth” [*M*])
(k)	רֹאשׁ	רֹאשׁ	רָאשִׁים	רָאשֵׁי	(“head” [*M*])

(3) Because of the wide range of possibilities in irregular nouns, it is often necessary to consult a lexicon to determine a noun’s gender. It is not necessary at this point to attempt to memorize all the irregularities described above. As these nouns are encountered in reading, their irregularities will become familiar.

3. Function of nouns

A noun is a substantive that can function in three ways: (1) nominatively, as in the case of the subject of a verb or a predicate nominative; (2) genitivally, as an absolute noun limiting a construct noun; or (3) accusatively, as in the case of the object of a verb or the object of a preposition.

- The hypothetical sentence רָאָה הַכֹּהֵן הָאָדָם בָּהָר contains a verb (רָאָה = “he saw”) followed by three nouns. The first noun (הַכֹּהֵן = “the priest”) functions nominatively as the subject of the verb, and the second and third nouns function accusatively as the object of the verb (הָאָדָם = “the man”) and the object of a preposition (בָּהָר = “by the mountain”). The meaning of the sentence is “The priest saw the man by the mountain.”

- In the hypothetical verbless sentence דָּוִד מֶלֶךְ־יִשְׂרָאֵל ("David was the king of Israel") the proper noun דָּוִד ("David") is the subject, and the construct noun מֶלֶךְ־ ("king of") is the predicate nominative. יִשְׂרָאֵל ("Israel") is an absolute proper noun functioning genitivally to limit the meaning of מֶלֶךְ־.
- In the phrase עַם־קֹדֶשׁ (literally, "a people of holiness" [Da 12:7]) the construct noun עַם־ ("people of") is limited by the genitival, absolute noun קֹדֶשׁ ("holiness"). In this situation the absolute noun has the force of an adjective, so that the phrase may be translated "a holy people." Since a construct word does not take a definite article, definiteness may be implied by the context, in which case the meaning is "the holy people," as it is in Da 12:7. However, definiteness can also be expressed by attaching the article to the absolute word, as in עַם־הַקֹּדֶשׁ ("the holy people" [Is 62:12]).

Lesson 7: Exercises

a. Reproduce from memory the common endings for nouns (section 7A.2b(1)) and the dual endings (section 7A.2c(1)).

b. The following regular nouns employ the common or dual endings. For each word identify the gender, number, and state (absolute or construct) and give a translation. In this exercise consider masculine, singular and feminine, plural nouns to be construct only if they have a *maqqef*. The translation of the lexical form of each word (that is, the masculine or feminine, singular, absolute form) appears in parentheses as an aid for determining the translation of the word as it appears in this exercise.

   - *Example:* אָהֳלֵי ("tent") ⇒ *Answer:* masculine, plural, construct, "tents of"

	Word	*Translation of lexical form*		*Word*	*Translation of lexical form*
(1)	גְּבוּל־	("boundary")	(6)	אַרְבַּעַת	("four")
(2)	נְבִיאִים	("prophet")	(7)	מִלְחָמוֹת	("war")
(3)	חֲמִשָּׁה	("five")	(8)	כְּלֵי	("vessel")
(4)	שְׂפָתַיִם	("lip" [*F*])	(9)	זָהָב	("gold")
(5)	כֹּל	("all")	(10)	עֹלוֹת־	("burnt offering")

(11) פָּנִים ("face")
(12) אַלְפַּיִם ("thousand"[*M*])
(13) אֱמוּנָה ("firmness")
(14) נַחֲלוֹת ("possession")
(15) לֶב־ ("heart")
(16) מוֹעֲדֵי ("appointed time")
(17) גִּבְעַת ("hill")
(18) מֵאוֹת ("hundred")

c. Learn to recognize, pronounce, and translate the following vocabulary.

	Word	*Translation*	*Notes*[1]
(1)	אִישׁ	man, husband (*NMS*)	*P:* אֲנָשִׁים, אַנְשֵׁי[2]
(2)	אִשָּׁה	woman, wife (*NFS*)	*Cs:* אֵשֶׁת; *P:* נָשִׁים, נְשֵׁי
(3)	בֵּן	son, child (*NMS*)	*Cs:* בֶּן־, בִּן־; *P:* בָּנִים, בְּנֵי
(4)	בַּת	daughter (*NFS*)	*P:* בָּנוֹת, בְּנוֹת
(5)	יָד	hand (*NFS*)	*Cs:* יַד; *Du:* יָדַיִם, יְדֵי; *P:* יָדוֹת, יְדוֹת
(6)	יוֹם	day (*NMS*)	*Du:* יוֹמַיִם; *P:* יָמִים, יְמֵי
(7)	קֹדֶשׁ	holiness (*NMS*)	*P:* קֳדָשִׁים, קָדְשֵׁי
(8)	רוּחַ	spirit, breath, wind (*NFS*)	
(9)	שָׁנָה	year (*NFS*)	*Du:* שְׁנָתַיִם; *MP:* שָׁנִים, שְׁנֵי; *FP:* שְׁנוֹת

d. The following biblical phrases and sentences are presented with an interlinear-style English translation. The blanks represent places in the Hebrew text where words from the vocabulary lists have been omitted. Rewrite the Hebrew phrases, supplying the missing words. Be sure to write Hebrew nouns with their appropriate common endings, as suggested by the English translation.

✓ Clues: When the English translation below includes the word "of," it is translating a Hebrew noun that is construct. A Hebrew construct noun never takes a definite article, even when its translation includes an implied article; however, an absolute Hebrew noun must have a definite article (in this exercise) if its translation indicates an article is present.

(1)

מְעַט	חִבֻּק	______	
"A little	folding of	both hands."	(Pr 6:10)

(2)

______	אָבִי	הִוא	
"The daughter of	my father	she is."	(Ge 20:12)

[1] Singular construct or plural forms are given under *Notes* in vocabulary lists if those forms are irregular or difficult to recognize. Dual forms are always listed where they occur.

[2] When two forms follow *P* (plural) or *Du* (dual), the first is absolute and the second is construct.

(3)

וְאַשְׁבִּיעֲךָ	______	______	הַשָּׁמַיִם	______	______	אֲשֶׁר
"And I will make you swear	by the LORD,	the God of	the heavens	and the God of	the earth,	that

לֹא־תִקַּח	______	לִבְנִי	______	הַכְּנַעֲנִי	
you will not give	a wife	to my son	from the daughters of	the Canaanites."	(Ge 24:3)

(4)

וַיִּשְׁתַּחוּ	______	______	______	־חֵת	
"And he [Abraham] bowed down	to the people of	the earth,	to the sons of	Heth."	(Ge 23:7)

(5)

וַיִּקְרָא־	בוֹ	. . .	______	־הָאוֹר	עַד־מַחֲצִית	______
"And he [Ezra] read	from it [the law]		from	the light (of day)	until the middle of	the day

נֶגֶד	______	______	
in front of	the men	and the women."	(Ne 8:3)

e. Read aloud and write a translation for the following words [numbers (1)-(9)] and sentences [numbers (10)-(18)]. Any noun that is followed by a *maqqef* should be translated as a construct, although not every construct in this exercise has a *maqqef.*

✓ In earlier lessons three verbs were introduced in their masculine, singular forms for the perfect tense. The same verbs are listed below with their corresponding feminine, singular, perfect forms, which appear in the following sentences. Note that the feminine, singular, perfect forms of these verbs end with ◌ָה, like the common ending for feminine, singular, absolute nouns.

בָּא	= "he came, went," etc.	בָּאָה	= "she came, went," etc.
יָשַׁב	= "he dwelled, sat"	יָשְׁבָה	= "she dwelled, sat"
רָאָה	= "he saw"	רָאֲתָה	= "she saw"

(1) הַר | הַר־ | הָרִים | הָרֵי (2) בֵּן | בֶּן־ | בָּנִים | בְּנֵי (3) בַּת | בַּת־ |
בָּנוֹת | בְּנוֹת־ (4) שָׁנָה | שְׁנַת | שָׁנִים | שְׁנוֹת | שְׁנָתַיִם (5) יוֹם־יִשְׂרָאֵל |
יְמֵי־יִשְׂרָאֵל (6) אֵשֶׁת אֱלֹהִים | נְשֵׁי אֱלֹהִים (7) מֶלֶךְ־הָאָרֶץ | מַלְכֵי הָאָרֶץ

(8) יַד הַכֹּהֵן | יְדֵי־הַכֹּהֵן | יְדוֹת־הַכֹּהֲנִים (9) אֱלֹהֵי־קֹ֫דֶשׁ | הַר־קֹ֫דֶשׁ | גּוֹי־
הַקֹּ֫דֶשׁ (10) וְרָאָה יִשְׂרָאֵל אַרְצוֹת־הַגּוֹיִם (11) יָֽשְׁבָה רוּחַ־אֱלֹהִים בִּבְנֵי
אֲנָשִׁים (12) רָאָה הַכֹּהֵן יַד־יְהוָה בִּשְׁנֵי[1]־הַמֶּ֫לֶךְ (13) וּבָא יוֹם־יְהוָה אֶל־בְּנֵי־
יִשְׂרָאֵל וְאֶל־בְּנוֹת־יִשְׂרָאֵל (14) יָשַׁב בֶּן־הָאִשָּׁה בַּמֶּ֫לֶךְ לְיוֹמַ֫יִם (15) בָּא עַם־
הַקֹּ֫דֶשׁ אֶל־אֶ֫רֶץ־יִשְׂרָאֵל וַיהוָה הַמֶּ֫לֶךְ לַגּוֹי (16) רָֽאֲתָה הָאִשָּׁה כִּי בָ֫אָה
רוּחַ־אָדָם מֵרוּחַ־אֱלֹהִים (17) הַנָּשִׁים בְּנוֹת־הַמֶּ֫לֶךְ וְהָֽאֲנָשִׁים בְּנֵי־הַכֹּהֵן
(18) יָֽשְׁבָה הָאִשָּׁה בָּאָ֫רֶץ כְּרֹאשׁ־הָעָם לִשְׁנָתַ֫יִם

[1] The word שְׁנֵי can either be the masculine, plural, construct form of שָׁנָה ("year") or the masculine, dual, construct form of שְׁנַ֫יִם ("two"). One can determine which is intended by the context in which the word appears; the former is the appropriate translation in this sentence.

Lesson 8

ADJECTIVES, SIGN OF THE OBJECT

8A ADJECTIVES

1. Inflection of adjectives

a. Adjectives, like nouns, are inflected with endings. The adjectival endings designate the gender as masculine or feminine, the number as singular or plural, and the state as absolute or construct. There are no dual endings for adjectives.

b. The adjectival endings are the same as the common endings for nouns, as listed in the following chart. These endings are employed with nearly all adjectives.[1]

	SINGULAR		PLURAL	
	Absolute	*Construct*	*Absolute*	*Construct*
M	[none]	[none]	◌ִים	◌ֵי
F	◌ָה	◌ַת	וֹת	וֹת

c. The following chart provides illustrations of the occurrence of these endings with three of the most common adjectives. Their translations appear in parentheses. The simplest form of the adjective is the masculine, singular, absolute; it is also the lexical form.

	SINGULAR		PLURAL		
	Absolute	*Construct*	*Absolute*	*Construct*	
M	טוֹב	טוֹב	טוֹבִים	טוֹבֵי	("good")
F	טוֹבָה	טוֹבַת	טוֹבוֹת	טוֹבוֹת	
M	גָּדוֹל	גְּדוֹל	גְּדוֹלִים	גְּדֹלֵי	("great")
F	גְּדוֹלָה	גְּדוֹלַת	גְּדֹלוֹת	גְּדֹלוֹת	

[1] The only common adjective with an irregular ending is אֶחָד ("one" [*MS*]), whose feminine, singular form in both the absolute and construct states is אַחַת. See Lesson 12, exercise c.

M	רַב	רַב	רַבִּים	רַבֵּי	("many, much, great")
F	רַבָּה	רַבַּת	רַבּוֹת	רַבּוֹת	

✓ The preceding chart illustrates the fact that the spelling of adjectives may undergo alterations when endings are added. For example, the masculine, singular, absolute adjective גָּדוֹל becomes גְּדֹלוֹת in feminine, plural, absolute and construct. The addition of the וֹת ending causes the *qames* to reduce to *sheva* (under the first consonant) and the *holem-vav* to *holem* (with the second consonant).

2. Function of adjectives

a. Adjectives can function in three ways: attributively, predicatively, and substantivally.

b. Attributive

(1) An attributive adjective modifies a noun in the sense of describing an attribute of that noun.

(2) When functioning attributively, an adjective normally follows the noun it modifies[1] and agrees with that noun in terms of gender, number, and definiteness. The agreement in terms of definiteness means that the definite article will appear on the adjective if the noun which it modifies has the article. Since there is no dual number for the adjective, the plural form of the adjective is used to modify a dual noun.

- The phrase אִשָּׁה גְדוֹלָה (2Ki 4:8) is made up of a noun (אִשָּׁה = "woman") followed by an adjective (גְדוֹלָה = "great"), which is functioning attributively. The two words agree in that they are both feminine, singular, and indefinite (lacking the definite article). The phrase is translated "a great woman."
- The phrase הַדְּבָרִים הַטּוֹבִים (Jos 23:14) also has a noun (הַדְּבָרִים = "the words") followed by an attributive adjective (הַטּוֹבִים = "the good"). Both words are masculine, plural, and definite (having the definite article). The phrase is translated "the good words."
- The phrase נָשִׁים רַבּוֹת (Eze 16:41) has a noun (נָשִׁים = "women")

[1] Occasionally an attributive adjective precedes the noun it modifies. When this is the case the irregular positioning of the adjective may serve to emphasize its significance in a phrase or clause.

followed by an attributive adjective (רַבּוֹת = "many"). Both words are feminine, plural, and indefinite. Note that even though the ending of the feminine noun is irregular (◌ִים), the ending of the feminine adjective is regular (וֹת). The phrase is translated "many women."

- In יָדַיִם רָפוֹת ("weak hands" [Is 35:3]) the noun (יָדַיִם = "hands") is feminine, dual. The attributive adjective (רָפוֹת = "weak") is feminine, plural, since an adjective cannot take a dual ending.[1]

c. Predicative

(1) An adjective may function in a predicative manner, that is, as a predicate adjective in a verbless sentence. (See Lesson 5A.3b(2).)

(2) When functioning predicatively, an adjective normally precedes the noun it modifies (although it occasionally follows the noun). A predicate adjective, like an attributive adjective, agrees with the noun it modifies in gender and number; however, a predicate adjective does not take an article, even if the noun is articular. Since a predicate adjective appears in a verbless sentence, a state-of-being verb must be supplied in translation.

- The verbless sentence טוֹב יְהוָה (Ps 34:9) has a predicate adjective followed by the noun it modifies; neither word has a definite article. The sentence means "good is the LORD," or "the LORD is good."
- In גָדוֹל הַיּוֹם ("great is the day" [Jer 30:7]) the predicate adjective (גָדוֹל = "great") comes before the noun it modifies (הַיּוֹם = "the day") and agrees with that noun in gender and number. However, the predicate adjective cannot have an article, even when the noun does.
- While the predicate adjective normally precedes the noun it modifies, this order is sometimes reversed, as in הָעָם רָב ("the people are many" [Jdg 7:4]). The adjective agrees with the noun in gender and number, but it does not have an article since a predicate adjective cannot be articular. In fact, the absence of the article with רָב is a clue that it is predicative instead of attributive.

---

[1] For other examples of special situations of agreement between nouns and attributive adjectives, see Bruce K. Waltke and M. O'Connor, *An Introduction to Biblical Hebrew Syntax* (Winona Lake, IN: Eisenbrauns, 1990), §14.2c-d.

d. Substantival

(1) An adjective may function as a substantive, that is, like a noun. Rather than modifying a noun, a substantival adjective stands in the place of a noun, serving any of the roles in which a noun may serve.

(2) When functioning substantivally, an adjective may or may not take the article.

- In כְּשֵׁם הַגְּדוֹלִים ("like the name of the great" [1Ch 17:8]) a substantival adjective (הַגְּדוֹלִים = "the great") is serving as an absolute noun that limits a construct noun (כְּשֵׁם = "like the name of"). The phrase could be translated "like the name of the great ones" or "like the name of the great men," depending on whether it appears in a context in which the adjective refers to people in general or to men in particular (since the masculine, plural ending can be used for either group).
- תַּעֲשֶׂה הַטּוֹב ("you will do the good" [Dt 12:28]) has a substantival adjective (הַטּוֹב = "the good"), which functions as the object of a verb (תַּעֲשֶׂה = "you will do"). The clause could be translated, "you will do the good thing."
- In רַבַּת הַמְּהוּמָה ("much of the tumult" [Eze 22:5]) a construct substantival adjective (רַבַּת = "much of") is limited by an absolute noun (הַמְּהוּמָה = "the tumult"). The phrase could be translated "full of tumult."

3. Degrees of Comparison

a. Hebrew has a number of ways to express comparison, some of which employ adjectives.[1] While adjectives in English can be inflected to show comparative and superlative degrees (as in "great," "greater," and "greatest"), no such forms exist for Hebrew adjectives. They can, however, express ideas of comparison by means of particular grammatical constructions, some of which are mentioned here.

b. The comparative degree can be expressed by an adjective followed by the preposition מִן (normally in the prefixed form). In this situation מִן has the meaning "than."

- The hypothetical sentence שְׁלֹמֹה חָכָם מִפַּרְעֹה (roughly translated,

[1] For fuller discussions of various comparative and superlative constructions see Horsnell, 197-201; and Waltke and O'Connor, §14.4-14.5.

"Solomon wise from Pharaoh") means "Solomon was wiser than Pharaoh." The adjective (חָכָם = "wise") is followed by a prefixed מִן preposition.

- וְרָאִיתָ . . . עַם רַב מִמְּךָ (roughly translated, "and you will see . . . a people many from you" [Dt 20:1]) means "and you will see . . . a people more than you" or ". . . greater than you."
- מַה־מָּתוֹק מִדְּבַשׁ (roughly translated, "what sweet from honey?" [Jdg 14:18]) means "what is sweeter than honey?"
- אַחֶ֫יךָ . . . הַטּוֹבִים מִמְּךָ (roughly translated, "your brothers . . . the good from you" [2Ch 21:13]) means "your brothers . . . who are better than you."

c. The following are two ways in which adjectives can express the superlative.

(1) The superlative can be communicated by an articular adjective. In this sort of construction the adjective is often followed by the prefixed preposition בְּ.

- The hypothetical sentence יִשְׂרָאֵל הַקָּטֹן בַּגּוֹיִם (roughly translated "Israel the small in [among] the nations") means "Israel was the smallest of the nations." The articular adjective (הַקָּטֹן = "the small") is followed by the בְּ preposition on a noun.
- [אַתָּה][1] הַיָּפָה בַּנָּשִׁים (roughly translated, "[you], the beautiful in [among] the women" [SS 1:8]) means "[you] who are the most beautiful of women."
- הָאִישׁ הָרַךְ בְּךָ (roughly translated, "the man, the gentle in [among] you" [Dt 28:54]) means "the gentlest man among you." In this phrase the articular adjective (הָרַךְ = "the gentle") is followed by a בְּ preposition with a suffix meaning "you."
- בִּתִּי הַגְּדוֹלָה (roughly translated, "my daughter, the great [1Sa 18:17]) means "my eldest daughter." In this phrase the adjective is not followed by a בְּ preposition, but the idea of comparison with other daughters is implied.

(2) The superlative can also be expressed by a construct adjective, often followed by a definite noun (that is, a noun made definite by an article or some other grammatical element).

[1] The brackets indicate an implied word that is inserted in the biblical example for the sake of clarity.

- The hypothetical sentence דָּוִד גְּדוֹל־הַמְּלָכִים בָּאָֽרֶץ (roughly translated "David, great of the kings in the earth") means "David was the greatest of the kings in the earth." A construct adjective (גְּדוֹל־ = "great of") is followed by an articular noun.
- יְהוֹאָחָז קְטֹן בָּנָיו ("Jehoahaz, the small of his sons" [2Ch 21:17]) means "Jehoahaz, the youngest of his [father's] sons." While the noun בָּנָיו has no article, it is made definite by a ו suffix, which means "his." (See section 9A.1d.)

8B Sign of the Object

The typical word order for a verb sentence with a stated subject and a direct object is that the verb is first, followed by the subject, followed by the object of the verb. (See Lesson 5A.3b(1).) This order designates which word is the subject of the sentence and which is the direct object. Often another indicator is used to identify the object of a verb, namely, the sign of the object. This sign is אֵת, or, when followed by a *maqqef*, it is אֶת־. The sign of the object is placed immediately before a direct object. It is not translated, but simply serves as a grammatical marker.

- In the hypothetical sentence רָאָה יְהוָה עֳנִי יִשְׂרָאֵל, a verb (רָאָה = "he saw") is followed by three nouns. The word order indicates that the first noun (יְהוָה = "the LORD") is the subject and the next two nouns (עֳנִי יִשְׂרָאֵל = "the distress of Israel") form a construct phrase that serves as the object of the verb. The sentence could also be written with the sign of the object to even more clearly identify that the construct phrase is the direct object, as in רָאָה יְהוָה אֶת־עֳנִי יִשְׂרָאֵל (2Ki 14:26). The translation is the same with or without the sign of the object, since אֶת־ is an untranslatable marker of the verb's object. The sentence means "the LORD saw the affliction of Israel."
- The hypothetical sentence בָּרָא אֱלֹהִים הַשָּׁמַיִם וְהָאָֽרֶץ begins with a verb (בָּרָא = "he created") followed by three nouns. According to the order of the nouns, the first one (אֱלֹהִים = "God") serves as the subject and the other two as the double object of the verb (הַשָּׁמַיִם וְהָאָֽרֶץ = "the heavens and the earth"). To provide additional clarity, the sentence could also be written using the sign of the object: בָּרָא אֱלֹהִים אֵת הַשָּׁמַיִם וְאֵת הָאָֽרֶץ (Ge 1:1). The sentence means "God created the heavens and the earth."

Lesson 8: Exercises

a. Learn to recognize, pronounce, and translate the following vocabulary.

	Word	Translation	Notes
(1)	אֵת	[sign of the object – no translation] (*particle*[1])	*Cs:* אֶת, אֶת־
(2)	גָּדוֹל	great (*adj MS*)	*MS Cs:* גְּדוֹל; *MP:* גְּדוֹלִים, גְּדֹלֵי; *FS:* גְּדוֹלָה; *FP:* גְּדֹלוֹת
(3)	הָיָה	he was, became, existed (*V*)	With an impersonal subject = "it/there was, happened, occurred"
(4)	טוֹב	good (*adj MS*)	
(5)	יָדַע	he knew (*V*)	
(6)	לֵב[2]	heart, will, mind (*NMS*)	*Cs:* לֵב, לֶב־; *P:* לִבּוֹת
(7)	רַב	many, much, great *(adj MS)*	*MP:* רַבִּים, רַבֵּי; *FS:* רַבָּה, רַבַּת; *FP:* רַבּוֹת
(8)	שֵׁם	name (*NMS*)	*Cs:* שֵׁם, שֶׁם־; *P:* שֵׁמוֹת; שְׁמוֹת

b. The following interlinear-style translation of the biblical text omits some vocabulary words (including prefixed forms) and names. Rewrite the translation, supplying the missing data. Also identify the function of each adjective as attributive, predicative, substantival, comparative, or superlative. Then provide a smoother translation, consulting an English version if necessary. The gender and number of some nouns appears in brackets beside their translations to aid in identifying the adjectives which agree with them.

(1) וַיָּגָר אַבְרָהָם בְּאֶרֶץ פְּלִשְׁתִּים יָמִים רַבִּים

(Ge 21:34) ______." ______ ______ ______ ______, "And he lived as a foreigner,

(2) עַתָּה יָדַעְתִּי כִּי־ גָדוֹל יְהוָה מִכָּל־ הָאֱלֹהִים

(Ex 18:11) ______." ___ all of ______ ______ ______ I know "Now

---

[1] A particle is a short word that is normally indeclinable and cannot be classified as any other part of speech.

[2] This noun can also be spelled as לֵבָב (*Cs:* לְבַב; *P:* לְבָבוֹת).

(3) לְמַ֫עַן תֵּלֵךְ בְּדֶ֫רֶךְ טוֹבִים

"In order that | you may walk | ___ the way of | ______." (Pr 2:20)

(4) וְעָשִׂ֫תִי לְךָ שֵׁם גָּדוֹל כְּשֵׁם הַגְּדֹלִים אֲשֶׁר בָּאָ֫רֶץ

"___ I will make | for you | ______ | ______ | ______ | ______ | who are | ______." (2Sa 7:9)

(5) כִּי־ טוֹבַת מַרְאֶה הִיא

"______ | ______ | appearance | was she [Rebekah]." (Ge 26:7)

(6) הָאֵמִים לְפָנִים יָ֫שְׁבוּ בָהּ עַם גָּדוֹל וְרַב וָרָם כָּעֲנָקִים

"______ | previously | lived | in it [the land], | ______ | ______ | ______ | ___ being tall | ______." (Dt 2:10)

(7) וַיִּירְאוּ מְאֹד כִּי עִיר גְּדוֹלָה גִּבְעוֹן . . . וְכִי הִיא גְדוֹלָה מִן־ הָעַי[1]

"And they [the Canaanites] were afraid | greatly | ______ | a city [*FS*] | ______ | was Gibeon | . . . | ______ | it [*FS*] | ______ | ______ | ______." (Jos 10:2)

(8) וַיְהִי־לוֹ צֹאן רַבּוֹת[2]

"And there were for him [Jacob] | flocks [*FS*] | ______." (Ge 30:43)

(9) וַיֹּ֫אמֶר הֵן עוֹד הַיּוֹם גָּדוֹל

"And he [Jacob] said, | 'Look | still | ______ | ______.'" (Ge 29:7)

---

[1] The name of this city is typically spelled with a definite article. The article may be omitted in the translation, since it is not required in English.

[2] A singular, collective noun, like צֹאן, can be modified by either a singular or a plural adjective, since the noun is singular in form yet plural in meaning. In this verse the singular, collective noun is modified by a plural adjective.

c. Read aloud, pronounce and translate the following words or phrases [numbers (1)-(5)] and sentences [numbers (6)-(21)]. Also identify the function of each adjective as attributive, predicative, substantival, comparative, or superlative.

✓ These feminine, singular, perfect verbs occur in the sentences:

בָּ֫אָה = "she came, went," etc.   יָֽדְעָה = "she knew"

הָֽיְתָה = "she was, became," etc.

(1) כֹּהֵן גָּדוֹל | הַכֹּהֵן הַגָּדוֹל | כֹּהֲנִים גְּדוֹלִים | הַכֹּהֲנִים הַגְּדוֹלִים (2) אֶ֫רֶץ
רַבָּה | אֲרָצוֹת רַבּוֹת | הָאֲרָצוֹת הָרַבּוֹת (3) אִשָּׁה גְדוֹלָה | הַגְּדוֹלָה[1] | גְּדֹלוֹת
(4) הָאֲנָשִׁים הַטּוֹבִים | טוֹבִים | הַטּוֹב (5) יָד טוֹבָה | הַיָּד הַטּוֹבָה | הַיָּדוֹת
הַטּוֹבוֹת | הַיָּדַ֫יִם הַטּוֹבוֹת (6) יָדַע עַם־הָגּוֹיִם הָרַבִּים אֵת הַמֶּ֫לֶךְ הַטּוֹב
(7) טוֹב אֱלֹהִים[2] אֶל־בְּנֵי־אָדָם (8) יָשַׁב אִישׁ־אֱלֹהִים בָּעָם וְהָיָה כְּכֹהֵן לָעָם
(9) יָֽדְעָה טוֹבַת יִשְׂרָאֵל אֶת־שֵׁם־הַר־יְהוָה (10) הָיָה[3] רוּחַ גְּדוֹלָה בְּאֶ֫רֶץ
יִשְׂרָאֵל (11) לֶב־אֱלֹהִים גָּדוֹל מִלֶּב־אָדָם (12) רָאָה הַכֹּהֵן הַטּוֹב אֶת־הָאִשָּׁה
וְיָדַע כִּי הָֽיְתָה גְדוֹלַת־רוּחַ[4] (13) גְּדוֹלָה וְטוֹבָה יַד־יְהוָה כִּי בָ֫אָה אֶל־עַם־
הָאָ֫רֶץ (14) מֶ֫לֶךְ־יִשְׂרָאֵל הַגָּדוֹל בְּמַלְכֵי־הַגּוֹיִם (15) גְּדוֹלָה רוּחַ־יְהוָה וְטוֹב
שֵׁם־יְהוָה (16) בֶּן־הַמֶּ֫לֶךְ גָּדוֹל מִבֶּן־הַכֹּהֵן (17) הָיָה אֶ֫רֶץ רַבָּה לְעַם־אֱלֹהִים
(18) יָֽדְעָה בַּת־הָאִשָּׁה כִּי טוֹב־לֵב הַכֹּהֵן (19) רַבּוֹת הַשְׁנוֹת כִּי יָשַׁב הַטּוֹב
כְּרֹאשׁ־הָעָם (20) שֵׁם־יְהוָה גָּדוֹל־הַשְּׁמוֹת בָּאָ֫רֶץ (21) רָאָה כֹּהֵן־הַקֹּ֫דֶשׁ אֵת
גְּדֹלוֹת[5]־הַגּוֹי וְיָדַע כִּי טוֹבוֹת הַנָּשִׁים

---

[1] Since this adjective stands alone, one can assume it is substantival. Because it is feminine, singular, absolute, it may be translated "the great one," "the great woman," or "the great thing."

[2] When אֱלֹהִים functions as a singular noun (referring to "God") it is modified by a singular adjective (טוֹב in this sentence).

[3] הָיָה means "there was" in this sentence. רוּחַ cannot be the subject of this verb since it is feminine and הָיָה is masculine.

[4] The last clause of this sentence may be rendered "that she had a great spirit."

[5] Here גְּדֹלוֹת refers to women who are great by virtue of their social position (nobility).

Lesson 9

PRONOMINAL SUFFIXES ON NOUNS

9A PRONOMINAL SUFFIXES ON NOUNS

1. Introduction

a. A pronominal suffix can be attached to the end of a word to communicate the concept of a pronoun in relationship with that word. A pronominal suffix may be placed on nouns, substantival adjectives, prepositions, verbs, adverbs, and particles.

b. When attached to nouns, pronominal suffixes usually serve the function of possessive pronouns ("my," "your," "his," "her," "our," and "their"). There are two sets of forms for pronominal suffixes used with nouns. One set is employed with singular nouns; the other set with plural nouns.

c. The pronominal suffixes are attached to the construct forms of singular and plural nouns; they cannot be attached to absolute forms.

d. Since a pronominal suffix can appear only on a construct noun, and a construct noun cannot take a definite article, a noun with such a suffix can never be articular. However, a noun with a pronominal suffix is made definite by its suffix. For example, רֹאשִׁי ("my head") is a construct noun with a first person, singular, pronominal suffix ("my"). While this noun has no definite article, it is nevertheless definite because it has a suffix that refers to a particular head: "my head." In fact this noun and pronominal suffix can be translated "the head of me." Since a noun with a pronominal suffix is definite, an attributive adjective which follows such a noun will take the definite article.[1]

2. Pronominal suffixes for singular nouns

a. The following chart presents the forms of the pronominal suffixes which are commonly used with singular nouns, along with translations of those suffixes.[2]

---

[1] Kelley, 71.

[2] Alternate forms of some of the pronominal suffixes for singular nouns do occur in rare situations. See Joüon, §94h.

The bracketed forms occur in special cases, as discussed below.

	Form	Translation
1CS[1]	◌ִי	"my"[2]
2MS	◌ְךָ	"your"
2FS	◌ֵךְ	"your"
3MS	וֹ [הוּ, ו]	"his, its"[3]
3FS	◌ָהּ [הָ]	"her, its"

	Form	Translation
1CP	◌ֵ֫נוּ	"our"
2MP	◌ְכֶם	"your"
2FP	◌ְכֶן	"your"
3MP	◌ָם [הֶם]	"their"
3FP	◌ָן [הֶן]	"their"

b. Notes concerning the pronominal suffixes for singular nouns

(1) Most singular, construct nouns, to which pronominal suffixes are added, end with a consonant. The first form listed for each pronominal suffix in the preceding chart either is a vowel or begins with a vowel which is attached to the last consonant of a noun.

- יַד ("hand" *NMS,Cs*[4]) + ◌ְךָ ("your") = יָדְךָ ("your hand") The *sheva* of the suffix ◌ְךָ is placed under the final consonant of יַד.
- יַד ("hand" *NMS,Cs*) + וֹ ("his") = יָדוֹ ("his hand")
- יַד ("hand" *NMS,Cs*) + ◌ָהּ ("her") = יָדָהּ ("her hand")

(2) The singular, construct forms of a few nouns end with a vowel. In such cases the initial vowel of the pronominal suffixes may be omitted or altered, or the optional spellings of the suffixes, which appear in brackets in the chart, may be used.

- אֲבִי ("father" *NMS,Cs*) + ◌ְךָ ("your") = אָבִיךָ ("your father"). Since this construct noun ends with a vowel (*hireq-yod*), when the *2MS* pronominal suffix ◌ְךָ is attached, the initial vowel of the suffix (*sheva*) is dropped.
- אֲבִי ("father" *NMS,Cs*) + הוּ or ו ("his") = אָבִיהוּ or אָבִיו ("his father"). While nouns which end with consonants usually take the *3MS* pronominal

[1] *1CS* = first person, common (that is, masculine or feminine), singular; *2MS* = second person, masculine, singular; *2FS* = second person, feminine, singular; etc.

[2] The pronominal suffixes with nouns may also be translated "of me, of you, of him," etc., depending upon the context.

[3] While there is no neuter in Hebrew, English translations of the *3MS* and *3FS* pronominal suffixes may use the word "its" when referring to that which is neuter in English.

[4] *NMS,Cs* = noun, masculine, singular, construct.

suffix of וֹ, this noun, because it ends with a vowel, takes either of the alternate forms of הוּ or ו.

- אָבִי ("father" *NMS,Cs*) + הָ ("her") = אָבִיהָ ("her father"). Again, since this noun ends with a vowel, it takes the form of the *3FS* pronominal suffix that begins with a consonant (הָ).

(3) The *3FS* pronominal suffix has a *mappiq* (הּ◌ָ), which aids in distinguishing it from similar forms, such as the common ending for feminine, singular, absolute nouns (ה◌ָ).

(4) All the second person endings of the pronominal suffixes have a *kaf*, which aids in recognizing them.

c. The charts[1] below illustrate the occurrence of the pronominal suffixes with the masculine, singular noun סוּס ("horse") and the feminine, singular noun סוּסָה ("mare"). The construct forms of these singular nouns (to which the pronominal suffixes are added) are סוּס and סוּסַת.

(1) *NMS,Ab:*[2] סוּס ("horse"), *Cs:* סוּס

1CS	סוּסִי ("my horse")
2MS	סוּסְךָ ("your horse")
2FS	סוּסֵךְ ("your horse")
3MS	סוּסוֹ ("his horse")
3FS	סוּסָהּ ("her horse")

1CP	סוּסֵנוּ ("our horse")
2MP	סוּסְכֶם ("your horse")
2FP	סוּסְכֶן ("your horse")
3MP	סוּסָם ("their horse")
3FP	סוּסָן ("their horse")

(2) *NFS,Ab:* סוּסָה ("mare"), *Cs:* סוּסַת

1CS	סוּסָתִי ("my mare")
2MS	סוּסָתְךָ ("your mare")
2FS	סוּסָתֵךְ ("your mare")
3MS	סוּסָתוֹ ("his mare")
3FS	סוּסָתָהּ ("her mare")

1CP	סוּסָתֵנוּ ("our mare")
2MP	סוּסַתְכֶם ("your mare")
2FP	סוּסַתְכֶן ("your mare")
3MP	סוּסָתָם ("their mare")
3FP	סוּסָתָן ("their mare")

[1] Some forms in these and other charts are hypothesized for the sake of illustration.

[2] *NMS,Ab* = noun, masculine, singular, absolute

✓ When pronominal suffixes are added to a word, vowel alterations may occur in that word. The changes are due to the fact that the suffixes create new final syllables which are accented. This shifting of a word's accent may cause certain vowels to reduce or lengthen. To illustrate, chart (2) above indicates that the vowel before the ת in סוּסַת lengthens to a *qames* with the addition of most of the pronominal suffixes. At this stage the student need not be concerned with the rules by which these vowels change, but simply be aware that alterations may occur as suffixes are added.

3. Pronominal suffixes for plural nouns

a. The following chart presents the forms of the pronominal suffixes which are commonly used with plural nouns, along with the translations of those suffixes.[1] The forms in brackets are less frequently used.

	Form	*Translation*
1CS	◌ַי	"my"
2MS	◌ֶ֫יךָ	"your"
2FS	◌ַ֫יִךְ	"your"
3MS	◌ָיו	"his, its"
3FS	◌ֶ֫יהָ	"her, its"

	Form	*Translation*
1CP	◌ֵ֫ינוּ	"our"
2MP	◌ֵיכֶם	"your"
2FP	◌ֵיכֶן	"your"
3MP	◌ֵיהֶם [◌ָם]	"their"
3FP	◌ֵיהֶן [◌ָן]	"their"

b. Notes concerning the pronominal suffixes for plural nouns

(1) The regular pronominal suffixes for plural nouns appear to be a combination of the masculine, plural, construct noun ending ◌ֵי plus certain forms of the pronominal suffixes for singular nouns.[2] Consequently, every form contains a *yod*. Each of the most common plural forms of these suffixes for plural nouns (*1CP* suffix, *2MP* suffix, *2FP* suffix, etc.) retains the ◌ֵי. However, in the singular forms (*1CS* suffix, *2MS* suffix, *2FS* suffix, etc.) the vowel before the *yod* is altered. To illustrate the point:

- ◌ֵי (*NMP, Cs* ending) + הֶם (*3MP* indicator) = ◌ֵיהֶם (*PS 3MP*[3])

---

[1] For rare forms of the pronominal suffixes on plural nouns, see Joüon, §94i.

[2] For a more detailed discussion of this matter see Joüon, §94d.

[3] *PS 3MP* = pronominal suffix, third person, masculine, plural.

- □ֵי (*NMP,Cs* ending) + הָ (*3FS* indicator) = □ֶ֫יהָ (*PS 3FS*)
- □ֵי (*NMP,Cs* ending) + □ִי (*1CS* indicator) = □ַי (*PS 1CS*)

(2) Since the spelling of the suffixes in the preceding chart already incorporates the masculine, plural, construct ending of □ֵי, when a construct noun has that ending, as in מַלְכֵי, the □ֵי on the noun is dropped before the suffixes are added. To illustrate:

- מַלְכֵי (*NMP,Cs*) + □ֵיהֶם (*PS 3MP*) = מַלְכֵיהֶם ("their kings"). The form cannot be מַלְכֵיֵיהֶם, which appears to have two □ֵי endings before הֶם.
- מַלְכֵי (*NMP,Cs*) + □ֶ֫יהָ (*PS 3FS*) = מְלָכֶ֫יהָ ("her kings")
- מַלְכֵי (*NMP,Cs*) + □ַי (*PS 1CS*) = מְלָכַי ("my kings")

(3) Two bracketed suffixes appear in the chart: □ָם and □ָן. They are short forms of the *3MP* and *3FP* pronominal suffixes for plural nouns (and are identical to the *3MP* and *3FP* suffixes for singular nouns). These short forms have no feature which represents the incorporation of the *NMP,Cs* ending of □ֵי, as all the other suffixes have. □ָם and □ָן are employed as pronominal suffixes on plural nouns only in situations where it is obvious that the noun is plural, such as when a noun has the feminine, plural noun ending of וֹת. For example, שְׁמוֹתָם ("their names") is obviously a plural noun because of the feminine plural ending before the short *3MP* pronominal suffix. (See section 9A.4a(5).)

c. The charts below illustrate the occurrence of the pronominal suffixes on the masculine, plural noun סוּסִים ("horses"), and the feminine, plural noun סוּסוֹת ("mares"). The construct forms of these plural nouns (to which the pronominal suffixes are added) are סוּסֵי and סוּסוֹת.

(1) *NMP,Ab:* סוּסִים ("horses"), *Cs:* סוּסֵי

1CS	סוּסַי ("my horses")	*1CP*	סוּסֵ֫ינוּ ("our horses")
2MS	סוּסֶ֫יךָ ("your horses")	*2MP*	סוּסֵיכֶם ("your horses")
2FS	סוּסַ֫יִךְ ("your horses")	*2FP*	סוּסֵיכֶן ("your horses")
3MS	סוּסָיו ("his horses")	*3MP*	סוּסֵיהֶם ("their horses")
3FS	סוּסֶ֫יהָ ("her horses")	*3FP*	סוּסֵיהֶן ("their horses")

(2) *NFP,Ab:* סוּסוֹת ("mares"), *Cs:* סוּסוֹת

1CS	סוּסוֹתַי	("my mares")
2MS	סוּסוֹתֶיךָ	("your mares")
2FS	סוּסוֹתַיִךְ	("your mares")
3MS	סוּסוֹתָיו	("his mares")
3FS	סוּסוֹתֶיהָ	("her mares")

1CP	סוּסוֹתֵינוּ	("our mares")
2MP	סוּסוֹתֵיכֶם	("your mares")
2FP	סוּסוֹתֵיכֶן	("your mares")
3MP	סוּסוֹתֵיהֶם	("their mares")
3FP	סוּסוֹתֵיהֶן	("their mares")

✓ When a construct plural noun has an ending of וֹת (as with סוּסוֹת in chart (2) above), the suffixes are simply added to that ending. For example, סוּסוֹת (*NMS,Cs*) + ◌ֵיהֶם (*PS 3MP*) = סוּסוֹתֵיהֶם ("their mares"). The result is a word which appears to have both a feminine, plural, construct ending (וֹת) and a masculine, plural, construct ending (◌ֵי) before הֶם.

d. The following clues aid in recognizing when pronominal suffixes appear on plural nouns.

(1) The *1CS* pronominal suffix on plural nouns is ◌ַי.

(2) All the other pronominal suffixes for plural nouns also have a *yod* (◌ֶיךָ, ◌ַיִךְ, ◌ָיו, ◌ֶיהָ, ◌ֵינוּ, ◌ֵיכֶם, ◌ֵיכֶן, ◌ֵיהֶם, and ◌ֵיהֶן).

(3) An exception can occur with nouns that have the plural ending of וֹת or ◌ֹת. Such nouns may take the pronominal suffixes of ◌ָם (*3MP*) and ◌ָן (*3FP*), in which case the suffixes have no *yod* (as in שְׁמוֹתָם or שְׁמוֹתָן = "their names").

4. More nouns with pronominal suffixes

a. The following charts provide further illustrations of the occurrence of pronominal suffixes on nouns. The charts on the left side of the page illustrate the suffixes on singular nouns; the charts on the right illustrate the suffixes on the plural forms of the same nouns.

SINGULAR NOUNS	PLURAL NOUNS
(1) *NMS,Ab*: דָּבָר ("word"), *Cs*: דְּבַר	*NMP,Ab*: דְּבָרִים ("words"), *Cs*: דִּבְרֵי

1CS	דְּבָרִי	*1CP*	דְּבָרֵנוּ
2MS	דְּבָרְךָ	*2MP*	דְּבַרְכֶם

1CS	דְּבָרַי	*1CP*	דְּבָרֵינוּ
2MS	דְּבָרֶיךָ	*2MP*	דִּבְרֵיכֶם

2FS	דְּבָרֵךְ	*2FP*	דְּבַרְכֶן	*2FS*	דְּבָרַיִךְ	*2FP*	דִּבְרֵיכֶן
3MS	דְּבָרוֹ	*3MP*	דְּבָרָם	*3MS*	דְּבָרָיו	*3MP*	דִּבְרֵיהֶם
3FS	דְּבָרָהּ	*3FP*	דְּבָרָן	*3FS*	דְּבָרֶיהָ	*3FP*	דִּבְרֵיהֶן

(2) *NFS,Ab*: צְדָקָה ("righteousness"), *Cs*: צִדְקַת

NFP,Ab: צְדָקוֹת ("righteous acts"), *Cs:* צִדְקוֹת

1CS	צִדְקָתִי	*1CP*	צִדְקָתֵנוּ	*1CS*	צִדְקֹתַי	*1CP*	צִדְקֹתֵינוּ
2MS	צִדְקָתְךָ	*2MP*	צִדְקַתְכֶם	*2MS*	צִדְקֹתֶיךָ	*2MP*	צִדְקֹתֵיכֶם
2FS	צִדְקָתֵךְ	*2FP*	צִדְקַתְכֶן	*2FS*	צִדְקֹתַיִךְ	*2FP*	צִדְקֹתֵיכֶן
3MS	צִדְקָתוֹ	*3MP*	צִדְקָתָם	*3MS*	צִדְקֹתָיו	*3MP*	צִדְקֹתֵיהֶם
3FS	צִדְקָתָהּ	*3FP*	צִדְקָתָן	*3FS*	צִדְקֹתֶיהָ	*3FP*	צִדְקֹתֵיהֶן

✓ When pronominal suffixes are attached to plural, construct nouns which end in וֹת, the *holem vav* may reduce to a *holem*, so that the construct plural ending appears as ֹת before the pronominal suffix, as illustrated by the preceding word.

(3) *NFS,Ab:* בֵּן ("son"), *Cs:* בֶּן־, בִּן־

NFP,Ab: בָּנִים ("sons"), *Cs:* בְּנֵי

1CS	בְּנִי	*1CP*	בְּנֵנוּ	*1CS*	בָּנַי	*1CP*	בָּנֵינוּ
2MS	בִּנְךָ	*2MP*	בִּנְכֶם	*2MS*	בָּנֶיךָ	*2MP*	בְּנֵיכֶם
2FS	בְּנֵךְ	*2FP*	בִּנְכֶן	*2FS*	בָּנַיִךְ	*2FP*	בְּנֵיכֶן
3MS	בְּנוֹ	*3MP*	בְּנָם	*3MS*	בָּנָיו	*3MP*	בְּנֵיהֶם
3FS	בְּנָהּ	*3FP*	בְּנָן	*3FS*	בָּנֶיהָ	*3FP*	בְּנֵיהֶן

(4) *NFS,Ab:* בַּת ("daughter"), *Cs*: בַּת

NFP,Ab: בָּנוֹת ("daughters"), *Cs:* בְּנוֹת

1CS	בִּתִּי	*1CP*	בִּתֵּנוּ	*1CS*	בְּנֹתַי	*1CP*	בְּנוֹתֵינוּ[1] בְּנֹתֵינוּ

[1] Some words, like this one, have alternate spellings when certain pronominal suffixes are added.

2MS	בִּתְּךָ	*2MP*	בִּתְּכֶם	*2MS*	בְּנוֹתֶיךָ בְּנֹתֶיךָ	*2MP*	בְּנוֹתֵיכֶם בְּנֹתֵיכֶם
2FS	בִּתֵּךְ	*2FP*	בִּתְּכֶן	*2FS*	בְּנוֹתַיִךְ בְּנֹתַיִךְ	*2FP*	בְּנוֹתֵיכֶן
3MS	בִּתּוֹ	*3MP*	בִּתָּם	*3MS*	בְּנוֹתָיו בְּנֹתָיו	*3MP*	בְּנוֹתֵיהֶם בְּנֹתֵיהֶם בְּנֹתָם
3FS	בִּתָּהּ	*3FP*	בִּתָּן	*3FS*	בְּנוֹתֶיהָ בְּנֹתֶיהָ	*3FP*	בְּנוֹתֵיהֶן

(5) *NMS,Ab:* שֵׁם ("name"), *Cs:* שֵׁם, שֶׁם־

NMP,Ab: שֵׁמוֹת ("names"), *Cs:* שְׁמוֹת

1CS	שְׁמִי	*1CP*	שְׁמֵנוּ	*1CS*	שְׁמוֹתַי	*1CP*	שְׁמוֹתֵינוּ
2MS	שִׁמְךָ	*2MP*	שִׁמְכֶם	*2MS*	שְׁמוֹתֶיךָ	*2MP*	שְׁמוֹתֵיכֶם
2FS	שְׁמֵךְ	*2FP*	שִׁמְכֶן	*2FS*	שְׁמוֹתַיִךְ	*2FP*	שְׁמוֹתֵיכֶן
3MS	שְׁמוֹ	*3MP*	שְׁמָם	*3MS*	שְׁמוֹתָיו	*3MP*	שְׁמוֹתָם שְׁמֹתָם
3FS	שְׁמָהּ	*3FP*	שְׁמָן	*3FS*	שְׁמוֹתֶיהָ	*3FP*	שְׁמוֹתָן

✓ The plural forms of the masculine noun שֵׁם are irregular in that they take the ending of וֹת (which typically appears on feminine, plural nouns). The plural, construct ending of וֹת remains in place when the pronominal suffixes are added to the plural form of this word, as with the paradigm of סוּסוֹת. (See section 9A.3c(2).)

(6) *NFS,Ab:* עִיר ("city"), *Cs:* עִיר

NFP,Ab: עָרִים ("cities"), *Cs:* עָרֵי

1CS	עִירִי	*1CP*	עִירֵנוּ	*1CS*	עָרַי	*1CP*	עָרֵינוּ
2MS	עִירְךָ	*2MP*	עִירְכֶם	*2MS*	עָרֶיךָ	*2MP*	עָרֵיכֶם
2FS	עִירֵךְ	*2FP*	עִירְכֶן	*2FS*	עָרַיִךְ	*2FP*	עָרֵיכֶן
3MS	עִירוֹ	*3MP*	עִירָם	*3MS*	עָרָיו	*3MP*	עָרֵיהֶם
3FS	עִירָהּ	*3FP*	עִירָן	*3FS*	עָרֶיהָ	*3FP*	עָרֵיהֶן

- ✓ The feminine noun עִיר is irregular in its singular and plural forms. The singular, construct has no ending (as is typical with regular masculine nouns). Consequently, the pronominal suffixes on the singular form of this word follow the paradigm of סוּס above in section 9A.2c(1). The plural construct of this word employs the ending which is typical for regular masculine nouns (◌ֵי), and when the pronominal suffixes are added, this word follows the paradigm of סוּסִים above in section 9A.3c(1).

b. Flexibility in gender and number is not uncommon in pronominal suffixes. For example, a plural suffix is typically used to refer to a singular, collective antecedent, and masculine suffixes can take priority over feminine ones. Not only is a masculine suffix used with reference to a masculine antecedent, but also for an antecedent that is both masculine and feminine, and even sometimes to refer to a feminine antecedent.[1]

c. When adjectives function substantivally (that is, like nouns), they can take the same pronominal suffixes that are used with nouns.

- ‣ In גַּם טוֹבֹתָיו הָיוּ אֹמְרִים ("They were also speaking of his good deeds" [Neh 6:19]) the substantival adjective טוֹבֹתָיו ("his good deeds") has a pronominal suffix.

Lesson 9: Exercises

a. Reproduce from memory all the options for pronominal suffixes on singular nouns (section 9A.2a).

b. Reproduce from memory the three clues for recognizing pronominal suffixes on plural nouns (section 9A.3d).

c. Identify which pronominal suffix appears on the following words (for example, *PS 1CS*, *PS 2MS*, *PS 2FS*, etc.) and give a translation of each word. The translation of the lexical form of each word (that is, the masculine or feminine, singular, absolute form) appears in parentheses. Do the exercise without looking at a list of the pronominal suffixes.

- ‣ *Example:* שַׁעֲרֵיהֶם ("gate") ⇒ *Answer: PS 3MP*, "their gates"

[1] See Kautzsch, §135o.

	Word	*Translation of lexical form*		*Word*	*Translation of lexical form*
(1)	יַמָּה	("sea")	(21)	גִּבְעָתָהּ	("hill")
(2)	נַחֲלַתְכֶם	("possession")	(22)	קַדְמָתָן	("former state")
(3)	שִׂפְתוֹתֶיךָ	("lip")	(23)	מִנְחֹתֵיכֶם[1]	("gift")
(4)	מָעֻזְּכֶן	("fortress")	(24)	יָמַיִךְ	("day")
(5)	עֲצָתָם	("counsel")	(25)	יַלְדֵיהֶם	("child")
(6)	גְּבוּלִי	("boundary")	(26)	דָּמוֹ	("blood")
(7)	מִשְׁפָּטָן	("judgment")	(27)	גִּלּוּלֵיכֶן	("idol")
(8)	אֲדֹנֵינוּ	("lord")	(28)	שִׂמְחָתֵךְ	("joy")
(9)	אִמֵּךְ	("mother")	(29)	צֹאנֵנוּ	("flock")
(10)	אַדְמָתוֹ	("land")	(30)	עֵינַיִךְ	("eye")
(11)	לְבוּשְׁכֶן	("clothing")	(31)	נְבִיאָיו	("prophet")
(12)	אֲנָשַׁי	("man")	(32)	מַרְאֵיהֶן	("appearance")
(13)	נְעָרֶיךָ	("young man")	(33)	מִצְוֹתַי	("commandment")
(14)	לַחְמָם	("bread")	(34)	חַצְרֹתֵיהֶם	("court")
(15)	אֲבוֹתֵינוּ	("father")	(35)	אַרְצְךָ	("land")
(16)	כֵּלֶיהָ	("vessel")	(36)	עַבְדֵיכֶם	("servant")
(17)	פַּרְסֵיהֶן	("hoof")	(37)	דְּמוּתֵנוּ	("likeness")
(18)	מִשְׁפַּחְתִּי	("clan")	(38)	נַעֲרֹתֶיהָ	("girl")
(19)	גְּבֻלְכֶם	("border")	(39)	שַׂרְכֶם	("leader")
(20)	בְּהֶמְתְּךָ	("animal")	(40)	חַרְבוֹתָיו	("sword")

d. Learn to recognize, pronounce, and translate the following vocabulary.

	Word	*Translation*	*Notes*
(1)	דָּבָר	word, speech, thing (*NMS*)	*Cs:* דְּבַר *P:* דְּבָרִים, דִּבְרֵי
(2)	נָשָׂא	he lifted, lifted up, carried (*V*)	
(3)	עִיר	city, town (*NFS*)	*P:* עָרִים, עָרֵי
(4)	קוֹל	voice, sound (*NMS*)	*P:* קֹלוֹת or קֹלֹת
(5)	קָרָא	he called, met (*V*)	

[1] This word and others in this exercise have a plural, construct ending of ֹת before the pronominal suffix. It is a shortened form of the common feminine plural ending וֹת. See section 9A.4a(2).

e. The following biblical verses, written with an interlinear-style translation, have some missing words. Rewrite the Hebrew verses, filling in the blanks with words from the vocabulary lists. Pay close attention to the occurrence of pronominal suffixes on singular and plural nouns. When the English translation employs a second person, pronominal idea, the gender and number will appear in parentheses in order to indicate which pronominal suffix is required in Hebrew. If necessary, consult the paradigms in this lesson and vocabulary lists for help with vowel pointing. When finished, check the work against the Hebrew Bible.

(1)	וַיִּשְׁמַע	______	______־	______	______	
	"And he heard,	the LORD,	[sign of the object]	the voice of	your [*MP*] words."	(Dt 1:34)

(2)	אַף־	______	עוֹלֹת	תִּפְעָלוּן	______	חֲמַס	______	תְּפַלֵּסוּן	
	"No,	in heart,	injustices	you do;	in the land	violence	your [*MP*] hands	weigh out."	(Ps 58:3; *Eng*[1] 58:2)

(3)	וַיֹּאמֶר	יִצְחָק	______־	______	מַה־	זֶּה	מִהַרְתָּ	לִמְצֹא
	"And he said,	Isaac,	to	his son	'How is	this	(that) you have been so quick	to find (the wild game),
	______	וַיֹּאמֶר	______	הִקְרָה	______	______	לְפָנָי	
	my son?'	And he [Jacob] said,	'Because	he made it happen,	the LORD	your [*2MS*] God,	for me.'"	(Ge 27:20)

(4)	וַיֹּאמֶר	______	לֹא־יָדוֹן	______	______	לְעֹלָם	...	וְהָיוּ	______
	"And he said,	the LORD,	'It will not strive,	my spirit,	with the humankind	forever,		and they will be	his days
	מֵאָה	וְעֶשְׂרִים	______						
	one hundred	and twenty	year.'"[2]	(Ge 6:3)					

[1] The versification of the English Bible [*Eng*] sometimes varies from that of the Hebrew Bible.

[2] As this translation reflects, the Hebrew word for "year" is singular in this verse, where it has a collective meaning.

(5)

וַיֹּאמֶר	לָהּ	אֶלְקָנָה	______	חַנָּה	לָמָה	תִבְכִּי	. . .	הֲלוֹא	אָנֹכִי
"And he said	to her,	Elkanah,	her husband,	'Hannah,	why	do you weep?		Am not	I

______	לָךְ	מֵעֲשָׂרָה	______	
better [good]	to you	than ten	sons?'"	(1Sa 1:8)

(6)

וַיַּךְ	יֵהוּא	______	. . .	לְבֵית־	אַחְאָב	בְּיִזְרְעֶאל	וְכָל־	______
"And he struck,	Jehu,	[sign of the object]		the house of	Ahab	in Jezreel	and all of	his great ones,[1]

וּמְיֻדָּעָיו	______	
and his close friends,	and his preists."	(2Ki 10:11)

(7)

______	מִסְפַּר	______	הָיוּ	______	יְהוּדָה	
"For	the number of	your [*MS*] cities,	they are (like the number of)	your [*MS*] gods,	O Judah."	(Jer 11:13)

(8)

מֵאֵלֶּה	נִפְרְדוּ	אִיֵּי	______	______	אִישׁ	לִלְשֹׁנוֹ
"From these	they separated,	the distant regions of	the nations,	in their lands,	(all) people	according to their language,

לְמִשְׁפְּחֹתָם	______	
according to their families,	in their nations."	(Ge 10:5)

f. Read aloud and translate the following sentences.

✓ Several of the following sentences employ the masculine plural forms of some of the perfect verbs which have been introduced in vocabulary lists. Below are the relevant verbs with their masculine singular forms on the left and their plural forms on the right. Note that a *shureq* suffix is characteristic of the plural forms.

בָּא	= "he came, went," etc.	בָּ֫אוּ	= "they came, went," etc.
יָשַׁב	= "he dwelled, sat"	יָשְׁבוּ	= "they dwelled, sat"
נָשָׂא	= "he lifted," etc.	נָשְׂאוּ	= "they lifted," etc.

[1] A substantival adjective can take a pronominal suffix just as a noun does.

קָרָא	= "he called, met"	קָֽרְאוּ	= "they called, met"
רָאָה	= "he saw"	רָאוּ	= "they saw"

✓ The feminine, singular forms of two of these verbs also occur in the following sentences: נָשְׂאָה ("she lifted," etc.) and רָאֲתָה ("she saw").

(1) גָּדוֹל שִׁמְךָ יְהוָה[1] (2) רַבִּים כֹּהֲנֶיךָ בְּיִשְׂרָאֵל (3) נָשְׂאָה הַטּוֹבָה אֵת קוֹלָהּ אֶל־מַלְכָּהּ (4) עִירֵךְ עִירִי וְאַרְצֵךְ אַרְצִי (5) בָּא הַכֹּהֵן לַיהוָה וְקָרָא אֵת שֵׁם־קָדְשׁוֹ[3] (6) טוֹב אֱלֹהַי לְבָנָיו וְלִבְנוֹתָיו לִדְבָרוֹ[2] (7) יְהוָה מַלְכְּכֶם וְיִשְׂרָאֵל אַרְצְכֶם (8) טוֹבָה עִיר־קָדְשֵׁנוּ (9) רַבִּים וְטוֹבִים דְּבָרֶיךָ מַלְכִּי (10) בְּנוֹתֵינוּ הַגְּדֹלוֹת בַּנָּשִׁים בָּעִיר (11) רָאֲתָה הָאִשָּׁה כִּי קָרָא הַמֶּלֶךְ אֶת־בְּנָהּ וְאֶת־בִּתָּהּ[5] בִּשְׁמוֹתָם (12) קָֽרְאוּ אַנְשֵׁי־יִשְׂרָאֵל לֵאלֹהֵיהֶם וּבָא לְעַמּוֹ[4] כִּי קָֽרְאוּ (13) בָּנַיִךְ רָאשֵׁינוּ וְטוֹבִים בָּנַיִךְ לְעַמֵּנוּ (14) גְּדוֹלִים שְׁמוֹתָן בָּאָרֶץ וּשְׁמוֹתֵיכֶן[6] גְּדוֹלִים מִשְּׁמוֹתָן (15) בָּאוּ הָאִישׁ וְאִשְׁתּוֹ אֶל־בְּנָם וְיָֽשְׁבוּ בְּאַרְצוֹ לְיָמִים רַבִּים (16) רָאוּ הַמְּלָכִים כִּי יָֽשְׁבוּ גְּדֹלֵיהֶם וּגְדֹלוֹתֵיהֶם בֶּעָרִים בֶּהָרִים

[1] יְהוָה is used here as a vocative (direct address).

[2] The prefixed preposition ל can mean "according to."

[3] In the phrase שֵׁם־קָדְשׁוֹ the noun קָדְשׁוֹ is functioning adjectivally (see the last example in section 7A.3), consequently, the phrase is translated "his holy name." Also note that when the pronominal suffix is added to קֹדֶשׁ, the accent shifts to the last syllable and the *holem* under the ק shortens to a *qames-hatuf.*

[4] The second consonant of עַם is doubled when it is plural or has a suffix.

[5] בַּת becomes בִּת when a suffix is added.

[6] The *vav* conjunction means "but" in this sentence.

Lesson 10

Prepositions with Pronominal Suffixes

10A Prepositions with Pronominal Suffixes

As stated previously, the pronominal suffixes can be attached to prepositions. When this occurs, the suffixes serve as pronominal objects of prepositions (“me,” “you,” “him,” “her,” “us,” “them”). Some prepositions take the forms of the pronominal suffixes which are used with singular nouns; others take the forms which are used with plural nouns. Several patterns for pronominal suffixes on prepositions are illustrated below.

1. **Prepositions with the forms of the pronominal suffixes used with singular nouns**

   a. The two charts below give the simplest pattern: the pronominal suffixes with the prefixed prepositions בְּ (“in, by, with”) and לְ (“to, for, according to”).

	Form	*Translation*		*Form*	*Translation*
1CS	בִּי	“in me”	*1CP*	בָּנוּ	“in us”
2MS	בְּךָ	“in you”	*2MP*	בָּכֶם	“in you”
2FS	בָּךְ	“in you”	*2FP*	בָּכֶן	“in you”
3MS	בּוֹ	“in him”	*3MP*	בָּהֶם or בָּם	“in them”
3FS	בָּהּ	“in her”	*3FP*	בָּהֶן	“in them”

1CS	לִי	“to me”	*1CP*	לָנוּ	“to us”
2MS	לְךָ	“to you”	*2MP*	לָכֶם	“to you”
2FS	לָךְ	“to you”	*2FP*	לָכֶן	“to you”
3MS	לוֹ	“to him”	*3MP*	לָהֶם	“to them”
3FS	לָהּ	“to her”	*3FP*	לָהֶן	“to them”

✓ When the pronominal suffixes are attached to prepositions, they are sometimes spelled the same as they appear in the paradigm for the suffixes on singular nouns (Lesson 9A.2a). However, the vowels with which the suffixes begin are sometimes altered when they are attached to prepositions, as with several forms in the preceding charts (*2FS* and most plural forms). Since the consonants of the suffixes remain consistent, they are easily recognizable even when initial vowels change.

b. When the pronominal suffixes are added to the prefixed preposition כְּ ("like, as") and to מִן ("from, out of"), the spelling of the prepositions is irregular, as the charts below indicate.

	Form	Translation
1CS	כָּמ֫וֹנִי	"like me"
2MS	כָּמ֫וֹךָ	"like you"
2FS	כָּמוֹךְ	"like you"
3MS	כָּמ֫וֹהוּ	"like him"
3FS	כָּמ֫וֹהָ	"like her"

	Form	Translation
1CP	כָּמ֫וֹנוּ	"like us"
2MP	כָּכֶם	"like you"
2FP	כָּכֶן	"like you"
3MP	כָּהֵם	"like them"
3FP	כָּהֵן or כָּהֵ֫נָּה	"like them"

✓ As stated previously, the prefixed preposition כְּ is derived from the independent preposition כְּמוֹ, which has the same meaning. When the pronominal suffixes are added to כְּ, the spelling of the preposition reverts to its original form of כְּמוֹ in most cases (the singular forms and *1CP*). Since כְּמוֹ ends with a vowel, it requires suffixed forms which begin with a consonant. As a result, the *1CS* suffix employs a נ buffer before the □ִי ending. Also note that the *3MP* and *3FP* forms (which take the shortened spelling of the כְּ preposition) employ altered spellings of the pronominal suffix. They are, however, similar enough to the spellings of the suffixes with singular nouns that they can be easily recognized.

1CS	מִמֶּ֫נִּי	"from me"
2MS	מִמְּךָ	"from you"
2FS	מִמֵּךְ	"from you"
3MS	מִמֶּ֫נּוּ	"from him"
3FS	מִמֶּ֫נָּה	"from her"

1CP	מִמֶּ֫נּוּ	"from us"
2MP	מִכֶּם	"from you"
2FP	מִכֶּן	"from you"
3MP	מֵהֶם	"from them"
3FP	מֵהֶן or מֵהֵ֫נָּה	"from them"

✓ Most forms of מִן with pronominal suffixes employ a מּ (*mem* with a *dagesh-forte*) as a buffer between the initial מ of the preposition and the suffixes. In *1CS*, *3MS*, and *3FS* there is also a נ buffer. In the case of *3FS* the ה lacks the *mappiq* that normally appears. In addition, note that the forms for *1CP* and *3MS* are identical: מִמֶּ֫נּוּ. One can determine which is intended by the context in which the word appears.

c. The two charts below indicate the pattern which is followed when the pronominal suffixes are added to the independent prepositions אֵת ("with")[1] and עִם ("with").

	Form	Translation		Form	Translation
1CS	אִתִּי	"with me"	*1CP*	אִתָּ֫נוּ	"with us"
2MS	אִתְּךָ	"with you"	*2MP*	אִתְּכֶם	"with you"
2FS	אִתָּךְ	"with you"	*2FP*	אִתְּכֶן	"with you"
3MS	אִתּוֹ	"with him"	*3MP*	אִתָּם	"with them"
3FS	אִתָּהּ	"with her"	*3FP*	אִתָּן	"with them"

1CS	עִמִּי or עִמָּדִי[2]	"with me"	*1CP*	עִמָּ֫נוּ	"with us"
2MS	עִמְּךָ	"with you"	*2MP*	עִמָּכֶם	"with you"
2FS	עִמָּךְ	"with you"	*2FP*	עִמָּכֶן	"with you"
3MS	עִמּוֹ	"with him"	*3MP*	עִמָּם or עִמָּהֶם	"with them"
3FS	עִמָּהּ	"with her"	*3FP*	עִמָּן	"with them"

✓ A characteristic feature of the prepositions אֵת and עִם with the pronominal suffixes is the appearance of a *dagesh-forte* in the second consonant (תּ or מּ) in all forms.

2. Prepositions with the forms of the pronominal suffixes used with plural nouns.

a. אֶל ("to, into, toward") and עַל ("on, upon, over") are typical of the prepositions

[1] The preposition אֵת is spelled the same as the sign of the object. One can determine which is intended by the context in which the word appears. Both the preposition אֵת and the sign of the object can take the pronominal suffixes; however, the forms are spelled differently, as discussed in the next lesson.

[2] This longer form of the preposition with the *1CS* suffix may reflect an older spelling. See Kautzsch, §103c.

which employ the pronominal suffixes that are used with plural nouns, as the following charts illustrate.[1]

	Form	*Translation*		*Form*	*Translation*
1CS	אֵלַי	"to me"	*1CP*	אֵלֵינוּ	"to us"
2MS	אֵלֶיךָ	"to you"	*2MP*	אֲלֵיכֶם	"to you"
2FS	אֵלַיִךְ	"to you"	*2FP*	אֲלֵיכֶן	"to you"
3MS	אֵלָיו	"to him"	*3MP*	אֲלֵיהֶם	"to them"
3FS	אֵלֶיהָ	"to her"	*3FP*	אֲלֵיהֶן	"to them"

1CS	עָלַי	"on me"	*1CP*	עָלֵינוּ	"on us"
2MS	עָלֶיךָ	"on you"	*2MP*	עֲלֵיכֶם	"on you"
2FS	עָלַיִךְ	"on you"	*2FP*	עֲלֵיכֶן	"on you"
3MS	עָלָיו	"on him"	*3MP*	עֲלֵיהֶם	"on them"
3FS	עָלֶיהָ	"on her"	*3FP*	עֲלֵיהֶן	"on them"

b. Other very common prepositions which also take the forms of the pronominal suffixes for plural nouns are אַחַר ("after, behind"), עַד ("until"), and תַּחַת ("beneath, under, instead of").

Lesson 10: Exercises

a. Learn to recognize, pronounce, and translate the following vocabulary.

	Word	*Translation*	*Notes*
(1)	אֵת	with (*prep*)	*Cs:* אֵת אֶת־; spelled the same as the sign of the object; *PS:*[2] אִתִּי, אִתְּךָ, etc.
(2)	כֹּל	all, every (*NMS*)	*Cs:* כֹּל, כָּל־, *PS:* כֻּלּוֹ, כֻּלָּהּ, etc.

[1] These two prepositions have less common longer spellings of אֱלֵי and עֲלֵי, which appear in poetic literature. Pronominal suffixes are attached to these longer forms which have endings similar to masculine, plural, construct nouns (◌ֵי). See Joüon, §103m.

[2] The words following *PS:* in the *Notes* of vocabulary lists provide examples of spellings with pronominal suffixes.

(3)	מִשְׁפָּט	judgment, justice (*NMS*)	*Cs:* מִשְׁפַּט
(4)	נָתַן	he gave, put, set (*V*)	
(5)	עַל	on, upon, over (*prep*)	*PS:* עָלַי, עָלֶיךָ etc.
(6)	עִם	with (*prep*)	*PS:* עִמִּי or עִמָּדִי, עִמְּךָ, etc.
(7)	עָשָׂה	he did, made (*V*)	
(8)	רָעָה	evil (*NFS*)	
(9)	שָׁלַח	he sent (*V*)	
(10)	שָׁמַע	he heard, listened (*V*)	When followed by ל or ב (as in שָׁמַע בְּקוֹל or שָׁמַע לְקוֹל), can have the sense of "he listened to" or "he obeyed."

b. Rewrite the translations for the following biblical phrases, filling in the missing elements. Then identify which pronominal suffix appears on each preposition (for example, *PS 1CS*, *PS 2MS*, *PS 2FS*, etc.).

(1) וַתָּשֶׁת עָלַי כַּפֶּכָה
"And you placed ______ your hand." (Ps 139:5)

(2) אֵין כָּמוֹהָ
"There is none ______" (1Sa 21:10)

(3) כִּי אִתָּךְ נָשׁוּב
"______ ______ we will return" (Ru 1:10)

(4) נָתַן לָכֶם הַשַּׁבָּת
"______ ______ ___ sabbath" (Ex 16:29)

(5) וַתִּתֵּן גַּם־לְאִישָׁהּ עִמָּהּ
"And she also gave [the fruit] ______ ______" (Ge 3: 6)

(6) וְיַעְלְצוּ בְךָ
"And they will rejoice ______" (Ps 5:12)

(7) כַּאֲשֶׁר דִּבֶּר אֲלֵיהֶן
"As he said ______" (Ex 1:17)

(8) וַיִּמְלֹךְ עֲלֵיהֶם
"And he reigned ______" (1Ki 12:17)

(9) וְלֹא־נִרְאוּ כָהֵם
"___ nothing has been seen ______" (2Ch 9:11)

(10) כִּי יְהוָה עִמָּם
"______ ______ ______" (Zec 10:5)

	עֲבֹדָה	עָלֵינוּ	וַיִּתְּנוּ	(11)
(Dt 26:6)	labor”	______	“And they placed	

	אִתִּי	הָלַךְ	(12)
(Mal 2:6)	______”	“He walked	

	כָמֹונוּ	חֻלֵּיתָ	(13)
(Is 14:10)	______”	“They have become weak	

	אֵלַיִךְ	יִשְׁתַּחֲוּוּ	(14)
(Is 45:14)	______”	“They will bow down	

	אֱלֹהִים	רוּחַ	עָלָיו	וַתִּצְלַח	(15)
(1Sa 10:10)	______”	______	______	“And it rushed	

c. Read aloud and translate the following sentences.

✓ The following feminine and plural perfect verbs appear in the sentences below.

בָּאָה	=	“she came, went,” etc.	עָשׂוּ	=	“they did, made”
בָּאוּ	=	“they came, went,” etc.	קָרְאוּ	=	“they called, met”
הָיְתָה	=	“she was, became,” etc.	שָׁמְעָה	=	“she heard, listened”
יָשְׁבָה	=	“she dwelled, sat”	שָׁמְעוּ	=	“they heard, listened”
נָתְנָה	=	“she gave”			

(1) עָשָׂה אֱלֹהִים הָאָרֶץ וְכֹל בָּהּ (2) יַד־יְהוָה עָלֶיךָ (3) שָׁמְעָה הָאִשָּׁה לְקוֹל־
יְהוָה כִּי[2] קָרָא לָהּ (4) שָׁלַח רֹאשׁ־הָעָם אֵת[1] בְּנֵיכֶם מִכֶּם אֵלֵינוּ (5) טוֹבָה
הָאִשָּׁה וְטוֹבוֹת כָּל־בְּנוֹתֶיהָ כָּמוֹהָ (6) נָתַן אֱלֹהִים אֶת־רוּחוֹ[3] לָכֵן וְרוּחוֹ בָּכֶן
(7) קָרָא הַמֶּלֶךְ וּבָּאוּ אֲנָשָׁיו אֵת בְּנֵיהֶם לוֹ וּבָאוּ עִמּוֹ מִן־הָאָרֶץ (8) שָׁלַח
אֱלֹהִים אֵת אִישׁ־קֹדֶשׁ לָנוּ וְיָשַׁב הָאִישׁ עִמָּנוּ (9) נָתַן הַכֹּהֵן לָהֶם כָּל־דִּבְרֵי־
יְהוָה וְשָׁמְעוּ אַנְשֵׁי־הַגּוֹי אֶת־נְשֵׁיהֶם לְקוֹלוֹ (10) שָׁלַח רֹאשׁ־הַגּוֹי אֶת־בְּנוֹ אִתְּךָ

[1] Since אֵת (אֶת־) can either be the sign of the object or the preposition “with,” one must determine which is intended in the context. When אֵת follows a transitive verb (that is, a verb that can take a direct object), a practical method of determining its meaning is to first to read the sentence as if אֵת were the sign of the object (since it occurs more frequently) and then read the sentence as if it were the preposition. Whichever reading makes the most sense is the correct reading. In this sentence אֵת is the sign of the object.

[2] כִּי can mean “when.”

[3] The furtive *patah* which occurs with the lexical form רוּחַ cannot occur when a pronominal suffix is added because in such a case the ח is no longer the final consonant.

וְיָשַׁב עַל הָהָר כָּמ֫וֹךָ (11) שָׁמַע הַמֶּ֫לֶךְ לְקוֹל־אֱלֹהִים וְיָדַע כִּי טוֹבִים
הַדְּבָרִים מִמֶּ֫נּוּ (12) שָׁלַח יְהוָה מִשְׁפָּט עָלַי וְעַל אִשְׁתִּי[1] עִמִּי וְעָשָׂה טוֹב לְךָ
(13) יָשַׁב הַכֹּהֵן אִתִּי לְיָמִים רַבִּים וּבָא מִמֶּ֫נִּי אֲלֵיכֶם (14) נָתַן הָאִישׁ אֶת־
בִּתּוֹ לָאִשָּׁה הַטּוֹבָה וּבָ֫אָה אֵלֶ֫יהָ וְיָֽשְׁבָה אֶת־הָאִשָּׁה (15) עָשׂוּ כֹּהֲנֵי הָאָ֫רֶץ
אֶת־רָעָה וְעָשׂוּ[2] הָעָם אֶת־רָעָה כָּהֵם (16) קָֽרְאוּ בְנוֹת־יִשְׂרָאֵל אֶל אֱלֹהִים
וְנָתַן בָּנִים לָהֶן (17) כִּי הָיָה רָעָה בְּלִבּוֹת־אֲנָשִׁים[3] שָׁלַח יְהוָה אֶת־מִשְׁפָּט
עֲלֵיהֶם (18) קָֽרְאוּ נְשֵׁי הָעִיר עַל אֱלֹהִים וְשָׁמַע וּבָא אֲלֵיהֶן (19) נָֽתְנָה
הָאִשָּׁה אֶת־בְּנָהּ לָךְ וּבָא מִמֶּ֫נָּה וְיָשַׁב עִמָּךְ לְשָׁנִים רַבִּים וְהָיָה כְּבֵן אֵלַ֫יִךְ
(20) בָּא מִשְׁפַּט־יְהוָה עָלֵ֫ינוּ כִּי הָֽיְתָה רָעָה בָּ֫נוּ וְשָׁלַח יְהוָה אֶת רוּחוֹ אֲלֵיכֶן
כִּי הָיָה טוֹב בָּכֶן

[1] When the pronominal suffixes are added to nouns, they sometimes cause a change of vowels, as with this word, the lexical form of which is אִשָּׁה.

[2] As stated earlier (footnote 3 of Lesson 5, Exercise e), a singular, collective noun may take a singular verb; however, a collective noun may also take a plural verb, as this sentence illustrates.

[3] A subordinate clause (such as a כִּי clause) normally appears after the main clause of a sentence. However, for the purpose of emphasis a subordinate clause may come first, as it does in this sentence.

Lesson 11

Personal Pronouns, Sign of the Object with Pronominal Suffixes, Demonstrative Adjectives, Relative Clauses

11A Personal Pronouns

1. Hebrew personal pronouns are independent words which express subjective pronominal concepts ("I," "you," "he," "she," "we," and "they"). There are technically no objective personal pronouns; instead the sign of the object with pronominal suffixes serves that function, as discussed in the next section.
2. The chart below lists the personal pronouns and their translations.

	Form	*Translation*
1CS	אֲנִי or אָנֹכִי	"I"
2MS	אַתָּה	"you"
2FS	אַתְּ	"you"
3MS	הוּא	"he, it"[1]
3FS	הִיא	"she, it"

	Form	*Translation*
1CP	אֲנַחְנוּ	"we"
2MP	אַתֶּם	"you"
2FP	אַתֵּנָה or אַתֵּן	"you"
3MP	הֵמָּה or הֵם	"they"
3FP	הֵנָּה	"they"

3. Notes concerning the forms of the personal pronouns
   a. All of the second person forms (singular and plural) have a *tav* with a *dagesh-forte* (תּ).
   b. The *2FS* form אַתְּ (ʾatt) is unusual in its spelling. It has a final consonant with a *dagesh-forte* and a silent *sheva* at the end. The form is adapted from an older spelling.[2]

---

[1] While there is no neuter in Hebrew, English translations of the *3MS* and *3FS* personal pronouns may use the word "it" when referring to that which is neuter in English.

[2] See Joüon, §39a.

c. The *3FS* personal pronoun is sometimes spelled as הִוא rather than הִיא in the *MT*, particularly in the Pentateuch.[1]

4. The personal pronouns function like nouns in the nominative case.
   a. The personal pronouns most frequently occur as subjects in verbless clauses (see Lesson 5A.3).
      - אֲנִי יְהוָה = "I am the LORD" (Ge 15:7)
      - אַתְּ־אִשְׁתּוֹ = "You are his wife" (Ge 39:9)
      - אַתָּה הָאִישׁ = "You are the man" (2Sa 12:7)
   b. Sometimes the personal pronouns are used to emphasize the subjective pronominal elements of verbs. As stated previously (Lesson 5A.2b), the verb itself expresses the pronominal ideas of first, second or third person. The personal pronouns can be used with verbs to call special attention to these pronominal elements.
      - The verb בָּאָה by itself means "she came." The personal pronoun הִיא ("she") may be used with this verb to emphasize the *3FS* pronominal idea which is inherent in the verb. The result is הִיא בָּאָה (1Ki 14:17), which roughly translated is "she, she came," and may mean "*she* came" or "she herself came."
      - הָיוּ־לוֹ means "they were for him." The pronominal idea of the verb (הָיוּ = "they were") can be emphasized by adding a *3MP* personal pronoun, as in הֵמָּה הָיוּ־לוֹ (2Ch 22:4), which may be translated, "they themselves were for him."

5. Pronouns, like pronominal suffixes, can show flexibility in their usage with regard to gender. For example, masculine pronouns can take priority over feminine ones, as they are sometimes used to refer to feminine antecedents.

11B Sign of the Object with Pronominal Suffixes

1. As stated previously, pronominal suffixes can be used to express objective pronominal concepts, such as when they are attached to prepositions (see Lesson 10). The pronominal suffixes also have an objective function when they are attached to the sign of the object, which is the particle אֵת. When the pronominal suffixes are

---

[1] The consonantal text of the Pentateuch typically employed הוא for both the *3MS* and *3FS* personal pronouns. To distinguish the two, the *MT* uses the pointing of הִוא where the *3FS* form is intended.

attached to the sign of the object, words are formed which serve as the objects of verbs ("me," "you," "him," "her," "us," and "them"). Consequently, the function of the sign of the object with the pronominal suffixes is the same as the function of the objective personal pronouns in English when they are used as verbal objects.

2. The forms of the sign of the object (אֵת) with the pronominal suffixes appear in the chart below with translations.

	Form	*Translation*
1CS	אֹתִי	"me"
2MS	אֹתְךָ	"you"
2FS	אֹתָךְ	"you"
3MS	אֹתוֹ	"him, it"[2]
3FS	אֹתָהּ	"her, it"

	Form	*Translation*
1CP	אֹתָנוּ	"us"
2MP	אֶתְכֶם	"you"
2FP	אֶתְכֶן[1]	"you"
3MP	אֹתָם or אֶתְהֶם	"them"
3FP	אֹתָן or אֶתְהֶן	"them"

3. The forms of the sign of the object with the pronominal suffixes are spelled very similarly to the forms of the preposition אֵת ("with") when it has the suffixes. There is also a similarity with the second person, personal pronouns. However, each of these forms can be distinguished from one another.
   a. For the sake of comparison the column on the left in the following chart has the forms of the preposition אֵת with the pronominal suffixes; the center column has the forms of the second person, personal pronoun; and the right column has the forms of the sign of the object with the pronominal suffixes.

[1] This hypothetical form does not appear in the Hebrew Bible.

[2] While there is no neuter in Hebrew, English translations of the *3MS* and *3FS* forms as may use the word "it" when referring to that which is neuter in English.

	Preposition אֵת *+ PS*	*Personal Pronoun*	*Sign of the Object + PS*
1CS	אִתִּי ("with me")		אֹתִי ("me")
2MS	אִתְּךָ ("with you")	אַתָּה ("you")	אֹתְךָ ("you")
2FS	אִתָּךְ ("with you")	אַתְּ ("you")	אֹתָךְ ("you")
3MS	אִתּוֹ ("with him")		אֹתוֹ ("him")
3FS	אִתָּהּ ("with her")		אֹתָהּ ("her")
1CP	אִתָּנוּ ("with us")		אֹתָנוּ ("us")
2MP	אִתְּכֶם ("with you")	אַתֶּם ("you")	אֶתְכֶם ("you")
2FP	אִתְּכֶן ("with you")	אַתֵּן ("you")	אֶתְכֶן ("you")
3MP	אִתָּם ("with them")		אֶתְהֶם or אֹתָם ("them")
3FP	אִתָּן ("with them")		אֶתְהֶן or אֹתָן ("them")

b. The following clues are helpful in distinguishing the preceding forms from one another.

(1) Concerning the *tav* in each form:

[a] The preposition אֵת with the pronominal suffixes and the second person, personal pronouns always have a *dagesh-forte* in the *tav* (תּ).

[b] The sign of the object with the pronominal suffixes never has a *dagesh-forte* in the *tav* (ת).

(2) Concerning the vowel for the *alef* in each form:

[a] The preposition אֵת with the pronominal suffixes always has a *hireq* under the א.

[b] The second person personal pronouns always have a *patah* under the א.

[c] The sign of the object with the pronominal suffixes never has a *hireq* or *patah* under the א; instead it has either a *holem* or a *segol* (the latter occurring with the four "long" suffixes: כֶם, כֶן, הֶם, and הֶן).

(3) These clues concerning the pointing of the *alef* and *tav* in these forms can be abbreviated as follows.

אִ	=	preposition אֵת + *PS*
אַ	=	2nd person pronoun
אֹ or אֶ	=	sign of the object + *PS*
תּ	=	preposition אֵת + *PS or* 2nd person pronoun
ת	=	sign of the object + *PS*

4. As stated above, the sign of the object with the pronominal suffixes functions to indicate a pronominal object for a verb.[1]
   - The clause וַיְבָרֶךְ אֹתִי ("and he blessed me" [Ge 48:3]) has a finite verb followed by a the sign of the object with a *1CS* pronominal suffix (אֹתִי = "me").
   - The clause לָקַח אֹתוֹ אֱלֹהִים ("God took him" [Ge 5:24]) has a verb followed by the sign of the object with a *3MS* pronominal suffix (אֹתוֹ = "him"). The last word in the clause (אֱלֹהִים = "God") is the subject. While the word that appears immediately after a verb is often the subject of the verb, one can tell that אֹתוֹ is not the subject because it contains the sign of the object.
   - The phrase לְהָבִיא אֹתָנוּ ("to bring us" [Nu 20:5]) contains an infinitive, followed by the sign of the object with a *1CP* pronominal suffix (אֹתָנוּ = "us").
   - In the clause יוֹלֵךְ יְהוָה אֹתְךָ וְאֶת־מַלְכְּךָ ("the LORD will bring you and your king" [Dt 28:36]) the verb (יוֹלֵךְ = "he will bring") has a double direct object. The first is the sign of the object with a *2MS* pronominal suffix (אֹתְךָ = "you"), and the second is the sign of the object followed by a noun (וְאֶת־מַלְכְּךָ = "and your king").

11C Demonstrative Adjectives

1. The demonstrative adjectives are classified as near and remote.[2] The near demonstratives refer to someone or something which is near to hand ("this" or "these"), while the remote refer to someone or something which is more distant

[1] Another way of indicating a pronominal object for a verb is by attaching a pronominal suffix directly to the verb. See Lesson 19.

[2] Some grammarians refer to these forms as demonstrative pronouns.

("that" or "those"). The chart below gives the forms of the demonstrative adjectives and their translations.[1]

	Near Demonstratives		**Remote Demonstratives**	
	Form	*Translation*	*Form*	*Translation*
MS	זֶה	"this"	הוּא	"that"
FS	זֹאת	"this"	הִיא	"that"
MP	אֵלֶּה	"these"	הֵם or הֵמָּה	"those"
FP	אֵלֶּה	"these"	הֵנָּה	"those"

2. Notes concerning the forms of the demonstrative adjectives
   a. The *MP* and *FP* demonstrative adjectives employ the same form: אֵלֶּה.
   b. The forms of the remote demonstrative adjectives are spelled the same as the forms of the third person personal pronouns. In general, one may determine which is intended by the context in which the word appears. The function of the demonstrative adjectives, which is discussed below, also provides clues for identifying them.
3. A demonstrative adjective may function like other adjectives in an attributive, predicative, or substantival way.
   a. When functioning attributively, a demonstrative adjective follows the noun it modifies and agrees with that noun in gender, number, and definiteness (having the definite article). If a demonstrative adjective occurs with other adjectives which modify the same noun, the demonstrative appears last in the series of adjectives.
      - The phrase הָאִשָּׁה הַזֹּאת (roughly translated, "the woman, the this" [Dt 22:14]) has an articular noun followed by a near demonstrative adjective that is functioning attributively. The adjective agrees with the noun in gender, number, and definiteness. The phrase means "this woman."
      - The phrases הָאֲנָשִׁים הָהֵם ("those men" [Nu 14:38]) and הַגּוֹיִם הָאֵלֶּה ("these nations" [Dt 7:17]) each have articular nouns followed by demonstrative adjectives that agree in gender, number, and definiteness.

[1] For rare forms of the demonstratives see Waltke and O'Connor, §17.2.

- The phrase הָהָר הַטּוֹב הַזֶּה (roughly translated, "the mountain, the good, the this" [Dt 3:25]) has a noun followed by two attributive adjectives. The demonstrative adjective comes last in the series. The phrase means "this good mountain."

✓ One aid for distinguishing the remote demonstrative adjectives from the personal pronouns is the fact that the demonstratives, like other adjectives, can have an article; however, the personal pronouns cannot be articular. To say it another way, if the article appears on one of these shared forms – as in הַהוּא, הַהִיא, הָהֵמָּה, הָהֵם, or הָהֵנָּה – then the form must be a remote demonstrative adjective and not a personal pronoun.

b. When functioning predicatively, a demonstrative adjective typically appears in a verbless clause. It normally precedes the noun it modifies and agrees with the noun in gender and number. A predicative demonstrative cannot take an article.

- The clause זֶה הַיּוֹם עָשָׂה יְהוָה ("This is the day the LORD has made" [Ps 118:24]) begins with a near demonstrative adjective which is functioning predicatively. Both it and the noun it modifies (הַיּוֹם) are masculine, singular. However, the predicative demonstrative adjective cannot have an article, as the noun does.
- In the verbless clause זֹאת הָאָרֶץ ("this is the land" [Nu 34:2]) an indefinite, feminine, singular demonstrative adjective precedes an articular, feminine, singular noun.
- הִיא[1] זִמָּה ("that is wickedness" [Job 31:11]) has a feminine, singular, remote demostrative adjective followed by a feminine, singular noun.

c. A demonstrative adjective may also function substantivally (that is, in the place of a noun).

- In the clause זֶה יָצָא רִאשֹׁנָה ("this one came out first" [Ge 38:28]) a near demonstrative adjective (זֶה = "this") serves as the subject of a verb (יָצָא = "he came out").
- שִׁמְעוּ־נָא זֹאת ("now hear this" [Jer 5:21]) has a near demonstrative adjective (זֹאת = "this") functioning as the object of a verb (שִׁמְעוּ = "hear").

[1] The biblical text actually uses the alternative spelling of הִוא for the feminine, singular demonstrative adjective.

11D Relative Clauses

1. Relative clauses are usually introduced by the relative particle אֲשֶׁר. This particle cannot be declined – that is, it cannot be inflected to agree with its antecedent in gender or number. אֲשֶׁר serves the function of the relative pronouns in English; it therefore has a wide range of possible meanings, such as "who, whom, whose, which, where," or "when."[1]
2. The translation of אֲשֶׁר depends upon its antecedent and its usage in a sentence, as the following examples illustrate.
   - In יְהוָה אֲשֶׁר־פָּדָה אֶת־נַפְשִׁי ("the LORD who redeemed my life" [2Sa 4:9]) the relative particle (אֲשֶׁר = "who") is functioning as the personal subject of a verb clause.
   - וְהַגִּבּוֹרִים אֲשֶׁר לְדָוִד ("and the mighty men who were for David" or "who belonged to David" [1Ki 1:8]) uses אֲשֶׁר ("who") as the personal subject of a verbless clause.
   - In דְּבַר יְהוָה אֲשֶׁר דִּבֶּר ("the word of the LORD which he spoke" [1Ki 2:27]) אֲשֶׁר ("which") serves as the impersonal object of a verb clause.
   - In הָאִשָּׁה אֲשֶׁר נָתַתָּה עִמָּדִי ("the woman whom you gave to me" or "whom you gave to be with me" [Ge 3:12]) אֲשֶׁר ("whom") functions as the personal object of a verb (נָתַתָּה = "you gave").
   - הָאֱמֹרִי אֲשֶׁר אַתֶּם יֹשְׁבִים בְּאַרְצָם (roughly translated, "the Amorite who you are dwelling in their land" [Jos 24:15]) employs the relative particle in a genitival (possessive) sense. The clause may be translated, "the Amorite in whose (אֲשֶׁר) land you are dwelling."
   - In וּכְגַנָּה אֲשֶׁר־מַיִם אֵין לָהּ (roughly translated, "and like a garden which water there is not for it" [Isa 1:30]) the relative particle has a locative (location) sense. The clause may be translated, "and like a garden where (אֲשֶׁר) there is no water" (or "in which there is no water ").
   - וְהַיָּמִים אֲשֶׁר מָלַךְ דָּוִד (roughly translated, "and the days which he reigned, David" [1Ki 2:11]) employs the relative particle in a temporal sense. The clause may be translated, "and the days when (אֲשֶׁר) David reigned" (or "in which David reigned").

---

[1] In later biblical texts a prefixed relative particle שֶׁ also appears. For a discussion of its pointing and usage see Waltke and O'Connor, §19.2b, 19.4.

Lesson 11: Exercises

a. Reproduce from memory the clues for recognizing the distinctions between the preposition אֵת + pronominal suffixes, the personal pronoun, and the sign of the object + pronominal suffixes, as they appear in section 11B.3b(3).

b. Without looking at the paradigm charts in this lesson or the preceding one, identify the following words as a preposition + a pronominal suffix, a personal pronoun, or the sign of the object + a pronominal suffix. Also translate each word.

- *Example:* אֶתְכֶן ⇒ *Answer:* sign of object + *PS 2FP*, "you"

(1) אִתָּךְ	(6) אִתָּם	(11) אִתְּכֶן	(16) אֶתְהֶן
(2) אִתָּ֫נוּ	(7) אַתֵּן	(12) אֹתִי	(17) אֹתָהּ
(3) אִתָּהּ	(8) אֹתוֹ	(13) אֹתָם	(18) אַתֶּם
(4) אַתָּה	(9) אִתִּי	(14) אַתְּ	(19) אֹתָ֫נוּ
(5) אֶתְכֶם	(10) אֶתְהֶם	(15) אִתּוֹ	(20) אִתָּן

c. Learn to recognize, pronounce, and translate the following vocabulary.

	Word	*Translation*	*Notes*
(1)	אֵ֫לֶּה	these (*dem adj M/FP*)	
(2)	אֲנַ֫חְנוּ	we (*pron 1CP*)	
(3)	אָנֹכִי, אֲנִי	I (*pron 1CS*)	
(4)	אֲשֶׁר	who, whom, whose, which, where, when (*particle*)	
(5)	אַתְּ	you (*pron 2FS*)	
(6)	אַתָּה	you (*pron 2MS*)	
(7)	אַתֶּם	you (*pron 2MP*)	
(8)	אַתֵּן, אַתֵּ֫נָה	you (*pron 2FP*)	
(9)	הוּא	(a) he (*pron 3MS*) (b) that (*dem adj MS*)	
(10)	הִיא	(a) she (*pron 3FS*) (b) that (*dem adj FS*)	Sometimes הִוא in *MT*
(11)	הֵם, הֵ֫מָּה	(a) they (*pron 3MP*) (b) those (*dem adj MP*)	

(12)	הֵנָּה	(a) they (*pron 3FP*)
		(b) those (*dem adj FP*)
(13)	זֹאת	this (*dem adj FS*)
(14)	זֶה	this (*dem adj MS*)

d. Fill in the blanks in the following translations, using vocabulary words, forms from paradigm charts, and transliterated names. Some blanks also represent grammatical elements that are prefixed or suffixed to words whose translations are provided. Finally, give a smoother translation of the verses, consulting an English version if necessary.

(1)

וְהִנֵּה	דְבַר־	יְהוָה	אֵלָיו	לֵאמֹר	לֹא	יִירָשְׁךָ	זֶה[1]	כִּי־אִם
“___ behold	______	______	______	(came) saying,	‘Not	he will be your heir	______	but

אֲשֶׁר	יֵצֵא	מִמֵּעֶיךָ	הוּא	יִירָשֶׁךָ	
(one) ______	will come out	___ within ___	______	he will be your heir.’”	(Ge 15:4)

(2)

וַיֹּאמֶר	אֲנִי	יוֹסֵף	אֲחִיכֶם	אֲשֶׁר־	מְכַרְתֶּם	אֹתִי	מִצְרָיְמָה	
“And he said,	‘______	______	___ brother	______	you sold	______	to Egypt.’”	(Ge 45:4)

(3)

וַיִּשְׁלַח	אֹתָם	מֹשֶׁה	מִמִּדְבַּר	פָּארָן	עַל־	פִּי	יְהוָה
“And he sent	______	______	___ the wilderness of	______	______	the command of	______

כֻּלָּם	אֲנָשִׁים	רָאשֵׁי	בְנֵי־	יִשְׂרָאֵל	הֵמָּה	
______	______	______	______	______	______.”	(Nu 13:3)

(4)

וְלָמָה	יְהוָה	מֵבִיא	אֹתָנוּ	אֶל־	הָאָרֶץ	הַזֹּאת	לִנְפֹּל
“___ why is	______	bringing	______	______	______	______	___ fall

בַּחֶרֶב	נָשֵׁינוּ	וְטַפֵּנוּ	יִהְיוּ	לָבַז	הֲלוֹא	טוֹב	לָנוּ
___ sword?	______	___ our children	will be	___ spoils (of war).	Would it not be	______	______

---

[1] The antecedent for this word is “Eliezer.”

שׁוּב	מִצְרָיְמָה	
to return	to Egypt?”	(Nu 14:3)

(5)

וְטַפְּכֶם	אֲשֶׁר	אֲמַרְתֶּם	לָבַז	יִהְיֶה	וּבְנֵיכֶם	אֲשֶׁר	לֹא־יָדְעוּ
“___ your children	______	you said	___ spoils (of war)	will be	______	______	do not know

הַיּוֹם[1]	טוֹב	וָרָע	הֵמָּה	יָבֹאוּ	שָׁמָּה	וְלָהֶם	אֶתְּנֶנָּה	וְהֵם
______	______	___ evil	______	they will enter	there [the land]	______	I will give it	______

יִירָשׁוּהָ	
they will possess it.”	(Dt 1:39)

(6)

לֹא	אֶת־	אֲבֹתֵינוּ	כָּרַת	יְהוָה	אֶת־הַבְּרִית	הַזֹּאת	כִּי	אִתָּנוּ
“Not	______	___ fathers	did he make	______	___ covenant [*NFS*]	______	______	______

אֲנַחְנוּ	אֵלֶּה	פֹה	הַיּוֹם[2]	כֻּלָּנוּ	חַיִּים	
______	______	here	______	______	alive.”	(Dt 5:3)

(7)

וְאֶת־	בַּת־	פַּרְעֹה	הֶעֱלָה	שְׁלֹמֹה	מֵעִיר	דָּוִיד	לַבַּיִת	אֲשֶׁר
“______	______	______	he brought	______	______	______	to the house	______

בָּנָה־	לָהּ	כִּי	אָמַר	לֹא־תֵשֵׁב	אִשָּׁה	לִי	בְּבֵית
he built	______	______	he said,	‘She will not dwell	______	______	in the house of

דָּוִיד	מֶלֶךְ־	יִשְׂרָאֵל	כִּי־	קֹדֶשׁ[4]	הֵמָּה[3]	אֲשֶׁר־	בָּאָה	אֲלֵיהֶם
______	______	______	______	______	______	______	it has come	______

אֲרוֹן	יְהוָה	
the ark of [*NFS*]	______.’”	(2Ch 8:11)

---

[1] In this context the article makes this word definite in the sense of “today.”

[2] “Today” is the meaning of this word in this context.

[3] This personal pronoun refers to an unstated antecedent of “places.”

[4] This noun may be translated as an adjective (“holy”) in this verse.

d. Read aloud and translate the following sentences.

✓ The following feminine and plural perfect verbs appear in the sentences below.

בָּאָה = "she came, went," etc.
בָּאוּ = "they came, went," etc.
הָיוּ = "they were, became," etc.
יָדְעוּ = "they knew"
יָשְׁבוּ = "they dwelled, sat"
עָשׂוּ = "they did, made"
קָרְאוּ = "they called, met"
שָׁלְחוּ = "they sent"
שָׁמְעוּ = "they heard, listened"

(1) אַתְּ בַּת־הַמֶּלֶךְ וְהִיא בַּת־הַכֹּהֵן (2) אֲנִי יְהוָה הוּא שְׁמִי (3) יָשְׁבוּ הָאֲנָשִׁים
אִתְּכֶם וְהֵם כְּבָנִים לָכֶם (4) אַתֵּנָה הַגְּדֹלוֹת בְּכָל־בְּנוֹת־יִשְׂרָאֵל (5) בָּאוּ כָּל
הַכֹּהֲנִים אֲשֶׁר הָיוּ בָּאָרֶץ לַיהוָה וְשָׁמְעוּ[1] אֵלֶּה אֶת־קוֹלוֹ (6) זֶה דְּבַר־אֱלֹהִים
וְטוֹב הוּא (7) קָרְאוּ בְּנוֹת־הַמֶּלֶךְ לַיהוָה וְשָׁמַע אֹתָן (8) טוֹבוֹת־לֵב הַנָּשִׁים
הָאֵלֶּה וְרָעָה הַנָּשִׁים הָהֵנָּה (9) זֹאת בִּתִּי וְהוּא בְּנִי (10) כִּי אַתֶּם גְּדֹלֵי הַמֶּלֶךְ
שָׁלַח אֶתְכֶם לָנוּ (11) הֵמָּה אֲנָשֵׁינוּ וַאֲנַחְנוּ נְשֵׁיהֶם (12) שָׁלְחוּ הַכֹּהֲנִים הָהֵם
אֹתָנוּ אֵלֶיךָ כִּי אִישׁ־אֱלֹהִים אַתָּה (13) נָשָׂא הָעָם אֶת־שֵׁם־הַמֶּלֶךְ אֲשֶׁר יָשְׁבוּ
בְּאַרְצוֹ כִּי טוֹב הוּא לְעַמּוֹ (14) עַל הַיּוֹם הַהוּא קָרָא יְהוָה אֹתָךְ וְאֹתִי וְאֹתָךְ
שָׁלַח (15) קָרָא הַמֶּלֶךְ אֶת־הַכֹּהֵן הַטּוֹב הַהוּא בִּשְׁמוֹ כִּי הוּא יָדַע אֹתוֹ
(16) בָּאוּ הַנָּשִׁים הָהֵנָּה לָכֵן כִּי שָׁלְחוּ אַנְשֵׁי־הָעִיר אֹתָן (17) רָאָה הַמֶּלֶךְ אֹתָךְ
וְאֶת־בִּתֵּךְ וְאֶת־בְּנֵךְ אִתָּךְ (18) בָּאוּ הַכֹּהֲנִים וְהָעָם אִתָּם לְאַרְצֵנוּ וְיָשְׁבוּ
אִתָּנוּ (19) קָרָא הַמֶּלֶךְ אֶת־הָאֲנָשִׁים אֵלָיו וְשָׁלַח אֶתְהֶם מִן הָאָרֶץ לִשְׁנָתַיִם
כְּמִשְׁפָּט לָרָעָה אֲשֶׁר עָשׂוּ (20) קָרְאוּ הָאֲנָשִׁים הָאֵלֶּה אֶת הָאִשָּׁה הַהִיא
אֲלֵיהֶם כִּי יָדְעוּ אֶת הָאִשָּׁה אֲשֶׁר קָרְאוּ וְהִיא בָּאָה אִתָּם לְעִיר־הַקֹּדֶשׁ
(21) בָּא מִשְׁפַּט־אֱלֹהִים עַל־הָאִשָּׁה הַזֹּאת וְעַל־בְּנוֹתֶיהָ אִתָּהּ כִּי יָדַע אֱלֹהִים
כִּי הֵנָּה רָעָה

[1] The *vav* conjunction in this sentence means "but."

Lesson 12

Verbs in General, Perfect Conjugation of the Verb, Perfect Conjugation in the *Qal* Stem

12A Verbs in General

1. Verb roots

Most verbs have three basic consonants; for example, the verb מָשַׁל ("he ruled") is triconsonantal. The three consonants of a verb, written without vowels, comprise the verb's root. Thereby, משׁל is the root for מָשַׁל. The various forms of a verb are created by inflections or changes made to its root, such as the addition of certain vowels, prefixes, or suffixes; or the doubling of the middle consonant of the root.

2. Strong and weak verbs

Verbs are classified as strong (or regular) and weak. Strong verbs follow a fixed, regular pattern for the inflection of a triconsonantal verb root. Weak verbs follow irregular patterns of inflection and sometimes require the dropping of a consonant from a verb root. A weak verb is identified by the appearance of a weak consonant (א, ה, ו, ח, י, נ, ע, or ר [see Lesson 6C]) or a doubled consonant in a verb root. This Grammar will present the strong verb first.

3. Moods and tenses

a. Hebrew verbs appear in the indicative and imperative moods, which function in the same manner as they do in English. The indicative mood is declarative (making a statement), while the imperative expresses a command. Hebrew has no distinct subjunctive mood (expressing non-reality), as does English. Subjunctive notions are usually expressed by the context in which a Hebrew verb appears.[1] Indicative and imperative verbs are also called finite ("limited") verbs because they are limited to particular persons, genders, and numbers.

[1] Horsnell, 306.

b. The indicative mood of the Hebrew verb has two tenses: perfect and imperfect, as mentioned previously. These tenses do not denote the temporal ideas of past, present, and future, as English tenses do. Instead the Hebrew tenses suggest kinds of action or states. Simply put, the perfect tense typically indicates an action or state that is complete, while the imperfect indicates an action or state that is incomplete.[1]

4. Stems

a. The Hebrew verb appears in a number of what may be called "stems."[2] Each stem indicates something about the nature of the action (or state) of a verb. There are seven major stems that occur with strong verbs.

b. The simplest stem is called *qal*, the name of which is derived from the verb root קלל, which means "light." The *qal* stem is "light" in the sense that in the *3MS* form its spelling does not require the addition of a prefix or the doubling of a root consonant, as is the case in the other stems for strong verbs. The traditional names of these other stems are based upon the *3MS* forms of the verb root פעל in the various stems. The stem names are *nifal* (נִפְעַל), *piel* (פִּעֵל), *pual* (פֻּעַל), *hifil* (הִפְעִיל), *hofal* (הָפְעַל), and *hitpael* (הִתְפַּעֵל).[3]

c. The stems can convey a variety of connotations. In order to simplify the process of mastering the verb forms, only one connotation will be given for each stem while the strong verb is being introduced. A future lesson will discuss other meanings that the stems can have. (See Lesson 20A.2.)

(1) The *qal* stem denotes simple action in the active voice. (The action of this

---

[1] Since Hebrew verbs do not by themselves convey temporal ideas, it may be argued that they do not, strictly speaking, have the quality of tense. However, "tense" remains a useful term for describing certain basic qualities of the Hebrew verb. Some grammarians use alternate terms for the perfect and imperfect tenses – such as "suffix," "perfective," *qatal*, or *qtl* conjugation for the perfect; and "prefix," "non-perfective," *yiqtol*, or *yqtl* conjugation for the imperfect. For more detailed discussions of the connotations of the tenses see Horsnell, 47-48; Joüon, §111a-f; Waltke and O'Connor, §29.1-29.6, 30.1-30.4, 31.1; and Kautzsch, §106a, 107a.

[2] Some grammarians prefer the term "pattern" or "theme." See Horsnell, 44; and C.L. Seow, *A Grammar for Biblical Hebrew*, rev. ed. (Nashville: Abingdon, 1995), 89.

[3] As is typical in this Grammar, these Hebrew terms are spelled in a simplified form. Some grammarians use alternative terminology for the names of the stems; see Seow, 89-90; and Waltke and O'Connor, §21.1c.

stem is simple by comparison with the more complex kinds of action that occur in some of the other stems.)

- ‣ מָשַׁל is a perfect, *qal*, *3MS* verb, meaning "he ruled." It describes the subject's performance of a simple act.

(2) The *nifal* stem usually expresses the passive of *qal*, in which case it denotes simple action in the passive voice.

- ‣ While the perfect, *qal, 3MS* verb מָשַׁל means "he ruled," the corresponding *nifal* form נִמְשַׁל[1] means "he was ruled." *Nifal* depicts the subject as the one acted upon in a simple action.

(3) The *piel* stem is the most difficult to define. It always expresses the active voice but can convey a variety of connotations with regard to the nature of its action. No single category is an adequate description of the general notion of *piel*. (See Lesson 20A.2d.) However, to simplify the process of learning *piel* forms, only one connotation is introduced here: *piel* can serve to intensify the simple action of *qal*. That intensification may involve multiplying or strengthening the basic verbal idea in some way. Notions of intensification in *piel* verbs can be translated in a variety of ways; however, when no other expression is appropriate, this Grammar will use the default of indicating a *piel* verb by underlining its translation, as in the first example below.

- ‣ מִשֵּׁל is a perfect, *piel*, *3MS* verb, which may be translated "he <u>ruled</u>." The intensive action is performed by the subject.
- ✓ Some *piel* verbs lend themselves to more idiomatic expressions of intensity in English, as the next two examples illustrate.
- ‣ While the perfect, *qal*, *3MS* verb קָבַר means "he buried," the corresponding *piel* form קִבֵּר can mean "he buried many" – connoting intensity through repeated action.
- ‣ While the perfect, *qal, 3MS* verb שָׁאַל means "he asked," the corresponding *piel* verb שִׁאֵל may be translated "he begged" – suggesting intensity by strengthening or repeating the action.

---

[1] This Grammar uses the verb root משׁל ("rule") as a model for discussing the strong verb. Some hypothetical forms appear for the sake of illustration.

(4) The *pual* stem usually serves as the passive of *piel*.

- Where the perfect, *piel*, *3MS* verb מִשֵּׁל means "he <u>ruled</u>," the corresponding *pual* form מֻשַּׁל means "he was <u>ruled</u>." The action is happening to the subject.

(5) The *hifil* stem usually denotes causative action in the active voice. To say it another way, *hifil* typically expresses the causative of *qal*. Often the causative idea can be communicated by a translation that employs "cause" or "make."

- הִמְשִׁיל is a perfect, *hifil*, *3MS* verb, meaning "he caused to rule" or "he made to rule." It describes the subject's causation of an action.
- While the perfect, *qal*, *3MS* verb יָצָא means "he went out," the corresponding *hifil* form הוֹצִיא means "he caused to go out" or "he brought out."

(6) The *hofal* stem expresses the passive of *hifil*. When a *hifil* verb expresses causative action in the active voice, its *hofal* form denotes the same causation in the passive voice.

- While the perfect, *hifil*, *3MS* verb הִמְשִׁיל means "he caused to rule," the corresponding *hofal* form הָמְשַׁל means "he was caused to rule" or "he was made ruler." The causative action is happening to the subject.

(7) The *hitpael* stem usually denotes reflexive action; that is, it expresses action that the subject performs upon himself or herself.

- הִתְמַשֵּׁל is a perfect, *hitpael*, *3MS* verb, meaning "he ruled himself."
- ✓ In form *hitpael* is related to *piel* and *pual* in that all three require a doubling of the middle consonant of a verb root. These three are sometimes referred to as the "intensive stems."

d. Summary

(1) The meanings of the stems as described in this section:[1]

(a) *Qal* = simple action in the active voice

(b) *Nifal* = usually the passive of *qal*

(c) *Piel* = sometimes intensive action in the active voice

(d) *Pual* = usually the passive of *piel*

(e) *Hifil* = usually causative action in the active voice

---

[1] See Lesson 20A.2 for a more thorough discussion of the range of meanings which the stems can have.

(f) *Hofal* = passive of *hifil*

(g) *Hitpael* = usually reflexive

(2) Another way of classifying the stems:

(a) Active voice = *qal*, *piel*, and *hifil*

(b) Passive voice = *nifal*, *pual*, and *hofal*

(c) Reflexive = *hitpael*

12B Perfect Conjugation of the Verb

1. Meaning of perfect verbs

Since the Hebrew perfect verb connotes completed action rather than temporal action (temporal action being past, present, or future), a variety of English tenses may be used in translating a Hebrew perfect verb. The perfect may describe action completed in the past, in the present, or even in the future. The context of a Hebrew verb is the guide for understanding which English tense best conveys the meaning. While Hebrew perfect verbs may convey a variety of temporal meanings, it is often the case that they communicate action that has been completed in the past.[1] For now this Grammar will translate Hebrew perfect verbs with the English past tense for the sake of simplicity. A future lesson will explore other ways of translating the Hebrew perfect (Lesson 20A.1).

2. Perfect verb suffixes

a. All perfect verbs in Hebrew employ a particular set of suffixes. These suffixes convey not only the idea of the perfect tense but also the person, gender, and number of a verb (which agrees with the person, gender, and number of a verb's subject, if one is stated). The perfect suffixes are as follows.

3MS	[none]	*3CP* [2]	וּ
3FS	◌ָה		
2MS	תָּ	*2MP*	תֶּם
2FS	תְּ[3]	*2FP*	תֶּן
1CS	תִּי	*1CP*	נוּ

[1] It is for this reason that verbs presented in vocabulary lists in the perfect tense are translated with the English past tense.

[2] *3CP* = third person, common (either masculine and feminine), plural

[3] The spelling of תְּ is unusual in that it has a *dagesh-forte* and a silent *sheva*, similar to the personal pronoun אַתְּ (Lesson 11A.3). The unusual spelling is an adaptation from an older form.

b. The above chart begins with the *3MS* form, as do all of the perfect and imperfect verb charts in this Grammar. The reason for this approach (as opposed to beginning with the first person) is that the *3MS* form is the simplest – being the only one that does not require a suffix. All the other perfect forms have suffixes and are based upon the *3MS*. Since the perfect *3MS* is most basic, it is the lexical form for a strong verb (that is, the form by which a verb is listed in a lexicon).

12C Perfect Conjugation in the *Qal* Stem

1. The chart below presents the conjugation of the strong perfect verb in the *qal* stem. It employs the verb root משׁל ("rule") as a model, demonstrating how the above suffixes are added to this root.

3MS	מָשַׁל ("he ruled")
3FS	מָשְׁלָה ("she ruled")
2MS	מָשַׁלְתָּ ("you ruled")
2FS	מָשַׁלְתְּ ("you ruled")
1CS	מָשַׁלְתִּי ("I ruled")
3CP	מָשְׁלוּ ("they ruled")
2MP	מְשַׁלְתֶּם ("you ruled")
2FP	מְשַׁלְתֶּן ("you ruled")
1CP	מָשַׁלְנוּ ("we ruled")

2. Notes concerning the perfect, *qal* conjugation
   a. The perfect, *qal*, *3MS* form of a strong verb requires the vowels *qames* and *patah* (as in מָשַׁל).[1] This form is the basis upon which the other *qal* forms are built. The *patah* under the second consonant of the root appears in most of the *qal* conjugation (*3MS*, *2MS*, *2FS*, *1CS*, *2MP*, *2FP*, and *1CP*) and is known as the thematic vowel of this stem in the perfect tense.
   b. The addition of the perfect suffixes in *qal* causes the following changes in pointing.

[1] An exception occurs with stative verbs. (See Lesson 21A.)

(1) Two suffixes begin with (or are made up of) a vowel: וּ (*3CP*) and ◌ָה (*3FS*). When attached to a verb root, these suffixes, along with the last consonant of the root, form syllables which are accented – for משׁל the new syllables are לוּ (*3CP*) and לָה (*3FS*). The shifting accent causes the thematic vowel to reduce from a *patah* to a vocal *sheva* (as in שְׁ). The *qames* under the first consonant receives a *meteg* (as in מָֽ).

(2) The irregular suffix תְּ (*2FS*) involves the addition of only a consonant to a verb root. It is preceded by a silent *sheva* and creates an irregular final syllable that ends with two consonants – for משׁל the final syllable is שַׁלְתְּ. Since the suffix does not add another syllable to the verb, the accent is unchanged (remaining on the second and final syllable).

(3) Three suffixes form open syllables; they are תָּ (*2MS*), תִּי (*1CS*), and נוּ (*1CP*). When added to a verb they require a silent *sheva* under the last consonant of the root (as in לְ). The accent does not move to the suffix; it remains on the second syllable of the verb which retains its thematic vowel – for משׁל the accent remains above the שַׁ.

(4) Two suffixes form closed syllables; they are תֶּם (*2MP*) and תֶּן (*2FP*). When added to a verb root, these new final syllables receive the accent. They are also preceded by a silent *sheva*, which occurs under the last consonant of the root (as in לְ). In addition, these long suffixes require the *qames* under the first consonant of the root to reduce to a vocal *sheva* (as in מְ).

3. The chart below presents the perfect conjugation in *qal* for two other roots which follow the pattern of strong verbs: שׁמר ("keep") and קטל ("kill").

3MS	שָׁמַר ("he kept")	קָטַל ("he killed")
3FS	שָֽׁמְרָה ("she kept")	קָֽטְלָה ("she killed")
2MS	שָׁמַ֫רְתָּ ("you kept")	קָטַ֫לְתָּ ("you killed")
2FS	שָׁמַרְתְּ ("you kept")	קָטַלְתְּ ("you killed")
1CS	שָׁמַ֫רְתִּי ("I kept")	קָטַ֫לְתִּי ("I killed")
3CP	שָֽׁמְרוּ ("they kept")	קָֽטְלוּ ("they killed")

2MP	שְׁמַרְתֶּם	("you kept")
2FP	שְׁמַרְתֶּן	("you kept")
1CP	שָׁמַ֫רְנוּ	("we kept")

קְטַלְתֶּם	("you killed")
קְטַלְתֶּן	("you killed")
קָטַ֫לְנוּ	("we killed")

Lesson 12: Exercises

a. List from memory the seven major stems of the verb. Also indicate the meanings of these stems as described in section 12A.4d(1) (that is, whether the action of each is simple, intensive, or causative; and whether each is active, passive, or reflexive).

b. Reproduce from memory the perfect conjugation of משׁל ("rule") for the *qal* stem in each person, gender, and number (that is, in *3MS*, *3FS*, *2MS*, etc.), as in section 12C.1. Also give a translation for each form.

c. Learn to recognize, pronounce, and translate the following vocabulary.

	Word	*Translation*	*Notes*
(1)	אֶחָד	one (*adj MS*)	*Cs:* אַחַד; *FS, Ab & Cs:* אַחַת
(2)	לָקַט	he picked up, gathered (*V*)	
(3)	מָשַׁל	he ruled, reigned (*V*)	When followed by בְּ prep, בְּ = "over"
(4)	קָטַל	he killed (*V*)	
(5)	שָׁמַר	he kept, watched, guarded (*V*)	

d. Rewrite the Hebrew verses below, supplying the missing words based on the English translation that is provided. First attempt the exercise without assistance from charts or vocabulary lists in this Grammar or from a Hebrew Bible. Then, if necessary, consult such helps.

	______	______	______	־יֶשׁ־	______	(1)
(Ge 39:4)	in [into] his hand"	he gave	for him [belonging to him]	there was	"And all	

דָּוִיד	______	______ ־	______	(3)	בְּבַ֫יִת	[1] ______	לֹא	______ (2)

---

[1] For the sake of simplicity, this Grammar uses the symbol ◌֫ to refer to any sort of Hebrew accent. The system of accenting in *BHS* uses a variety of other symbols that have not yet been discussed; one of

(1Ch 11:7)	David	the city of	to [לֹ] it [*MS*]	"They called [named]	(2Sa 7:6)	in a house"	I dwelled	not	"For

	______	אִמְרֵי־	______	______	______	______	־	______	(4)
(Jos 24:27)	the LORD	the words of	all of	[sign of the object]	it [*FS*] heard	it [a stone] [*FS*]		"For	

	______[1]	לְפִי־אָכְלוֹ	______	(6)		______	______	לֹא	(5)
(Ex 16:18)	they gathered"	according to his need for food	"A man [each one]		(Pr 24:12)	this [*MS*]"	we knew	"Not	

	______	______	הֵ֫נָּה	______	______	______	לֹא	(7)
(Ge 45:8)	the God [sent me]"	that	here [rather it is]	me	you [*MP*] sent	you [*MP*]	"Not	

	מִטָּה־	______	______	(9)		______	דַּרְכֵי	______	(8)
(Eze 23:41)	a stately couch"	on	"And you [*FS*] sat		(2Sa 22:22)	the LORD"	the ways of	"I kept	

	______	צִוְּךָ־	______	______	______	לֹא	______	(10)
(1Sa 13:14)	the LORD"	he commanded you	which	[sign of the object]	you [*MS*] kept	not	"For	

e. Read aloud and translate the following words [numbers (1)-(5)] and sentences [numbers (6)–(18)].

(1) קָטַל | קָטַ֫לְנוּ | קָטַלְתְּ | קָֽטְלוּ (2) לְקַטְתֶּם | לָֽקְטָה | לָקַ֫טְתִּי | לְקַטְתֶּן
(3) מָשַׁלְתְּ | מָשַׁ֫לְתִּי | מָשַׁ֫לְתָּ | מָֽשְׁלוּ (4) אֲנִי[2] קָטַ֫לְתִּי | הוּא קָטַל | אֲנַ֫חְנוּ
קָטַ֫לְנוּ | הֵ֫נָּה קָֽטְלוּ (5) אַתֶּם לְקַטְתֶּם | אַתְּ לָקַטְתְּ | אַתֵּ֫נָה לְקַטְתֶּן | אַתָּה
לָקַ֫טְתָּ (6) שָֽׁמְרוּ הָאֲנָשִׁים אֶת בְּנֵיהֶם וְשָֽׁמְרוּ הַנָּשִׁים אֶת בְּנוֹתֵיהֶן (7) מָֽשְׁלוּ
מַלְכֵי־הַגּוֹיִם אֶת־הָעָם אֲשֶׁר יָֽשְׁבוּ בְּאַרְצֹתָם[3] בְּמִשְׁפָּט לְשָׁנִים רַבּוֹת

those accents appears on the second syllable of this word in the Hebrew text. Additional accents may be observed in *BHS* with other words in this exercise.

[1] In *BHS* the vowel under the second consonant of this word is lengthened from *sheva* to *qames* because of the sort of accent it has (one which indicates the end of the verse).

[2] See Lesson 11A.4b.

[3] The וֹ of אַרְצוֹת reduces to a *holem* when the suffix ◌ָם is added.

(8) שְׁמַרְתֶּן דִּבְרֵי־אֱלֹהִים בְּלִבּוֹתֵיכֶן וְעָשׂוּ[1] יְדוֹתֵיכֶן אֵת טוֹב כָּל־יְמֵיכֶן
(9) לָקַטְתִּי בָּנַי אֵלַי כִּי יָדַעְתִּי כִּי קָֽטְלוּ אֶת־בֶּן־הַמֶּלֶךְ אֲשֶׁר עָשָׂה אֶת־רָעָה
בְּעִירֵנוּ (10) יָשַׁבְנוּ בְּאֶרֶץ־יִשְׂרָאֵל לִשְׁנָתַיִם כִּי שָֽׁלְחָה רוּחַ־אֱלֹהִים אֹתָנוּ אֶל
הָאָרֶץ הַהִיא (11) אַתָּה לָקַטְתָּ כֹּהֲנֵי־יְהוָה לְעִירְךָ וְקָֽרְאוּ לְעַם־הָעִיר
וּבָאוּ[2] אֶל יְהוָה כְּעַם בְּלֵב אֶחָד (12) שָֽׁמְעָה אַחַת הַנָּשִׁים לְדִבְרֵי־אָדָם־
אֱלֹהִים וְשָֽׁמְרָה אֶת־בָּנֶיהָ וְאֶת־בְּנוֹתֶיהָ מֵרָעָה (13) לָקַטְתְּ אֶת־כָּל־הַנָּשִׁים
לָךְ מִן־הָעִיר וְשָׁמַרְתְּ אֹתָן אִתָּךְ לְכָל־הַיָּמִים כִּי מָשַׁל הַמֶּלֶךְ אֶת־הָעִיר
(14) אַתֶּם רָאשֵׁי הַגּוֹיִם וּבְמִשְׁפָּט מְשַׁלְתֶּם עַמֵּיכֶם כִּי שְׁמַרְתֶּם דְּבַר
אֱלֹהִים (15) שָׁלַחְנוּ אֶחָד מֵאַנְשֵׁי עִירֵנוּ אֶל עַם הָעִיר הַהִיא וְנָשָׂא אֶת־קוֹלוֹ
וְקָרָא אֹתָם לַיהוָה (16) נָתַן אִישׁ־אֱלֹהִים אֶת־כָּל־שְׁמוֹת־כֹּהֲנֵי־הָאָרֶץ
לַמֶּלֶךְ וּמֵהַשְּׁמוֹת הָהֵם קָרָא הַמֶּלֶךְ אֶת־אֶחָד כֹּהֵן לָעָם בֶּהָרִים וּבָא לָהֶם
וְיָשַׁב עִמָּם (17) שָׁמַעְתָּ לְקוֹל הַמֶּלֶךְ הַגָּדוֹל וְיָדַעְתָּ כִּי טוֹבִים דְּבָרָיו אֲשֶׁר
נָתַן לְךָ (18) לָקַט יְהוָה אֹתָנוּ אֵלָיו וְשָׁמַר אֹתָנוּ מִן רָעָה וּמָשַׁל אֹתָנוּ
בְּמִשְׁפָּט כִּי קָרָאנוּ[3] עַל שְׁמוֹ

[1] This is the *3CP* form of עָשָׂה, a weak verb which loses its last consonant when a suffix is added.

[2] This is the *3CP* form of בּוֹא ("[to] come"), a weak verb that loses its middle consonant when a suffix is added.

[3] In this weak verb the vowel under the ר lengthens to a *qames* and the א becomes quiescent.

Lesson 13

Perfect Conjugation in the Other Major Stems, Summary of the Perfect Conjugation

13A Perfect Conjugation in the Other Major Stems

1. Introduction

a. As stated previously, the strong verb occurs in seven major stems, each of which has its own connotations. The last lesson introduced all of the stems in general and the perfect, *qal* stem in particular. The purpose of this section is to introduce the forms of the strong perfect verb in the other six major stems.

b. The *qal* stem is the basis for the formation of the other stems. They, like *qal*, take the perfect suffixes, which indicate the person, gender, and number of a verb. The major accent of a perfect verb remains on the same syllable in the other stems as it does in *qal* – except for two forms in *hifil*. In addition to these common features, each stem has unique elements, as described in the following discussion.

2. Perfect conjugation in the *nifal* stem

a. The right column in the following chart presents the forms of the perfect, *nifal* verb for the root משׁל; the left column has the perfect, *qal* forms of this same verb for comparison. As indicated in the last lesson, the *nifal* stem usually serves as the passive of *qal*, in which case it conveys simple action in the passive voice, as the translation indicates.

	Perfect		
	Qal	*Nifal*	
3MS	מָשַׁל	נִמְשַׁל	("he was ruled")
3FS	מָשְׁלָה	נִמְשְׁלָה	("she was ruled")
2MS	מָשַׁלְתָ	נִמְשַׁלְתָ	("you were ruled")
2FS	מָשַׁלְתְ	נִמְשַׁלְתְ	("you were ruled")
1CS	מָשַׁלְתִי	נִמְשַׁלְתִי	("I was ruled")
3CP	מָשְׁלוּ	נִמְשְׁלוּ	("they were ruled")
2MP	מְשַׁלְתֶם	נִמְשַׁלְתֶם	("you were ruled")
2FP	מְשַׁלְתֶן	נִמְשַׁלְתֶן	("you were ruled")
1CP	מָשַׁלְנוּ	נִמְשַׁלְנוּ	("we were ruled")

b. Notes concerning the perfect, *nifal* conjugation

(1) The most distinctive feature of this stem is the נִ prefix. The prefixed נִ and the first consonant of the root create a closed syllable – in the case of משל the new syllable is נִמְ (nim). Note that the first consonant of the verb root receives a silent *sheva*.

(2) The vowel for the second consonant of the root in most forms is a *patah*, except when a vowel suffix is added (*3FS* and *3CP*), in which case the *patah* reduces to a vocal *sheva*. Since *qal* follows this same pattern, the *nifal* and *qal* stems are spelled the same beginning with the second consonant of the verb – שׁ in the case of משל, as a comparison of the two columns above indicates. In other words, the only difference between the perfect, *qal* and the perfect, *nifal* is in the spelling of the first syllable.

(3) The spelling of the stem name *nifal* (נִפְעַל) is reflected in the *3MS* form, which begins with *ni* and has an *a* vowel, as נִמְשַׁל (nim/šal) illustrates.

3. Perfect conjugation in the *piel* stem

a. The perfect, *piel* forms of משל appear in the following chart, along with the corresponding *qal* forms for comparison. As indicated in the last lesson, the *piel* stem can connote intensive action in the active voice, as suggested by the underlined translation.

	Perfect	
	Qal	*Piel*
3MS	מָשַׁל	מִשֵּׁל (“he <u>ruled</u>”)
3FS	מָשְׁלָה	מִשְּׁלָה (“she <u>ruled</u>”)
2MS	מָשַׁלְתָּ	מִשַּׁלְתָּ (“you <u>ruled</u>”)
2FS	מָשַׁלְתְּ	מִשַּׁלְתְּ (“you <u>ruled</u>”)
1CS	מָשַׁלְתִּי	מִשַּׁלְתִּי (“I <u>ruled</u>”)
3CP	מָשְׁלוּ	מִשְּׁלוּ (“they <u>ruled</u>”)
2MP	מְשַׁלְתֶּם	מִשַּׁלְתֶּם (“you <u>ruled</u>”)
2FP	מְשַׁלְתֶּן	מִשַּׁלְתֶּן (“you <u>ruled</u>”)
1CP	מָשַׁלְנוּ	מִשַּׁלְנוּ (“we <u>ruled</u>”)

b. Notes concerning the perfect, *piel* conjugation

(1) There are two major characteristics which appear in every form of this stem. One is a *hireq* under the first consonant of the root. The other is the doubling of the second root consonant by means of a *dagesh-forte* – something which also occurs in *pual* and *hitpael*.

(2) In *3MS* the second consonant of the root has a *sere*. This vowel reduces to a *patah* with the addition of a suffix that begins with a consonant (*2MS*, *2FS*, *1CS*, *2MP*, *2FP*, and *1CP*). This vowel further reduces to a vocal *sheva* when a vowel suffix is added (*3FS* and *3CP*).

(3) A comparison of the two columns above indicates that in the perfect, except for the *3MS* form, *piel* and *qal* verbs are spelled the same beginning with the second of the doubled consonants in *piel*. For example, compare the *piel*, *3FS* form מִשְּׁלָה (or מִשְׁשְׁלָה to spell it without the *dagesh-forte*) with the *qal*, *3FS* form מָשְׁלָה.

(4) The spelling of the stem name *piel* (פִּעֵל) is reflected in the *3MS* form, which has the vowels *i* and *e*, as מִשֵּׁל (miš/šēl) illustrates.

4. Perfect conjugation in the *pual* stem

a. The following chart presents the perfect, *pual* forms of משׁל, along with the *qal* forms of the same verb for the sake of comparison. As indicated in the last lesson, the *pual* stem usually serves as the passive of *piel,* as suggested by the underlined translation.

	Perfect	
	Qal	*Pual*
3MS	מָשַׁל	מֻשַּׁל ("he was ruled")
3FS	מָשְׁלָה	מֻשְּׁלָה ("she was ruled")
2MS	מָשַׁלְתָּ	מֻשַּׁלְתָּ ("you were ruled")
2FS	מָשַׁלְתְּ	מֻשַּׁלְתְּ ("you were ruled")
1CS	מָשַׁלְתִּי	מֻשַּׁלְתִּי ("I was ruled")
3CP	מָשְׁלוּ	מֻשְּׁלוּ ("they were ruled")
2MP	מְשַׁלְתֶּם	מֻשַּׁלְתֶּם ("you were ruled")
2FP	מְשַׁלְתֶּן	מֻשַּׁלְתֶּן ("you were ruled")
1CP	מָשַׁלְנוּ	מֻשַּׁלְנוּ ("we were ruled")

b. Notes concerning the perfect, *pual* conjugation

(1) Two major characteristics appear in every form of this stem: a *qibbus* under the first consonant of the root and a *dagesh-forte* in the second consonant.

(2) In most forms the second consonant of the root has a *patah.* This vowel reduces to a vocal *sheva* when a vowel suffix is added (*2FS* and *3CP*).

(3) A comparison of the two columns above indicates that in the perfect the *pual* stem is spelled the same as *qal* beginning with the second of the doubled consonants in *pual*. In addition, a comparison of *pual* and *piel* verbs in the perfect indicates that, outside of the *3MS* form, the two stems are spelled exactly the same except for the vowel under the first consonant. (See Appendix 3, paradigm 1). For example, compare the *pual*, *3FS* form מֻשְּׁלָה and the *piel*, *3FS* form מִשְּׁלָה.

(4) The spelling of the stem name *pual* (פֻּעַל) is reflected in the *3MS* form, which has the vowels *u* and *a*, as מֻשַּׁל (mŭš/šal) illustrates.

5. Perfect conjugation in the *hifil* stem

a. The perfect, *hifil* forms of משל appear in the following chart, along with the corresponding *qal* forms for comparison. As indicated in the last lesson, the *hifil* stem often conveys causative action in the active voice, as the translation indicates.

	Perfect		
	Qal	*Hifil*	
3MS	מָשַׁל	הִמְשִׁיל	("he caused to rule")
3FS	מָשְׁלָה	הִמְשִׁילָה	("she caused to rule")
2MS	מָשַׁלְתָּ	הִמְשַׁלְתָּ	("you caused to rule")
2FS	מָשַׁלְתְּ	הִמְשַׁלְתְּ	("you caused to rule")
1CS	מָשַׁלְתִּי	הִמְשַׁלְתִּי	("I caused to rule")
3CP	מָשְׁלוּ	הִמְשִׁילוּ	("they caused to rule")
2MP	מְשַׁלְתֶּם	הִמְשַׁלְתֶּם	("you caused to rule")
2FP	מְשַׁלְתֶּן	הִמְשַׁלְתֶּן	("you caused to rule")
1CP	מָשַׁלְנוּ	הִמְשַׁלְנוּ	("we caused to rule")

b. Notes concerning the perfect, *hifil* conjugation

(1) The key distinctive of the *hifil* stem is the הִ prefix. The prefix and the first consonant of the verb root create a closed syllable – in the case of משל the new syllable is הִמְ (him).

(2) In *3MS* the vowel for the second consonant of the verb root is the naturally-long vowel *hireq-yod*. That vowel is retained (does not reduce) with the addition of the vowel suffixes (*3FS* and *3CP*). Moreover, when these two suffixes are added, they do not draw the accent to themselves (as they do in the other stems). Thus in *3FS* and *3CP* the accent remains on the syllable which has the *hireq-yod*.

(3) When a suffix is added that begins with a consonant (*2MS*, *2FS*, *1CS*, *2MP*, *2FP*, and *1CP*), the vowel of the second consonant of the root in *3MS* (*hireq-yod*) reduces to a *patah*. Consequently, in these cases the spelling of *hifil* is the same as the spelling of *nifal* in the perfect except for the prefix consonant.

(See Appendix 3, paradigm 1). For example, compare the *hifil*, *2MS* form הִמְשַׁלְתָּ with the *nifal*, *2MS* form נִמְשַׁלְתָּ.

(4) The spelling of the stem name *hifil* (הִפְעִיל) is reflected in the *3MS* form, which begins with *hi* and has another *i* vowel, as הִמְשִׁיל (*him/šîl*) illustrates.

6. Perfect conjugation in the *hofal* stem

a. The following chart presents the perfect, *hofal* forms of משל along with the *qal* forms of this verb for comparison. As indicated in the last lesson, the *hofal* stem is the passive of *hifil*, which means *hofal* often connotes causative action in the passive voice, as the translation indicates.

	Perfect	
	Qal	*Hofal*
3MS	מָשַׁל	הָמְשַׁל ("he was caused to rule")
3FS	מָשְׁלָה	הָמְשְׁלָה ("she was caused to rule")
2MS	מָשַׁלְתָּ	הָמְשַׁלְתָּ ("you were caused to rule")
2FS	מָשַׁלְתְּ	הָמְשַׁלְתְּ ("you were caused to rule")
1CS	מָשַׁלְתִּי	הָמְשַׁלְתִּי ("I was caused to rule")
3CP	מָשְׁלוּ	הָמְשְׁלוּ ("they were caused to rule")
2MP	מְשַׁלְתֶּם	הָמְשַׁלְתֶּם ("you were caused to rule")
2FP	מְשַׁלְתֶּן	הָמְשַׁלְתֶּן ("you were caused to rule")
1CP	מָשַׁלְנוּ	הָמְשַׁלְנוּ ("we were caused to rule")

b. Notes concerning the perfect, *hofal* conjugation

(1) The key distinguishing feature of this stem is the הָ prefix. The vowel of this prefix is the short vowel *qames-hatuf.* The prefixed הָ and the first consonant of the verb root create a closed syllable – in the case of משל the new syllable is הָמְ (hom).

(2) The vowel for the second consonant of the root in most cases is a *patah*. However, when a vowel suffix is added (*3FS* and *3CP*), the *patah* reduces to a vocal *sheva*.

(3) In the perfect the spelling of *hofal* is the same as the spelling of *nifal* except for the prefix. (See Appendix 3, paradigm 1). For example, compare the *hofal,*

3MS form הָמְשַׁל with the *nifal, 3MS* form נִמְשַׁל.

(4) The spelling of the stem name *hofal* (הָפְעַל) is reflected in the *3MS* form, which begins with *ho* and has an *a* vowel, as הָמְשַׁל (hom/šal) illustrates.

7. Perfect conjugation in the *hitpael* stem

a. The following chart has the perfect, *hitpael* forms of משל along with the *qal* forms of this same verb for comparison. As indicated in the last lesson, the *hitpael* stem usually denotes reflexive action, as the translation indicates.

	Perfect	
	Qal	*Hitpael*
3MS	מָשַׁל	הִתְמַשֵּׁל ("he ruled himself")
3FS	מָשְׁלָה	הִתְמַשְּׁלָה ("she ruled herself")
2MS	מָשַׁלְתָּ	הִתְמַשַּׁלְתָּ ("you ruled yourself")
2FS	מָשַׁלְתְּ	הִתְמַשַּׁלְתְּ ("you ruled yourself")
1CS	מָשַׁלְתִּי	הִתְמַשַּׁלְתִּי ("I ruled myself")
3CP	מָשְׁלוּ	הִתְמַשְּׁלוּ ("they ruled themselves")
2MP	מְשַׁלְתֶּם	הִתְמַשַּׁלְתֶּם ("you ruled yourselves")
2FP	מְשַׁלְתֶּן	הִתְמַשַּׁלְתֶּן ("you ruled yourselves")
1CP	מָשַׁלְנוּ	הִתְמַשַּׁלְנוּ ("we ruled ourselves")

b. Notes concerning the perfect, *hitpael* conjugation

(1) There are three distinguishing features of this stem: a two-consonant prefix of הִת, a *patah* under the first consonant of the root, and a *dagesh-forte* in the second root consonant.

(2) As stated previously, the *hitpael* stem is formally related to *piel*. Besides sharing the characteristic of a doubled consonant, the two stems follow the same pattern with regard to the vowel for the second consonant of the root. In *3MS* the vowel is a *sere*. It reduces to a *patah* with the addition of a suffix that begins with a consonant (*2MS*, *2FS*, *1CS*, *2MP*, *2FP*, and *1CP*). This vowel further reduces to a vocal *sheva* when a vowel suffix is added (*2FS* and *3CP*).

(3) Beginning with the second consonant of the root, *hitpael* and *piel* are spelled the same in the perfect. (See Appendix 3, paradigm 1). For example, compare the *hitpael*, *3FS* form הִתְמַשְּׁלָה with the *piel*, *3FS* form מִשְּׁלָה

(4) The spelling of the stem name *hitpael* (הִתְפַּעֵל) is reflected in the *3MS* form, which begins with *hit* and has the vowels *a* and *e*, as הִתְמַשֵּׁל (*hiṯ*/maš/šēl) illustrates.

c. A peculiar feature of the perfect, *hitpael* is that when the prefix הִתְ is added to a verb root that begins with the sibilant consonants ס, צ, שׂ, or שׁ, the sibilant and the ת of the prefix change places, as the following example illustrates.[1]

- The perfect, *hitpael*, *3MS* form of שׁמר is הִשְׁתַּמֵּר, rather than הִתְשַׁמֵּר.

13B Summary of the Perfect Conjugation

1. It is imperative that the student learns to recognize the perfect verb in terms of its root, stem, person, gender and number, and learns to translate the verb. One key to accomplishing this goal is the mastery of the full conjugation of the perfect verb in the *qal* stem and also the *3MS* form of each of the other major stems. For the sake of convenience, these forms for משׁל appear in the chart below with their translations. Any strong verb root could be substituted for משׁל and the prefixes, suffixes, vowels, and accents would remain the same.

---

[1] There are other changes which can occur when the הִתְ prefix is attached to a verb root. (1) When a root begins with צ, the ת of the prefix not only changes places with the צ, it also changes from a ת to a ט. To illustrate, the perfect, *hitpael*, *3MS* form of the root צדק is הִצְטַדֵּק, instead of הִתְצַדֵּק. (2) When a root begins with ד, ט, or ת, then the ת of the prefix disappears and a compensating *dagesh-forte* appears in the first consonant of the root. To illustrate the perfect, *hitpael*, *3MS* form of the root תמם is הִתַּמֵּם, instead of הִתְתַּמֵּם. For other examples see Waltke and O'Connor, §26.1.16.

	Perfect						
	Qal	*Nifal*	*Piel*	*Pual*	*Hifil*	*Hofal*	*Hitpael*
3MS	מָשַׁל "he ruled"	נִמְשַׁל "he was ruled"	מִשֵּׁל "he ruled"	מֻשַּׁל "he was ruled"	הִמְשִׁיל "he caused to rule"	הָמְשַׁל "he was caused to rule"	הִתְמַשֵּׁל "he ruled himself"
3FS	מָשְׁלָה "she ruled"						
2MS	מָשַׁלְתָּ "you ruled"						
2FS	מָשַׁלְתְּ "you ruled"						
1CS	מָשַׁלְתִּי "I ruled"						
3CP	מָשְׁלוּ "they ruled"						
2MP	מְשַׁלְתֶּם "you ruled"						
2FP	מְשַׁלְתֶּן "you ruled"						
1CP	מָשַׁלְנוּ "we ruled"						

✓ The full conjugation of the perfect verb (with all persons, genders, and numbers in all the stems), using משל as a model, appears in Appendix 3, paradigm 1.

2. Another key to learning the perfect verb is mastery of the following clues for recognizing the forms of the perfect. (These clues appear in summary form in Appendix 1.)

✓ Where appropriate these clues are represented in symbol form.

□ = a consonant of a verb root

⊡ = a consonant of a verb root with a *dagesh-forte*

- *Example:* □ּ□□ represents the three consonants of a verb root with a *dagesh-forte* in the middle consonant.

a. General clues for recognizing strong perfect verbs

(1) In *3MS* the perfect verb has no suffix. The perfect, *3MS* verb also follows a particular pattern of vowel pointing and in some stems has a particular prefix. For example, □ָ□ַ□ is *3MS* in perfect, *qal*; and נִ□ְ□ַ□ is *3MS* in perfect, *nifal.*

(2) Outside of *3MS*, the presence of one of the perfect verb suffixes (□ָה, תָּ, תְּ, תִּי, וּ, תֶּם, תֶּן, or נוּ) indicates a perfect verb.

(3) The person, gender, and number of perfect verbs can be identified by their suffixes or by particular vowel pointing when there is no suffix (such as □ָ□ַ□ in *perf, qal, 3MS*).

b. Clues for recognizing the stems of strong perfect verbs

(1) *Qal*

(a) Most forms (but NOT all) have a *qames* under the first consonant of the root (□ָ□□).

(b) *Qal* can also be identified by the absence of the clues for the other stems.

(2) *Nifal:* נִ□ְ□□

All forms have a נִ prefix – a feature unique to *nifal.*

(3) *Piel*: □ִ□ּ□

(a) All forms have a *hireq* under the first consonant of the root – a feature unique to *piel.*

(b) All forms have a *dagesh-forte* in the second consonant of the root – a characteristic shared with *pual* and *hitpael.*

(4) *Pual:* □ֻ□ּ□

(a) All forms have a *qibbus* under the first consonant of the root – a feature unique to *pual.*

(b) All forms have a *dagesh-forte* in the second consonant of the root.

(5) *Hifil:* הִ□ְ□□

All forms have a הִ prefix – a feature unique to *hifil.*

(6) *Hofal:* הָ□ְ□□

All forms have a הָ (ho) prefix – a feature unique to *hofal*.

(7) *Hitpael:* הִתְ□ַ⊡□

(a) All forms have a הִתְ prefix – a feature unique to *hitpael*.

(b) All forms have a *patah* under the first consonant of the root.

(c) All forms have a *dagesh-forte* in the second consonant of the root.

Lesson 13: Exercises

a. Reproduce from memory the perfect conjugation of משל ("rule") in the *qal* stem in each person, gender, and number (*3MS*, *3FS*, *2MS*, etc.) and also reproduce the *3MS* forms only of the other major stems in the perfect conjugation of משל (as in section 13B.1). Finally, give a translation of each form.

b. While the forms requested above are the only ones the student must master, it is helpful to be familiar with all the forms of the perfect conjugation. Therefore, attempt to fill in the full practice chart for the perfect conjugation which appears in Appendix 3, item 16. (This chart may be duplicated by the student.) The student may need assistance from paradigm 1 in Appendix 3 in completing this assignment.

c. Below are symbolic representations of the clues for recognizing the stems of the perfect conjugation. Without consulting any charts, identify which stem is represented in each case (□ = a consonant of a verb root).

‣ *Example:* □ָ□□ ⇒ *Answer: qal*

(1) הָ□ְ□□ (3) הִתְ□ַ⊡□ (5) הִ□ְ□□

(2) □ִ⊡□ (4) נִ□ְ□□ (6) □ֻ⊡□

d. Without consulting any charts, identify the root, stem, person, gender and number of the following perfect verbs that have appeared in vocabulary lists. Then give a translation of each.

‣ *Example:* הָמְשַׁלְתְּ ⇒ *Answer:* > משל,[1] *hofal, 2FS*, "you were made to rule"

(1) קָֽרְאָה (5) הִלְקַ֫טְתִּי (9) הִקְרִיא

(2) שְׁלַחְתֶּם (6) נִשְׁלַ֫חְנוּ (10) נִשְׁמַרְתֶּן

(3) הִתְנַשְּׂאוּ (7) נָתַן (11) הִתְלַקַּ֫טְנוּ

(4) יָדַ֫עְתָּ (8) הָקְטַלְתְּ (12) יִשְׁבוּ

[1] The symbol > indicates that a verb root follows.

(13) נִשְׁמַ֫עְתָּ	(16) יֵדַ֫עְתִּי	(19) מְשְׁלָה
(14) מִשַּׁלְתְּ	(17) הָשְׁמַעְתֶּם	(20) הִקְטִ֫ילוּ
(15) הָיָה[1]	(18) הִשְׁתַּמַּרְתֶּן[2]	(21) יָשַׁ֫בְנוּ

e. Learn to recognize, pronounce, and translate the following vocabulary.

	Word	*Translation*	*Notes*
(1)	אָח	brother (*NMS*)	*Cs*: אֲחִי; *S* with *PS*: אָחִי, אָחִ֫יךָ, etc.; *P*: אַחִים, אֲחֵי; *P* with *PS:* אַחַי, אַחֶ֫יךָ, etc.
(2)	בֵּין	between (*prep*)	*PS:* בֵּינִי, בֵּינְךָ, etc.; or בֵּינֵ֫ינוּ, בֵּינֵיכֶם, etc.
(3)	לֹא	no, not (*particle*)	Also spelled לוֹא
(4)	עַד	(a) until (*prep*) (b) perpetuity (*NMS*)	*Prep* with *PS:* עָדַי, עָדֶ֫יךָ, etc.
(5)	שַׂר	ruler, prince, official (*NMS*)	*P*: שָׂרִים

f. Some biblical clauses with partial translations appear below. Vocabulary words have been omitted along with some verbs that have not yet appeared in vocabulary lists but whose meanings can be found in Appendix 4. Longer blanks stand for the translation of more than one Hebrew word. First supply the missing words; then attempt a smooth translation, consulting an English Bible if necessary.

(1) אָסַ֫פְתָּ כָל־עֶבְרָתֶ֫ךָ = "____________ your wrath" (Ps 85:4; *Eng* 85:3)

(1) עָמָל כִּתֵּ֫בוּ[3] = "Troublesome laws ______" (Is 10:1)

(2) כִּי רוּחַ עָבְרָה־בּוֹ = "____________" (Ps 103:16)

---

[1] This is a weak verb, one characteristic of which is that its lexical form has a *qames* as the vowel for the second root consonant instead of a *patah*.

[2] See section 13A.7c.

[3] The accent and corresponding lengthened vowel (*sere* instead of *sheva*) occur because this word stands at the end of the verse. The form conveys intensity in the sense of constant repetition.

(3) הֵם הִמְלִיכוּ וְלֹא מִמֶּנִּי = "___________" (Hos 8:4)

(4) בְּשַׁעֲרֵי שְׁאוֹל פֻּקַּדְתִּי = "To the gates of Sheol ______" (Is 38:10)

(5) כִּי לֹא־שָׁמַעַתְּ[1] בְּקוֹלִי = "___________" (Jer 22:21)

(6) וְנִכְרְתָה[2] מִפִּיהֶם = "______ from their mouths" (Jer 7:28)

(7) הַפִּקָּדוֹן אֲשֶׁר הָפְקַד אִתּוֹ = "The deposit ___________" (Lv 5:23; *Eng* 6:4)

(8) עָרוֹם הִלְּכוּ[3] בְּלִי לְבוּשׁ = "Naked ______ without clothes" (Job 24:10)

(9) אֱלֹהַי אֲשֶׁר־עָשִׂיתִי לְקַחְתֶּם = "___________ I have made ______" (Jdg 18:24)

(10) מִמְּעֵי אִמִּי הִזְכִּיר שְׁמִי = "From the womb of my mother ___________" (Is 49:1)

(11) כִּי־אָמַרְנוּ לַמֶּלֶךְ = "___________" (Ezr 8:22)

(12) וּבַשָּׁנָה הַשְּׁבִעִית הִתְחַזַּק יְהוֹיָדָע = "______ the seventh ______ Jehoiada" (2Ch 23:1)

(13) וּשְׁעָרֶיהָ אֻכְּלוּ בָאֵשׁ = "And its gates ______ in the fire" (Ne 2:3)

g. Read aloud and translate the following words [numbers (1)-(3)] and sentences [numbers (4)-(18)]. The student should be able to complete the exercise without consulting any charts or vocabulary lists.

(1) לָקַט | נִלְקְטָה | לִקַּטְתָּ | לֻקַּטְתְּ | הִלְקַטְתִּי (2) הָמְשְׁלוּ | הִתְמַשַּׁלְתֶּם
מְשַׁלְתֶּן | נִמְשַׁלְנוּ (3) אֲנִי שִׁמַּרְתִּי | הֵנָּה שֻׁמְּרוּ | הִיא הִשְׁמִירָה | אֲנַחְנוּ
הָשְׁמַרְנוּ (4) נִשְׁלְחוּ מִשְׁפְּטֵי קֹדֶשׁ עַל הַגּוֹיִם הָהֵם וְלֹא[4] שִׁמְּרוּ אֶת־לִבּוֹתָם
מִן־רָעָה (5) שֻׁמַּע הַקּוֹל בְּכָל־הָאָרֶץ כִּי הָיָה קוֹל־אִישׁ־יְהוָה (6) עַד הַיּוֹם
הַזֶּה לוֹא יָדַעְתִּי כִּי שֻׁלַּחְתָּ[5] לְעִירֵנוּ בַּאֲחִי־הַשַּׂר הַטּוֹב (7) הִתְמַשַּׁלְנוּ

---

[1] This is a weak verb in which the guttural ע requires an A-class vowel rather than a *sheva*.

[2] The antecedent for this verb is הָאֱמוּנָה ("truth" [*NFS*]).

[3] In this context the verb connotes the repeated activity of walking about.

[4] The *vav* conjunction means "but" in this clause.

[5] In this weak verb the guttural ח requires an A-class vowel rather than a *sheva*.

בְּדִבְרֵי אֱלֹהִים וְנָתַן רוּחַ־קָדְשׁוֹ אֵלֵינוּ (8) אַתֵּן אֲשֶׁר נְשֵׁי אֱלֹהִים הִשְׁמַעְתֶּן
אֶת־בְּנֵיכֶן לִדְבַר־הַכֹּהֵן אֲשֶׁר יָשַׁב בָּעִיר בֵּין הֶהָרִים (9) נִקְרָאוּ[1] אַחֵינוּ
בְּרוּחַ יְהוָה וְיִשְׁבוּ עַל הַר אֱלֹהִים לְיָמִים רַבִּים (10) הִשְׁמַרְתִּי בְּנֵי הַמֶּלֶךְ
מֵרָעָה וְעָשָׂה אֱלֹהִים אֹתָם כְּכֹהֲנָיו כִּי יָדְעוּ אֹתוֹ וְשָׁמְעוּ לוֹ (11) יְהוָה
לֹא מָשַׁלְתָּ בָּם לְטוֹב אֲשֶׁר לֹא נִקְרָאוּ בְשִׁמְךָ (12) אַתֶּם אֲשֶׁר שָׁלַח יְהוָה
כְּכֹהֲנֵינוּ הִקְטַלְתֶּם אַנְשֵׁי רָעָה (13) הִתְנַשֵּׂא שַׂר הַגּוֹי עַל עַמּוֹ וְנוֹדְעָה[2]
רָעַת הַשַּׂר בְּכָל־הָאָרֶץ (14) הָשְׁמַרְתְּ דְּבַר־יְהוָה כִּי נִתַּן[4] לִבֵּךְ[3] לַיהוָה
(15) אַתֶּם אֲשֶׁר מְשַׁלְתֶּם עַל הָאָרֶץ הַהִיא הִלְקַטְתֶּם אֵת עַמֵּיכֶם אֶל עָרֵיהֶם
כִּי הָיָה יוֹם־יְהוָה (16) בְּשָׂרֵי הָעָם עֶשָׂה[5] מִשְׁפָּט בֵּין הַנָּשִׁים אֲשֶׁר יֶשְׁבוּ
בָּעִיר הַזֹּאת וּבֵין הַנָּשִׁים אֲשֶׁר יֶשְׁבוּ בָּעִיר הַהִיא (17) שָׁלַחְתָּ עַם רַב אֶל
הֶעָרִים אֲשֶׁר מֶשְׁלוּ בַּשָּׂרִים הַגְּדוֹלִים (18) בַּיּוֹם הַהוּא הִתְלַקְטוּ כָּל־אַנְשֵׁי־
עָרֵינוּ עַל הַר אֶחָד וְשָׁמְעוּ הַמֶּלֶךְ אֲשֶׁר הוּא קָרָא עַל־שֵׁם־יְהוָה כִּי רָעָה
גְדוֹלָה בָּאָרֶץ

---

[1] In this weak verb the ר requires an A-class vowel rather than a *sheva*.

[2] The first root consonant of this weak verb (> ידע) changes to a *vav* with the addition of a prefix. If it were spelled like a strong verb it would be נִידְעָה.

[3] לֵב becomes לִב when a suffix is added.

[4] This weak verb (> נתן) loses its first root consonant when a prefix is added. If that consonant remained in place, it would be spelled נִנְתַּן.

[5] This weak verb requires the lengthening of the vowel before the ה in this form.

Lesson 14

Imperfect Conjugation of the Verb, Imperfect Conjugation in the *Qal* Stem, Analysis of the Verb

14A Imperfect Conjugation of the Verb

1. Meaning of imperfect verbs

Since the imperfect connotes incomplete action rather than temporal action, a variety of English tenses may be used in translating a Hebrew imperfect verb. The imperfect may describe action that is incomplete in the past, present, or future. The context of a Hebrew verb governs which English tense best conveys the meaning. While imperfect verbs may connote a variety of temporal meanings, it is often the case that they communicate action that is incomplete in the future. For now this Grammar will translate Hebrew imperfect verbs with the English future tense for the sake of simplicity. A future lesson will discuss other ways of translating the imperfect. (See Lesson 20A.1d).

2. Imperfect verb prefixes and suffixes

a. All imperfect verbs in Hebrew employ a particular set of prefixes and suffixes. These prefixes and suffixes indicate the person, gender, and number of a verb.

b. The following chart presents the prefixes that are used with imperfect verbs. (In *hitpael* they form the first consonant of the prefix.)

3MS	י	*3MP*	י
3FS	תּ	*3FP*	תּ
2MS	תּ	*2MP*	תּ
2FS	תּ	*2FP*	תּ
1CS	א	*1CP*	נ

(1) The consonants that appear as the prefixes in the preceding chart provide some clues for recognizing the form of an imperfect verb. Those clues are summarized in the following chart.

Prefix	=	**Person**	**Gender**	**Number**
י	=	*3*	*M*	*S* and *P*
תּ	=	*3* *2*	*F* *M* and *F*	*S* and *P* *S* and *P*
א	=	*1*	*C*	*S*
נ	=	*1*	*C*	*P*

✓ A *nun* prefix also occurs with a perfect, *nifal* verb. However, when a *nun* prefix appears, the other aspects of a verb distinguish whether it is perfect, *nifal* or imperfect, *1CP*. For example, the verb נִמְשַׁלְתְּ can be identified as a perfect, *nifal* rather than an imperfect *1CP*, because it has a perfect suffix.

(2) The consonantal prefixes listed above must also have vowels. Those vowels vary from stem to stem; therefore, they will be discussed as each of the imperfect stems is introduced.

c. Along with prefixes, imperfect verbs also employ the suffixes that appear in the following chart.

3MS	[none]
3FS	[none]
2MS	[none]
2FS	◌ִי
1CS	[none]

3MP	וּ
3FP	נָה
2MP	וּ
2FP	נָה
1CP	[none]

✓ Some of the imperfect suffixes are similar to the suffixes of the perfect conjugation. The perfect, *3CP* suffix וּ also appears in imperfect, *3MP* and *2MP*. The imperfect, *3FP* and *2FP* suffix נָה is similar to the perfect, *3FS* suffix ◌ָה. The suffix ◌ִי of imperfect, *2FS* is similar to the perfect, *1CS* suffix תִּי.

d. The prefixes and suffixes of the imperfect conjugation are presented together in symbolic form in the following chart (□ = a consonant of a verb root).

3MS	י□□□	*3MP*	י□□□וּ
3FS	תּ□□□	*3FP*	תּ□□□נָה
2MS	תּ□□□	*2MP*	תּ□□□וּ
2FS	תּ□□□ִי	*2FP*	תּ□□□נָה
1CS	א□□□	*1CP*	נ□□□

(1) Some of the preceding imperfect forms are identical to each other: *3FS* and *2MS* are the same, and *3FP* and *2FP* are the same. One can determine which is intended by the context of the verb.

(2) These preceding prefixes and suffixes occur in all the stems, with the exception that in *hitpael* the prefixes involve the consonants listed in the chart plus a *tav*. Thus the *hitpael* prefixes are ית, תת, את, and נת. (See section 15A.7.)

14B Imperfect Conjugation in the *Qal* Stem

1. The following chart presents the conjugation of the strong imperfect verb in the *qal* stem. It employs the verb משל as a model, demonstrating how the above prefixes and suffixes are added to this root.

3MS	יִמְשֹׁל	("he will rule")
3FS	תִּמְשֹׁל	("she will rule")
2MS	תִּמְשֹׁל	("you will rule")
2FS	תִּמְשְׁלִי	("you will rule")
1CS	אֶמְשֹׁל	("I will rule")
3MP	יִמְשְׁלוּ	("they will rule")
3FP	תִּמְשֹׁלְנָה	("they will rule")
2MP	תִּמְשְׁלוּ	("you will rule")
2FP	תִּמְשֹׁלְנָה	("you will rule")
1CP	נִמְשֹׁל	("we will rule")

2. Notes concerning the imperfect, *qal* conjugation
   a. In *qal* all the prefixes except one receive a *hireq*. The guttural א (*1CS*) takes a *segol* instead of a *hireq* because it prefers an E-class vowel to an I-class vowel.
   b. Since the imperfect prefixes are made up of a consonant and a short vowel (either a *hireq* or *segol*), the prefixes join with the first consonant of a verb root to form a closed syllable. As a result, the first root consonant receives a silent *sheva*.
   c. In *3MS* a *holem* appears above the second consonant of the root – above שׁ in the case of משׁל. This *3MS* form is the basis upon which the other *qal* forms are created, meaning that the *holem* appears in the other forms where possible (*3MS*, *3FS*, *2MS*, *1CS*, *3FP*, *2FP*, and *1CP*). Consequently, the *holem* is known as the thematic vowel of the imperfect, *qal* stem.
   d. Five forms have no suffix (*3MS*, *3FS*, *2MS*, *1CS*, and *1CP*), which means they are spelled exactly the same except for differing prefix consonants.
   e. Three forms involve the addition of a vowel suffix (*2FS*, *3MP*, and *2MP*). When attached to a verb root, these suffixes, along with the last consonant of the root, form syllables that are accented – for משׁל the new syllables are לִי (*2FS*) and לוּ (*3MP* and *2MP*). Because of the shifting accent, the thematic vowel reduces from a *holem* to a vocal *sheva* (as in שְׁ).
   f. Two forms involve the addition of the open syllable suffix נָה, which occurs in *3FP* and *2FP*. When it is attached to a verb root, the last consonant of the root takes a silent *sheva* (as in לְ). The accent does not move to the נָה suffix; it remains on the second syllable which also retains the thematic vowel *holem* – for משׁל the accented syllable is שֹׁ֫ל.
3. The following chart presents the imperfect conjugation in *qal* for two other roots that follow the pattern of strong verbs: שׁמר ("keep") and קטל ("kill").

3MS	יִשְׁמֹר	("he will keep")
3FS	תִּשְׁמֹר	("she will keep")
2MS	תִּשְׁמֹר	("you will keep")
2FS	תִּשְׁמְרִי	("you will keep")
1CS	אֶשְׁמֹר	("I will keep")

יִקְטֹל	("he will kill")
תִּקְטֹל	("she will kill")
תִּקְטֹל	("you will kill")
תִּקְטְלִי	("you will kill")
אֶקְטֹל	("I will kill")

3MP	יִשְׁמְרוּ	(“they will keep”)
3FP	תִּשְׁמֹרְנָה	(“they will keep”)
2MP	תִּשְׁמְרוּ	(“you will keep”)
2FP	תִּשְׁמֹרְנָה	(“you will keep”)
1CP	נִשְׁמֹר	(“we will keep”)

יִקְטְלוּ	(“they will kill”)
תִּקְטֹלְנָה	(“they will kill”)
תִּקְטְלוּ	(“you will kill”)
תִּקְטֹלְנָה	(“you will kill”)
נִקְטֹל	(“we will kill”)

14C Analysis Of The Verb

1. The verb can be analyzed in terms of its grammatical status. Such analysis for finite verbs identifies the following features.
   a. Root (the triconsonantal root of a verb)
   b. Conjugation (perfect, imperfect, or imperative)
   c. Stem (*qal*, *nifal*, *piel*, etc.)
   d. Person, gender, and number
   e. Additional features (such as a prefixed conjunction or pronominal suffix)
   f. Translation (of the verb form – not the root)
2. The order of the above list suggests the process through which one moves in analyzing a verb, as described below.
   a. The first task in analysis is determining the verb root. With strong verbs it can be identified as the three consonants which are left after removing any prefix or suffix, if any is present.
      - מָשַׁל has no prefix or suffix; its root is משל.
      - קְטַלְתֶּן has a suffix (תֶּן). When it is removed, the root קטל remains.
      - תִּלְקְטוּ has a prefix (תִּ) and a suffix (וּ). When they are removed, the root לקט remains.
   b. The second step in the analysis of a verb is to determine its conjugation. Thus far only the perfect and imperfect conjugations have been introduced.
      (1) All of the forms of the perfect conjugation, except for *3MS*, can be identified by the presence of one of the perfect suffixes and, in the case of some stems, the presence of a perfect prefix. When there is no prefix, a *3MS* form can be identified as perfect by its pointing.

(2) All of the forms of the imperfect conjugation can be identified by the presence of one of the imperfect prefixes and, in some cases, imperfect suffixes.

- מֻשַּׁל has no prefix or suffix; therefore, it cannot be an imperfect verb. The pointing identifies it as a perfect, *pual*, *3MS*.
- אֶשְׁמֹר has a prefix (א) that indicates it is an imperfect verb.
- הִתְקַטַּלְנוּ has a prefix (הִת) and a suffix (נוּ) that mark it as a perfect verb.

c. The third step in analyzing a verb is identifying its stem, based upon the presence of the clues for the various stems – that is, the occurrence of certain prefixes and pointing.

- הָקְטַלְתִּי is a perfect verb in the *hofal* stem, as indicated by the הָ prefix.
- נִמְשֹׁל is an imperfect verb in the *qal* stem, as evidenced by the *holem* above the second consonant of the root (the imperfect, *qal* thematic vowel). While a *nun* prefix also occurs with a perfect, *nifal* verb, it is obvious by the rest of the spelling of this word that it is imperfect, *qal*, *1CP*, rather than perfect, *nifal*.

d. The next step in verb analysis is determining person, gender, and number (*P/G/N*). This step can be accomplished by examining a verb's suffix in the case of the perfect conjugation (except where it is lacking in *3MS*) and a verb's prefix and sometimes suffix in the case of the imperfect conjugation.

- לָקַט is perfect, because it has no prefix, and it is *3MS* because it has no suffix.[1]
- יִקְטֹל has a prefix (יִ) which indicates that it is imperfect, third person, masculine. The lack of a suffix indicates that it is singular.
- מִשַּׁלְנוּ is perfect, as indicated by the suffix and lack of a prefix; the suffix also identifies it as *1CP*.
- תִּשְׁמְרִי is imperfect, as indicated by its prefix and suffix; they also mark it as *2FS*.

e. The fifth step in the analysis of a verb is identifying any additional features – namely, other prefixes or suffixes which may occur in addition to perfect and imperfect prefixes and suffixes.

[1] Some non-finite verb forms (certain infinitives and participles) also lack prefixes and suffixes. They can be distinguished from a perfect, *3MS* verb by their unique pointing, as discussed in future lessons.

- וְנִמְשַׁלְתָּ has a נִ prefix and תָּ suffix that identify it as perfect, *nifal*, *2MS*. It also has the additional feature of a prefixed *vav* conjunction (וְ).

f. The final step in analyzing a verb is its translation.

- וְנִמְשַׁלְתָּ means "and you were ruled."

3. The chart below further illustrates the analysis of the verb.

Word	Root	Conju-gation	Stem	P/G/N	Additional Features	Translation
וְלָקְטוּ (Nu 11:8)	> לקט	*perf*	*qal*	*3CP*	+ *vav conj*	"and they gathered"
תִּקְטֹל (Ps 139:19)	> קטל	*impf*	*qal*	*2MS*		"you will kill"
וְנִשְּׂאוּ (Ezr 8:36)	> נשׂא	*perf*	*piel*	*3CP*	+ *vav conj*	"and they lifted up"
יַשְׁמִיעוּ (Neh 8:15)	> שׁמע	*impf*	*hif*	*3MP*		"you will cause to hear"

Lesson 14: Exercises

a. Reproduce from memory the imperfect conjugation of משׁל in the *qal* stem in each person, gender, and number (*3MS*, *3FS*, *2MS*, etc.), as in section 14B.1. Also give a translation for each form.

b. The following are symbolic representations of verb roots with the prefixes and suffixes of imperfect verbs (□ = a consonant of a verb root). Without consulting any charts, identify the person, gender, and number in each case; if two options are possible, give them both.

- *Example:* □□□ת ⇒ *Answer: 3FS* or *2MS*

(1) ת□□□ִי   (3) י□□□   (5) א□□□

(2) ת□□□וּ   (4) ת□□□נָה   (6) י□□□וּ

c. Without consulting any charts, analyze the following verbs from vocabulary lists in terms of root, conjugation, stem, *P/G/N*, additional features, and translation. The student may wish to use the blank chart for the analysis of words at the end of Appendix 2; this chart may be duplicated by the student.

✓ For some verbs in this exercise there are two possibilities for *P/G/N*. Since the verbs are not presented with any context, either option is acceptable.

- *Example:* וְהִקְטַ֫לְנוּ ⇒ *Answer:* > קטל, *perf, hif, 1CP,* + *vav conj,* "and we caused to kill"

(1)	יִקְטֹל	(6)	הִתְקַטֵּל	(11)	יִשְׁמְעוּ
(2)	לָֽקְטָה	(7)	וְמִשְׁלוּ	(12)	תִּמְשֹׁל
(3)	הָמְשַׁ֫לְתָּ	(8)	נִלְקֹט	(13)	שְׁמַ֫רְתִּי
(4)	וְתִשְׁמְרוּ	(9)	נִשְׁמַרְתְּ	(14)	אֶקְטֹל
(5)	הִשְׁלַחְתֶּן	(10)	תִּמְשֹׁ֫לְנָה	(15)	וְתִלְקְטִי

d. Learn to recognize, pronounce, and translate the following vocabulary.

	Word	*Translation*	*Notes*
(1)	אָב	father (*NMS*)	*Cs:* אֲבִי ,אַב; *S* with *PS:* אָבִי, אָבִיךָ, etc.; *P:* אָבוֹת ,אֲבוֹת; *P* with *PS:* אֲבוֹתַי or אֲבֹתַי, אֲבוֹתֵיהֶם or אֲבוֹתָם, etc.
(2)	אָמַר	he said (*V*)	
(3)	בַּ֫יִת	house (*NMS*)	*Cs:* בֵּית; *P:* בָּתִּים ,בָּתֵּי
(4)	חֶ֫רֶב	sword, dagger (*NFS*)	*P:* חֲרָבוֹת ,חַרְבוֹת
(5)	שָׁמַ֫יִם	heavens, sky (*NMDu*)	Occurs only in dual

e. Some biblical clauses with partial translations appear below. The blanks represent words that either have appeared in vocabulary lists or can be found in Appendix 4. Longer blanks stand for the translation of more than one Hebrew word. First supply the missing words; then attempt a smooth translation, consulting an English Bible if necessary.

(1) אֲשֶׁר־יִלְקְטוּ יוֹם יוֹם[1] = "____________" (Ex 16:5)

(2) כַּסְפִּי וּזְהָבִי לְקַחְתֶּם = "____________" (Joel 4:5; *Eng* 3:5)

(3) אָֽמְרָה אָחִי הוּא = "____________" (Ge 20:5)

(4) כִּי־נִשְׁמֹר לַעֲשׂוֹת אֶת־כָּל־ הַמִּצְוָה הַזֹּאת = "____________ to do ____________ the commandment ______" (Dt 6:25)

(5) וְתִשְׁמַ֫עְנָה[2] הַגְּבָעוֹת קוֹלֶךָ = "______ the hills [*FP*] ______" (Mic 6:1)

---

[1] The repetition of this noun is an idiom for "daily."

[2] In this weak verb the guttural ע is preceded by an A-class vowel rather than a *holem*.

(6) תִּקְטֹל אֱלוֹהַּ[1] רָשָׁע = "____________" (Ps 139:19)

(7) כִּי־אָסַ֫פְתִּי אֶת־שְׁלוֹמִי מֵאֵת[2] הָעָם־הַזֶּה = "____________" (Jer 16:5)

(8) וְלֹא־נִפְקַד מִמֶּ֫נּוּ אִישׁ = "____________" (Nu 31:49)

(9) לֹא־אֶמְשֹׁל אֲנִי בָּכֶם וְלֹא־יִמְשֹׁל בְּנִי בָּכֶם = "____________" (Jdg 8:23)

(10) אַתָּה הִמְלַ֫כְתָּ אֶת־עַבְדְּךָ = "____________" (1Ki 3:7)

(11) מַה־תֹּאמְרִי[3] כִּי־יִפְקֹד עָלַ֫יִךְ ... אַלֻּפִים לְרֹאשׁ = "____________ . . . friends ______?" (Jer 13:21)

(12) שׁוּעָלִים הִלְּכוּ[4]־בוֹ = "Foxes ____________" (Lam 5:18)

(13) אַתֶּם לְכוּ קְחוּ לָכֶם תֶּ֫בֶן מֵאֲשֶׁר תִּמְצָ֫אוּ[5] = "______ go, take ______ straw ____________" (Ex 5:11)

(14) לֹא זָכַרְתְּ אַחֲרִיתָהּ = "____________ the end of it" (Is 47:7)

(15) וְהַנַּעֲרָה אֲשֶׁר תִּיטַב[6] בְּעֵינֵי הַמֶּ֫לֶךְ תִּמְלֹךְ תַּ֫חַת וַשְׁתִּי = "And the young woman ____________ Vashti" (Est 2:4)

f. Read aloud and translate the following words [number (1)] and sentences [numbers (2)-(16)]. The student should be able to do the translation without consulting any charts or vocabulary lists.

---

[1] אֱלוֹהַּ (*NMS*) is not the subject of the verb but stands in apposition to it. In this context אֱלוֹהַּ is parallel in meaning to אֱלֹהִים.

[2] This word is a preposition with another preposition prefixed to it.

[3] In this weak verb the א quiesces and the prefix takes a *holem* instead of a *hireq*.

[4] In this context the verb implies intensity in the sense of prowling.

[5] In this weak verb the guttural א is preceded by an A-class vowel rather than a *sheva*. The accent appears where it does because this verb comes at the midpoint of the verse.

[6] In this weak verb (> יטב) the י quiesces (losing its *sheva*) and the vowel for the last syllable reduces from a *holem* to a *patah*.

(1) יִקְטֹל | תִּקְטְלוּ | נִקְטֹל | תִּקְטֹל[1] | תִּקְטֹלְנָה | אֶקְטֹל | תִּקְטְלִי | יִקְטְלוּ
(2) נִמְשֹׁל אַרְצֹתֵינוּ בְּמִשְׁפָּט כַּאֲשֶׁר[2] מָֽשְׁלוּ אֲבוֹתֵינוּ אֶת הָאֲרָצוֹת הָאֵלֶּה לְיָמִים
רַבִּים (3) אַתֶּם אֲשֶׁר כֹּהֲנִים אֲמַרְתֶּם[3] לָנוּ כִּי עָשָׂה אֱלֹהִים אֵת הַשָּׁמַיִם וְאֵת
הָאָרֶץ (4) תִּשְׁלְחִי אָבִיךְ אֶל בֵּיתֵנוּ וְיִשְׁמַע[4] דְּבָרֵינוּ כִּי לֹא נִשְׁמַעְנוּ בָּךְ
(5) בַּיּוֹם הַהוּא אַתָּה תִּרְאֶה[5] בֶּן־אָדָם בַּשָּׁמַיִם בְּחֶרֶב בְּיָדוֹ (6) הִלְקִיטוּ
רָאשֵׁי יִשְׂרָאֵל אֶת־בְּנֵיהֶם וְאֶת־נְשֵׁי־בְנֵיהֶם מִן בָּתֵּיהֶם וּבָאוּ[6] לְעִיר־הַקֹּדֶשׁ
(7) אֵלֶּה הָאֲנָשִׁים אֲשֶׁר יִקְטְלוּ אֵת הַכֹּהֵן אֲשֶׁר לֹא עָשָׂה כַּאֲשֶׁר אָמַר אֱלֹהִים
(8) אֶלְקֹט בְּנוֹתַי אֶל־בֵּיתִי וּבָנַי אֶשְׁלַח אֶל־הַמֶּלֶךְ וְיִשְׁמֹר אֹתָם מִן־רָעָה
(9) זֶה בֵּית יְהוָה וְתִשְׁמְרוּ רָעָה מִמֶּנּוּ כַּאֲשֶׁר אָמַר כֹּהֵן יְהוָה לָכֶם
(10) תִּשְׁמַעְנָה בְּנוֹת הַמֶּלֶךְ אֶת־קוֹלוֹתֵינוּ כִּי נֹאמַר[7] אֲלֵיהֶן כִּי לֹא הָיָה מִשְׁפָּט
בְּאַרְצֵנוּ (11) נָשָׂא אָבִינוּ אֵת שֵׁם־יְהוָה בְּבֵיתֵנוּ וְנִשְׁמַע קוֹלוֹ בָּנוּ אֲשֶׁר בָּנָיו
וְתַעֲשֶׂינָה[8] יְדוֹתֵינוּ טוֹב וְלֹא רָעָה (12) נָשָׂא אָבִיךְ אֶת־שֵׁם־אֱלֹהִים לַשָּׁמַיִם
וְשָׁמַע אֱלֹהִים אֹתוֹ וְלֹא בָּאָה הַחֶרֶב לְבֵיתְךָ (13) תִּשְׁמַעְנָה אֵת דִּבְרֵי שָׂרֵיכֶן
אֲשֶׁר יֹאמְרוּ אֲלֵיכֶן וְתִשְׁמֹרְנָה דִּבְרֵיהֶן בְּלִבּוֹתֵיכֶן (14) לֹא תִמְשֹׁל אֶת־עִיר־
אָבִיהָ לְיָמִים רַבִּים כִּי יִשְׁלְחוּ מַלְכֵי הֶעָרִים בֶּהָרִים אֶת־הַחֶרֶב עַל[9] בֵּיתָהּ
(15) הִתְלַקְּטוּ אַחֵינוּ לְבֵית־יְהוָה כִּי נִקְרָאוּ[10] בְּרוּחַ־אֱלֹהִים (16) יִשְׁלַח הַגּוֹי הַזֶּה
אֵת בָּנָיו בַּחֲרָבוֹת עַל הַגּוֹי הַהוּא וְלֹא יִרְאוּ[11] עַמֵּי הָאָרֶץ אֶת־מִשְׁפָּט לְשָׁנִים
רַבִּים

---

[1] When a word has more than one possibility for translation and appears without any context, as with this word, then any of the options is acceptable.

[2] This word literally means "as which," but a more idiomatic translation is simply "as."

[3] In this weak verb the guttural א requires a composite *sheva* rather than a simple one.

[4] In this weak verb the guttural ע is preceded by an A-class vowel rather than a *holem*. Observe the same principle occurring in later sentences with the weak verb שלח.

[5] In this weak verb the ה is preceded by a *segol* rather than *holem*.

[6] This weak verb from the root בּוֹא ("[to] come") loses its middle consonant when a suffix is added. The same principle applies to this verb when it appears in a later sentence with a feminine, singular suffix.

[7] In this weak verb the guttural א quiesces, and the imperfect נ prefix takes a *holem*. The ר, like a guttural, is preceded by an A-class vowel rather than a *holem*. A similar phenomenon occurs in a later sentence when this verb root has a י prefix.

[8] This weak verb (> עשׂה) loses its final consonant in this form, which is imperfect, *qal*, *3FP*.

[9] Here the preposition means "against."

[10] In this weak verb the guttural א is preceded by a *qames* rather than *patah*.

[11] This weak verb (> ראה) loses its last consonant when a verb suffix is added.

Lesson 15

Imperfect Conjugation in the Other Major Stems, Summary of the Imperfect Conjugation

15A Imperfect Conjugation in the Other Major Stems

1. Introduction

a. The preceding lesson introduced the imperfect conjugation in the *qal* stem; this section introduces the other major stems of the strong imperfect verb.

b. Each stem in the imperfect requires the addition of the imperfect prefixes and suffixes, which indicate an imperfect verb's person, gender, and number. The major accent of an imperfect verb remains on the same syllable in the other stems as it does in *qal* – except for three forms in *hifil*. In addition to these common features, each stem has unique elements, as described in the following discussion.

2. Imperfect conjugation in the *nifal* stem

a. The right column in the following chart presents the forms of the imperfect, *nifal* for the root משׁל; the column on the left presents the imperfect, *qal* for comparison. Since *nifal* usually expresses the passive of *qal*, it often conveys simple action in the passive voice, as the translation indicates.

	Imperfect	
	Qal	*Nifal*
3MS	יִמְשֹׁל	יִמָּשֵׁל ("he will be ruled")
3FS	תִּמְשֹׁל	תִּמָּשֵׁל ("she will be ruled")
2MS	תִּמְשֹׁל	תִּמָּשֵׁל ("you will be ruled")
2FS	תִּמְשְׁלִי	תִּמָּֽשְׁלִי ("you will be ruled")
1CS	אֶמְשֹׁל	אֶמָּשֵׁל ("I will be ruled")
3MP	יִמְשְׁלוּ	יִמָּֽשְׁלוּ ("they will be ruled")

3FP	תִּמְשֹׁ֫לְנָה	תִּמָּשַׁ֫לְנָה ("they will be ruled")
2MP	תִּמְשְׁלוּ	תִּמָּֽשְׁלוּ ("you will be ruled")
2FP	תִּמְשֹׁ֫לְנָה	תִּמָּשַׁ֫לְנָה ("you will be ruled")
1CP	נִמְשֹׁל	נִמָּשֵׁל ("we will be ruled")

b. Notes concerning the imperfect, *nifal* conjugation

(1) There are two key features which distinguish this stem: a *dagesh-forte* appears in the first consonant of the verb root, and a *qames* occurs beneath the same consonant. When followed by a *sheva*, the *qames* has a *meteg* to distinguish it from a *qames-hatuf* (in *2FS*, *3MP*, and *2MP* – the forms that have a vowel suffix).

(2) When the imperfect prefixes appear in *nifal*, they require the same vowels that they do in *qal* – that is, *hireq* in every case except with the **א** (*1CS*), which takes a *segol* instead. (Compare the spelling of the *qal* and *nifal* prefixes in the preceding chart.)

(3) In *3MS* the second consonant of the root has a *sere*. This vowel reduces to a *patah* when the syllabic suffix נָה is added (*3FP* and *2FP*). This vowel further reduces to a vocal *sheva* when a vowel suffix is added (*2FS*, *3MP*, and *2MP*).

3. Imperfect conjugation in the *piel* stem

a. The right column in the following chart presents the forms of the imperfect, *piel* for the root משׁל; the column on the left has the imperfect, *qal* for comparison. The underlined translation suggests one connotation of *piel:* intensive action in the active voice.

	Imperfect	
	Qal	*Piel*
3MS	יִמְשֹׁל	יְמַשֵּׁל ("he will rule")
3FS	תִּמְשֹׁל	תְּמַשֵּׁל ("she will rule")
2MS	תִּמְשֹׁל	תְּמַשֵּׁל ("you will rule")
2FS	תִּמְשְׁלִי	תְּמַשְּׁלִי ("you will rule")
1CS	אֶמְשֹׁל	אֲמַשֵּׁל ("I will rule")

3MP	יִמְשְׁלוּ	יְמַשְּׁלוּ (“they will rule”)
3FP	תִּמְשֹׁלְנָה	תְּמַשֵּׁלְנָה (“they will rule”)
2MP	תִּמְשְׁלוּ	תְּמַשְּׁלוּ (“you will rule”)
2FP	תִּמְשֹׁלְנָה	תְּמַשֵּׁלְנָה (“you will rule”)
1CP	נִמְשֹׁל	נְמַשֵּׁל (“we will rule”)

b. Notes concerning the imperfect, *piel* conjugation

(1) There are three distinguishing features of this stem. One is that the imperfect prefixes take a *sheva*. A composite *sheva* occurs with the guttural prefix **א** (*1CS*); a vocal *sheva* appears with all the other prefixes. (This feature also occurs in *pual*). The second distinguishing feature is that the vowel for the first consonant of the root in every form is a *patah*. The third feature is the appearance of a *dagesh-forte* with the second consonant of the root. (This characteristic occurs in *piel*, *pual*, and *hitpael* in both the perfect and the imperfect conjugations.)

(2) The vowel for the second consonant of the root in this stem is a *sere* in all forms except those that have a vowel suffix (*2FS*, *3MP*, and *2MP*). The vowel suffix requires the reduction of the *sere* to a *sheva*.

4. Imperfect conjugation in the *pual* stem

a. The right column in the following chart presents the forms of the imperfect, *pual* for the root משׁל; the left column has the imperfect, *qal* for comparison. The *pual* usually functions as the passive of *piel*, as suggested by the underlined translation.

	Imperfect	
	Qal	*Pual*
3MS	יִמְשֹׁל	יְמֻשַּׁל (“he will be ruled”)
3FS	תִּמְשֹׁל	תְּמֻשַּׁל (“she will be ruled”)
2MS	תִּמְשֹׁל	תְּמֻשַּׁל (“you will be ruled”)
2FS	תִּמְשְׁלִי	תְּמֻשְּׁלִי (“you will be ruled”)
1CS	אֶמְשֹׁל	אֲמֻשַּׁל (“I will be ruled”)
3MP	יִמְשְׁלוּ	יְמֻשְּׁלוּ (“they will be ruled”)

3FP	תִּמְשֹׁלְנָה	תְּמֻשַּׁלְנָה ("they will be ruled")
2MP	תִּמְשְׁלוּ	תְּמֻשְּׁלוּ ("you will be ruled")
2FP	תִּמְשֹׁלְנָה	תְּמֻשַּׁלְנָה ("you will be ruled")
1CP	נִמְשֹׁל	נְמֻשַּׁל ("we will be ruled")

b. Notes concerning the imperfect, *pual* conjugation

(1) Two features of imperfect, *piel* also occur in *pual:* the prefixes take a *sheva* (simple or composite), and a *dagesh-forte* appears in the second root consonant.

(2) The most distinctive feature of *pual* in both the perfect and the imperfect conjugations is that the first consonant of the root takes a *qibbus*. (Compare the perfect, *pual* and the imperfect, *pual* in Appendix 3, paradigm 1.)

(3) The second consonant of the root in imperfect, *pual* is a *patah* in all forms except those that have a vowel suffix (*2FS*, *3MP*, and *2MP*). The vowel suffix requires a reduction of the *patah* to a *sheva*.

5. Imperfect conjugation in the *hifil* stem

a. The right column in the following chart presents the forms of the imperfect, *hifil* for the root משׁל; the left column has the imperfect, *qal* for comparison. The translation below communicates a common meaning of *hifil:* causative action in the active voice.

	Imperfect	
	Qal	*Hifil*
3MS	יִמְשֹׁל	יַמְשִׁיל ("he will cause to rule")
3FS	תִּמְשֹׁל	תַּמְשִׁיל ("she will cause to rule")
2MS	תִּמְשֹׁל	תַּמְשִׁיל ("you will cause to rule")
2FS	תִּמְשְׁלִי	תַּמְשִׁילִי ("you will cause to rule")
1CS	אֶמְשֹׁל	אַמְשִׁיל ("I will cause to rule")
3MP	יִמְשְׁלוּ	יַמְשִׁילוּ ("they will cause to rule")
3FP	תִּמְשֹׁלְנָה	תַּמְשֵׁלְנָה ("they will cause to rule")
2MP	תִּמְשְׁלוּ	תַּמְשִׁילוּ ("you will cause to rule")
2FP	תִּמְשֹׁלְנָה	תַּמְשֵׁלְנָה ("you will cause to rule")
1CP	נִמְשֹׁל	נַמְשִׁיל ("we will cause to rule")

b. Notes concerning the imperfect, *hifil* conjugation

(1) The key distinguishing feature of this stem is the occurrence of a *patah* as the vowel for each of the imperfect prefixes.

(2) A *hireq-yod* appears with the second consonant of the root in most forms. This feature also characterizes some forms of *hifil* in the perfect conjugation. (Compare perfect, *hifil* with imperfect, *hifil* in Appendix 3, paradigm 1.) The only imperfect, *hifil* forms which do not have a *hireq-yod* with the second consonant of the root are those which have the syllabic suffix נָה (*3FP* and *2FP*), in which case the *hireq-yod* reduces to a *sere*.

(3) The forms which have a vowel suffix (*2FS*, *3MP*, and *2MP*) do not draw the accent to themselves, as they do in the other stems. Instead the accent remains on the syllable which has the *hireq-yod*. (This characteristic also occurs in perfect, *hifil*.) To say it another way, the second syllable in every imperfect, *hifil* form is accented.

6. Imperfect conjugation in the *hofal* stem

a. The right column in the following chart presents the forms of the imperfect, *hofal* for the root משׁל; the left column has the imperfect, *qal* for comparison. Since *hofal* is the passive of *hifil*, it often conveys causative action in the passive voice, as the translation indicates.

	Imperfect	
	Qal	*Hofal*
3MS	יִמְשֹׁל	יָמְשַׁל (“he will be caused to rule”)
3FS	תִּמְשֹׁל	תָּמְשַׁל (“she will be caused to rule”)
2MS	תִּמְשֹׁל	תָּמְשַׁל (“you will be caused to rule”)
2FS	תִּמְשְׁלִי	תָּמְשְׁלִי (“you will be caused to rule”)
1CS	אֶמְשֹׁל	אָמְשַׁל (“I will be caused to rule”)
3MP	יִמְשְׁלוּ	יָמְשְׁלוּ (“they will be caused to rule”)
3FP	תִּמְשֹׁ֫לְנָה	תָּמְשַׁ֫לְנָה (“they will be caused to rule”)
2MP	תִּמְשְׁלוּ	תָּמְשְׁלוּ (“you will be caused to rule”)

2FP	תִּמְשֹׁ֫לְנָה	תָּמְשַׁ֫לְנָה ("you will be caused to rule")
1CP	נִמְשֹׁל	נָמְשַׁל ("we will be caused to rule")

b. Notes concerning the imperfect, *hofal* conjugation

(1) The key distinguishing feature of this stem is that the imperfect prefixes take a *qames-hatuf*, just as the ה prefix in perfect, *hofal* takes a *qames-hatuf*.

(2) A *patah* appears as the vowel for the second consonant of the root in every form except those with a vowel suffix (*2FS*, *3MP*, and *2MP*), in which case the *patah* reduces to a vocal *sheva*. In this regard the imperfect, *hofal* is identical to the perfect, *hofal*. (Compare perfect, *hofal* with imperfect, *hofal* in Appendix 3, paradigm 1.)

7. Imperfect conjugation in the *hitpael* stem

a. The right column in the following chart presents the forms of the imperfect, *hitpael* for the root משׁל; the left column has the imperfect, *qal* forms for comparison. The translation communicates the common meaning of *hitpael:* reflexive action in the active voice.

	Imperfect	
	Qal	*Hitpael*
3MS	יִמְשֹׁל	יִתְמַשֵּׁל ("he will rule himself")
3FS	תִּמְשֹׁל	תִּתְמַשֵּׁל ("she will rule herself")
2MS	תִּמְשֹׁל	תִּתְמַשֵּׁל ("you will rule yourself")
2FS	תִּמְשְׁלִי	תִּתְמַשְּׁלִי ("you will rule yourself")
1CS	אֶמְשֹׁל	אֶתְמַשֵּׁל ("I will rule myself")
3MP	יִמְשְׁלוּ	יִתְמַשְּׁלוּ ("they will rule themselves")
3FP	תִּמְשֹׁ֫לְנָה	תִּתְמַשֵּׁ֫לְנָה ("they will rule themselves")
2MP	תִּמְשְׁלוּ	תִּתְמַשְּׁלוּ ("you will rule yourselves")
2FP	תִּמְשֹׁ֫לְנָה	תִּתְמַשֵּׁ֫לְנָה ("you will rule yourselves")
1CP	נִמְשֹׁל	נִתְמַשֵּׁל ("we will rule ourselves")

b. Notes concerning the imperfect, *hitpael* conjugation

(1) There are three distinguishing features of this stem in both the perfect and the

imperfect conjugations. One is the appearance of a two-consonant prefix. In the imperfect, *hitpael* this prefix is made up of the regular imperfect prefixes (יִ, תִּ, אֶ, or נִ), each of which has a *hireq* or *segol*, followed by a ת with a silent *sheva*. The second distinguishing feature is the appearance of a *patah* as the vowel for the first consonant of the root, and the third feature is a *dagesh-forte* in the second root consonant.

(2) The vowel for the second consonant of the root in this stem is a *sere* in the forms which have no suffix (*3MS*, *3FS*, *2MS*, *1CS*, and *1CP*). The *sere* reduces to a *patah* with the addition of the syllabic suffix נָה (*3FP* and *2FP*), and to a *sheva* with a vowel suffix (*2FS*, *3MP*, and *2MP*).

(3) Excepting the prefix, most imperfect forms of *hitpael* are spelled the same as *piel*. This similarity occurs because *hitpael* is based upon *piel*.

c. In the imperfect, *hitpael* (as with the perfect, *hitpael*) when the prefix is added to a verb root that begins with the sibilant consonant ס, צ, שׂ, or שׁ, the sibilant and the ת of the prefix change places.[1]

- *Impf, hit, 3MS* > שׁמר = יִשְׁתַּמֵּר (rather than יִתְשַׁמֵּר).

15B Summary of the Imperfect Conjugation

1. It is imperative that the student learn to recognize the imperfect verb in all its forms. One key to accomplishing this goal is the mastery of the full conjugation of the imperfect verb in the *qal* stem and also the *3MS* form of each of the other major stems. For the sake of convenience, these forms for משׁל appear in the following chart with their translations. Any strong verb root could be substituted for משׁל and the prefixes, suffixes, vowels, and accents would remain the same.

[1] Some verb roots undergo additional changes in this stem; see the footnote for Lesson 13A.7c.

	Imperfect						
	Qal	*Nifal*	*Piel*	*Pual*	*Hifil*	*Hofal*	*Hitpael*
3MS	יִמְשֹׁל "he will rule"	יִמָּשֵׁל "he will be ruled"	יְמַשֵּׁל "he will rule"	יְמֻשַּׁל "he will be ruled"	יַמְשִׁיל "he will cause to rule"	יָמְשַׁל "he will be caused to rule"	יִתְמַשֵּׁל "he will rule himself"
3FS	תִּמְשֹׁל "she will rule"						
2MS	תִּמְשֹׁל "you will rule"						
2FS	תִּמְשְׁלִי "you will rule"						
1CS	אֶמְשֹׁל "I will rule						
3MP	יִמְשְׁלוּ "they will rule"						
3FP	תִּמְשֹׁלְנָה "they will rule"						
2MP	תִּמְשְׁלוּ "you will rule"						
2FP	תִּמְשֹׁלְנָה "you will rule"						
1CP	נִמְשֹׁל "we will rule"						

✓ Note: The full conjugation of the imperfect verb, using משל as a model, appears in Appendix 3, paradigm 1.

2. Another key to learning the imperfect verb is the mastery of the following clues for recognizing the forms of the imperfect. Where appropriate these clues are represented in symbol form (□ = a consonant of a verb root; ◁ = an imperfect prefix). (These clues appear in summary form in Appendix 1.)

   a. General clues for recognizing strong imperfect verbs

      (1) The presence of an imperfect prefix (י, ת, א, or נ) identifies a verb as imperfect.

(2) In the case of the נ prefix (*1CP*), which is also a prefix in perfect, *nifal*, the pointing of a verb indicates whether or not it is imperfect.

- נִמְשֹׁל can be identified as a *1CP* imperfect verb by the *holem* over the שׁ – a characteristic of imperfect, *qal* verbs that does not occur in perfect, *nifal*.
- נִמָּשֵׁל can be identified as an *1CP* imperfect verb by the *dagesh-forte* and *qames* – characteristics of imperfect, *nifal* verbs that do not occur in perfect, *nifal*.

(3) The person, gender, and number of imperfect verbs can be identified by the imperfect prefixes and suffixes. (See Lesson 14A.2d.)

b. Clues for recognizing the stems of strong imperfect verbs

(1) *Qal*: □□□ְ◁ִ or □□□ְ◁ֶ

(a) All forms have a *hireq* or *segol* under the prefix – a characteristic shared with *nifal*.

(b) Most forms (but NOT all) have a *holem* above the second consonant of the root (□□ֹ□ְ◁ִ) – a feature unique to *qal*.

(c) *Qal* can also be identified by the absence of the clues for the other stems.

(2) *Nifal*: □□□ָּ◁ִ or □□□ָּ◁ֶ

(a) All forms have a *hireq* or *segol* under the prefix.

(b) All forms have a *dagesh-forte* and a *qames* with the first consonant of the root – features unique to *nifal*.

(3) *Piel*: □□ּ□ַ◁ְ or □□ּ□ַ◁ֲ

(a) All forms have a *sheva* (either a simple *sheva* or a *hatef-patah*) under the prefix – a characteristic shared with *pual*.

(b) All forms have a *patah* under the first consonant of the root – a characteristic shared with *hitpael*.

(c) All forms have a *dagesh-forte* in the second consonant of the root – a characteristic shared with *pual* and *hitpael*.

(4) *Pual*: □□ּ□ֻ◁ְ or □□ּ□ֻ◁ֲ

(a) All forms have a *sheva* (either a simple *sheva* or a *hatef-patah*) under the prefix.

(b) All forms have a *qibbus* under the first consonant of the root – a feature unique to *pual*.

(c) All forms have a *dagesh-forte* in the second consonant of the root.

(5) *Hifil*: ◁ַ□ְ□□

All forms have a *patah* under the prefix – a feature unique to *hifil*.

(6) *Hofal*: ◁ָ□ְ□□

All forms have a *qames-hatuf* under the prefix – a feature unique to *hofal*.

(7) *Hitpael*: ◁ִתְ□ַ□ּ□ or ◁ֶתְ□ַ□ּ□

(a) All forms have a two consonant prefix, the second consonant of which is always ת – a feature unique to *hitpael*.

(b) All forms have a *patah* under the first consonant of the root.

(c) All forms have a *dagesh-forte* in the second consonant of the root.

Lesson 15: Exercises

a. Reproduce from memory the imperfect conjugation of מושׁל in the *qal* stem in each person, gender, and number (*3MS*, *3FS*, *2MS*, etc.) and also reproduce the *3MS* forms only of the other major stems in the imperfect conjugation (as in section 15B.1). Finally, give a translation of each form.

✓ Once the student has learned these forms of the imperfect conjugation, it will be necessary to review the same forms of the perfect to make sure the two conjugations are not confused with one another.

b. While the forms requested above are the only ones the student must master, it is helpful to be familiar with all the forms of the imperfect conjugation. Therefore, attempt to fill in the full practice chart for the imperfect conjugation which appears in Appendix 3, item 16. (This chart may be duplicated by the student.) The student may need assistance from paradigm 1 in Appendix 3 in completing this assignment.

c. Without consulting any charts, identify the following symbolic forms in terms of conjugation (*perf* or *impf*) and person, gender, and number (□ = a consonant of a verb root). Do not assume the forms have any other prefixes or suffixes than the ones that actually appear. If more than one answer is possible, give all options.

▸ *Example:* ת□□□ ⇒ *Answer: Impf, 2MS* or *Impf, 3FS*

(1) י□□□	(6) א□□□	(11) נ□□□[1]
(2) □□□תָ	(7) □□□תְּ	(12) □□□תִּי
(3) □□□ָה	(8) □□□תֶּם	(13) ת□□□ִי
(4) ת□□□וּ	(9) □□□וּ	(14) □□□תֶּן
(5) □□□נוּ	(10) י□□□וּ	(15) ת□□□נָה

d. Without consulting any charts, identify the following symbolic forms in terms of conjugation (*perf* or *impf*) and stem (*qal*, *nif*, *piel*, etc.) (◁ = an imperfect prefix consonant).

✓ This exercise does not intend to indicate particular *P/G/N*, as suggested by the lack of suffixes. It is concerned with indicating the clues for conjugations and stems.

▸ *Example:* ◁ִ□ָּ□□ ⇒ *Answer: Impf, nif*

(1) ◁ִ□ְ□□	(7) ◁ִתְ□ַ□ּ□	(13) ◁ֲ□ַ□ּ□
(2) □ִ□ּ□	(8) ◁ֲ□ֻ□ּ□	(14) הִ□ְ□□
(3) הִתְ□ַ□ּ□	(9) נִ□ְ□□	(15) ◁ָ□ְ□□
(4) ◁ְ□ַ□ּ□	(10) □ֻ□ּ□	(16) ◁ְ□ֻ□ּ□
(5) ◁ֵ□ָּ□□	(11) ◁ַ□ְ□□	(17) ◁ֶתְ□ַ□ּ□
(6) הָ□ְ□□	(12) ◁ֶ□ְ□□	

e. Without consulting any charts, analyze the following verbs from vocabulary lists in terms of root, conjugation, stem, *P/G/N*, additional features, and translation. More than one answer may be possible for some of these words. Since they appear with no context, either option is acceptable.

▸ *Example:* וּתְשַׁמַּעְנָה ⇒ *Answer:* > שׁמע, *impf*, *pual*, *2FP*, + *vav conj*, "and you will be heard" (or *3FP*, "and they will be heard")

(1) מָשְׁלָה	(7) נִקְטַל	(13) וְהָשְׁלַחְתֶּם
(2) הִקְטַלְנוּ	(8) שִׁמְעוּ	(14) יִשָּׁמְעוּ
(3) תַּשְׁמִעִי	(9) וְתַשְׁלִיחוּ	(15) וּנְשַׁמֵּר
(4) וְשָׁלַחְתִּי	(10) שָׁמַרְתָּ	(16) הִתְקַטַּלְתֶּן
(5) תָּקְטַל	(11) תִּתְמַשְּׁלוּ	(17) הִלְקַטְתְּ
(6) אֶתְמַשֵּׁל	(12) תִּלְקֹט	(18) תְּשַׁלַּחְנָה

[1] Two answers are possible if one assumes that a particular stem is implied. A similar situation arises in the next exercise.

f. Learn to recognize, pronounce, and translate the following vocabulary.

	Word	*Translation*	*Notes*
(1)	אִם	if (*particle*)	
(2)	כֵּן	thus, so (*adv*)	With ל *prep:* לָכֵן = "therefore"
(3)	עוֹלָם	eternity, antiquity, forever, a long time (*NMS*)	
(4)	פָּנִים	face, faces, presence (*NMP*)	No *S; P* can mean "face"; with ל *prep:* לִפְנֵי = "before"
(5)	תַּ֫חַת	beneath, under, instead of (*prep*)	*PS:* תַּחְתַּי, תַּחְתֶּ֫יךָ, etc.

g. Some biblical clauses with partial translations appear below. The blanks represent words that either have appeared in vocabulary lists or can be found in Appendix 4. Longer blanks stand for the translation of more than one Hebrew word. First supply the missing words; then attempt a smooth translation, consulting an English Bible if necessary.

(1) אֵ֫לֶּה הַדְּבָרִים אֲשֶׁר תְּדַבֵּר[1] אֶל־בְּנֵי יִשְׂרָאֵל = "____________" (Ex 19:6)

(2) עַל־חוֹמֹתַ֫יִךְ יְרוּשָׁלַ֫םִ הִפְקַ֫דְתִּי שֹׁמְרִים = "______ your walls ____________ watchmen" (Is 62:6)

(3) כָּל־צִדְקֹתָיו אֲשֶׁר־עָשָׂה לֹא תִזָּכַ֫רְנָה = "______ his righteous acts [*NFP*] ____________" (Eze 18:24)

(4) כְּבוֹד יְהוָה נִרְאָה[2] בֶּעָנָן = "____________ in the cloud (Ex 16:10)

(5) וּמַדּוּעַ תִּתְנַשְּׂאוּ עַל־קְהַל יְהוָה = "And why ____________ the congregation of ______?" (Nu 16:3)

(6) לֹא־יִשְׁלְחוּ הַצַּדִּיקִים בְּעַוְלָ֫תָה יְדֵיהֶם = "____________ in injustice ______" (Ps 125:3)

(7) לֹא־נַמְלִיךְ אִישׁ = "____________" (2Ki 10:5)

---

[1] Moses is the antecedent for the subject of this verb.

[2] In this weak verb the vowel before the ה lengthens from *patah* to *qames*.

(8) וּתְבֻקְשִׁי[1] וְלֹא־תִמָּצְאִי עוֹד לְעוֹלָם = "____________" (Eze 26:21)

(9) אִישׁ אֶת־שְׁמוֹ תִּכְתֹּב[2] עַל־מַטֵּהוּ = "____________" (Nu 17:17; *Eng* 17:2)

(10) הַכֶּסֶף אֲשֶׁר לֻקַּח־לָךְ[3] = "____________" (Jdg 17:2)

(11) וְאָזְנֶיךָ תִּשְׁמַעְנָה[4] דָּבָר = "And your ears ____________" (Is 30:21)

(12) וַאֲנִי אֲחַזֵּק אֶת־לִבּוֹ וְלֹא יְשַׁלַּח[5] אֶת־הָעָם = "____________" (Ex 4:21)

(13) הֲלוֹא[6] נֶגֶד עֵינֵינוּ אֹכֶל נִכְרָת[7] = "______ before ______ food [*NFS*] ______?" (Joel 1:16)

(14) אַכְבִּיד אֶת־עֻלְּכֶם = "______ your yoke" (2Ch 10:14)

(15) מִלֵּא אֹתָם חָכְמַת־לֵב = "____________ with wisdom of ______" (Ex 35:35)

(16) כִּי אָמְרָה אַל־אֶרְאֶה[8] בְּמוֹת הַיָּלֶד = "____________ on the death of the child" (Ge 21:16)

h. Read aloud and translate the following words [number (1)] and sentences [numbers (2)-(19)]. The student should be able to complete the exercise without consulting any charts or vocabulary lists.

(1) יִמְשֹׁל | תִּמָּשֵׁל | תְּמַשְּׁלִי | אֲמַשֵּׁל | יַמְשִׁילוּ | תָּמְשַׁלְנָה | תִּתְמַשְּׁלוּ | נִמְשֹׁל

(2) כִּדְבַר־הַמֶּלֶךְ כֵּן הוּא בְּכֹל הָאָרֶץ (3) לֹא תִקָּטַלְנָה הַנָּשִׁים הָהֵנָּה כִּי לֹא

---

[1] *BHS* lacks the *dagesh-forte*.

[2] Moses is the antecedent for the subject of this verb.

[3] In this context the prefixed preposition means "from."

[4] In this weak verb the guttural ע is preceded by an A-class vowel rather than a *holem*.

[5] In this weak verb the guttural ח is preceded by an A-class vowel rather than a *sere*.

[6] The prefix הֲ on this word has no translation; it simply indicates that the clause is interrogative (expressing a question).

[7] In *BHS* the last syllable of this word has an accent that causes its vowel to lengthen from a *patah* to *qames*.

[8] In this weak verb the ה is preceded by a *segol* rather than a *holem*.

תֵּעָשֶׂה[2] רָעָה בָהֶן (4) בָּאָה[1] הָעִיר הַהִיא תַּחַת חֶרֶב־הַמֶּלֶךְ וְנִקְטְלוּ כָל־
אֲנָשֶׁיהָ (5) אִם אַתְּ אִשְׁתִּי[4] וְתֵשְׁבִי[3] אִתִּי וְעַמִּי עַמֵּךְ (6) יִשְׁמֹר יְהוָה אֶתְכֶם
מֵרָעָה אִם תִּקְרְאוּ עַל שְׁמוֹ (7) אַתָּה וּבָנֶיךָ הַכֹּהֲנִים אֲשֶׁר תֵּשְׁבוּ לִפְנֵי
אֱלֹהִים עוֹלָם (8) עַד בָּא אִישׁ אֱלֹהִים לֹא הָיָה אֶחָד תַּחַת הַשָּׁמַיִם אֲשֶׁר
עָשָׂה אֶת־טוֹב לְלֵב יְהוָה (9) יִשְׁמְרוּ אֶת־דְּבַר־אֱלֹהִים כִּי הֵמָּה יָבוֹאוּ[5] לִפְנֵי
שָׂרֵי הַכֹּהֲנִים וְיֹאמְרוּ[6] שָׂרֵי הַכֹּהֲנִים אֲלֵיהֶם (10) עַל הַיּוֹם הַהוּא יְשַׁלְּחוּ
בָּנַי לְבֵיתְךָ וְתִשָּׁמֵר בָּם (11) תִּמְשֹׁל אֶת הַגּוֹי תַּחַת אָחִיךָ כִּי לֹא קָרָא אָחִיךָ
עַל שֵׁם יְהוָה וְלֹא הָיָה בוֹ רוּחַ יְהוָה (12) אֲנַחְנוּ גְדוֹלִים מִכָּל־בְּנֵי־יִשְׂרָאֵל
כִּי נִשְׁתַּמֵּר מִן־רָעָה (13) אִם לֹא תַעֲשׂוּ[7] כַּאֲשֶׁר אָמַר יְהוָה וּתְקָטְלוּ אַתֶּם
וּבְנֵיכֶם בַּחֶרֶב (14) כִּי הֵבֵיאתָ[8] רָעָה עַל בֵּיתִי כֵּן אָבִיא רָעָה עָלֶיךָ וְעַל
בֵּיתְךָ (15) יִתְלַקְּטוּ עַם־עִירְךָ לִפְנֵי הַמֶּלֶךְ הַגָּדוֹל בְּמַלְכֵי הָאָרֶץ וְיִמָּשְׁלוּ
בוֹ (16) אֲנִי אֶעֱשֶׂה[9] אֶת מִשְׁפָּט בֵּין הֵנָּה אֲשֶׁר טוֹבוֹת וּבֵין הֵנָּה אֲשֶׁר לֹא
(17) תָּשְׁלְחוּ בְנֵיכֶם לְאַרְצֵנוּ לִדְבַר־הַמֶּלֶךְ וְהֵם אַנְשֵׁי בְנוֹתֵינוּ (18) נָשָׂא
הַמֶּלֶךְ אֶת פְּנֵי בִתּוֹ אֲשֶׁר לָהּ נֶעֶשְׂתָה[10] רָעָה (19) לָכֵן אַתֵּנָה תְּלַקֵּטְנָה
אֶת־בְּנוֹתֵיכֶן עִמָּכֶן אֶל בֵּית אֱלֹהֵיכֶן עַל הַיּוֹם הַגָּדוֹל הַהוּא וְתִשְׁמַעְנָה
דְּבַר־יְהוָה אֲשֶׁר יֹאמַר[11] הַכֹּהֵן לָכֶן

---

[1] This weak verb (> בוא; *perf, qal, 3MS* = בָּא) loses the middle consonant of its root in this form.

[2] This weak verb (> עשׂה) is *impf, nif.*

[3] A *vav* conjunction can mean "then" when it follows a clause introduced by אם ("if"). This *impf, qal* weak verb (> ישׁב) loses the first consonant of its root when a prefix is added; the loss also changes the prefix vowel from *hireq* to *sere*. The same phenomenon occurs with this root in a future sentence.

[4] The first clause of this sentence is verbless and requires a future tense, state-of being verb ("will be") in English.

[5] This weak verb (> בוא; *perf, qal, 3MS* = בָּא) is *impf, qal.*

[6] In this weak verb the quiescent א loses its vowel, and the prefix takes a *holem* rather than *hireq*.

[7] This weak verb (> עשׂה) is *impf, qal*. The third root consonant drops out with a suffix, and the first two vowels change because of the guttural ע.

[8] This weak verb (> בוא; *perf, qal, 3MS* = בָּא) is *perf, hif.* The same verb appears again in this sentence where it is *impf, hif.*

[9] This weak verb (> עשׂה) is *impf, qal*.

[10] This weak verb (> עשׂה) is *perf, nif.*

[11] In this weak verb the א quiesces and the prefix receives a *holem* rather than *hireq*. The ר is preceded by a A-class vowel rather than a *holem*.

Lesson 16

Vav with Perfect and Imperfect Verbs, Orientation to The Hebrew Bible and Lexicon

16A *Vav* with Perfect and Imperfect Verbs

1. Introduction

a. When the *vav* is added to perfect and imperfect verbs, it can function in two different ways: either as a simple *vav* conjunction or as a *vav* consecutive.

b. The simple *vav* conjunction (*vav conj*) on perfect and imperfect verbs has already appeared many times in this Grammar. The *vav* is pointed according to the rules in Lesson 6B.2b, and is translated by "and" or some other appropriate English conjunction.

- מָשַׁל + *vav conj* = וְמָשַׁל ("And he ruled")
- יִמְשֹׁל + *vav conj* = וְיִמְשֹׁל ("And he will rule")

c. Perfect and imperfect verbs can also take a *vav* consecutive (*vav cons*) which has two functions. One is to convey the idea of a conjunction, just as the simple *vav conj* does. The other function is to invert the meaning of the verb's tense, so that a perfect verb with a *vav cons* has generally the same meaning as an imperfect, and an imperfect verb with a *vav cons* has roughly the same meaning as a perfect verb.[1] To say it another way, a *vav* consecutive typically changes the action of a perfect verb from complete to incomplete, and it changes the action of an imperfect from incomplete to complete.

2. *Vav* consecutive with perfect verbs

a. A *vav cons* on a perfect verb is pointed in the same way as the simple *vav conj*. The *vav cons*, however, does in some cases impact the accent of the verb to which

---

[1] While this Grammar maintains the traditional terminology of "*vav* consecutive," others have used such terms as "*vav* conversive," "*vav* inversive," and "relative *vav*." See Joüon, §117; and Waltke and O'Connor, §32.1.1a.

it is attached. When a perfect verb is accented on the penultimate (next to last) syllable, as it is in *1CS* and *2MS*, the *vav cons* may move the accent to the last syllable. For example, compare the following *perf, qal, 1CS* verb with *vav conj* and *vav cons*.

- מָשַׁלְתִּי + *vav conj* = וּמָשַׁלְתִּי ("And I ruled")
- מָשַׁלְתִּי + *vav cons* = וּמָשַׁלְתִּי ("And I will rule")

Outside of the recognition of this occasional shift of accent, one can identify the occurrence of the perfect with *vav cons* (*perf* + *vav cons*) by the context in which the verb appears.

b. A *perf* + *vav cons* typically follows another clause or phrase which establishes the action in a text as incomplete, then the *perf* + *vav cons* continues the incomplete action. As the term "consecutive" implies, *vav cons* usually appears in a language sequence that is governed by the temporal sense of a preceding verb or phrase.[1]

(1) Most often the pattern is one in which an imperfect verb, indicating future action, is followed by a *perf* + *vav cons* which continues the future action.

- אִם אֶת־הַדָּבָר הַזֶּה תַּעֲשֶׂה וְצִוְּךָ אֱלֹהִים וְיָכָלְתָּ עֲמֹד = "If you will do this thing, and God will command you, then you will be able to endure" (Ex 18:23)

  The imperfect verb (תַּעֲשֶׂה = "you will do") and the succeeding *perf* + *vav cons* verbs (וְצִוְּךָ = "and God will command you"; וְיָכָלְתָּ = "and you will be able") all convey incomplete action in the future.

- שֵׁשֶׁת יָמִים תַּעֲבֹד וְעָשִׂיתָ כָּל־מְלַאכְתֶּךָ = "Six days you will labor and do all of your work" (Ex 20:9)

  This verse begins with an imperfect verb (תַּעֲבֹד = "you will labor") whose action is future; a *perf* + *vav cons* verb (וְעָשִׂיתָ = "and you will do") continues the same temporal idea.

(2) A *perf* + *vav cons* can succeed other language elements besides an imperfect verb. The following examples illustrate a few of the possibilities.

- אֲנִי יְהוָה דִּבַּרְתִּי וְעָשִׂיתִי = "I, the LORD, have spoken, and I will do it" (Eze 17:24)

[1] For the examples of the *perf* + *vav cons* that follow and for others see Joüon, §119c-zb; and Waltke and O'Connor, §32.2.1-32.2.6.

The first clause has a perfect verb (דִּבַּ֫רְתִּי = "I have spoken"), followed by a *perf + vav cons* (וְעָשִׂ֫יתִי = "and I will do") which states a future consequence of the first clause.

- וּבֹ֫קֶר וּרְאִיתֶם אֶת־כְּבוֹד יְהוָה = "And in the morning you will see the glory of the LORD" (Ex 16:7)

  This quotation begins with a temporal phrase which places the action in the future (וּבֹ֫קֶר = "and in the morning"), then a *perf + vav cons* (וּרְאִיתֶם = "you will see") continues the future notion.

- שִׁמְעוּ אֶת־דִּבְרֵי הַבְּרִית הַזֹּאת וַעֲשִׂיתֶם אוֹתָם = "Hear the words of this covenant, and then you will do them" (Jer 11:6)

  In this verse an imperative verb (שִׁמְעוּ = "hear") is followed by a *perf + vav cons* (וַעֲשִׂיתֶם = "then you will do"). The second verb could be translated as an imperative: "and do them."

✓ In a *perf + vav cons* construction the *vav* may be translated with a wide range of options, depending on its context, or may require no translation at all, as the preceding examples illustrate.

c. While a *perf + vav cons* normally follows another language element which governs its temporal sense, the form can occur at the beginning of a text where there is no connection with a preceding temporal notion.

- וְהָיָה בְּאַחֲרִית הַיָּמִים = "It will be in the last days" (Is 2:2)

  This clause initiates a prophetic oracle with a *perf + vav cons* (וְהָיָה = "it will be"). Since there is no dependency on preceding material, the *vav* is left untranslated.

3. *Vav* consecutive with imperfect verbs

a. A *vav cons* on an imperfect verb differs in appearance from a simple *vav conj* on an imperfect.

(1) With regard to the *vav cons* that is attached to an imperfect:

(a) The *vav* is usually pointed with a *patah* and followed by a *dagesh-forte* in the first consonant of the imperfect verb (וַ__ּ__).

- וַיִּמְשֹׁל = "And he ruled"

(b) Before א (*1CS* imperfect prefix), which cannot take a *dagesh-forte*, the vowel under the *vav* lengthens to a *qames* (וָא__).

- ▸ וָאֶמְשֹׁל = "And I ruled"

(c) Before יְ (and certain other situations of vocal *sheva*) the *vav* takes a *patah* and is not followed by *dagesh-forte* (וַיְ__).

- ▸ וַיְהִי = "And it was"

✓ The distinctive pointing of the *vav cons* on the imperfect (וַ__ּ__ , וָא__ or וַיְ__) means that this form can be readily distinguished from *impf* + *vav conj*.

(2) With regard to the imperfect verb to which the *vav cons* is attached:

(a) The imperfect sometimes appears in a shortened form after *vav cons.*[1]

[1] In strong verbs the shortening only occurs in certain *hifil* forms where *hireq-yod* becomes *sere*. Compare the following.

- ▸ יַמְשִׁיל + *vav conj* = וְיַמְשִׁיל ("And he will cause to rule")
- ▸ יַמְשִׁיל + *vav cons* = וַיַּמְשֵׁל ("And he caused to rule")

[2] When *vav cons* is attached to weak verbs, shortened forms appear in other stems besides *hifil.*[2] The shortening may involve the loss of a consonant as well as the reduction of a vowel, as the following example illustrates.

- ▸ *Impf, qal, 3MS* forms from the root היה:

  Without *vav cons:* יִהְיֶה = "he will be"

  With *vav cons:* וַיְהִי = "and he was"

(b) The *vav cons* also tends to move the accent of the imperfect from the last syllable to the penultimate in some verbs.

---

[1] Some grammarians theorize that these so-called "shortened imperfect" forms are actually not imperfects at all, but represent a third conjugation in Hebrew called the "preterite." The preterite employs the same prefixes as the imperfect but conveys simple action in the past. According to the theory, it is a verb in the preterite conjugation (rather than *impf* + *vav cons*) which appears with a *vav* to indicate completed action in the past. The preterite occasionally appears in ancient texts without a *vav*. In such cases it resembles the imperfect (because of the prefix), but connotes simple past action. (For example: אַעֲלֶה in Jdg 2:1; יָשֶׁת in Ps 18:12; and אִוָּלֶד in Job 3:3). See Joüon, §117b-c; Waltke and O'Connor, §31.1.1, 33.1.2; and Ronald J. Williams, *Hebrew Syntax, An Outline* (Toronto: University of Toronto Press, 1967), §176-7. Rather than presenting a third, preterite conjugation, this Grammar takes the traditional approach that the *vav cons* appears on the imperfect (whose form is often shortened), with the result that *impf* + *vav cons* conveys completed action. While this approach may involve some oversimplification, it is an appropriate one for this stage of learning the language.

[2] See Waltke and O'Connor, §33.1.1b.

- *Impf, piel, 3MS* forms from the root ברך:

  Without *vav cons:* יְבָרֵךְ = "he will bless"

  With *vav cons:* וַיְבָרֶךְ = "and he blessed"

b. An imperfect with *vav cons* (*impf* + *vav cons*) typically follows another clause or phrase which establishes the action in a text as completed, then the *impf* + *vav cons* continues the notion of completed action.[1]

(1) Usually the pattern is one in which a perfect verb, indicating past action, is followed by an *impf* + *vav cons* that conveys consecutive action in the past. This pattern is quite common in narrative materials.

- הִקְשַׁבְתִּי וָאֶשְׁמָע = "I have given heed and I have listened" (Jer 8:6)

  The first verb is a perfect and the second is an *impf* + *vav cons*; both convey completed action in the past.

- וְהַנָּחָשׁ הָיָה עָרוּם . . . וַיֹּאמֶר אֶל־הָאִשָּׁה = "Now the serpent was crafty . . . and he said to the woman" (Ge 3:1)

  Again, a perfect verb conveying completed action (הָיָה) is followed by an *impf* + *vav cons* (וַיֹּאמֶר), wherein the second verb continues the kind of action indicated by the first.

(2) An *impf* + *vav cons* can follow other language elements besides a perfect verb, as the following illustrate.

- וְלוֹ שְׁתֵּי נָשִׁים . . . וַיְהִי לִפְנִנָּה יְלָדִים = "And he had two wives . . . and Peninah had children" (1Sa 1:2)

  The first clause is verbless and requires a past tense verb in translation; the second clause has an *impf* + *vav cons* (וַיְהִי) which continues the past tense narrative.

- כִּי נַעַר יִשְׂרָאֵל וָאֹהֲבֵהוּ – "When Israel was a boy, I loved him" (Hos 11:1)

  The verse begins with a temporal clause that sets the action in the past, then the *impf* + *vav cons* (וָאֹהֲבֵהוּ) continues the temporal sense.

- בְּקָרְבָתָם לִפְנֵי־יְהוָה וַיָּמֻתוּ = "In their approaching the LORD, when they died" (Le 16:1)

---

[1] For the examples of the *impf* + *vav cons* that follow and for others see Joüon, §118c-v; and Waltke and O'Connor, §33.2.1-33.3.5.

In this verse an *impf* + *vav cons* (וַיָּמֻ֫תוּ) follows an infinitival phrase (בְּקָרְבָתָם). The context places the action in the past.

c. While an *impf* + *vav cons* normally follows another language element which governs its temporal sense, the verb construction can occur at the beginning of a text where there is no close connection with a preceding temporal notion. In fact, an *impf* + *vav cons* even appears at the beginning of some biblical books. For example, Numbers begins with וַיְדַבֵּר יְהוָה אֶל־מֹשֶׁה = "The LORD spoke to Moses." The *impf* + *vav cons* expression וַיְהִי (> הָיָה) = "and there was" or "and it happened" very commonly occurs at the beginning of narratives to signal the recital of past events. The book of Ruth begins with וַיְהִי בִּימֵי שְׁפֹט = "It happened in the days of the judges" or "In the days when the judges were ruling."

4. Analysis of verbs with *vav* consecutives

While a *vav cons* normally inverts the meaning of a perfect or imperfect verb, it does not actually change the form of a verb. In other words, a perfect verb with a *vav cons* is still analyzed as a perfect, and likewise with an imperfect. The *vav cons* is included as an additional feature in the analysis, as the following illustrate.

Word	Root	Conju-gation	Stem	P/G/N	Additional Features	Translation
וְלָקַחְתָּ֫ (Ge 24:4)	> לקח	*perf*	*qal*	*2MS*	+ *vav cons*	"and you will take"
וַיַּמְלֵךְ (2Ki 24:17)	> מלך	*impf*	*hif*	*3MS*	+ *vav cons*	"and he made to reign"

✓ Note that in the first example above the accent is on the last syllable, indicating it is a *perf* + *vav cons* rather than a *perf* + *vav conj* (which would be accented on the penultimate). Also note that the second example has a shortened final vowel (*sere* instead of *hireq*), which is characteristic of *impf* + *vav cons* in *hifil.*

16B Orientation to the Hebrew Bible and Lexicon

The exercises beginning with this lesson will require the student to translate verses directly from the Hebrew Bible, using the aid of a lexicon. To facilitate the task, this section provides some orientation to these two works.

1. The Hebrew Bible

a. The Hebrew Bible is divided into three large sections:

(1) *Torah* (תּוֹרָה = "law") including Genesis, Exodus, Leviticus, Numbers, and Deuteronomy

(2) *Nebiim* (נְבִיאִים = "prophets") which is further divided into the "Former Prophets" of Joshua, Judges, Samuel, and Kings; and the "Latter Prophets" of Isaiah, Jeremiah, Ezekiel, and "the 12" (i.e., Hosea, Joel, Amos, Obadiah, Jonah, Micah, Nahum, Habakkuk, Zephaniah, Haggai, Zechariah, and Malachi)

(3) *Ketubim* (כְּתוּבִים = "writings") which includes the remaining books of the canon: Psalms, Job, Proverbs, Ruth, Song of Songs (Canticles), Ecclesiastes, Lamentations, Esther, Daniel, Ezra, Nehemiah, and Chronicles.

The first letters of these three major sections provide an abbreviated term for the Hebrew Bible: *T* (ת) *N* (נ) *K* (כ) which is vocalized as *Tanak.*

b. Several editions of the Hebrew Bible are available. The most popular for students is the *Biblia Hebraica Stuttgartensia* (*BHS*), edited by Elliger and Rudolph and published by the German Bible Society.[1] This critical edition is based on the oldest Masoretic manuscript of the entire Hebrew Bible. It contains not only the biblical text but also Masoretic notes (in the outside margins and immediately below the text) and a critical apparatus with alternate readings (at the bottom of the page). *BHS* begins with a lengthy prolegomena in several languages, including English, followed by lists of abbreviations and symbols with interpretation in Latin. English translations of the Latin lists are available in several resources, such as *The Text of the Old Testament*, by Würthwein, or *A Simplified Guide to BHS*, by Scott.[2]

c. The first task for the student is becoming familiar with the biblical text itself. A few of the markings that accompany the text are explained below.

(1) The system of dividing scripture into chapters and verses was introduced by Medieval Christian scholars. The Masoretes indicated divisions in the text by

---

[1] Karl Elliger and Wilhelm Rudolph, eds., *Biblia Hebraica Stuttgartensia* (Stuttgart: Deutsche Bibelgesellschaft, 1967-77).

[2] Ernst Würthwein, *The Text of the Old Testament*, 2d ed, trans. Erroll R. Rhodes (Grand Rapids: William B. Eerdmans, 1995); and William R. Scott, *A Simplified Guide to BHS*, 3d ed. (N. Richland Hills, TX: BIBAL Press, 1987).

other means. One is the marking of *sedarim*, or lessons. Looking at Ge 1:1 as an example, the large ס at the right margin marks the beginning of a *seder* ("order"); the small א indicates this is the first *seder*. The Masoretes indicated paragraphs by means of a single פ (= *petuha* ["open"]), as at the end of Ge 1:5, or by a ס (= *setuma* ["closed"]), as at the end of Ge 3:15. The small circles that appear above the Hebrew words are keys for moving to the Masoretic notes in the margin. (These notes will be discussed in connection with the exercises of Lesson 18.)

(2) The remaining marks around the words of the text are accents. For the sake of simplicity this Grammar has employed a single mark for any Hebrew accent, which is ◌֫. The Hebrew Bible actually has dozens of specific kinds of accents. In fact, there are two accentual systems: one contains 21 accents used in the poetic books of Psalms, Proverbs, and Job, and the other has the 27 accents employed in the rest of the *MT*. Every Hebrew word (or word group when *maqqef* appears) has a major accent, and some words also have a secondary stress. The accents are not only an aid to pronunciation but also to interpretation. Accents function either disjunctively (separating words) or conjunctively (joining words) to indicate the distinct parts of a verse from the perspective of the Masoretes. Since Hebrew has no punctuation marks, the accents can be significant aids for translation and interpretation.[1] The student should consult the table of accents inserted in *BHS* to become familiar with the appearance of all the accents. However, at this point it is necessary to learn the significance of only two disjunctive accents in particular.

(a) A *silluq* (סִלּוּק = "end") appears as ◌ֽ beneath the final accented syllable of a verse. (While it resembles a *meteg*, its function is so different that the two are easily distinguished from one another.) A word with a *silluq* is also followed by another kind of mark called a *sof passuq* (׃). Note that the final word of Ge 1:1 (הָאָֽרֶץ׃) contains these two marks.

(b) An *atnah* (אַתְנָח = "rest") appears as ◌֑ and marks the mid-point of a verse. Note the occurrence of this accent with the third word in Ge 1:1 (אֱלֹהִ֑ים). (While this accent normally stands to the left of a vowel, it

[1] Kelley, 16.

sometimes appears to the right in this Grammar.)

(3) A word that is marked with *silluq* or *atnah* (as well as certain other accents) is a word in "pause." As the name suggests, a pausal word indicates where to break the reading of the text. In pausal forms the accent tends to move to the penultimate syllable, and if the accented vowel is short it often lengthens, as the following illustrate.

Non-pausal Form	*Pausal Form*
אֲנִי ("I")	אָֽנִי׃ (Ge 27:24)
אֶ֫רֶץ ("land")	אָ֑רֶץ (Jer 22:29)
אַתָּה ("you")	אָ֑תָּה (Ge 3:11)
בַּ֫יִת ("house")	בָּֽיִת׃ (1Ch 14:1)
יִשְׁמְעוּ ("they will hear")	יִשְׁמָ֑עוּ (Dt 18:14)
לְךָ ("to you" [*MS*])	לָ֑ךְ[1] (Ge 33:5)

✓ As the last example illustrates, when a syllable with a *2MS* pronominal suffix is in pause, the *sheva* usually lengthens to a *qames* and the final *kaf* takes a silent *sheva*. Thus, when the *2MS* pronominal suffix is in pause, it looks exactly like the *2FS* pronominal suffix (◌ָךְ). In such cases the context in which the form appears indicates which gender is intended.

2. Hebrew Lexicons

a. An essential tool for the beginner in translating the Hebrew Bible is a Hebrew-English lexicon. One widely used lexicon is *A Hebrew and English Lexicon of the Old Testament*, edited by Brown, Driver, and Briggs (*BDB*).[2] Although it is quite old and some of its research outdated, *BDB* is the most thorough one-volume lexicon available. This lexicon is arranged in such a way that words (verbs, nouns, adjectives, etc.) are listed under the roots from which they come, so far as can be determined. For example, to find the meaning of the word מִשְׁפָּט one does not look in the *mem* section of the lexicon but under the verb root שָׁפַט ("judge"),

---

[1] In *MT* the *lamed* has a *dagesh-forte* which links it to the preceding word. In this verse it is obvious that the pronominal suffix is masculine because its antecedent is Jacob.

[2] Francis Brown, S. R. Driver, and Charles A. Briggs, *A Hebrew and English Lexicon of the Old Testament* (Oxford: Clarendon Press, 1907).

which appears on page 1047. מִשְׁפָּט, a noun meaning "judgment," is the fourth entry under שָׁפַט (page 1048). This noun has been formed by attaching a מ to the verb root (מ being a very common noun prefix, as discussed in Lesson 23). One of the values of organizing a lexicon based on roots is that it makes apparent how words are related to one another. However, the scheme can also make some words difficult to find because of the challenge of uncovering their roots. This Grammar will offer some clues along the way to help in the process.

✓ While the entries for words in *BDB* are arranged by roots, many words also appear in alphabetic order with a note indicating the root. For example, a note appears in the *mem* section of the lexicon on page 606 which says, "מִשְׁפָּט v. שׁפט" (v. = "see").

b. A few other comments are helpful as a general orientation to *BDB*.

(1) The list of abbreviations, beginning on page xiii, is an indispensable guide to which the user will want to refer frequently. The lexicon also contains an Aramaic-English section beginning on page 1078.

(2) Note the general arrangement of an entry for a verb, using אָבַד on page 1 as an example. The verb is listed by its lexical form (*perf, qal, 3MS*); "vb." identifies the part of speech. Then a gloss (or general meaning) for the verb comes next, followed by some data in bold parentheses related to etymology and cognate languages. The entry then moves to discussing this verb in each stem where it occurs. Under the heading **Qal**, examples of verb forms with references appear in the categories of perfect, imperfect, infinitive, and participle. The fact that there is no listing for the imperative conjugation indicates that this verb does not occur in *qal*, imperative. After the illustrative Hebrew forms come various meanings of the verb in *qal*. The entry continues with *piel* and *hifil* forms and meanings. Since no other stems are listed, one can assume that this verb occurs only in *qal, piel,* and *hifil*. It is important to realize that the general meaning of a word that appears after the lexical form and part of speech ("perish" in the case אָבַד) may or may not be appropriate for a particular passage. When translating a verb one must pay close attention to the lexicon's discussion of the meanings which that verb can have in various stems and then select the meaning which best fits the context in which

the word appears.

- ✓ Note that following the entry for אָבַד there are four nouns which are derived from the root of this verb.

(3) Observe the general arrangement of a noun entry by looking at אָב on page 3. This noun does not appear in the lexicon in alphabetic order but under a conjectured root "II. אבה," which is the second of two roots with this spelling. The ה of the root, which is a weak consonant, has dropped out in the noun form. In time the student will become familiar with the ways in which weak roots are modified in derived noun forms. (For now a little random searching around the place where a noun would appear alphabetically sometimes leads to a discovery of its root, as it would in the case of this word.) As with a verb, the entry for the noun אָב begins with its lexical form, followed by indication of the part of speech, a gloss (general meaning) for the noun, and some etymological information. Then come various forms of the noun in the singular – absolute, construct, and suffixed (with pronominal suffixes). The same follows for the plural. Finally, the lexicon explains the various meanings of the noun in particular contexts.

(4) The page headers in *BDB* indicate the first and last entries on each page. Since words are listed under their roots, it is often the case that the headers do not follow alphabetic order. For example, if one looks in the *alef* section of the lexicon on page 20, the header above the left column is תאנים, and above the right column is אופיר. In other words, the headers indicate the entries on a page, not the alphabetic order of roots. Finding alphabetized roots may require searching backward or forward through a few pages.

c. Several other lexicons are available besides *BDB;* two are mentioned here. *The Hebrew and Aramaic Lexicon of the Old Testament* by Koehler and Baumgartner is a much more thorough and up-to-date lexicon than *BDB*. Originally published in five volumes, it can also be found in a condensed two-volume format. Koehler and Baumgarter's work has the advantage of presenting most Hebrew words in an alphabetical arrangement, rather than attempting to place them all under their roots. However, the size of this lexicon makes it significantly more expensive than *BDB*. A much briefer work, based on Koehler and Baumgartner's lexicon, is

A Concise Hebrew and Aramaic Lexicon of the Old Testament, by Holladay. Holladay's popular lexicon has several benefits: size, cost, arrangement, and up-to-date information; however, its discussions (e.g., of grammatical forms) are not as thorough as those in *BDB* and Koehler-Baumgartner.[1]

Lesson 16: Exercises

a. Learn to recognize, pronounce, and translate the following vocabulary.

	Word	*Translation*	*Notes*
(1)	אֲדָמָה	land, ground, earth (*NFS*)	*Cs:* אַדְמַת
(2)	אֹהֶל	tent (*NMS*)	*P:* אֹהָלִים
(3)	אָסַף	he gathered, removed (*V*)	
(4)	בֹּקֶר	morning (*NMS*)	*P:* בְּקָרִים
(5)	בְּרִית	covenant (*NFS*)	
(6)	זָכַר	he remembered (*V*)	
(7)	כָּרַת	he cut off, cut down (*V*)	
(8)	מַחֲנֶה	camp, army (*NM/FS*[2])	*Cs:* מַחֲנֵה; *MP:* מַחֲנִים; *FP:* מַחֲנוֹת
(9)	מַיִם	water, waters (*NMDu*)	Occurs only in *Du*
(10)	סָבִיב	(a) around, all around (*adv* or *prep*) (b) circuit, neighborhood (*NM/FS*[2])	*Cs:* סְבִיב; *MP:* סְבִיבִים; *FP:* סְבִיבוֹת; *P* with *PS:* סְבִיבֶיהָ (*M*), סְבִיבוֹתַי (*F*), etc.
(11)	צַדִּיק	righteous, just (*adj MS*)	
(12)	תּוֹרָה	instruction, direction, law (*NFS*)	

---

[1] Ludwig Koehler and Walter Baumgartner, *The Hebrew and Aramaic Lexicon of the Old Testament*, trans. and ed. M.E.J. Richardson (Leiden: E. J. Brill, 1994-2000); and William L. Holladay, *A Concise Hebrew and Aramaic Lexicon of the Old Testament*. Grand Rapids: William B. Eerdmans, 1971.

[2] This word is sometimes masculine and at other times feminine.

b. Analyze the following verbs, nouns, and adjectives, using a lexicon as necessary. The analysis of verbs has been discussed previously; however, this is the first exercise calling for the analysis of nouns and adjectives. Their analysis involves identification of: (1) root (not the lexical form, but the root from which the noun comes, if one can be determined), (2) part of speech (*N* or *adj*), (3) gender (*M* or *F*) and number (*S* or *P*), (4) state (*Ab* or *Cs*), and (5) any additional features. Then provide a translation of the word (not its lexical form). The student may want to consult Appendix 2 for a summary of the steps in analyzing verbs, nouns, and adjectives. The blank analysis chart at the end of Appendix 2 may be used for this exercise.

- *Example:* וּמִמִּקְדָּשִׁי (Eze 9:6) ⇒ *Answer:* > קדשׁ, *NMS, Cs* + *prep* מִן, *vav conj*, & *PS 1CS*, “and from my sanctuary”

(1)	לְאַדְמָתוֹ	(Ps 146:4)	(11)	יִתְחַטָּא	(Nu 31:23)
(2)	וְיִשְׁמַע	(Jdg 9:7)	(12)	וְתוֹרוֹת	(Ne 9:13)
(3)	וּלְרִשְׁעֵי	(Eze 7:21)	(13)	הַצַּדִּיקִים	(Ps 125:3)
(4)	וַתִּלָּקַח	(Est 2:8)	(14)	וְנָטַעְתִּי	(Ecc 2:5)
(5)	וְאָסַפְתִּי	(Jer 21:4)	(15)	וִיסַלֵּף	(Ex 23:8)
(6)	בַּמַּחֲנוֹת	(Zec 14:15)	(16)	מִבְּרִיתֵךְ׃	(Eze 16:61)
(7)	וְשָׁאַלְתָּ	(1Ki 3:11)	(17)	וְזָכַרְתָּ	(Dt 5:15)
(8)	רִכְבָּהּ	(Na 2:14; *Eng* 2:13)	(18)	אָהֳלֵיכֶם	(Jos 22:8)
(9)	הַבָּיִת	(2Ch 7:3)	(19)	וָאֲבַקֵּשׁ	(Eze 22:30)
(10)	וַיַּכְרֵת	(Jos 11:21)	(20)	מִזְבְּחֶךָ׃	(Dt 33:10)

c. Read aloud and translate Genesis 1:1-5 from the Hebrew Bible, using a lexicon as necessary. Also provide an analysis of all verbs.

✓ The following notes provide help with grammatical forms that have not yet been introduced, including weak verbs. Weak verbs can lose root consonants in some forms, and they often employ vowel pointing that diverges from the paradigm of strong verbs. The following notes identify missing root consonants, and a lexicon will aid in recognizing the stems of verbs whose vowels are irregular.

Verse 2:

(1) In הָיְתָה (> הָיָה) the final ה of the root strengthens to a ת with the addition of a verb suffix.

(2) מְרַחֶ֫פֶת (> רחפ) is participle, *piel.* It has a מְ prefix and a feminine, singular participial suffix (◌ֶת). Consult a lexicon for its translation.

Verse 3:

יְהִי (> הָיָה) has lost its final root consonant. It is a special imperfect form known as a jussive (as discussed in Lesson 17). In this context its translation requires use of the auxiliary verb "let."

Verse 4:

וַיַּ֫רְא (> רָאָה) has lost its final root consonant. While the prefix vowel of *patah* makes it look like *hifil*, the verb is actually *qal*. The *patah* prefix vowel appears because ר, like gutturals, prefers an A-class vowel before it.

Lesson 17

Jussive and Cohortative, Imperative Conjugation, Verbs of Prohibition, Analysis of Volitional Verb Forms

17A Jussive and Cohortative

1. Introduction

a. Hebrew has three ways of expressing volition (the will of someone). They are the jussive, cohortative, and imperative. The imperative mood expresses direct, positive commands; it will be discussed in the next section.

b. The jussive and cohortative usually convey more indirect, or more subtle, expressions of volition than the imperative does. The jussive and cohortative are not distinct conjugations but are specialized expressions of the imperfect.

2. Jussive

a. The jussive occurs only in the imperfect and usually in the third person, singular or plural.[1]

(1) In some verb roots the jussive has a shortened imperfect form.

(a) The shortened imperfect of the jussive resembles the shortened forms of the imperfect which sometimes appear with the *vav* consecutive. (See Lesson 16A.3a(2)(a).) Like the shortened imperfect with the *vav* consecutive, the shortened jussive forms sometimes move the accent from the last syllable to the penultimate.

(b) In strong verbs the shortening of the jussive occurs only in *hifil* forms which normally have a *hireq-yod* in the second syllable. In these forms the jussive tends to shorten the *hireq-yod* to a *sere*, as the following illustrates.

- *Impf, hif, 3MS* forms from the root מׁשל:

---

[1] The jussive occurs in the second person in prohibitions (see section 17C.2) and on rare occasions in the first person. See Joüon, §114g.

Non-jussive: יַמְשִׁיל = "he will rule"

Jussive: יַמְשֵׁל = "let him rule" or "may he rule"

(c) In weak verbs the shortening of the imperfect in jussive can occur in other stems besides *hifil* and can involve the loss of a consonant as well as the reduction of a vowel, as the following illustrates.

- *Impf, qal, 3MS* forms from the root היה:

  Non-jussive: יִהְיֶה = "he will be"

  Jussive: יְהִי = "let him be"

(2) For most verb roots, however, the jussive and non-jussive forms of the imperfect are spelled the same. In such cases the context of the verb is the key to recognizing the presence of a jussive, as illustrated by most of the examples in the next paragraph.

b. The jussive may convey a wide range of volitional ideas, such as desire, wish, request, advice, invitation, exhortation, order, or command. While there are a variety of English expressions which can convey the nuances of the jussive, it is often useful to employ such auxiliary verbs as "let" or "may." In the following examples the jussive verbs appear in parentheses in the translations.[1]

- יֵלֶךְ־נָא אֲדֹנָי בְּקִרְבֵּנוּ = "Please let the Lord go (יֵלֶךְ) in our midst" (Ex 34:9)
- כָל־מֹצְאִי יַהַרְגֵנִי[2] = "Anyone who finds me may kill me (יַהַרְגֵנִי) (Ge 4:14)
- יַחַד הָרִים יְרַנֵּנוּ = "Let the hills sing (יְרַנֵּנוּ) together for joy" (Ps 98:8)
- יְבָרֶכְךָ יְהוָה וְיִשְׁמְרֶךָ = "May the LORD bless you (יְבָרֶכְךָ) and keep you (וְיִשְׁמְרֶךָ)" (Nu 6:24)
- וַיֹּאמְרוּ יְחִי הַמֶּלֶךְ = "And they said, 'Long live (יְחִי) the king!'" (1Sa 10:24)

---

[1] The term "jussive" comes from a Latin verb that means "to order." For these and other jussive examples see Joüon, §114h-l; and Waltke and O'Connor, §34.3a-d.

[2] The symbol □̂ is used in this and succeeding lessons to mark a pausal accent, whether the accent in *BHS* is an *atnah, silluq,* or a more minor accent.

✓ Note that the first example above uses the particle נָא with a jussive verb. This particle often appears in volitional expressions and can therefore be a clue to the presence of a jussive, cohortative, imperative, or prohibitive verb. Grammarians have traditionally assigned an entreaty function to this particle and translated it with such words as "please," "now," or "I pray." However, it is sometimes best to leave the particle untranslated.[1]

3. Cohortative

a. The cohortative can occur only in the first person, singular or plural, of the imperfect. It is formed by adding a ◌ָה suffix to the first person imperfect, as the following examples illustrate.

	Imperfect, *1CS & 1CP*	
	Non-Cohortative	*Cohortative*
Qal	אֶמְשֹׁל ("I will rule")	אֶמְשְׁלָה ("May I rule")
	נִמְשֹׁל ("We will rule")	נִמְשְׁלָה ("Let us rule")
Hifil	אַמְשִׁיל ("I will cause to rule")	אַמְשִׁ֫ילָה ("Let me cause to rule")
	נַמְשִׁיל ("We will cause to rule")	נַמְשִׁ֫ילָה ("May we cause to rule")

b. Notes concerning the cohortative

(1) The *qal* examples above show that when the cohortative suffix is attached to a word it creates a new syllable that receives the accent, and the preceding vowel (under second consonant of the root) reduces from *holem* to *sheva*. However, the *hifil* examples indicate that when the vowel before the suffix is naturally-long (*hireq-yod*), the accent does not move to the syllable with the suffix, and the naturally-long vowel does not reduce.

(2) Note that the second cohortative verb in the preceding chart (נִמְשְׁלָה = "Let us rule") is spelled the same as the perfect, *nifal, 3FS* form ("She will be ruled"). Whether the cohortative or the perfect, *nifal* is intended can be determined from the context in which the verb appears.

c. The cohortative, like the jussive, can convey a wide range of volitional ideas, such as desire, intention, request, resolve, or encouragement. While there are a variety

[1] See Kautzsch, §105b; and Lambdin, 170.

of English expressions which can communicate the nuances of the cohortative, it is often useful to translate a cohortative with such auxiliary verbs as "let" or "may." In the following examples the cohortative verbs appear in parentheses in the translations.[1]

- לְכוּ־נָא וְנִוָּכְחָה = "Come now, and let us reason together (וְנִוָּכְחָה)" (Is 1:18)
- הַצִּילֵנִי מִטִּיט וְאַל־אֶטְבָּעָה אִנָּצְלָה = "Rescue me from the mire, that I may not sink (אֶטְבָּעָה); let me be rescued (אִנָּצְלָה)" (Ps 69:15; *Eng* 69:14)
- נְנַתְּקָה אֶת־מוֹסְרוֹתֵימוֹ וְנַשְׁלִיכָה מִמֶּנּוּ עֲבֹתֵימוֹ = "Let us rip off (נְנַתְּקָה) their bonds, and let us throw (וְנַשְׁלִיכָה) their cords from us" (Ps 2:3)
- וְהָבִיאָה לִּי וְאֹכֵלָה = "And bring it to me, that I may eat (וְאֹכֵלָה)" (Ge 27:4)
- אוּלַי אֲכַפְּרָה בְּעַד חַטַּאתְכֶם = "Perhaps I can make atonement (אֲכַפְּרָה) for your sin" (Ex 32:30)

d. While the jussive and the cohortative have similar volitional connotations, they are distinct from one another in that the jussive normally occurs in the third person, imperfect, and the cohortative occurs only in the first person, imperfect.

17B Imperative Conjugation of the Verb

1. Introduction

a. As stated earlier, the imperative – like the jussive and cohortative – is a volitional verb form. It expresses volition in the form of a command. The Hebrew imperative, however, is used only for positive commands. Prohibitions, or negative commands, employ the imperfect conjugation, as discussed later in this lesson.

b. The imperative occurs in two forms: a regular form, which is most common, and a long form. The regular form is presented first.

[1] The term "cohortative" literally refers to mutual encouragement. For these and other cohortative examples see Joüon, §114b-f; and Waltke and O'Connor, §34.5.1-2.

2. Regular imperative conjugation in the major stems

a. The imperative verb occurs only in the second person and typically not in the *pual* and *hofal* stems. Since there is no *3MS* imperative, the *2MS* form is the simplest in each stem and the one on which the other forms are based. The following chart presents the conjugation of the regular imperative verb, using the strong root משל as a model. It provides all forms for the *qal* stem and the *2MS* forms for the other relevant stems. Mastery of these forms is one key to learning the imperative conjugation. The translations convey common meanings of the imperative in the various stems; other connotations are also possible.

	Imperative						
	Qal	*Nifal*	*Piel*	*Pual*	*Hifil*	*Hofal*	*Hitpael*
2MS	מְשֹׁל "rule"	הִמָּשֵׁל "be ruled"	מַשֵּׁל "<u>rule</u>"		הַמְשֵׁל "cause to rule"		הִתְמַשֵּׁל "rule yourself"
2FS	מִשְׁלִי "rule"						
2MP	מִשְׁלוּ "rule"						
2FP	מְשֹׁלְנָה "rule"						

✓ The full conjugation of the imperative verb, using משל as a model, appears in Appendix 3, paradigm 1.

b. Notes concerning the imperative conjugation

(1) The imperative verb is similar to the second person imperfect verb. In fact, all forms of the imperative, *piel* are spelled exactly like the imperfect, *piel* minus the imperfect prefix.

- תְּמַשֵּׁל (*impf, piel, 2MS*) minus prefix = מַשֵּׁל (*impv, piel, 2MS*) The same pattern is followed in *2FS, 2MP,* and *2FP.*

(2) The imperative, *qal* also resembles the imperfect, *qal* without the prefix. One additional difference in *qal* is that the *2FS* and *2MP* imperatives require a *hireq* under the first consonant of the root instead of the *sheva* which appears

under the first root consonant in the imperfect (else there would be the impossible situation of the imperative forms beginning with two *shevas*).

- תִּמְשֹׁל (*impf, qal, 2MS*) minus prefix = מְשֹׁל (*impv, qal, 2MS*). The same pattern is followed in *2FP*.
- תִּמְשְׁלִי (*impf, qal, 2FS*) minus prefix (= מְשְׁלִי) + lengthening of first vowel = מִשְׁלִי (*impv, qal, 2FS*). The same pattern is followed in *2MP*.

(3) The other imperative stems also employ spellings which are very similar – but not identical – to the pointings of the imperfect verb.

(a) In *nifal* the imperative and imperfect are spelled the same except that the imperative employs a הִ prefix, while the imperfect has prefixes of יִ, תִּ, אֶ, or נִ.

✓ Note that the prefix הִ also occurs in perfect, *hifil;* however, the imperative, *nifal* can easily be distinguished from the perfect, *hifil* by the pointing of the first root consonant.

- *Perf, hif, 3MS:* הִמְשִׁיל
- *Impv, nif, 2MS:* הִמָּשֵׁל

(b) In *hifil* the imperative is spelled the same as the imperfect except for two differences. One is that the imperative employs a הַ prefix, while the imperfect has prefixes of יַ, תַּ, אַ, or נַ. Also, imperative *hifil, 2MS* has a final vowel of *sere*, rather than the *hireq-yod* which appears in imperfect, *hifil, 2MS*.

✓ Note that in *hifil* the imperative and imperfect employ the same prefix vowel (*patah*), while the imperative and perfect employ the same prefix consonant (ה).

(c) In *hitpael* the imperative is like the imperfect except that the imperative employs a הִתְ prefix, while the imperfect has prefixes of יִתְ, תִּתְ, אֶתְ, or נִתְ.

✓ Note that the imperative and the perfect employ the same prefix in this stem (הִתְ). In fact, in *hitpael* the imperative *2MS* form (הִתְמַשֵּׁל) is identical to the perfect *3MS*, and the imperative *2MP* (הִתְמַשְּׁלוּ) is the same as the perfect *3CP*. The context in which these forms appear make clear which conjugation is intended.

c. Another key to learning the imperative verb is mastery of the following clues for recognizing the forms of the imperative. (These clues appear in summary form in Appendix 1.)

(1) General clues for recognizing regular imperative verbs from strong roots

(a) Imperative verbs have some vowels that are similar to the imperfect and they employ the same suffixes; however, imperatives never have the prefixes of the imperfect.

(b) All imperative verbs are second person; their gender and number can be identified by the presence of the same suffixes that are used with the imperfect.

2MS	□□□	*2MP*	□□□וּ
2FS	□□□ִי	*2FP*	□□□ְנָה

(c) As stated previously, the particle נָא often occurs with volitional verb forms; therefore, it can be a clue to the presence of an imperative.

(2) Clues for recognizing the stems of regular imperative verbs from strong roots

(a) *Qal:* □ְ□ֹ□ or □ְ□ַ□

✓ *Sheva* and *holem* appear beneath the first two root consonants in *2MS* and *2FP*. The first two vowels are *hireq* and *sheva* in *2FS* and *2MP*.

(b) *Nifal:* הִ□ָּ□ֵ□

(c) *Piel:* □ַ□ֵּ□

(d) *Hifil:* הַ□ְ□ֵ□

(e) *Hitpael:* הִתְ□ַ□ֵּ□

3. Long form of the imperative

a. The *2MS* imperative sometimes appears in a longer form which involves the addition of a □ָה suffix (also called a paragogic ["added"] ה). While this form may have originally served as an emphatic imperative, it seems to have lost that nuance. Thus, in the Hebrew Bible it appears to have the same meaning as the regular imperative.[1]

[1] Joüon, §143d; Lambdin, 114.

b. The ◌ָה suffix can appear in *2MS* in any stem of the imperative, although it usually appears in *qal*. The suffix causes certain changes in pointing, as the following examples illustrate.

	Imperative, *2MS*	
	Regular Form	*Long Form*
Qal	מְלֹךְ	מָלְכָה ("reign")
	שְׁמֹר	שָׁמְרָה ("keep")
	שְׁלַח	שִׁלְחָה ("send")
Nifal	[none]	הִשָּׁבְעָה ("swear")
Piel	מַהֵר	מַהֲרָה ("hurry")

c. Notes concerning the long form of the imperative

(1) In the long form the first consonant of the root in *qal* usually takes a *qames-hatuf*, as the first two examples in the preceding chart indicate. The third example illustrates a weak verb (with a final guttural consonant) which takes a first vowel of *hireq* in the long form. The *nifal* example only appears in the long form, and the *piel* example is a weak verb, whose second consonant cannot take a *dagesh-forte*.

(2) Sometimes the long form of the imperative is similar to forms in other conjugations. For example, in some verbs the long form resembles the perfect, *qal, 3FS*. For example, compare the following:

מָלְכָה = *impv, qal, MS* + ה suffix [long form] ("reign")

מָֽלְכָה = *perf, qal, 3FS* ("she reigned").

The two forms can be distinguished by the fact that the imperative has a *qames-hatuf* as the first vowel, and the perfect has a *qames*. A *meteg* helps make this distinction when it appears with the perfect verb; otherwise the context of the verb is the clue to recognizing its form.

(3) While the long form of the imperative and the cohortative take the same suffix (◌ָה), they can easily be distinguished from one another since the cohortative has either the *1CS* or *1CP* imperfect prefix (**א** or **נ**).

17C Verbs of Prohibition

Prohibition, or a negative command, is not expressed by the imperative conjugation, but by a second person imperfect with one of two negative particles.

1. The negative particle לֹא with an imperfect often expresses the concept of absolute or permanent prohibition.
   - לֹא תִּגְנֹב = "You will not steal" or "Never steal" (Ex 20:15)
2. The negative particle אַל appears with jussives to express prohibitions that are less direct or aimed at stopping something immediately or temporarily.
   - אַל־תִּירְאוּ אֶת־עַם הָאָרֶץ = "Do not fear (stop fearing) (אַל־תִּירְאוּ) the people of the land" (Nu 14:9)
   - אַל־נָא תַעֲבֹר מֵעַל עַבְדֶּךָ = "Please do not pass (אַל־נָא תַעֲבֹר) by your servant" (Ge 18:3)

✓ Note that the second example above employs נָא as a particle of entreaty.

17D Analysis of Volitional Verb Forms

The analysis of volitional verb forms – the jussive, cohortative, and imperative – is illustrated in the following chart. Jussive and cohortative verbs are part of the imperfect conjugation but also require indication of their unique forms as jussives (*juss*) and cohortatives (*cohort*). Imperative verbs require indication of their conjugation (*impv*), and the long forms are identified by means of the additional feature of a ה suffix.

Word	Root	Conju-gation	Stem	P/G/N	Additional Features	Translation
יֵרֶא (2Ch 24:22)	> ראה	*impf, juss*	*qal*	*3MS*		"may he see"
וַאֲבָרְכָה (Ge 12:3)	> ברך	*impf, cohort*	*piel*	*1CS*	+ *vav conj*	"and let me bless"
דַּבְּרוּ (Ge 50:4)	> דבר	*impv*	*piel*	*2MP*		"speak"
וְאָכְלָה (Ge 27:19)	> אכל	*impv*	*qal*	*2MS*	+ *vav conj* & ה suffix	"and eat"
אַל־יִחַר (Ex 32:22)	> חרה	*impf, juss*	*qal*	*3MS*	+ אַל	"do not burn with anger"

Lesson 17: Exercises

a. Reproduce from memory the imperative forms of משׁל for the *qal* stem in all persons, genders, and numbers (that is, *2MS*, *2FS*, *2MP*, and *2FP*) and the *2MS* imperative forms of this verb for the other major stems. Then give a translation of all forms. (Appendix 3, item 16, has an imperative practice chart.)

b. Without consulting any charts, identify the following symbolic forms in terms of conjugation (*perf, impf,* or *impv*) and person, gender, and number. Do not assume the forms have any other prefixes or suffixes than the ones that actually appear. If more than one answer is possible, give all options.

- *Example:* □□□ו ⇒ *Answer: impv, 2mp;* or *perf, 3CP*

(1) □□□ִי
(2) י□□□וּ
(3) א□□□
(4) □□□תִּי
(5) ת□□□ִי
(6) □□□תֶּן
(7) נ□□□
(8) □□□תְּ
(9) □□□ְנָה
(10) □□□ָה
(11) י□□□
(12) □□□תָּ
(13) □□□נוּ
(14) ת□□□ְנָה
(15) ת□□□
(16) □□□תֶּם
(17) ת□□□וּ

c. Without consulting any charts, identify the following symbolic forms in terms of conjugation (*perf, impf,* or *impv*) and stem (*qal, nif, piel,* etc.). Do not assume the occurrence of a *dagesh-forte* except where indicated. If more than one answer is possible, give all options.

✓ This exercise does not intend to indicate particular *P/G/N*, as suggested by the lack of suffixes. It is concerned with indicating the clues for conjugations and stems.

- *Example:* הִתְ□ַ⊡□ ⇒ *Answer: Impv, hit;* or *perf, hit*

(1) הִ□ְ□□
(2) □ַ⊡□
(3) ◁ִ⊡□□
(4) ◁ְ□ֻ⊡□
(5) ◁ֶ□ְ□□
(6) נִ□ְ□□
(7) □ְ□ֹ□
(8) ◁ֲ□ַ⊡□
(9) ◁ַ□ְ□□
(10) הִ⊡ָ□□
(11) □ִ⊡□
(12) ◁ִתְ□ַ⊡□
(13) הָ□ְ□□
(14) הַ□ְ□□
(15) ◁ֲ□ֻ⊡□
(16) ◁ֶ⊡ָ□□
(17) ◁ְ□ַ⊡□
(18) ◁ִ□ְ□□
(19) □ִ□ְ□
(20) □ֻ⊡□
(21) ◁ָ□ְ□□
(22) ◁ֶתְ□ַ⊡□

d. Learn to recognize, pronounce, and translate the following vocabulary.

	Word	*Translation*	*Notes*
(1)	אַל	no, not (*particle*)	
(2)	גָּלָה	he uncovered, revealed, went into exile (*V*)	
(3)	חָיָה	he lived, revived (*V*)	
(4)	נָא	please, now, I pray (*particle*)	Usually employed with *cohort, juss*, or *impv*
(5)	עֶ֫בֶד	servant, slave (*NMS*)	*PS:* עַבְדִּי, עַבְדְּךָ, etc.; *P:* עֲבָדִים, עַבְדֵי
(6)	עַ֫יִן	eye (*NFS*)	*Du:* עֵינַ֫יִם
(7)	צוה[1]	צִוָּה (*piel*): he commanded, ordered (*V*)	Only occurs in *piel* and *pual*
(8)	שְׁנַ֫יִם (*M*), שְׁתַּ֫יִם[2] (*F*)	two (*N M/F Du*)	Occurs only in *Du; Cs:* שְׁנֵי (*M*), שְׁתֵּי (*F*); שֵׁנִי (*M*), שֵׁנִית (*F*) = "second"
(9)	תָּ֫וֶךְ	midst, middle (*NMS*)	*Cs:* תּוֹךְ

e. Analyze the following verbs, using a lexicon as necessary. When more than one option is possible, consult the biblical text to determine which is appropriate in context.

- *Example:* אַל־תִּשְׂמַח (Hos 9:1) ⇒ *Answer:* > שׂמח, *impf, juss, qal, 2MS* + אַל, "stop rejoicing"

---

[1] Since this verb never occurs in *qal*, its lexical form cannot be the *perf, qal, 3MS* form; instead the root (without vowels) serves as the lexical form.

[2] The numbers from two to ten occur as both masculine and feminine nouns. The ordinal numbers from two to ten also have related cardinals ("second," "third," etc.), which are formed by means of the suffixes ◌ִי (*M*) or ◌ִית (*F*). The spelling of the feminine ordinal number שְׁתַּ֫יִם (šta/yim = "two") is irregular. The *sheva* is silent and the תּ has a *dagesh-lene*. The same is true for the construct form of this word: שְׁתֵּי (štê). See Kautzsch, §97b.

(1)	צַוֵּה	(Jos 4:16)	(8)	אִנָּצֵלָה	(Ps 69:15; *Eng* 69:14)
(2)	לֹא תִּגְנֹב	(Ex 20:15)	(9)	קִרְאוּ	(Jdg 16:25)
(3)	הִשָּׁמְרִי	(Jdg 13:4)	(10)	מָֽצְאָה	(Lv 25:28)
(4)	וְנִזְבְּחָה	(Ex 3:18)	(11)	אַל־יִמְשְׁלוּ	(Ps 19:14; *Eng* 19:13)
(5)	יַכְרֵת	(Ps 12:4; *Eng* 12:3)	(12)	וַאֲגַדְּלָה	(Ge 12:2)
(6)	וְאָכְלָה	(Ge 27:19)	(13)	הַקְשִׁיבָה	(Ps 5:3; *Eng* 5:2)
(7)	שְׁמַעְנָה	(Is 32:9)	(14)	הִתְחַזְּקוּ	(1Sa 4:9)

f. Read aloud and translate the following texts from the Hebrew Bible with the help of a lexicon. Also provide an analysis of all verbs.

✓ The following notes aid in identifying certain weak verb roots and unfamiliar grammatical forms. Consult a lexicon for assitance in identifying the stems of weak verbs whose vowels differ from those of strong verbs.

(1) Genesis 1:6-8

Verse 6

(a) יְהִי < היה

(b) מַבְדִּיל (> בדל) is a participle, *hifil*. The מַ prefix and the *hireq-yod* are typical in participle, *hifil*. Consult a lexicon for its translation.

Verse 7

Even though וַיַּעַשׂ (> עשׂה) has a יַ prefix, it is not a *hifil* verb, as indicated by the fact that the lexicon lists no *hifil* forms for this verb. The guttural consonant ע requires the A-class prefix vowel.

(2) Psalm 119:17-19

Verse 18

(a) גַּל (> גלה) loses its final root consonant in this form; the *patah* is the clue to this verb's conjugation and stem.

(b) וְאַבִּיטָה (> נבט) loses its first root consonant in this form; the נ is assimilated into the בּ by means of a *dagesh-forte*.

(c) נִפְלָאוֹת (> פלא) is a participle, *nifal*, feminine, plural; it serves as the object of a verb. See a lexicon for its meaning.

Lesson 18

Infinitive, Participle

18A Infinitive

1. Introduction

a. As stated previously, perfect, imperfect, and imperative verbs are finite. Their action is limited by inflection (through prefixes and suffixes) to particular persons, genders, and numbers. Hebrew has two additional conjugations that are not finite: the infinitive and the participle. These two conjugations are non-finite in that they lack the typical inflectional limitations of finite verbs. This section will consider the infinitive, and the next the participle.

b. The infinitive is a verbal noun, which means that it shares some characteristics of verbs and some of nouns. In form it is like a verb in that it is built on a verb root and appears in the verb stems. However, the infinitive is unlike a verb in that it has no person, gender, or number. One way the infinitive is like the noun is that it sometimes takes prefixed prepositions; other similarities to nouns will be discussed later.

c. Hebrew infinitives appear in two states: construct and absolute. While these two terms are also used of nouns, they have different meanings when applied to infinitives. The infinitive construct, which is much more common, is discussed first.

2. Infinitive construct

a. The following chart presents the conjugation of the infinitive construct in the major stems where it occurs, using the strong verb root מָשַׁל as a model. Since infinitives have no person, gender, or number, each stem has only one form. The infinitive construct is used in ways similar to the English infinitive ("to rule") and gerund ("ruling"). These two notions are suggested by the translations; other connotations are also possible.

Infinitive Construct						
Qal	*Nifal*	*Piel*	*Pual*	*Hifil*	*Hofal*	*Hitpael*
מְשֹׁל "(to) rule/ ruling"	הִמָּשֵׁל "(to) be ruled/being ruled"	מַשֵּׁל "(to) rule/ ruling"		הַמְשִׁיל "(to) cause to rule/ causing to rule"		הִתְמַשֵּׁל "(to) rule one's self/ ruling one's self"

b. Notes concerning the infinitive construct conjugation

(1) In *qal, nifal, piel,* and *hitpael,* the form of the infinitive construct is identical to the *2MS* imperative. The *hifil* forms in these two conjugations differ in that the infinitive construct takes a *hireq-yod* in the last syllable (הַמְשִׁיל), while the *2MS* imperative has a *sere* (הַמְשֵׁל). (See the chart in section 18A.4a.) The infinitive construct of the strong verb does not appear in the other major stems.

(2) The infinitive construct often has a prefixed preposition ל ("to"). However, the prepositional idea can be implied even when there is no prefixed preposition. Consequently, the English preposition "to" appears in parentheses in the translations of the preceding chart. The infinitive construct can also take other prefixed prepositions, as discussed below.

c. Function of the infinitive construct[1]

(1) The infinitive construct can function like a verb in the sense of having a subject or object. (The infinitive appears in parentheses after its translation in the following examples.)

- לָמוּת שָׁם אֲנַחְנוּ וּבְעִירֵנוּ = "to die (לָמוּת) there, we and our cattle," or more idiomatically, "so that we and our cattle would die there" (Nu 20:4).

  The infinitive has a double subject (אֲנַחְנוּ וּבְעִירֵנוּ). Its root has a middle *vav* (מוּת). In weak verbs of this sort the *vav* becomes a vowel in infinitive, *qal*, construct.

- לְנַשֵּׁק לְבָנַי וְלִבְנֹתָי = "to kiss (לְנַשֵּׁק) my sons and daughters" (Ge 31:28).

  In this phrase the infinitive has a double object (לְבָנַי וְלִבְנֹתָי).

[1] This discussion follows the approach of Lambdin, 128-29. For the following examples and others see Joüon, §124; Waltke and O'Connor, §36.2-36.3; and Williams, §192-200.

(2) The infinitive construct – sometimes accompanied by a subject or object – can function substantivally (like a noun) in a sentence. Usually it serves as a subject or predicate nominative in a verbless clause. However, it can serve other substantival roles, such as the object of a verb or a genitive in a construct phrase.[1]

- הִנֵּה שְׁמֹעַ מִזֶּבַח טוֹב לְהַקְשִׁיב מֵחֵלֶב אֵילִים = "Behold, to obey (שְׁמֹעַ) is better than sacrifice; to heed (לְהַקְשִׁיב) better than the fat of rams" (1Sa 15:22).

  In this verse two infinitives serve as subjects of verbless clauses; the first one without a preposition, the second one with a prefixed לְ.

- וְזֶה הַחִלָּם לַעֲשׂוֹת = "And this is (the) beginning of them (הַחִלָּם) to do," or more idiomatically, "And this is what they are beginning to do" (Ge 11:6).

  The first infinitive (הַחִלָּם) is *hifil*, construct with a pronominal suffix; it serves as a predicate nominative in this clause.

- לֹא אֵדַע צֵאת וָבֹא = "Not I know to go out (צֵאת) or to come in (וָבֹא)," or more idiomatically, "I do not know how to go out or to come in" (1Ki 3:7).

  The verb in this clause (אֵדַע) has two infinitives as objects. Both are *qal*, construct and come from weak roots.

- בְּיוֹם אֲכָלְךָ = "in the day of your eating (אֲכָלְךָ)" (Ge 2:17).

  The construct noun (בְּיוֹם) is followed by an infinitive that functions genitively in the construct phrase. The infinitive is *qal*, construct with a pronominal suffix.

(3) Most often the infinitive construct is connected to a preposition. It can follow an independent preposition, but more frequently it has one of the prefixed prepositions בְּ, כְּ, or לְ. With these prepositions an infinitive construct can function verbally and substantivally, as illustrated previously. However, very commonly such constructions serve to modify or complement verbs.

(a) With the prepositions בְּ and כְּ an infinitive construct usually serves the role of a temporal clause in English.

---

[1] Lambdin, 128-29.

- בְּעָמְדוֹ לִפְנֵי פַּרְעֹה = "in his standing (בְּעָמְדוֹ) before Pharaoh," or more idiomatically, "when he stood before Pharaoh" (Ge 41:46).

  The infinitive, *qal*, construct (בְּעָמְדוֹ) has a pronominal suffix, which affects its vowel pointing.
- וַיְהִי כְּבוֹא אַבְרָם מִצְרָיְמָה = "And it happened as coming (כְּבוֹא), Abram, to Egypt," or more idiomatically, "And it happened as soon as Abram came to Egypt" (Ge 12:14).

(b) Infinitive constructs appear quite often with ל to complement or explain verbs in a wide variety of ways.

- וַיְמָאֵן לְהִתְנַחֵם = "And he refused to comfort himself (לְהִתְנַחֵם)," or "And he refused to be comforted" (Ge 37:35).
- וְשָׁמְרוּ בְנֵי־יִשְׂרָאֵל אֶת־הַשַּׁבָּת לַעֲשׂוֹת אֶת־הַשַּׁבָּת = "And the children of Israel will keep the sabbath to do (לַעֲשׂוֹת) the sabbath," or more idiomatically, "And the children of Israel will keep the sabbath by observing it" (Ex 31:16).
- וַיְדַבֵּר אֱלֹהִים אֶל־נֹחַ לֵאמֹר = "And God spoke to Noah saying (לֵאמֹר)" (Ge 8:15).

  The infinitive construct אֱמֹר with ל is a special case. It is spelled irregularly in that the א becomes quiescent and the preposition takes a *sere* as compensation: לֵאמֹר. When introducing a quotation, as in this verse, it is an idiom for "saying."

✓ The preceding examples illustrate the fact that prepositions are quite flexible in their connotations. Their meanings are impacted by their usages in sentences and by the meanings of accompanying verbs.

3. Infinitive absolute

a. The infinitive absolute, like the infinitive construct, cannot be inflected to show person, gender, or number. The forms of the infinitive absolute appear in the following chart, using the strong verb משל as a model. The translations suggest one option for the meanings of the infinitive absolute in the major stems; other connotations are also possible, as discussed below.

Infinitive Absolute						
Qal	*Nifal*	*Piel*	*Pual*	*Hifil*	*Hofal*	*Hitpael*
[1] מָשׁוֹל	נִמְשֹׁל or [2] הִמָּשֵׁל	מַשֹּׁל or מַשֵּׁל	מֻשֹּׁל	הַמְשֵׁל	הָמְשֵׁל	הִתְמַשֵּׁל
"ruling"	"being ruled"	"ruling"	"being ruled"	"causing to rule"	"being caused to rule"	"ruling one's self"

b. Notes concerning the infinitive absolute conjugation

(1) Two patterns commonly occur with regard to the infinitive absolute in *nifal* and *piel*. The second option in *piel* (מַשֵּׁל) is spelled exactly like the infinitive construct and the *2MS* imperative in this stem.

(2) Three other forms of the infinitive absolute are spelled the same as forms in other conjugations: one of the infinitive, *nifal,* absolute forms (נִמְשֹׁל) is identical to the imperfect, *qal, 1CP;* the infinitive, *hifil,* absolute (הַמְשֵׁל) is the same as the imperative, *hifil, 2MS;* and the infinitive, *hitpael,* absolute (הִתְמַשֵּׁל) is the same as *hitpael* forms in the infinitive construct, the *3MS* perfect, and the *2MS* imperative. (See the chart in section 18A.4a.)

c. Function of the infinitive absolute[3]

(1) The infinitive absolute functions in ways that have little parallel in English grammar. It usually serves an adverbial role and as a rule does not take prefixed prepositions.

(2) Most frequently the infinitive absolute appears along with a finite verb (*perf, impf,* or *impv*) and serves to intensify or complement the verb in some way. It usually precedes a cognate verb – that is, a verb of the same root as the infinitive. Less frequently the infinitive absolute follows a verb, which may or

[1] In some verbs this form is spelled according to the pattern of מָשֹׁל.

[2] Sometimes the spelling of the infinitive, *nifal,* construct (הִמָּשֵׁל) is employed as the infinitive, *nifal,* absolute, especially for the sake of assonance (similarity of sound). Such may occur, for example, in a situation like הִמָּשֵׁל יִמָּשֵׁל. Joüon, §51b.

[3] For the following examples and others see Waltke and O'Connor, §35.2-35.5; and Williams, §201-212.

may not be a cognate.[1] When the infinitive absolute intensifies a verb, that intensity may be translated in a wide variety of ways, depending upon the verb's meaning and its context. Often it is useful in translation to use such terms as "indeed," "certainly," or "really." To illustrate, in הַמְשֵׁל יַמְשִׁיל (= "causing to rule, he will cause to rule") an infinitive, *hifil,* absolute precedes an imperfect, *hifil* verb. The phrase may be translated "He will certainly cause to rule." In מָשַׁל מָשׁוֹל (= "he ruled, ruling") an infinitive, *qal,* absolute follows a perfect, *qal* verb. It may be translated "He indeed ruled." Biblical examples follow.

- אָמוֹר אָמַרְתִּי בֵּיתְךָ וּבֵית אָבִיךָ יִתְהַלְּכוּ לְפָנַי = "Saying (אָמוֹר), I said that your house and your father's house will walk before me," or more idiomatically, "Indeed, I have promised that your house and your father's house will minister before me" (1Sa 2:30).

  An infinitive, *qal,* absolute (אָמוֹר) precedes a cognate perfect, *qal* verb (אָמַרְתִּי), intensifying its action.

- שָׁמוֹר תִּשְׁמְרוּן אֶת־מִצְוֺת יְהוָה = "Keeping (שָׁמוֹר), you will keep the commandments of the LORD," or more idiomatically, "You must keep the commandments of the LORD" (Dt 6:17).

  Here an infinitive, *qal,* absolute (שָׁמוֹר) precedes and intensifies an imperfect, *qal* that is a cognate verb (תִּשְׁמְרוּן).

- שִׁמְעוּ שָׁמוֹעַ וְאַל־תָּבִינוּ = "Hear, hearing (שָׁמוֹעַ), but do not comprehend," or "Hear indeed, but do not understand" (Is 6:9).

  An infinitive, *qal,* absolute (שָׁמוֹעַ) follows a cognate imperative, *piel* (שִׁמְעוּ). The infinitive intensifies the action of the verb.

- קְבוּרַת חֲמוֹר יִקָּבֵר סָחוֹב וְהַשְׁלֵךְ = "With the burial of a donkey he will be buried, dragging off (סָחוֹב) and casting away (וְהַשְׁלֵךְ)," or more idiomatically, "He will be buried like a donkey, dragged off and cast away" (Jer 22:19).

[1] In the past grammarians concluded that when the infinitive absolute follows a finite verb it gives a durative or repetitive quality to the verb. More recent grammarians have tended to move away from such a view, claiming instead that when the infinitive absolute appears after a verb it does not necessarily convey a different nuance than when it occurs before a verb. See Waltke and O'Connor, §35.3.1d.

An imperfect, *nifal* (יִקָּבֵר) is followed by two infinitive constructs that are not cognates. The infinitives (סָחוֹב and וְהַשְׁלֵךְ) complement the action of the verb.

(3) An infinitive absolute sometimes serves the role of a finite verb, most commonly replacing an imperative.

- זָכוֹר אֶת־יוֹם הַשַּׁבָּת = "Remember (זָכוֹר) the Sabbath day" (Ex 20:8).

  This infinitive, *qal,* absolute serves the function of an imperative in this clause.

- כֹּה אָמַר יְהוָה אָכֹל וְהוֹתֵר = "Thus the LORD says, 'Eating (אָכֹל) and having some leftover (וְהוֹתֵר),'" or more idiomatically, "Thus the LORD says, 'They will eat and have some leftover'" (2Ki 4:43).

  Two infinitive absolutes – the first *qal* (אָכֹל) and the second *hifil* (וְהוֹתֵר) – serve the role of imperfect verbs in this verse.

(4) Occasionally an infinitive absolute functions like a substantive, such as the subject of a clause, a predicate nominative, or a genitive following a construct noun.

- אָכֹל דְּבַשׁ הַרְבּוֹת לֹא־טוֹב = "Eating (אָכֹל) too much honey is not good" (Pr 25:27).

  This infinitive, *qal,* absolute is the subject of the clause.

- מוּסַר הַשְׂכֵּל = "the discipline of being prudent (הַשְׂכֵּל)" (Pr 1:3).

  This infinitive, *hifil,* absolute functions genitively in relationship with a construct noun.

4. Summary of the infinitive construct and absolute

a. As suggested by the following chart, it is helpful to compare the forms of the infinitive construct and absolute with one another and with certain forms of the imperative, perfect, and imperfect in order to note similarities and differences.

Infinitive Construct						
Qal	*Nifal*	*Piel*	*Pual*	*Hifil*	*Hofal*	*Hitpael*
מְשֹׁל	הִמָּשֵׁל	מַשֵּׁל		הַמְשִׁיל		הִתְמַשֵּׁל
Infinitive Absolute						
מָשׁוֹל	נִמְשֹׁל or הִמָּשֵׁל	מַשֹּׁל or מַשֵּׁל	מֻשֹּׁל	הַמְשֵׁל	הָמְשֵׁל	הִתְמַשֵּׁל
Imperative *2MS*						
מְשֹׁל	הִמָּשֵׁל	מַשֵּׁל		הַמְשֵׁל		הִתְמַשֵּׁל
Perfect *3MS*						
						הִתְמַשֵּׁל
Imperfect *1CP*						
	נִמָּשֵׁל					

b. A key to learning the infinitive is mastery of the following clues for recognizing their forms and distinguishing them from other conjugations. (These clues appear in summary form in Appendix 1.)

(1) General clues for recognizing the infinitive construct and absolute

(a) Neither the infinitive construct nor absolute can take the verb suffixes that indicate person, gender, and number. Consequently, any imperative form that has a verb suffix (□ִי, וּ, or נָה) can be easily distinguished from the infinitive. All imperative forms except *2MS* have such suffixes.

(b) Infinitive constructs are often connected to independent or prefixed prepositions. Perfects, imperatives, and (usually) infinitive absolutes do not take prefixed prepositions or stand as the objects of independent prepositions.

(c) Other than these clues, one can distinguish between similar forms of the infinitive construct, infinitive absolute, imperative, and perfect by means of the context in which the word appears.

(2) Clues for recognizing the stems of infinitives from strong verb roots

(a) *Qal*

[1] Construct: □ְ□ֹ□

[2] Absolute: □ָ□וֹ□

(b) *Nifal*

[1] Construct: הִ□ָּ□ֵ□

[2] Absolute: נִ□ְ□ֹ□ or הִ□ָּ□ֹ□

(c) *Piel*

[1] Construct: □ַ□ֵּ□

[2] Absolute: □ַ□ֹּ□ or □ַ□ֵּ□

(d) *Pual* absolute: □ֻ□ֹּ□

(e) *Hifil*

[1] Construct: הַ□ְ□ִי□

[2] Absolute: הַ□ְ□ֵ□

(f) *Hofal* absolute: הָ□ְ□ֵ□

(g) *Hitpael*

[1] Construct: הִתְ□ַ□ֵּ□

[2] Absolute: הִתְ□ַ□ֵּ□

18B Participle

1. Introduction

a. The participle, like the infinitive, is a non-finite verb form. It lacks the kind of verbal inflections that appear in finite verbs (*perf, impf,* and *impv*) to indicate person, gender, and number.

b. The participle is a verbal adjective, which means that it has some of the characteristics of both verbs and adjectives. In form it is like a verb in that it is built on a verb root and appears in verb stems. A participle is like an adjective (and also a noun) in that it takes the common endings that indicate gender, number, and state for nouns and adjectives. A participle can also appear with the definite article and prefixed prepositions.

2. Participle conjugation in the major stems

a. *Qal* participle

(1) The *qal* stem of the participle is unique in that it has both active and passive forms, something that occurs in no other conjugation. Outside of *qal*, the other stems of the participle are either active or passive, but not both. In other words the *piel*, *hifil*, and *hitpael* participles are active; and the *nifal*, *pual*, and *hofal* participles are passive. The passive form of the *qal* participle, like the *nifal*,

expresses simple action in the passive voice.[1]

(2) As stated above, the participles in all stems take the common endings for nouns and adjectives. The following paradigm presents the forms of the participle, *qal,* active and passive in all genders, numbers, and states, using the strong verb root משׁל.

<table>
<tr><th></th><th colspan="5">Participle, Qal</th></tr>
<tr><th rowspan="2"></th><th colspan="2">Singular</th><th colspan="2">Plural</th><th rowspan="2">Translation</th></tr>
<tr><th>Absolute</th><th>Construct</th><th>Absolute</th><th>Construct</th></tr>
<tr><td></td><td colspan="5">Active</td></tr>
<tr><td>M</td><td>מֹשֵׁל[2]</td><td>מֹשֵׁל</td><td>מֹשְׁלִים</td><td>מֹשְׁלֵי</td><td rowspan="2">“ruling/one(s) ruling”</td></tr>
<tr><td>F</td><td>מֹשֶׁ֫לֶת or מֹשְׁלָה</td><td>מֹשֶׁ֫לֶת or מֹשְׁלַת</td><td>מֹשְׁלוֹת</td><td>מֹשְׁלוֹת</td></tr>
<tr><td></td><td colspan="5">Passive</td></tr>
<tr><td>M</td><td>מָשׁוּל[3]</td><td>מְשׁוּל</td><td>מְשׁוּלִים</td><td>מְשׁוּלֵי</td><td rowspan="2">“being ruled/ one(s) being ruled”</td></tr>
<tr><td>F</td><td>מְשׁוּלָה</td><td>מְשׁוּלַת</td><td>מְשׁוּלוֹת</td><td>מְשׁוּלוֹת</td></tr>
</table>

✓ Two forms appear for the feminine, singular, absolute participle. The most common in *qal* active is ◌ֶת, while ◌ָה is typical for *qal* passive.

b. Participles in all the major stems

Participles in every stem can occur with any of the common noun endings that are illustrated in the preceding chart. However, for the sake of simplicity, the following paradigm presents only the masculine, singular, absolute forms of the participle in all of the stems, again using the strong verb root משׁל as a model. The translations indicate two common options for translating participles in various stems.

[1] Joüon, §417q, suggests that the participle, *qal,* passive connotes completed action, while the participle, *nifal* implies action that is in process.

[2] In some verbs this form is spelled according to the pattern of מוֹשֵׁל.

[3] In some verbs this form is spelled according to the pattern of מָשֻׁל.

Participle, *MS*, Absolute						
Qal	*Nifal*	*Piel*	*Pual*	*Hifil*	*Hofal*	*Hitpael*
Active						
מֹשֵׁל “ruling/ one ruling”		מְמַשֵּׁל “ruling/ one ruling”		מַמְשִׁיל “causing to rule/ one causing to rule”		מִתְמַשֵּׁל “ruling himself/ one ruling himself”
Passive						
מָשׁוּל “being ruled/one being ruled”	נִמְשָׁל “being ruled/one being ruled”		מְמֻשָּׁל “being ruled/one being ruled”		מָמְשָׁל “being caused to rule/one being caused to rule”	

c. Notes concerning the participle conjugation

(1) Five stems of the participle – *piel*, *pual*, *hifil*, *hofal*, and *hitpael* – have the following:

(a) A מ prefix (or מִתְ in the case of *hitpael*)

(b) A pointing which resembles the pointing of the imperfect verb.

(2) All of the passive participle forms in the preceding chart, with the exception of the *qal* passive, have a *qames* as the vowel for the second root consonant in absolute forms.

(a) This pattern is typically followed in all absolute participles in the non-*qal*, passive stems, as illustrated by the following *nifal* absolute forms.

Participle, *nifal*: *MS Ab:* נִמְשָׁל
FS Ab: נִמְשָׁלָה (less often: נִמְשֶׁלֶת)
MP Ab: נִמְשָׁלִים
FP Ab: נִמְשָׁלוֹת

✓ Note that the vowel under the second root consonant distinguishes the participle, *nifal, MS, Ab* (נִמְשָׁל) from the perfect, *nifal, 3MS* (נִמְשַׁל).

Pual and *hofal* absolute participle forms follow the same pattern as the preceding *nifil* forms with regard to the *qames* under the second root consonant.

(b) The *qames* under the second root consonant typically reduces in the construct participle forms of the non-*qal,* passive stems, as illustrated with the following *nifal* construct forms.

Participle, *nifal:* *MS Cs:* נִמְשַׁל
FS Cs: נִמְשְׁלַת (less often: נִמְשֶׁ֫לֶת)
MP Cs: נִמְשְׁלֵי
FP Cs: נִמְשְׁלוֹת

Pual and *hofal* construct participles usually follow the same pattern with regard to the second root consonant.

d. A key to learning the participle is mastery of the following clues for recognizing its forms. (These clues appear in summary form in Appendix 1.)

(1) General clues for recognizing the participle

(a) The appearance of the common endings for nouns and adjectives helps to distinguish the participle from other verb forms outside of the *MS* absolute and construct (which have no ending). The *MS* forms can be recognized by their unique pointing, as described below.

(b) The מ prefix which appears on the in *piel*, *pual*, *hifil*, *hofal*, and *hitpael* readily distinguishes these participles from all other verb forms.

(c) In the absolute forms of the participle in *nifal,* the *qames* under the second root consonant distinguishes it from other verb forms.

(2) Clues for recognizing the stems of strong verb participles

(a) *Qal*

[1] Active: □□□̇

All forms have the unique feature of a *holem* with the first root consonant.

[2] Passive: □וּ□□

All forms have the unique feature of a *shureq* after the second root consonant.

(b) *Nifal*: נִ□ְ□ָ□

In construct forms (*MS, MP, FS,* and *FP*) the *qames* reduces.

(c) *Piel*: מְ□ַ□ּ□

(d) *Pual*: מְ□ֻ□ּ□

(e) *Hifil*: מַ□ְ□□

(f) *Hofal*: מָ□ְ□□

(g) *Hitpael*: מִתְ□ַ□ּ□

3. Function of the participle[1]

a. A participle often functions in the ways that an adjective functions: attributively, predicatively, and substantivally.

(1) When functioning attributively, a participle (like an adjective) follows the noun it modifies and agrees with it in gender, number, and definiteness. It is often useful to translate an attributive participle with a relative clause.

- אֵשׁ אֹכְלָה = "a fire, a consuming (אֹכְלָה)," which means "a consuming fire" (Dt 4:24).
- כָּל־הַכֶּסֶף הַנִּמְצָא = "all of the money, the being found (הַנִּמְצָא)," which means "all of the money which was found" (Ge 47:14).

(2) When a participle functions predicatively it appears in a verbless clause, usually with a stated subject. The predicative participle, which does not take an article, agrees with the subject it modifies in gender and number (like an adjective).

- עֲזֻבוֹת עָרֵי עֲרֹעֵר = "being abandoned (עֲזֻבוֹת) the cities of Aroer," which in its context means "the cities of Aroer will be abandoned" (Is 17:2).

(3) A substantival participle stands in the place of a noun, serving such roles as a subject, predicate nominative, or the object of a verb or preposition. Like a noun, a substantival participle may take the article. Substantival participles may be translated in various ways, sometimes by supplying "one(s)" as the subject of the participle's action, by a relative clause, or simply by a noun which incorporates the verbal notion of the participle. For example, one might

[1] For the examples that follow and others see Horsnell, 78-83; Waltke and O'Connor, §37.1-37.7; and Williams, §213-222.

translate the participle, *qal,* active הַמֹּשֵׁל as "the ruling one," "the one who rules," or "the ruler," depending upon the context in which the word appears.

- וַיִּרְאוּ הַשֹּׁמְרִים אִישׁ = "And the watching ones (הַשֹּׁמְרִים) saw a man," or more idiomatically, "And those who were watching [the city of Bethel] saw a man," or "And the spies saw a man" (Jdg 1:24).

  The participle, *qal,* active (הַשֹּׁמְרִים) is the subject of the verb in this clause.

- וָאֶשְׁמַע אֵת מִדַּבֵּר אֵלָי = "And I heard one speaking (מִדַּבֵּר) to me" (Eze 2:2).

  The participle (מִדַּבֵּר) is serving as the object of a verb. Its stem is *hitpael*. The ת of the מִתְ prefix has been assimilated into the first root consonant by means of a *dagesh-forte*, since the "t" and "d" sounds blend together in speech. A full spelling of the form would be מִתְדַּבֵּר.

- לְשֹׁמְרֵי בְרִיתוֹ = "to keeping ones (לְשֹׁמְרֵי) of his covenant," or more idiomatically, "to those who keep his covenant" (Ps 103:18).

  This participle, *qal,* active (לְשֹׁמְרֵי) is *MS* construct and is limited by the absolute noun that follows it. The participle also serves as the object of a preposition.

b. A participle may also function like a finite verb (*perf, impf,* or *impv*). In this role it often conveys continuous action in the present or past, or it may suggest imminent action.[1] The temporal state of the action is implied by the participle's context. When functioning like a finite verb, a participle can take an object or adverbial complement of some sort.

- כִּי יֹדֵעַ אֱלֹהִים כִּי בְּיוֹם אֲכָלְכֶם מִמֶּנּוּ = "For God knows (יֹדֵעַ) that in the day you eat from it" (Ge 3:5).
- בָּרָק רֹדֵף אֶת־סִיסְרָא = "Barak was pursuing (רֹדֵף) Sisera" (Jdg 4:22).
- וַאֲנִי הִנְנִי מֵבִיא אֶת־הַמַּבּוּל = "And I, behold I, will cause to come (מֵבִיא) the flood," or more idiomatically, "Behold, I will bring the flood" (Ge 6:17).

  מֵבִיא (> בוא) is participle, *hifil,* conveying imminent action.

✓ When a participle does not have an object or adverbial complement, it may be

[1] Williams, §213-214

difficult to distinguish whether it is functioning like a finite verb or a predicate adjective. In such cases it makes little difference which classification is chosen.

18C Analysis of Infinitives and Participles

1. The analysis of infinitives involves identification of the verb root, conjugation (*inf*), stem, state (*Cs* or *Ab*), any additional features, and the translation of the infinitive.
2. The analysis of participles requires identification of the verb root, conjugation (*part*), stem, gender, number, state, any additional features, and the translation of the participle. In the case of a participle, *qal,* it is also necessary to indicate the voice (*act* or *pass*). With other stems no indication of voice is necessary, since they can only be either active or passive.

Word	Root	Conju-gation	Stem[1]	G/N	State	Additional Features	Translation
לְחַזֵּק (Jos 11:20)	חזק <	*inf*	*piel*	--	*Cs*	+ *prep* לְ	"to harden"
הֵאָכֹל (Lv 7:18)	אכל <	*inf*	*nif*	--	*Ab*		"being eaten"
הַהֹלְכִים (Ex 10:8)	הלך <	*part*	*qal act*	*MP*	*Ab*	+ *art*	"the ones going"
מַזְכֶּרֶת (Nu 5:15)	זכר <	*part*	*hif*	*FS*	*Ab*		"causing to remember"

✓ A summary of the steps involved in analyzing infinitives and participles appears in Appendix 2.

Lesson 18: Exercises

a. Reproduce from memory the following forms for משׁל and give a translation for each form.

(1) Participle, *qal*, active, masculine, singular, absolute

(2) Participle, *qal*, passive, masculine, singular, absolute

(3) Infinitive, *qal*, construct

(4) Infinitive, *qal*, absolute

[1] When a participle is in the *qal* stem, also indicate in this column whether it is active or passive.

b. Without consulting any charts, identify the following symbolic forms in terms of conjugation (*perf, impf, impv, inf,* or *part*) and stem (*qal, nif, piel,* etc.). In the case of an infinitive also identify whether the form is construct or absolute. In the case of a participle, *qal,* also identify the voice as active or passive. Do not assume the occurrence of a *dagesh-forte* except where indicated. If more than one answer is possible, give all options.

✓ This exercise is concerned with the general clues for conjugations and stems. The clues are intended as indicators for all the forms of a particular conjugation and stem, not simply one form (with a few exceptions, as in *impv, qal* where one clue [□ְ□ֹ□] applies to two forms and another [□ְ□□] to two forms).

- *Example:* הִ□ָּ□ֵ□ ⇒ *Answer: inf, nif, Cs*

  This example is not identified as the general clue for *impv, nif* because it applies to only one form in that stem and conjugation – only *2MS* has a *sere* under the second consonant of the root. Instead, the general clue for *impv, nif* (which applies to all forms of that conjugation and stem) is הִ□ָּ□□. Similarly, while הִ□ָּ□□ is an accurate clue for *inf, nif, Cs,* הִ□ָּ□ֵ□ is a more precise clue, since it also indicates the vowel which always appears under the second root consonant.

(1) □ֹ□□
(2) נִ□ְ□ֹ□
(3) ◁ִ□ָּ□□
(4) מַ□ְ□□
(5) □ִ□ְ□
(6) □ָ□וֹ□
(7) □ֵ□ּ□
(8) ◁ְ□ֶ□ּ□
(9) הָ□ְ□ֵ□
(10) מְ□ַ□ּ□
(11) ◁ַ□ְ□□
(12) □ֶ□ֹּ□
(13) ◁ֱ□ְ□□
(14) הִ□ָּ□ֹ□
(15) נִ□ְ□ָ□
(16) ◁ָ□ְ□□
(17) מִתְ□ַ□ּ□
(18) □ֶ□ּ□
(19) □ַ□ֹּ□
(20) □□וּ□
(21) הִ□ְ□□
(22) □ְ□ֹ□
(23) הִתְ□ַ□ֵּ□
(24) ◁ְ□ַ□ּ□
(25) מָ□ְ□□
(26) ◁ֲ□ֶ□ּ□
(27) □ַ□ֵּ□
(28) נִ□ְ□□
(29) הַ□ְ□ִי□
(30) □ַ□ּ□
(31) ◁ִתְ□ַ□ּ□
(32) הִ□ָּ□□
(33) הַ□ְ□ֵ□
(34) ◁ִ□ְ□□
(35) מְ□ֶ□ּ□
(36) הָ□ְ□□
(37) הִתְ□ַ□ּ□
(38) ◁ֲ□ַ□ּ□
(39) הַ□ְ□□

c. Learn to recognize, pronounce, and translate the following vocabulary.

	Word	*Translation*	*Notes*
(1)	דבר[1]	דִּבֶּר (*piel*): he spoke (*V*)	Usually *piel;* in *qal* only as *inf* and *part*
(2)	זֶרַע	seed, offspring, sowing (*NMS*)	*S* with *PS:* זַרְעִי, זַרְעֲךָ, etc.
(3)	יָם	sea (*NMS*)	*P:* יַמִּים
(4)	מָלַךְ	he reigned, was/became king (or *F:* she was/ became queen) (*V*)	
(5)	מָקוֹם	place (*NMS*)	*P:* מְקֹמוֹת
(6)	מֹשֶׁה	Moses (*proper N*)	
(7)	עוֹד	yet, still, again, besides (*adv*)	
(8)	עֵץ	tree, trees, wood (*NMS*)	
(9)	שָׁלֹשׁ, שָׁלוֹשׁ (*M*); שְׁלֹשָׁה (*F*)	three (*N M/F S*)	*MS Cs:* שְׁלֹשׁ; *FS Cs:* שְׁלֹשֶׁת; *P:* שְׁלֹשִׁים = "thirty";[2] שְׁלִישִׁי (*M*), שְׁלִישִׁית (*F*) = "third"

d. Analyze the following words without consulting charts or clues. Use the lexicon only where necessary for translation. When more than one option for analysis is possible, consult the biblical text to determine which is appropriate in context. Some weak verbs appear with vowels that vary slightly from the משׁל paradigms in this lesson; however, the forms of these verbs are similar enough to be easily recognized.

- *Example:* מְלֻבָּשִׁים (1Ki 22:10) ⇒ *Answer:* > לבשׁ, *part, pual, MP, Ab,* "being clothed"

---

[1] This verb's root serves as its lexical form since the verb never occurs in *perf, qal, 3MS*.

[2] The plural forms of the numerals from "three" to "nine" make up the numerals from "thirty" to "ninety."

(1) יֹדַ֫עַת (Nu 31:17)
(2) לְלַקֵּט (Ru 2:15)
(3) הַנִּקְרָא (Is 43:7)
(4) מְשַׁלֵּחַ (Ge 43:4)
(5) בִּקֵּעַ (Job 28:10)
(6) נִשְׁאֹל (1Sa 20:6)
(7) בְּהִתְנַשֵּׂא (Pr 30:32)
(8) וְהָפְדֵּה (Lv 19:20)
(9) הַכְּתוּבוֹת (2Ch 34:24)
(10) וְנִגְזְלָה (Pr 4:16)
(11) מִתְנַבְּאִים (1Ki 22:10)
(12) וּלְהַגְדִּיל (Am 8:5)
(13) זְרוּעָה (Jer 2:2)
(14) וְהִדְרִיךְ (Is 11:15)
(15) מְסֻתָּֽרֶת (Pr 27:5)
(16) לְהִנָּתֵן (Est 3:14)
(17) מָעֳמָד (1Ki 22:35)
(18) וְהַכְבֵּד (Ex 8:11; *Eng* 8:15)
(19) מַלֵּט (Jer 39:18)
(20) כִּמְלַקֵּט (Is 17:5)

e. Read aloud and translate the following texts from the Hebrew Bible with the help of a lexicon. Also provide an analysis of all finite verbs (*perf, impf,* or *impv*), infinitives, and participles.

(1) Genesis 1:9-13

Verse 9

(a) יִקָּווּ > II קוה

(b) The ר in וְתֵרָאֶה cannot take the *dagesh-forte* that would normally appear in this stem. To compensate, the preceding vowel (under the prefix) has lengthened from *hireq* to *sere*.

Verse 10

וּלְמִקְוֵה > II קוה Note that this noun, like many others, is formed by prefixing a מ to a verb root. The resulting form resembles a participle.

Verse 11

This verse provides an appropriate place for some introductory observations about the *Masora* and the critical apparatus in *BHS*.[1]

(a) *Masora*

[1] As the name suggests, the marginal *Masora* (or *Masora marginalis*) refers to Masoretic notes in the margins of the Hebrew Bible. One part,

[1] For fuller discussions see Scott; Würthwein; and Reinhard Wonneberger, *Understanding BHS: A Manual for the Users of Biblia Hebraica Stuttgartensia*, 3d rev. ed., trans. Dwight R. Daniels (Rome: Pontifical Biblical Institute, 2001).

the *Masora parva* (*Mp*) (= "small *Masora*"), consists of the notes that appear in the outside margins of *BHS*. The other part, the *Masora magna* (*Mm*) (= "large *Masora*"), is comprised mostly of concordance-like lists that originally appeared in the upper and lower margins of the *MT*. The *Mm* notes themselves do not appear in *BHS* but are published separately. The notations that appear immediately below the Hebrew text in *BHS* make reference to relevant material in the separately published *Mm*.

[2] It is helpful for beginning students to familiarize themselves with certain features of the *Mp*. The small circles above words in the Hebrew text refer to notes in the *Mp*. A circle spaced between words, as between the first two words in verse 11 (וַיֹּ֣אמֶר אֱלֹהִ֗ים), indicates that a note in the *Mp* relates to two or more words. Since the circle between the first two words in verse 11 is the first one on the line, it refers to the first note in the *Mp*, which appears in the left margin. The second superscript circle in verse 11 stands above a single word (תַּֽדְשֵׁ֤א), indicating that the second *Mp* note relates to this word. *Mp* notes are separated by periods and are written in abbreviated Aramaic and Hebrew. The prolegomena to *BHS* translates the abbreviations into Latin; English translations are also available.[1] In the *Mp,* Hebrew letters with dots above them usually refer to numbers. For example, the first *Mp* note relating to verse 11 has the letters כ and ה with dots above them, which stands for the number "25," indicating how many times the phrase וַיֹּ֣אמֶר אֱלֹהִ֗ים occurs elsewhere in the Hebrew Bible. The superscript "10" after כה directs the reader to the paragraph immediately below the Hebrew text and a reference to material in the *Mm*. The second circle in the verse, above תַּֽדְשֵׁ֤א, refers to the *Mp* note of ל with a dot above it. It stands for "no other," meaning that this is the only occurrence of this particular word in the Hebrew Bible.

[1] A handy, inexpensive source is Scott's *A Simplified Guide to BHS;* see pages 37-51.

(b) Critical apparatus

[1] The critical apparatus in *BHS* appears in the paragraph at the bottom of the page. Superscript English letters in the Hebrew text refer to critical notes in the apparatus. A superscript letter immediately after a word indicates that the note relates only to that word. For example, the superscript "b" after עֵץ in verse 11 means that note "b" relates to this word. When the same superscript letter appears before and after a group of words, as the letter "a" occurs before and after דֶּשֶׁא עֵשֶׂב in verse 11, it indicates that the critical note relates to the whole phrase. If a letter appears at the beginning of a verse and is not repeated, then the critical note deals with the entire verse. In the critical apparatus two parallel lines separate notes, and verse numbers appear in a bold font. The critical notes themselves employ symbols and abbreviations that are interpreted in Latin in the *BHS* prolegomena; English translations are also available.[1]

[2] To illustrate a critical note, locate note "b" for verse 11 in the critical apparatus (the second note on the last line). It gives a variant reading for עֵץ, which begins "read ('l') with ('c')" and then lists the external evidence for the variant in symbolic form. The evidence is "a few ('pc') manuscripts of the Hebrew Bible ('Mss'), the Samaritan Pentateuch, the Septuagint, the Syriac version, the Targum Pseudo-Jonathan, and the Vulgate." The critical note then gives the variant: וְעץ, which alters the text by adding a *vav* conjunction to the word. (Only vowels that are different from the text appear with the variant. Since the *sere* under the *ayin* is not altered, it is not repeated in the critical note.) Finally, the note offers some internal textual evidence to support the variant: "compare ('cf') with verse 12," where in a parallel expression עֵץ has a *vav* conjunction.

Verse 12

וַתּוֹצֵא > יצא In this root, as with most verb roots that begin with a *yod*, the first consonant becomes a *holem-vav* in the *hifil* stem.

[1] Ibid., 61-87.

(2) Psalm 119:9

(a) בַּמֶּה is the interrogative pronoun מה with a preposition.

(b) Interpret the notes for this verse in the critical apparatus.

✓ Sometimes a variant appears in an abbreviated form, giving only enough consonants of a word to make clear what the alteration is. Such is the case with the critical notes for this verse. For example, the variant for לִשְׁמֹר appears as בִּשׁ, indicating that the only change is with regard to the prefixed preposition.

(3) Numbers 25:5

(a) Note "b" in the critical apparatus provides a clue to the function of אֲנָשָׁיו in the verse.

(b) לְבַ֫עַל פְּע֑וֹר is a proper noun with a preposition.

(4) Genesis 37:8

(a) הֲמָלֹךְ begins an interrogative clause, as indicated by the prefix הֲ. This interrogative ה, which is discussed later (in Lesson 20), has no translation; it simply indicates that the clause should be translated in the form of a question.

(b) אִם also functions in this verse as an interrogative particle. It requires no translation but simply indicates that the following clause is interrogative.

(c) וַיּוֹסִפוּ is a *hifil* verb from the root יסף.

Lesson 19

Pronominal Suffixes on Finite Verbs, Pronominal Suffixes on Non–Finite Verbs

19A Pronominal Suffixes on Finite Verbs

1. Introduction

a. Pronominal suffixes can appear on verbs, as they do with other parts of speech. When pronominal suffixes occur with finite verbs – perfect, imperfect, or imperative – they function as the objects of the verbal action. As discussed previously, a verb can have an object comprised of the sign of the object with a pronominal suffix, as in מָשַׁל אֹתָם = "He ruled them." Another way of expressing the same thing is to place the pronominal suffix directly on the verb, as in מְשָׁלָם = "He ruled them." Pronominal suffixes normally appear on finite verbs that are active; therefore, the following discussion will focus on pronominal suffixes with verbs in three stems: *qal, piel,* and *hifil.*[1]

b. The following verbs, with analysis below them, illustrate the usage of pronominal suffixes on finite verbs.

- הִמְלַכְתִּיךָ = "I made you king" (2Ch 1:11).
  Perf, hif, 1CS + pronominal suffix *2MS* (*PS 2MS*)
- יִמְצָאֻהוּ = "They will find him" (Job 20:8).
  Impf, qal, 3MP + PS 3MS
- בָּרְכֵנִי = "Bless me" (Ge 27:34).
  Impv, piel, 2MS + PS 1CS

2. Pronominal suffixes on perfect verbs

a. The following chart indicates the typical spelling of the pronominal suffixes as

---

[1] It is possible, although rare, for pronominal suffixes to appear in the passive stems of some verbs. For example, וְנָעָבְדֵם (= "let us be made to serve them" or "let us serve them" [Dt 13:3]) is an *imperfect, hofal* verb with a *PS 3MP*.

they appear on perfect verbs. Two sets of forms are given: one for verbs ending with vowels (such as מָשַׁלְתָּ) and the other for verbs ending with consonants (such as מָשַׁל).[1] In the latter case a variety of connecting vowels can appear between the consonantal endings of verbs and the consonants of the suffixes.

	Pronominal Suffixes for Perfect Verbs		
	On verbs ending with vowels	*On verbs ending with consonants*[2]	*Translation*
1CS	נִי	◌ַנִי	"me"
2MS	ךָ	◌ְךָ	"you"
2FS	ךְ	◌ֶךְ, ◌ֵךְ	"you"
3MS	ו, הוּ	◌ָהוּ, וֹ	"him, it"
3FS	הָ	◌ָהּ	"her, it"
1CP	נוּ	◌ָנוּ	"us"
2MP	כֶם	◌ְכֶם	"you"
2FP[3]	כֶן	◌ְכֶן	"you"
3MP	ם	◌ַם, ◌ָם	"them"
3FP	ן	◌ַן, ◌ָן	"them"

✓ Most forms of the pronominal suffixes for verbs resemble the suffixes for singular nouns. (See Lesson 9A.2a.) One difference is that the *1CS* suffix for verbs has a *nun* before the *hireq-yod,* which does not typically occur with nouns. Another difference is that the suffixes for verbs that end with consonants (in the second column of forms) sometimes employ different connecting vowels than the suffixes for nouns. Note also that perfect verbs have a preference for A-class connecting vowels with the suffixes. (See *1CS, 3MS, 3FS, 1CP, 3MP,* and *3FP* in the second column of suffixes above.)

[1] There are a few other rare forms. See Horsnell, 264-65; Kautzsch, §58a; Lambdin, 260; and Seow, 197.

[2] A silent *sheva* may also appear before the first consonant of the suffixes in *1CS, 3MS,* and *1CP.*

[3] *PS 2FP* for verbs is hypothetical, since it does not occur in the Hebrew Bible. Kautzsch, §58a

b. Forms of the perfect verb to which pronominal suffixes are attached[1]

(1) When pronominal suffixes are attached to verbs, certain changes occur in vowels and accenting. The chart below uses משל to illustrate the major changes that occur in the spelling of strong perfect verbs when pronominal suffixes are attached. The second column for each stem presents the vowel pointing of the verb to which the suffixes are attached. (The symbol __ represents a pronominal suffix at the end of a verb.) The first column under each stem gives the normal spelling of perfect verbs without suffixes for the sake of comparison.

	Perfect					
	Qal		*Piel*		*Hifil*	
P/G/N of verb:	*Without PS*	*Before PS*	*Without PS*	*Before PS*	*Without PS*	*Before PS*
3MS	מָשַׁל	מְשָׁל__	מִשֵּׁל	מִשְּׁל__ or מִשֶּׁל__	הִמְשִׁיל	הִמְשִׁיל__
3FS	מָשְׁלָה	מְשָׁלַת__ or מְשָׁלָת__	מִשְּׁלָה	מִשְּׁלַת__	הִמְשִׁילָה	הִמְשִׁילַת__
2MS	מָשַׁלְתָּ	מְשַׁלְתּ__	מִשַּׁלְתָּ	מִשַּׁלְתּ__	הִמְשַׁלְתָּ	הִמְשַׁלְתּ__
2FS	מָשַׁלְתְּ	מְשַׁלְתִּי__	מִשַּׁלְתְּ	מִשַּׁלְתִּי__	הִמְשַׁלְתְּ	הִמְשַׁלְתִּי__
1CS	מָשַׁלְתִּי	מְשַׁלְתִּי__	מִשַּׁלְתִּי	מִשַּׁלְתִּי__	הִמְשַׁלְתִּי	הִמְשַׁלְתִּי__
3CP	מָשְׁלוּ	מְשָׁלוּ__	מִשְּׁלוּ	מִשְּׁלוּ__	הִמְשִׁילוּ	הִמְשִׁילוּ__
2MP	מְשַׁלְתֶּם	מְשַׁלְתּוּ__	מִשַּׁלְתֶּם	מִשַּׁלְתּוּ__	הִמְשַׁלְתֶּם	הִמְשַׁלְתּוּ__
2FP	מְשַׁלְתֶּן	מְשַׁלְתּוּ__	מִשַּׁלְתֶּן	מִשַּׁלְתּוּ__	הִמְשַׁלְתֶּן	הִמְשַׁלְתּוּ__
1CP	מָשַׁלְנוּ	מְשַׁלְנוּ__	מִשַּׁלְנוּ	מִשַּׁלְנוּ__	הִמְשַׁלְנוּ	הִמְשַׁלְנוּ__

(2) Notes concerning the forms of the perfect with pronominal suffixes

(a) When the suffixes are attached to perfect, *qal* verbs, an initial vowel of *qames* reduces to *sheva* and the second vowel sometimes lengthens to *qames*.

(b) The *3FS* verb ending ◌ָה changes to ◌ַת or ◌ָת before the pronominal

[1] See Horsnell, 267-71; and Seow, 196.

suffixes. This is the same sort of change that occurs with *FS* nouns before the suffixes.

(c) The *2FS* verb ending תְּ becomes תִּי before pronominal suffixes, so that it has the same spelling as the *1CS* verb.

(d) In *2MP* and *2FP* the characteristic final consonants (ם and ן) are replaced by וּ, so that they both have the same ending of תוּ֫ before pronominal suffixes.

(e) In some forms the accent remains where it stands when the verb has no pronominal suffix; in others it shifts to the ultimate or penultimate syllable.

c. Examples of the perfect verb with pronominal suffixes, using מ֫שׁל to illustrate[1]

(1) Perfect, *qal, 3MS* verb with pronominal suffixes

Perfect, qal, 3MS: מָשַׁל			
PS:		*PS:*	
1CS	מְשָׁלַ֫נִי ("he ruled me")	*1CP*	מְשָׁלָ֫נוּ ("he ruled us")
2MS	מְשָׁלְךָ֫ ("he ruled you")	*2MP*	מְשָׁלְכֶ֫ם ("he ruled you")
2FS	מְשָׁלֵךְ ("he ruled you")	*2FP*	מְשָׁלְכֶ֫ן ("he ruled you")
3MS	מְשָׁלוֹ or מְשָׁלָ֫הוּ ("he ruled him")	*3MP*	מְשָׁלָם ("he ruled them")
3FS	מְשָׁלָהּ ("he ruled her")	*3FP*	מְשָׁלָן ("he ruled them")

(2) Examples of perfect, *qal* verbs in other persons, genders, and numbers with pronominal suffixes

- *3FS* verb מָֽשְׁלָה + selected *PS* = מְשָׁלַ֫תְנִי, מְשָׁלַ֫תּוּ or מְשָׁלַ֫תְהוּ, מְשָׁלָ֫תַם ("she ruled me," etc.)
- *2MS* verb מָשַׁ֫לְתָּ + selected *PS* = מְשַׁלְתָּ֫הּ, מְשַׁלְתָּ֫נוּ, מְשַׁלְתָּ֫ן ("you ruled her," etc.)
- *2FS/1CS* verbs מָשַׁ֫לְתִּי/מָשַׁלְתְּ + selected *PS* = מְשַׁלְתִּ֫יהָ, מְשַׁלְתִּ֫ינוּ, מְשַׁלְתִּ֫ים ("you/I ruled her," etc.)

[1] Some hypothetical forms appear for the sake of illustration. See Horsnell, 267-70; Kelley, 154-56; Lambdin, 261-62, 266-67; and Weingreen, 123-27.

- *3CP* verb מָשְׁלוּ + selected *PS* = מְשָׁלוּנִי[1], מְשָׁלוּהוּ, מְשָׁלוּנוּ ("they ruled me," etc.)

(3) Examples of the perfect, *piel* verb with pronominal suffixes

- *3MS* verb מִשֵּׁל + selected *PS* = מִשְּׁלַנִי, מִשֶּׁלְךָ, מִשֶּׁלְכֶם ("he ruled me," etc.)
- *2MS* verb מִשַּׁלְתָּ + selected *PS* = מִשַּׁלְתּוֹ, מִשַּׁלְתָּהּ, מִשַּׁלְתָּם ("you ruled him," etc.)
- *3CP* verb מִשְּׁלוּ + selected PS = מִשְּׁלוּהוּ, מִשְּׁלוּנוּ, מִשְּׁלוּן ("they ruled him," etc.)

(4) Examples of the perfect, *hifil* verb with pronominal suffixes

- *3MS* verb הִמְשִׁיל + selected *PS* = הִמְשִׁילַנִי, הִמְשִׁילֵךְ, הִמְשִׁילָן ("he made me rule," etc.)
- *1CS* verb הִמְשַׁלְתִּי + selected *PS* = הִמְשַׁלְתִּיךָ, הִמְשַׁלְתִּיו, הִמְשַׁלְתִּים ("I made you rule," etc.)
- *3CP* verb הִמְשִׁילוּ + selected *PS* = הִמְשִׁילוּהָ, הִמְשִׁילוּנוּ, הִמְשִׁילוּכֶם ("they made her rule," etc.)

3. Pronominal suffixes on imperfect and imperative verbs

a. Since the imperative conjugation is very similar to the imperfect conjugation without the imperfect prefixes, the same patterns are followed for attaching pronominal suffixes to imperfects and to imperatives.

b. Forms of the pronominal suffixes for imperfect and imperative verbs

The following chart presents the pronominal suffixes that usually appear on imperfect and imperative verbs. Two sets of forms are given: one for verbs ending with vowels (such as יִמְשְׁלוּ or מִשְׁלִי) and the other for verbs ending with consonants (such as תִּמְשֹׁל or מְשֹׁל).[2]

---

[1] When pronominal suffixes are added to a verb ending in וּ, sometimes the וּ reduces to a *qibbus*, as in מְשָׁלֻנִי (*perf, qal, 3CP + PS 1CS*).

[2] See Horsnell, 266; Kelley, 158; Lambdin, 271; and Seow, 248.

	Pronominal Suffixes for Imperfect & Imperative Verbs		
	On verbs ending with vowels	*On verbs ending with consonants*	*Translation*
1CS	נִי	□ֵ֫נִי	"me"
2MS	ךָ	□ְךָ	"you"
2FS	ךְ	□ֵךְ	"you"
3MS	ו, הוּ	□ֵ֫הוּ	"him, it"
3FS	הָ	□ָהּ, □ֶ֫הָ	"her, it"
1CP	נוּ	□ֵ֫נוּ	"us"
2MP	כֶם	□ְכֶם	"you"
2FP[1]	כֶן	□ְכֶן	"you"
3MP	ם	□ֵם	"them"
3FP	ן	□ֵן	"them"

✓ The suffixes in the first column (for imperfect and imperative verbs ending with vowels) are the same suffixes that are used on perfect verbs ending with vowels. Note in the second column of suffixes that E-class connecting vowels are typically employed with imperfect and imperative verbs ending with consonants, in contrast to perfect verbs which prefer A-class connecting vowels.

c. Forms of the imperfect to which pronominal suffixes are attached[2]

When pronominal suffixes are attached to imperfect verbs, certain changes can occur in vowel pointing and accenting. The changes, however, are much less dramatic than those which occur in perfect verbs, with one exception. The *3FP* and *2FP* forms of the imperfect verb before pronominal suffixes are spelled the same as the *2MP* imperfect. The following chart uses משׁל to illustrate the changes that occur in the spelling of strong imperfects when pronominal suffixes are attached. Under each stem the second column has the forms of representative imperfects before the suffixes, while the first column has the normal spelling of imperfect verbs without suffixes.

[1] *PS 2FP* for verbs is hypothetical, since it does not occur in the Hebrew Bible. Kautzsch, §58a.

[2] See Horsnell, 272.

	Imperfect					
	Qal		*Piel*		*Hifil*	
P/G/N of verb:	*Without PS*	*Before PS*[1]	*Without PS*	*Before PS*	*Without PS*	*Before PS*
3MS	יִמְשֹׁל	יִמְשְׁל__	יְמַשֵּׁל	יְמַשְּׁל__	יַמְשִׁיל	יַמְשִׁיל__
2FS	תִּמְשְׁלִי	תִּמְשְׁלִי__	תְּמַשְּׁלִי	תְּמַשְּׁלִי__	תַּמְשִׁילִי	תַּמְשִׁילִ__
3MP	יִמְשְׁלוּ	יִמְשְׁלוּ__	יְמַשְּׁלוּ	יְמַשְּׁלוּ__	יַמְשִׁילוּ	יַמְשִׁילוּ__
3FP	תִּמְשֹׁלְנָה	תִּמְשְׁלוּ__	תְּמַשֵּׁלְנָה	תְּמַשְּׁלוּ__	תַּמְשֵׁלְנָה	תַּמְשִׁילוּ__
2MP	תִּמְשְׁלוּ	תִּמְשְׁלוּ__	תְּמַשְּׁלוּ	תְּמַשְּׁלוּ__	תַּמְשִׁילוּ	תַּמְשִׁילוּ__
2FP	תִּמְשֹׁלְנָה	תִּמְשְׁלוּ__	תְּמַשֵּׁלְנָה	תְּמַשְּׁלוּ__	תַּמְשֵׁלְנָה	תַּמְשִׁילוּ__

✓ In *3FP* and *2FP,* imperfect verbs before pronominal suffixes exchange their normal verb suffix of נָה for a וּ suffix (which also occurs in *2MP*), with the result that three plural forms are identical: *3FP, 2MP,* and *2FP.*

d. Examples of the imperfect verb with pronominal suffixes, using משׁל to illustrate[2]

(1) Imperfect, *qal, 3MS* verb with pronominal suffixes

Imperfect, qal, 3MS: יִמְשֹׁל			
PS:		*PS:*	
1CS	יִמְשְׁלֵנִי ("he will rule me")	*1CP*	יִמְשְׁלֵנוּ ("he will rule us")
2MS	יִמְשָׁלְךָ[3] ("he will rule you")	*2MP*	יִמְשָׁלְכֶם ("he will rule you")
2FS	יִמְשְׁלֵךְ ("he will rule you")	*2FP*	יִמְשָׁלְכֶן ("he will rule you")
3MS	יִמְשְׁלֵהוּ ("he will rule him")	*3MP*	יִמְשְׁלֵם ("he will rule them")
3FS	יִמְשְׁלֶהָ or יִמְשְׁלָהּ ("he will rule her")	*3FP*	יִמְשְׁלֵן ("he will rule them")

✓ The preceding pattern is also followed with the other imperfects that have no

---

[1] With a few pronominal suffixes the vowel under the second root consonant is a *qames-hatuf* instead of a *sheva,* as illustrated in charts that follow.

[2] See Horsnell, 272-275; Kelley, 156-59; Lambdin, 271-73; and Weingreen, 130-31.

[3] The vowel under the second root consonant is a *qames-hatuf* in this form and those with *2MP* and *2FP* pronominal suffixes. Weingreen, 130.

verb suffix: *3FS, 2MS, 1CS,* and *1CP*.

(2) Examples of imperfect, *qal* verbs in other persons, genders, and numbers with pronominal suffixes

- *2FS* verb תִּמְשְׁלִי + selected *PS* = תִּמְשְׁלִיהוּ, תִּמְשְׁלִיהָ, תִּמְשְׁלִינוּ ("you will rule him," etc.)
- *3MP* verb יִמְשְׁלוּ+ selected *PS* = יִמְשְׁלוּנִי, יִמְשְׁלוּךָ, יִמְשְׁלוּם ("they will rule me," etc.)
  - ✓ The pattern of the *3MP* verb is followed in the other imperfects that end in *shureq* before the pronominal suffixes: *2MP, 3FP,* and *2FP*.

(3) Examples of imperfect, *piel* and *hifil* verbs with pronominal suffixes

- *Piel, 3MS* verb יְמַשֵּׁל + selected *PS* = יְמַשְּׁלֵנִי, יְמַשֶּׁלְךָ, יְמַשְּׁלֵם ("he will rule me," etc.)
- *Hif, 3MS* verb יַמְשִׁיל + selected *PS* = יַמְשִׁילֵהוּ, יַמְשִׁילֶהָ, יַמְשִׁילְכֶם ("he will make him rule," etc.)

e. Forms of the imperative to which pronominal suffixes are attached[1]

(1) The following chart uses משׁל to illustrate the typical changes that occur in the spelling of strong imperatives when pronominal suffixes are attached. The imperative without suffixes also appears for the sake of comparison.

	Imperative					
	Qal		*Piel*		*Hifil*	
P/G/N of verb:	*Without PS*	*Before PS*	*Without PS*	*Before PS*	*Without PS*	*Before PS*
2MS	מְשֹׁל	מָשְׁל__	מַשֵּׁל	מַשְּׁל__	הַמְשֵׁל	הַמְשִׁיל__
2FS	מִשְׁלִי	מִשְׁלִי__	מַשְּׁלִי	מַשְּׁלִי__	הַמְשִׁילִי	הַמְשִׁיל__
2MP	מִשְׁלוּ	מִשְׁלוּ__	מַשְּׁלוּ	מַשְּׁלוּ__	הַמְשִׁילוּ	הַמְשִׁילוּ__
2FP	מְשֹׁלְנָה	מִשְׁלוּ__	מַשֵּׁלְנָה	מַשְּׁלוּ__	הַמְשֵׁלְנָה	הַמְשִׁילוּ__

(2) Notes concerning the forms of the imperative to which pronominal suffixes are attached

[1] See Horsnell, 275-79.

(a) In *qal 2MS* the *sheva* under the first consonant usually lengthens to a *qames-hatuf,* as it does in the long form of the imperative when a ◌ָה suffix is attached.

(b) In *hifil 2MS* the vowel for the second root consonant lengthens from *sere* to *hireq-yod.*

(c) In *2FP* the suffix changes from נָה to וּ in all the stems, as it does in the imperfect. The result is that the *2MP* and *2FP* forms are identical before pronominal suffixes.

f. Examples of the imperative verb with pronominal suffixes[1]

(1) Examples of imperative, *qal* verbs with pronominal suffixes

PS:	*Impv, qal, 2MS:* מְשֹׁל
1CS	מָשְׁלֵנִי ("rule me")
3MS	מָשְׁלֵהוּ ("rule him")
3FS	מָשְׁלֶהָ or מָשְׁלָהּ ("rule her")
1CP	מָשְׁלֵנוּ ("rule us")
3MP	מָשְׁלֵם ("rule them")

PS:	*Impv, qal, 2MP/2FP:* מְשֹׁלְנָה / מִשְׁלוּ
1CS	מִשְׁלוּנִי ("rule me")
3MS	מִשְׁלוּהוּ ("rule him")
3FP	מִשְׁלוּהָ ("rule her")
1CP	מִשְׁלוּנוּ ("rule us")
3MP	מִשְׁלוּם ("rule them")

(2) Examples of imperative, *piel* and *hifil* verbs with pronominal suffixes

- *Piel, 2MS* verb מַשֵּׁל + selected *PS* = מַשְּׁלֵהוּ, מַשְּׁלֵנוּ, מַשְּׁלֵם ("rule him," etc.")
- *Hif, 2MS* verb הַמְשֵׁל + selected *PS* = הַמְשִׁילֵנִי, הַמְשִׁילֶהָ, הַמְשִׁילֵם ("make me rule," etc.)

g. Imperfect and imperative pronominal suffixes with an energic *nun*

When pronominal suffixes are attached to imperfect and imperative verbs that end in a consonant, an additional *nun,* usually called an energic *nun,* can appear in some pronominal suffix forms. The phenomenon occurs in the *1CS, 2MS, 3MS, 3FS,* and *1CP* suffixes. The energic *nun* undergoes assimilation with another consonant of the pronominal suffix by means of a *dagesh-forte,*

[1] See Horsnell, 276-79; and Lambdin, 273.

as the following chart indicates.[1] The additional *nun* does not alter the meaning of the pronominal suffixes.

	PS with energic nun	*Example with impf, qal, 3MS:* יִמְשֹׁל
1CS	◌ֶ֫נִּי	יִמְשְׁלֶ֫נִּי ("he will rule me")
2MS	◌ֶ֫ךָּ	יִמְשְׁלֶ֫ךָּ ("he will rule you")
3MS	◌ֶ֫נּוּ	יִמְשְׁלֶ֫נּוּ ("he will rule him")
3FS	◌ֶ֫נָּה	יִמְשְׁלֶ֫נָּה ("he will rule her")
1CP	◌ֶ֫נּוּ	יִמְשְׁלֶ֫נּוּ ("he will rule us")

✓ In *2MS* the energic *nun* is assimilated into the ךּ with a *dagesh-forte*. The ךָ still retains its *qames*. In *3MS* the ה of the normal suffix הוּ is assimilated into the *nun* with a *dagesh-forte*. The result is that the *3MS* and *1CP* suffixes are identical.

19B Pronominal Suffixes on Non-Finite Verbs

Pronominal suffixes can also be attached to two non-finite verbs: the infinitive construct and the participle. Infinitive absolutes do not take pronominal suffixes. Since infinitive constructs are verbal nouns and participles are verbal adjectives, it is not surprising that they usually take the same forms of the pronominal suffixes that are used with singular nouns and substantival adjectives. (See Lesson 9A.2a.)

1. Pronominal suffixes on infinitive constructs

a. When pronominal suffixes appear on infinitive constructs, they can serve one of two functions: either as the subject or the object of the infinitive. One can determine which is intended by the context of the infinitive.

(1) Since an infinitive has no subjective inflection indicating person, gender, and number, a pronominal suffix can function as its subject.

- וּכְעָמְדוֹ תִּשָּׁבֵר מַלְכוּתוֹ וְתֵחָץ . . . וְלֹא כְמָשְׁלוֹ = "And when he arises (or "and as his arising") (וּכְעָמְדוֹ) his kingdom will be broken, and it will be divided . . . but not according to the way he ruled (or "as his ruling") (כְּמָשְׁלוֹ)" (Da 11:4)

[1] See Horsnell, 266, 284; and Kelley, 159. Similar pronominal suffixes with an energic *nun* appear with the preposition מִן. See Lesson 10A.1b.

This verse has two infinitive, *qal,* constructs with pronominal suffixes (וּכְעָמְדוֹ and וּכְמָשְׁלוֹ). In both cases the pronominal suffixes serve as subjects for the infinitives.

(2) When a pronominal suffix on an infinitive construct is objective, it functions in the same manner as a pronominal suffix functions with finite verbs.

- וַיַּנִּחֵהוּ בְגַן־עֵדֶן לְעָבְדָהּ וּלְשָׁמְרָהּ = "And he [God] placed him in the garden of Eden to cultivate it (לְעָבְדָהּ) and to keep it (וּלְשָׁמְרָהּ)" (Ge 2:15)

  This verse also has two infinitive, *qal,* constructs with pronominal suffixes (לְעָבְדָהּ and וּלְשָׁמְרָהּ). In both cases the suffixes serve as objects of the infinitives.

b. Forms of the infinitive construct with pronominal suffixes[1]

(1) The following chart illustrates the typical spelling of representative infinitive, *qal,* constructs with pronominal suffixes. Since the suffixes can serve either as subjects or objects of infinitive constructs, both options are given for translation.

PS:	*Infinitive, qal, construct:* מְשֹׁל	
1CS	מָשְׁלִי or מָשְׁלֵנִי	("my ruling/ruling me")
2MS	מְשָׁלְךָ or מָשְׁלְךָ	("your ruling/ruling you")
2FS	מָשְׁלֵךְ	("your ruling/ruling you")
3MS	מָשְׁלוֹ	("his ruling/ruling him")
3FS	מָשְׁלָהּ	("her ruling/ruling her")
1CP	מָשְׁלֵנוּ	("our ruling/ruling us")
2MP	מְשָׁלְכֶם or מָשְׁלְכֶם	("your ruling/ruling you")
3MP	מָשְׁלָם	("their ruling/ruling them")
3FP	מָשְׁלָן	("their ruling/ruling them")

✓ Some forms of the infinitive, *qal,* construct in the preceding chart resemble the imperative, *qal, 2MS* with pronominal suffixes. (See section 19A.3f(1).) Both conjugations have a common form of מָשְׁל__ before the

[1] See Horsnell, 279-80; and Kautzsch, §61d.

suffixes. The infinitive, *qal,* construct also has an alternate spelling of מְשָׁל-- before some suffixes.

(2) The following words illustrate the appearance of pronominal suffixes on infinitive constructs in other stems than *qal*. One option for translation is provided for each. Since pronominal suffixes can function subjectively with infinitive constructs, they may appear on infinitives in *nifal,* something which does not occur with finite verbs.

- הִמָּשְׁלֶךָ = *inf, nif, Cs, + PS 2MS,* "you (are) being ruled"
- מַשְׁלֵהוּ = *inf, piel, Cs, + PS 3MS,* "ruling him"
- הַמְשִׁילֵנוּ = *inf, hif, Cs, + PS 1CP,* "making us rule"
- הִתְמַשְּׁלָם = *inf, hit, Cs + PS 3MP,* "ruling themselves"

2. Pronominal suffixes on participles

a. A pronominal suffix on a participle can function in several ways. For example, it may serve a genitival role as it does with nouns; it may function as the object of the participle's action; or it may qualify the action of the participle in some way. The following examples illustrate these functions.

- וְעַל־נִכְבַּדֶּיהָ יַדּוּ גוֹרָל = "And lots were cast over her nobles (or "ones of her being honorable") (נִכְבַּדֶּיהָ)" (Nah 3:10)

  This *nifal* participle (נִכְבַּדֶּיהָ) has a *3FS* pronominal suffix which functions genitively as a possessive pronoun.

- הִנְנִי מַאֲכִילָם = "Behold, I am feeding them (or "causing them to eat") (מַאֲכִילָם)" (Jer 9:14; *Eng* 9:15)

  The participle is *hifil* and has a *3MP* pronominal suffix that serves as the object of the participle.

- כִּי מְבֹרָכָיו יִירְשׁוּ אָרֶץ וּמְקֻלָּלָיו יִכָּרֵתוּ = "For the ones being blessed by him (מְבֹרָכָיו) will inherit the land, but the ones being cursed by him (וּמְקֻלָּלָיו) will be cut off" (Ps 37:22)

  This verse has two *pual* participles (מְבֹרָכָיו and וּמְקֻלָּלָיו), each with a *3MS* pronominal suffix that qualifies the action of the participle.

b. Pronominal suffixes can only be attached to the construct forms of participles, just as they are attached to construct nouns. The following forms of משל illustrate the spelling of participles with pronominal suffixes in various stems.

- מֹשְׁלֵיכֶם = *part, qal, act, MP, Cs + PS 2MP,* "(ones) ruling you"
- מְשֻׁלֵ֫נוּ = *part, qal, pass, MS, Cs + PS 1CP*, "(one) being ruled by us"
- נִמְשָׁלְתֵךְ = *part, nif, FS, CS + PS 2FS,* "(one) being ruled by you"
- מְמַשְׁלֶ֫יהָ = *part, piel, MP Cs + PS 3FS,* "(ones) ruling her"
- מְמֻשָּׁלֵ֫נוּ = *part, pual, MP, Cs + PS 1CP,* "(ones) being ruled by us"
- מַמְשִׁילוֹתַי = *part, hif, FP, Cs + PS 1CS,* "(ones) making me rule"
- מִתְמַשְּׁלוֹ = *part, hit, MS, Cs + PS 3MS,* "(one) ruling himself"

Lesson 19: Exercises

a. Learn to recognize, pronounce, and translate the following vocabulary.

	Word	*Translation*	*Notes*
(1)	אָדוֹן	lord, master (*NMS*)	אֲדֹנָי (literally "my lord") usually means "Lord"; substitute for יהוה
(2)	אַחַר	after, behind (*prep, adv,* or *conj*)	*PS* on *prep:* אַחֲרֶ֫יךָ, אַחֲרָיו, etc.
(3)	אָכַל	he ate (*V*)	
(4)	אַף	anger, nose, nostril (*NFS*)	*S* with *PS:* אַפִּי, אַפְּךָ; *Du:* אַפַּיִם = "face"; *Du* with *PS:* אַפֶּ֫יךָ, אַפָּיו, etc.
(5)	אַרְבַּע (*M*), אַרְבָּעָה (*F*)	four (*NM/FS*)	*P:* אַרְבָּעִים = "forty"; רְבִיעִי (*M*), רְבִיעִית (*F*) = "fourth"
(6)	אֵשׁ	fire *(NFS)*	No *P*
(7)	בקשׁ	בִּקֵּשׁ (*piel*): he sought, asked (*V*)	Never occurs in *qal*
(8)	ברך	בֵּרַךְ (*piel*): he blessed (*V*)	Usually occurs in *piel*
(9)	דָּם	blood (*NMS*)	*Cs:* דַּם
(10)	כֹּה	thus (*adv*)	
(11)	לַ֫יְלָה	night (*NMS*)	*Ab* also לַ֫יִל; *Cs:* לֵיל

(12) מוֹעֵד meeting place, meeting, appointed time (*NMS*)

(13) עַתָּה now (*adv*)

(14) פֶּה mouth (*NMS*) *Cs:* פִּי; *P:* פִּיּוֹת

b. Analyze the following words, working without the help of paradigm charts or a lexicon so far as possible. When there is more than one option for analysis, consult the biblical text to determine which is appropriate in context.

- *Example:* וְגֹאֲלֵךְ (Is 54:5) ⇒ *Answer:* > גאל, *part, qal, act, MS, Cs, + vav conj + PS 2FS,* "and one redeeming you" or "and your redeemer"

(1)	לְמָכְרָהּ	(Ex 21:8)	(12)	לְהַכְעִיסוֹ	(Dt 4:25)
(2)	הִפְקַדְתִּיךָ	(Jer 1:10)	(13)	עֲלֻמֵנוּ	(Ps 90:8)
(3)	אֹמְנַיִךְ	(Is 49:23)	(14)	וּנְבַקְשֶׁנּוּ[1]	(SS 6:1)
(4)	דִּרְשׁוּנִי	(Am 5:4)	(15)	מַאֲכִילָם	(Jer 9:14; *Eng* 9:15)
(5)	מִתְעַבְּרוֹ	(Pr 20:2)	(16)	בְּאַמְּצוֹ	(Pr 8:28)
(6)	וְלַמְּדָהּ	(Dt 31:19)	(17)	נִפְלְאוֹתֶיךָ	(Ps 9:2; *Eng* 9:1)
(7)	הִבָּרַאֲךָ	(Eze 28:15)	(18)	וְקִדְּשׁוֹ	(Lv 16:19)
(8)	וְלָכְדָהּ	(2Sa 12:28)	(19)	וְהַעֲמִידֶהָ	(Eze 24:11)
(9)	וַיִּבְחָרֶךָּ	(Is 49:7)	(20)	וּמְאַסִּפְכֶם	(Is 52:12)
(10)	וּמְאֻשָּׁרָיו	(Is 9:15; *Eng* 9:16)	(21)	נְגַעֲנוּךָ	(Ge 26:29)
(11)	בְּהִתְעַטְּפָם	(La 2:12)	(22)	וַיַּמְלִיכֶהָ	(Est 2:17)

c. Read aloud and translate the following texts from the Hebrew Bible, using a lexicon as necessary. Also provide an analysis of all finite verbs (*perf, impf,* or *impv*) and non-finite verbs (*inf* and *part*).

(1) Genesis 1:14-19

Verse 14

(a) מְאֹרֹת > אור The common *NFP* ending of וֹת sometimes reduces to ת◌ֹ, as it does in this word. Similarly, in words derived from a verb with a

---

[1] The *dagesh-forte* which would normally occur in the ק does not appear here; the consonant has a vocal *sheva.*

middle vowel of וֹ (such as אוֹר), the וֹ can reduce to a *holem*, as it does in מְאֹרֹת.

(b) היה > וְהָיוּ

(c) לְאֹתֹת is a plural noun derived from the root אוה.

Verse 15

אור > לְהָאִיר

Verse 17

נתן < וַיִּתֵּן When an imperfect prefix is attached to a verb root beginning with *nun*, the *nun* is typically assimilated into the second root consonant by means of a *dagesh-forte*, as demonstrated by this verb.

(2) Genesis 32:27 (*Eng* 32:26)

(3) Deuteronomy 28:20

(a) Interpret the *Mp* note for הַמִּגְעֶרֶת.

(b) Determine what the variant readings are for יָדְךָ in the critical apparatus.

(4) Isaiah 49:19

צרר I < תֵּצְרִי

Lesson 20

Connotations of Verb Tenses and Stems

20A Connotations of Verb Tenses and Stems

In order to simplify the process of learning the verb, the discussion thus far has focused on one basic meaning for each of the tenses (perfect and imperfect) and stems (*qal, nifal,* etc.). However, verb tenses and stems are actually capable of expressing a broad range of connotations, which is the subject of this lesson.

1. Connotations of verb tenses

a. As previously discussed, the perfect and imperfect tenses of the indicative verb do not convey the temporal ideas of past, present, or future in the way that English tenses do. Instead the Hebrew perfect typically indicates a completed action or state, while the imperfect usually indicates an incomplete action or state. The following chart elaborates on these basic distinctions.[1]

Perfect	*Imperfect*
(1) The perfect implies the perspective of an outsider, viewing an event or state as a unity or whole from beginning to end.	(1) The imperfect implies the perspective of an insider, viewing an event or state as something that is unfolding
(2) The perfect usually connotes an action or state that is instantaneous and singular. It may view a series of events as a unified whole.	(2) The imperfect connotes an action or state that is continuing. It often conveys a pluraity of events that are repetitive or that extend over a period of time.

b. While Hebrew tenses are not limited to temporal notions of past, present, or future, English tenses arc. Thus a translator must determine which English tense appropriately conveys the notion of a Hebrew verb based upon the context in

[1] See Joüon, §111c; Kautzsch, §106a, 107a; and Seow, 147.

which the verb appears. Up to this point the student has translated a Hebrew perfect (or *impf* + *vav cons*) with an English past tense and a Hebrew imperfect (or *perf* + *vav cons*) with an English future. However, the options for translation are much more complex. The following describes some of the more common nuances of the Hebrew tenses in terms of the temporal categories of English.

c. Connotations of the perfect[1]

(1) Past time

(a) Most often the Hebrew perfect conveys the notion of a simple past tense verb in English.

- אַבְרָם יָשַׁב בְּאֶרֶץ־כְּנָעַן = "Abram dwelled (יָשַׁב) in the land of Canaan" (Ge 13:12).

(b) Sometimes the Hebrew perfect connotes the ideas of the perfect past or pluperfect in English.

- כֻּלָּנוּ כַּצֹּאן תָּעִינוּ = "All of us like sheep have gone astray (תָּעִינוּ)" (Is 53:6).
- רָחֵל גְּנָבָתַם = "Rachel had stolen them (גְּנָבָתַם)" (Ge 31:32).

(2) Present time

(a) Some perfect verbs require a present tense English translation because they express an action that is complete or whole but has effects that continue into the present. Such is especially true of Hebrew verbs that express an attitude, perception, attribute, or experience.

- יְדַעְתֶּן כִּי בְּכָל־כֹּחִי עָבַדְתִּי אֶת־אֲבִיכֶן = "You know (יְדַעְתֶּן) that with all my strength I have served your father" (Ge 31:6).

(b) Hebrew perfect verbs expressing a general or proverbial truth may be translated by an English present tense. The action is viewed as a whole but also has continuing validity.

- כָּלָה עָנָן = "A cloud vanishes (כָּלָה)" (Job 7:9).

(c) Some Hebrew verbs convey an instantaneous occurrence that requires an English present tense translation. The action is completed in the moment it

---

[1] For these examples and others see J.C.L. Gibson, *Davidson's Introductory Hebrew Grammar – Syntax*, 4th ed., (Edinburgh: T&T Clark, 1994), §56-59; Joüon, §112c-m; Kautzsch, §106b-p; Waltke and O'Connor, §30.5.1-30.5.2; and Williams, §161-66.

occurs.

- הִגַּ֫דְתִּי הַיּוֹם = "I declare (הִגַּ֫דְתִּי) today" (Dt 26:3).

(3) Future time

(a) The Hebrew perfect can be used to speak of a future event that is already completed in the mind of the speaker. For example, what may be called a "prophetic perfect" expresses a future event in the perfect tense because the speaker is so certain of its accomplishment.

- הָעָם הַהֹלְכִים בַּחֹ֫שֶׁךְ רָאוּ אוֹר גָּדוֹל = "The people who are walking in darkness will see (רָאוּ) a great light" (Is 9:1; *Eng* 9:2).

(b) A Hebrew perfect verb can express a future perfect idea that is viewed as an accomplished event even though it has not yet happened.

- אֶשְׁאָב עַד אִם־כִּלּוּ לִשְׁתֹּת = "I will draw water (for your camels) until they will have finished (כִּלּוּ) drinking" (Ge 24:19).

(4) Hypothetical statements can employ the Hebrew perfect to express unreal situations in the past or unfulfilled desires.

- לוּ־מַתְנוּ בְּאֶ֫רֶץ מִצְרַ֫יִם = "If only we had died (מַתְנוּ) in the land of Egypt" (Nu 14:2).

(5) A verb that is imperfect + *vav* consecutive can have a similar range of connotations as those described here for the perfect tense. (See Lesson 16A.3.)

d. Connotations of the imperfect[1]

(1) Future time

(a) Most often the imperfect can be translated with a simple English future tense verb. The future action of the Hebrew imperfect is frequently repetitive or continual.

- וְנָמֵר עִם־גְּדִי יִרְבָּץ = "And the leopard will lie down (יִרְבָּץ) with the kid" (Is 11:6).
- אִם־יַעֲלֶה הָעָם הַזֶּה = "If this people will continue to go up (יַעֲלֶה)" (1Ki 12:27).
- אַךְ טוֹב וָחֶ֫סֶד יִרְדְּפוּנִי כָּל־יְמֵי חַיָּי = "Surely goodness and mercy will follow me (יִרְדְּפוּנִי) all the days of my life" (Ps 23:6).

[1] For these and other examples see Gibson, §63-64; Joüon, §113b-h; Kautzsch, §107; Waltke and O'Connor, §31.2-31.6; and Williams, §167-175.

(b) The imperfect can also express a future idea from a past perspective.

- שָׁמְעוּ כִּי־שָׁם יֹאכְלוּ לָחֶם = "They heard that they would eat (יֹאכְלוּ) bread there" (Ge 43:25).

(c) The imperfect can convey the idea of the English future perfect, something that the Hebrew perfect tense can also do.

- עֵקֶב תִּשְׁמְעוּן אֵת הַמִּשְׁפָּטִים . . . וְשָׁמַר יְהוָה . . . אֶת־הַבְּרִית = "Because you will have kept (תִּשְׁמְעוּן) the ordinances . . . the LORD will keep . . . the covenant" (Dt 7:12).

(2) Present time

(a) The imperfect can express present tense action that is repetitive or is continuing for a period of time, whether brief or lengthy.

- יוֹם לְיוֹם יַבִּיעַ אֹמֶר = "Day to day they pour forth (יַבִּיעַ) speech" (Ps 19:3; *Eng* 19:2).
- לָמָּה תַעֲמֹד בַּחוּץ = "Why are you standing (תַעֲמֹד) outside" (Ge 24:31).
- לָמָּה־לִּי רֹב־זִבְחֵיכֶם יֹאמַר יְהוָה = "'What are your many sacrifices to me,' says (יֹאמַר) the LORD" (Is 1:11).

(b) The imperfect can even express action that has technically been completed, but continues to be relevant. (The perfect can be used in a similar manner. See section 20A.1c(2)(a).)

- לָמָּה זֶּה תִּשְׁאַל לִשְׁמִי = "Why is it that are you are asking (תִּשְׁאַל) my name?" (Ge 32:30; *Eng* 32:29).

(3) Past time

(a) The imperfect can convey repeated or continuing action in the past.

- וְכֵן יַעֲשֶׂה שָׁנָה בְשָׁנָה = "And so he used to do (יַעֲשֶׂה) year by year" (1Sa 1:7).
- וְהַבַּיִת יִמָּלֵא עָשָׁן = "And the house was filling (יִמָּלֵא) with smoke" (Is 6:4).

(b) Occasionally the imperfect is used in an uncharacteristic fashion to convey the simple past in a manner like the perfect. This usage mainly occurs in poetic passages.[1]

- יָשֶׁת חֹשֶׁךְ סִתְרוֹ = "He made (יָשֶׁת) darkness his covering" (Ps 18:12; *Eng* 18:11).

(4) The imperfect can express a variety of hypothetical or contingent ideas. The translation of these ideas may require the use of auxiliary verbs, such as "may, might, can, could, would," or "should." Often these connotations of the imperfect are introduced by certain conjunctions or interrogative words, such as אִם ("if"), כִּי ("that"), פֶּן ("lest"), מִי ("who?"), or לָמָּה ("why?").[2]

- יְהוָה מִי־יָגוּר בְּאָהֳלֶךָ מִי־יִשְׁכֹּן בְּהַר קָדְשֶׁךָ = "LORD, who may abide (יָגוּר) in your tent? Who may dwell (יִשְׁכֹּן) on your holy mountain?" (Ps 15:1).
- וְהוֹרֵיתִי אֶתְכֶם אֵת אֲשֶׁר תַּעֲשׂוּן = "And I will teach you what you should do (תַּעֲשׂוּן)" (Ex 4:15).

✓ The imperfect verb in the last example (תַּעֲשׂוּן) is *2MP* and has an "extra" *nun* on the end, called a paragogic ("extending") *nun*. When a paragogic *nun* occurs, it usually appears on an imperfect verb that would otherwise end with וּ. Like the energic *nun*, the *paragogic nun* does not affect the meaning of a word.[3]

(5) A verb that is perfect + *vav* consecutive can have a similar range of meanings to those described here for the imperfect tense. (See Lesson 16A.2.)

2. Connotations of verb stems

a. While learning the verb it has been helpful to concentrate on only one connotation of each of the major stems. However, now that the forms of the verb have been discussed, it is possible to consider the variety of connotations that the stems can express. The common meanings of the stems that were presented earlier are repeated in this section along with additional connotations. The intention is not to describe every possible meaning for the stems but rather the ones that occur with some degree of frequency.

---

[1] In this usage the imperfect usually appears in a shortened form, as it does with a *vav* consecutive. As mentioned previously, some grammarians conclude that this form represents a preterite ("past") conjugation distinct from the perfect and imperfect. See Lesson 16A.3a(2)(a). Horsnell, 60.

[2] Ibid.

[3] See Waltke and O'Connor, §31.7.

b. *Qal*

Qal connotes simple action in the active voice.

- כָּרַת = "He cut down" (Jdg 6:30).

c. *Nifal*

(1) *Nifal* most commonly expresses the passive of *qal*, or simple action in the passive voice.

- נִכְרַת = "It is cut off" (Joel 1:5).

(2) *Nifal* sometimes serves as the reflexive of *qal* (in which case the subject is acting on itself).

- נִשְׁמְרוּ = "They kept themselves" (1Sa 21:5; *Eng* 21:4).

(3) A special usage of the reflexive with a plural verb is the reciprocal *nifal*, in which case the subjects of the verb perform the action on themselves reciprocally.

- נִלְחֲמוּ = "They will fight one another" (see Is 19:2).[1]

(4) With some verbs *nifal* functions as the passive or reflexive of other stems than *qal*.[2]

- The root כבד in *qal* = "be honored"; in *piel* = "make honorable." In *nifal* = "be made honorable" (see Is 26:15) or "make oneself honorable" (see 2Sa 6:20). The *nifal* form of this verb expresses the passive or reflexive of *piel*.
- סתר does not occur in *qal*, but in *hifil* = "hide." In *nifal* = "be hidden" (see Ge 4:14) or "hide oneself" (see Pr 27:12), expressing the passive or reflexive of *hifil.*

(5) For a few verbs which do not typically occur in the *qal* stem, *nifal* serves the function of *qal*, communicating simple action in the active voice.

- מלט does not occur in *qal* but does appear commonly in *nifal* with the simple, active meaning "escape" (see Jdg 3:26).[3]

---

[1] When "see" precedes a scripture reference it indicates that the verse may not have exactly the same form or meaning as the example but does illustrate the point of the example.

[2] Joshua Blau, *A Grammar of Biblical Hebrew* (Wiesbaden: Otto Harrassowitz, 1976), 51; and Waltke and O'Connor, §23.6.

[3] Weingreen, 103.

d. *Piel*

(1) *Piel* is the most controversial stem because of the difficulty of generalizing about its basic meaning. Beyond saying that *piel* expresses the active voice, it is not possible to identify one basic connotation which underlies all the nuances of the stem.[1] Traditionally grammarians have categorized *piel* as an intensification of *qal*. Intensification, especially in the sense of multiplying action, is an appropriate description of some verbs in *piel*, although it is not accurate to say that this nuance applies broadly to verbs in the *piel* stem. In spite of this limitation, intensification has served as a useful example of *piel* meaning while introducing the forms of this stem. However, the student should recognize that verbs express diverse connotations in *piel*, and one must rely on a lexicon and on a verb's context when determining meaning. Several possible connotations of this stem are described below.

(2) As discussed previously, some verbs employ *piel* as an intensification of *qal*. Thus far this Grammar has indicated intensification by the convention of an underlined translation, as with מִשֵּׁל = "he <u>ruled</u>." However, the intensification of *piel* can be expressed with a variety of nuances. It often involves some sort of multiplication of action, in which case it may be called a "frequentative" *piel*.[2]

- שׁבר in *qal* = "break"; in *piel* = "<u>break</u>, shatter, smash" (see Ex 9:25).
- נשׁק in *qal* = "kiss"; in *piel* = "<u>kiss</u>, kiss earnestly" or "kiss repeatedly" (see Ge 45:15).
- הלך in *qal* = "walk"; in *piel* = "walk about" (see Job 30:28).

(3) A common connotation of *piel* is causation, in a manner similar to *hifil*.[3]

- אבד in *qal* = "perish"; in *piel* = "cause to perish" or "destroy" (see 2Ki 21:3).
- למד in *qal* = "learn"; in *piel* = "cause to learn" or "teach" (see Ecc 12:9).
- קדשׁ in *qal* = "be holy"; in *piel* = "cause to be holy" or "consecrate" (see 1Ki 8:64).

---

[1] Joüon, §52d. See also Waltke and O'Connor, §24.1.

[2] See Waltke and O'Connor, §24.5.

[3] "Causation" is used here as a broad category encompassing several more technical categories that grammarians sometimes use. See for example Waltke and O'Connor, §24.2-24.3.

(4) Occasionally *piel* expresses the notion of deprivation, or the removal of something.[1]

- חטא in *qal* = "sin"; in *piel* = "remove sin" (see Eze 43:22).
- סקל in *qal* = "stone"; in *piel* it can mean "clear of stones" (see Is 5:2).

(5) For some verbs which do not typically occur in *qal,* the *piel* stem serves the function of *qal*, communicating simple action in the active voice.

- דִּבֶּר = "He spoke" (Ge 12:4).
- בִּקֵּשׁ = "He sought" (1Sa 13:14).

e. *Pual*

(1) *Pual* normally serves as the passive of *piel.* In this role it can have a range of meanings corresponding to *piel.*

- קדשׁ in *piel* = "cause to be holy" or "consecrate"; in *pual* = "be consecrated" (see 2Ch 26:18).
- סקל in *piel* can mean "clear of stones"; in *pual* = "be cleared of stones" (see 1Ki 21:14).
- בקשׁ in *piel* = "seek"; in *pual* = "be sought" (see Jer 50:20).

(2) A few *pual* verbs function as the passive of *qal.*[2]

- לקח in *qal* = "take." The root does not appear in *piel* but does occur in *pual* with the meaning "be taken," which serves as the passive of *qal* (see Ge 3:23).

✓ The *pual* stem infrequently occurs in the Hebrew Bible.

f. *Hifil*

(1) The *hifil* stem most commonly serves as the causative of *qal* in the active voice.

- משׁל in *qal* = "rule"; the *hifil* form הִמְשִׁילָם = "he caused them to rule" (see Da 11:39). In this example the causative *hifil* verb is transitive (having an object).
- זקן in *qal* = "be old," and in *hifil* = "grow old" or "cause oneself to be

---

[1] See Joüon, §52d; and Williams, §145.

[2] These *pual* forms are likely the remnants of an old *qal* passive form which used to exist in the perfect conjugation, but which the Masoretes treated as *pual*. Likewise, a few imperfect and participle forms of the antiquated *qal* passive probably appear in the *MT* as *hofal*. See Waltke and O'Connor, §22.6b.

old" (see Job 14:8). In this example the causative *hifil* is intransative (having no object).

(2) Some *hifil* verbs convey a simple active meaning, like *qal*. In most cases these verbs do not occur in *qal*.[1]

- These *hifil* verbs do not occur in *qal*:
  - הוֹשִׁיעַ (> ישׁע) = "He saves" (Ps 20:7; *Eng* 20:6).
  - יַסְתִּיר (> סתר) = "He will hide" (see 1Sa 20:2).
  - הִשְׁמִיד (> שׁמד) = "He destroyed" (see Dt 2:22).
- כרת = "cut down, cut off" in both *qal* (see 1Sa 24:6; *Eng* 24:5) and *hifil* (see 1Sa 28:9).

g. *Hofal*

The *hofal* stem is the passive of *hifil;* therefore, it has a range of meanings corresponding to *hifil*.

- מלך in *hifil* is causative, as in הִמְלִיךְ אֶת־שָׁאוּל = "He made Saul king" (1Sa 15:35). In *hofal* this verb is causative and passive: הָמְלַךְ = "He was made king" (Da 9:1).
- שׁלך does not occur in *qal.* In *hifil* = "cast out" (see Ne 9:11), and in *hofal* = "be cast out" (see Is 14:19).

✓ The *hofal* stem occurs in the Hebrew Bible less frequently than any other stem.

h. *Hitpael*

(1) The *hitpael* stem usually connotes reflexive action. In form it is the reflexive of *piel* (as indicated by the *dagesh-forte* in both stems), but *hitpael* may also serve as the reflexive of *qal* and *hifil*.[2]

- קדשׁ in *piel* and *hifil* = "make holy, consecrate"; in *hitpael* = "consecrate oneself" (see Ex 19:22).
- נדב in *qal* = "incite, impel"; in *hitpael* = "volunteer" or "incite oneself to action" (see 1Ch 29:17).
- חבא in *hifil* = "hide"; in *hitpael* = "hide oneself" (see 1Sa 14:11).

---

[1] For these and other examples see Kelley, 111-12.

[2] See Horsnell, 108-9; Lambdin, 249; and Waltke and O'Connor, §26.2.

(2) A special use of the reflexive with a plural verb is the reciprocal *hitpael*.

- ראה in *qal* = "look"; in *hitpael* = "look at one another" (see 2Ki 14:8).

(3) Occasionally *hitpael* serves as the passive of another stem.

- רפא in *qal* = "heal"; in *hitpael* = "be healed" (see 2Ki 8:29).

(4) *Hitpael* also occasionally has an intensive function in the sense of an action that is repeated or continued over a period of time.

- הלך in *qal* = "walk"; in *hitpael* = "walk about, wander, roam" (see Ex 21:19 and 1Sa 30:31). In *piel* this verb has an intensive meaning that is similar to *hitpael*. (See section 20A.2d(2).)

(5) Some verbs in *hitpael* express a simple, active meaning like the *qal* stem.

- יִתְנַבֵּא (> נבא) = "He prophecies (1Ki 22:8).
- הִתְפַּלֵּל (> פלל) = "He prayed" (2Ch 30:18).

i. A number of verbs in various stems are classified as "denominative." The classification means that these verbs have been derived from a noun (or other part of speech), in contrast to the typical pattern of nouns being derived from verbs. Denominative verbs appear in a variety of stems, as the following illustrate.

- From the noun מֶ֫לֶךְ ("king") comes the *qal* verb מָלַךְ = "he was king" (Jos 13:10).
- From the noun שֶׁ֫בַע ("seven") comes the *nifal* verb נִשְׁבַּע = "he swore ("he bound himself seven times") (Ge 24:7).
- From the noun כֹּהֵן ("priest") comes the *piel* verb כִּהֵן = "he served as priest" (1Ch 5:36; *Eng* 6:10).
- From the noun מָטָר ("rain") comes the *hifil* verb הִמְטִיר = "he caused to rain" (Ge 2:5).
- From the noun אַף ("nose, anger") comes the *hitpael* verb הִתְאַנַּף = "he was angry" or "showed himself angry" (Dt 1:37).

✓ *BDB* usually places denominative verbs after the nouns (or other parts of speech) from which they are derived. (By contrast, when a noun is derived from a verb, *BDB* places the noun after the verb root.)

j. The preceding discussion summarizes a number of basic connotations of the major verb stems. Because of the variety of possible meanings, one must rely upon a lexicon to discover the range of connotations which any particular verb may have. Then one must select the connotation that is most appropriate for the context in which a verb appears.

Lesson 20: EXERCISES

a. Learn to recognize, pronounce, and translate the following vocabulary.

	Word	*Translation*	*Notes*
(1)	אַהֲרֹן	Aaron (*proper N*)	
(2)	אָיַב	he was an enemy (*V*)	
(3)	אֵם	mother (*NFS*)	*S* with *PS:* אִמִּי, אִמְּךָ, etc. *P* with *PS:* אִמֹּתָם, אִמֹּתֵנוּ, etc.
(4)	חָטָא	he sinned, missed (*V*)	
(5)	חַטָּאת	sin, sin offering (*NFS*)	*Cs:* חַטַּאת; *P:* חַטָּאוֹת
(6)	חַי	alive, living (*adj MS*)	*FS:* חַיָּה; *P:* חַיִּים; חַיָּה is also *NFS* = "living thing, animal"; חַיִּים is also *NMP* = "life"
(7)	חָמֵשׁ (*M*), חֲמִשָּׁה (*F*)	five (*NM/FS*)	P: חֲמִשִּׁים = "fifty"; חֲמִישִׁי (*M*), חֲמִישִׁית (*F*) = "fifth"
(8)	יָלַד	he brought forth, gave birth (*V*)	
(9)	כָּתַב	he wrote (*V*)	
(10)	לֶחֶם	bread, food (*NMS*)	*S* with *PS:* לַחְמִי, לַחְמְךָ, etc.
(11)	נְאֻם	utterance, oracle (*NMS Cs*)	Occurs only in *S Cs*
(12)	נֶפֶשׁ	living being, soul, person, self (*NFS*)	*P:* נַפְשׁוֹת, נְפָשׁוֹת
(13)	צָבָא	army, host, war, warfare (*NMS*)	*P:* צְבָאוֹת
(14)	שָׁלוֹם	wholeness, well-being, prosperity, peace (*NMS*)	*Cs:* שְׁלוֹם ; *P:* שְׁלוֹמִים
(15)	שְׁלֹמֹה	Solomon (*proper N*)	

b. Read aloud and translate the following texts from the Hebrew Bible, using a lexicon as necessary. Also provide an analysis of all finite verbs (*perf, impf,* or *impv*) and non-finite verbs (*inf* and *part*).

(1) Genesis 1:20-23

Verse 20

יְעוֹפֵף (> עוף) is a weak verb with a middle root consonant of *vav*. Roots with a middle *vav* consonant can have some unique stems that require a doubling of the third consonant instead of the second consonant (as occurs with strong verbs in *piel*, *pual*, and *hitpael*). יְעוֹפֵף has a doubled third consonant and is in the *polel* stem, a stem that is equivalent to *piel* with strong verbs.

Verse 22

פְּרוּ (> פרה) and וּרְבוּ (> רבה) are imperative weak verbs that have lost their final consonants. Another verb form from the root רבה appears later in the verse.

(2) Job 9:20

(3) Psalm 34:4 (*Eng* 34:3)

וּנְרוֹמְמָה (> רום) is a weak verb that appears in a stem called *polel*, which is equivalent to *piel* in its range of meanings. See Lesson 25A.1g.

(4) Isaiah 1:24

(5) Isaiah 9:5 (*Eng* 9:6)

(a) נִתַּן (> נתן) In this form the first root consonant of נ has assimilated into the ת as a *dagesh-forte* because of the addition of a נ prefix.

(b) וַתְּהִי (> היה)

(c) Interpret the significance of note "b" for this verse in the critical apparatus.

(d) Read אֲבִיעַד as two words: אֲבִי עַד.

(6) Judges 8:19

הַחֲיִתֶם (> חיה)

(7) Numbers 9:18

(a) יִסְעוּ (> נסע) In this form the first root consonant of נ has dropped out with the addition of a י prefix.

(b) יַחֲנוּ (> חנה)

Lesson 21

Stative Verbs, Introduction to Weak Verbs

21A Stative Verbs

1. Thus far the verb discussion has concentrated on verbs that express action or motion. Such verbs are called "fientive," which is to say that they describe an activity.[1] For example, מָשַׁל = "he ruled" is a fientive verb since it depicts an action performed by a subject. A few Hebrew verbs fall into another category called "stative"; they describe a state of existence rather than an activity. For example, כָּבֵד = "he is heavy" is a stative verb because it depicts a subject's state of being.
2. One way of classifying stative verbs is according to their meaning. The following stative verbs from vocabulary lists illustrate the categories.[2]

   a. Statives describing an attribute:

   - חָזַק = "he was strong"
   - יָטַב = "he was good"
   - יָכֹל = "he was able"
   - כָּבֵד = "he was heavy"
   - קָדַשׁ = "he was holy"
   - קָטֹן = "he was small"

   b. Statives describing a circumstance:

   - מָלֵא = "he was full"
   - מָלַךְ = "he was king"

   c. Statives describing an emotional or psychological state:

   - אָהֵב = "he loved"
   - יָרֵא = "he was afraid"

3. Vowel classes of stative verbs

   a. Another way to classify stative verbs is according to their vowels. This scheme

---

[1] "Fientive" comes from the Latin word *fiens* = "acting." See Waltke and O'Connor, §20.2k.

[2] See Horsnell, 121-22; and Joüon, §41f.

identifies statives by the second vowel of their lexical forms (*perf, qal, 3MS*).[1] The vowel classes for stative verbs (moving from the largest to the smallest class) are as follows.

E-class, as illustrated by אָהֵב, יָרֵא, כָּבֵד, and מָלֵא

A-class, as illustrated by חָזַק, יָטַב, מָלַךְ, and קָדַשׁ

O-class, as illustrated by יָכֹל and קָטֹן

b. Stative verbs of all three vowel classes are generally inflected according to the משל paradigm of strong verbs except in the *qal* stem. The principle differences in *qal* are illustrated in the following charts using כבד, קדשׁ, and קטן as models. (The charts indicate where statives differ from משל. See Appendix 3, paradigm 2, for all *qal* forms of the three classes of statives.)

(1) Perfect, *qal*

[a] E-class statives have a second vowel of *sere* in perfect, *qal, 3MS;* all other forms follow the משל paradigm.

Perfect, *Qal*		
	משל	*E-class*
3MS	מָשַׁל	כָּבֵד

[b] O-class statives in perfect, *qal* have a second vowel of either *holem* or *qames-hatuf* where משל has a *patah.*

Perfect, *Qal*		
	משל	*O-class*
3MS	מָשַׁל	קָטֹן
2MS	מָשַׁלְתָּ	קָטֹנְתָּ
2FS	מָשַׁלְתְּ	קָטֹנְתְּ
1CS	מָשַׁלְתִּי	קָטֹנְתִּי
2MP	מְשַׁלְתֶּם	קְטָנְתֶּם
2FP	מְשַׁלְתֶּן	קְטָנְתֶּן
1CP	מָשַׁלְנוּ	קָטֹנּוּ

[1] See Horsnell, 122-24.

✓ For קטן: in *2MP* and *2FP* the ◌ָ vowel is a *qames-hatuf*, and in *1CP* the final *nun* of the root has assimilated into the *nun* of the verb suffix by means of a *dagesh-forte*. The assimilation of the *nun* can be observed in other forms of קטן in the charts that follow.

[c] A-class statives are conjugated like משל in perfect, *qal*.

(2) Imperfect and imperative, *qal*

In the *qal* stem of the imperfect and imperative, all three vowel classes of statives normally take an A-class vowel for the second root consonant where משל has a *holem*.

Imperfect, *Qal*				
	משל	*E-class*	*A-class*	*O-class*
3MS	יִמְשֹׁל	יִכְבַּד	יִקְדַּשׁ	יִקְטַן
3FS	תִּמְשֹׁל	תִּכְבַּד	תִּקְדַּשׁ	תִּקְטַן
2MS	תִּמְשֹׁל	תִּכְבַּד	תִּקְדַּשׁ	תִּקְטַן
1CS	אֶמְשֹׁל	אֶכְבַּד	אֶקְדַּשׁ	אֶקְטַן
3FP	תִּמְשֹׁלְנָה	תִּכְבַּדְנָה	תִּקְדַּשְׁנָה	תִּקְטַנָּה
2FP	תִּמְשֹׁלְנָה	תִּכְבַּדְנָה	תִּקְדַּשְׁנָה	תִּקְטַנָּה
1CP	נִמְשֹׁל	נִכְבַּד	נִקְדַּשׁ	נִקְטַן

Imperative, *Qal*				
	משל	*E-class*	*A-class*	*O-class*
2MS	מְשֹׁל	כְּבַד	קְדַשׁ	קְטַן
2FP	מְשֹׁלְנָה	כְּבַדְנָה	קְדַשְׁנָה	קְטַנָּה

4. Stative verbs and adjectives

a. Several stative verbs in perfect, *qal* are spelled the same as their corresponding adjectival forms. For example, כָּבֵד can either be the verb "he was heavy" or the *MS* adjective "heavy," and קָטֹן can either be the verb "he was small" or the *MS* adjective "small." The context in which these words appear is the clue to recognizing their form. Because of this similarity, statives are sometimes referred to as "conjugated adjectives."

b. The close connection between stative verbs and adjectives is also reflected in the tendency for adjectival forms to serve in the place of stative participles. For example, the stative participle of שׁכח ("forget") appears in the phrase שֹׁכְחֵי אֱלוֹהַּ ("ones forgetting God" [Ps 50:22]), while a parallel phrase uses a related adjective instead: שְׁכֵחֵי אֱלֹהִים ("ones forgetting God" [Ps 9:18; *Eng* 9:17]).[1]

5. Connotations of stative verbs in the perfect and imperfect tenses[2]

a. In the perfect tense stative verbs can convey the meanings of either the past or present tense in English.

- חִזְּקוּ = "They made strong" (Jdg 9:24).
- קָטֹנְתִּי = "I am least (small)" (Ge 32:11; *Eng* 32:10).

b. In the imperfect tense statives normally express the idea of the future tense. However, other connotations (such as the present or past tense) are also possible for statives as they are for fientive verbs. (See Lesson 20A.1d.)

- אִירָא = "I will fear" (Ps 27:1).
- יַקְדִּישׁוּ = "They consecrate (make holy)" (Lv 22:3).
- תִּכְבַּד = "It was continually heavy (Ps 32:4).

21B Introduction to Weak Verbs

This lesson has already discussed one way to categorize verbs: as fientives or statives. Another manner of categorization is to identify verbs as strong or weak. Much of this Grammar has focused on describing the fixed patterns of the conjugations of the strong verb, as represented by משׁל. However, the majority of Hebrew verbs fall into the category of weak verbs, meaning that their roots contain particular consonants which cause their inflections to vary from those of the strong verb. The easiest way to learn the patterns of weak verbs is by noting how their inflections vary from the paradigm of the strong verb. This lesson will introduce the classification and general characteristics of weak verbs. Succeeding lessons will explore in more detail the inflection of various classes of these verbs.

---

[1] See Joüon, §50b.

[2] See ibid., §113a; and Horsnell, 126-27.

1. Classification of weak verbs

a. A weak verb is identified by one of two factors. One is the occurrence in a verb root of a guttural (א, ה, ח, or ע), a quiescent (א, ה, ו, or י), *nun*, or *resh* (which has some characteristics of gutturals). The other factor that indicates a weak verb is the appearance of the same consonant in the second and third positions of a verb root.

b. The following chart presents the traditional method of classifying weak verbs. This classification method is based upon the verb root פעל, whereby פ stands for the first consonant of a root, ע for the second, and ל for the third.

ל (*3rd root consonant*)	ע (*2nd root consonant*)	פ (*1st root consonant*)
Guttural	Guttural (including ר)	Guttural (including ר)
א	ו (middle vowel)	א
ה	י (middle vowel)	י
	עע[1] (double-*ayin*)	נ

(1) Notes concerning the chart for classifying weak verbs

(a) To illustrate the significance of the chart, if a verb root has a guttural in the פ (first consonant) position, it is called a *pe*-guttural weak verb. All weak verbs of this classification share certain characteristics. Verbs which have a ר in the פ position typically display at least some of the same characteristics.

- עָמַד ("he stood") is a *pe*-guttural weak verb since it has the guttural ע in the first consonant position.

(b) If a verb has an א in the פ (first consonant) position it is called a *pe-alef* weak verb. Since an א is a guttural, *pe-alef* weak verbs share cetain characteristics with other *pe*-guttural verbs; however, *pe-alef* verbs have additional features which are unique to themselves. Therefore, if a verb has an א in the פ position, it is properly called a *pe-alef* verb, since that is a more specific classification, rather than simply a *pe*-guttural.

[1] עע represents a doubling of any consonant (not necessarily ע), so that the consonant that appears in the ע (second consonant) position also appears in the ל (third consonant) position.

- ‏אָכַל‏ ("he ate") is a *pe-alef* (abbreviated ‏פ״א‏) weak verb.

(c) A verb which has a ו or י in the ע (second consonant) position is called an *ayin-vav* or *ayin-yod* weak verb. These verbs are also termed "middle vowel" verbs, since ו and י become naturally-long vowels in these verbs.

- ‏קוּם‏ ("to rise") is an *ayin-vav* (‏ע״ו‏) weak verb. This form is infinitive, *qal,* construct, which serves as the lexical form for this verb class.
- ‏שִׂים‏ ("to set") is an *ayin-yod* (‏ע״י‏) weak verb. This form is infinitive, *qal,* construct, which serves as the lexical form for this verb class.

(d) The classification of ‏עע‏ or double-*ayin* indicates a doubling of whatever consonant appears in the ע (second consonant) position. In other words, it refers to a verb root that has the same consonant, whatever that consonant may be, in the second and third positions.

- ‏סָבַב‏ ("he surrounded") is a double-*ayin* (‏עע‏) weak verb since a ב appears in the second and third consonant positions.

(e) Some verbs have more than one weakness.

- ‏יָצָא‏ ("he went out") is doubly weak, being *pe-yod* (‏פ״י‏) and *lamed-alef* (‏ל״א‏).
- ‏יָרֵא‏ ("he was afraid") is triply weak, being *pe-yod* (‏פ״י‏), *ayin-resh* (‏ע״ר‏), and *lamed-alef* (‏ל״א‏).

(2) Grammarians have proposed other schemas for identifying weak verbs than the traditional one presented above. For example, some use Roman numerals (I, II, and III) to designate the three places of a root consonant, as in I-*alef*, II-*vav*, or III-*he*. Others designate the root consonants with such terms as "initial," "middle," and "final," as is initial-*alef*, middle-*vav*, or final-*he*.[1]

2. Disappearance of consonants

a. A weak consonant in a verb can disappear in certain forms. The disappearance of a consonant may simply amount to the dropping of the weak consonant, or it may also involve the assimilation of the weak consonant into a neighboring consonant. In some cases of assimilation the neighboring consonant (that is, the one which accepts the assimilated consonant) receives a *dagesh-forte*. This *dagesh-forte*

---

[1] For example, see Kautzsch, §64, 66; and Seow, 24.

serves to compensate for the dropped consonant; it also provides a clue that a root consonant has fallen out.

- The *pe-yod* verb ישׁב ("sit") drops the י when certain verb prefixes are added. For example, the imperfect, *qal*, *1CS* form is אֵשֵׁב ("I will sit"). In this case no *dagesh-forte* appears to indicate assimilation.
- When certain verb prefixes are added to the *pe-nun* verb נשׂא ("lift"), the נ assimilates into the second consonant of the root, and that consonant receives a compensating *dagesh-forte*. To illustrate, the imperfect, *qal*, *3MS* form of this root is יִשָּׂא ("he will lift").
- When certain verb suffixes are added to the double-*ayin* verb קלל ("be light") the second ל assimilates into the first ל, and the first ל receives a compensating *dagesh-forte*. For example, the perfect, *qal*, *3MP* form of this root is קַלּוּ ("they were light").

b. Classifications of weak verbs that commonly lose a consonant when inflected

(1) The most challenging aspect of translating a weak verb is identifying a root consonant that drops out as the verb is inflected. Future lessons will describe the key situations in which various classifications of weak verbs drop or assimilate consonants. However, it is helpful at this point to recognize that six types of weak verbs very commonly experience the disappearance of a consonant at points in their conjugations. They are

Pe-yod *Pe-nun*
Ayin-vav *Ayin-yod* Double-*ayin*
Lamed-he

In certain situations other classes of weak verbs may lose a consonant when inflected; however, the preceding list represents most situations where a consonant disappears.

(2) In the lessons that follow a number of clues will be presented for identifying the roots of weak verbs that have lost a consonant. For now, one method for

identifying a root consonant that has disappeared is by using the preceding list of six classifications of weak verbs that commonly lose a consonant when inflected.

(a) For example, in order to translate the weak verb וַיִּבְכּוּ in Ge 50:3 one must identify this verb's root. The first step is to determine which of the consonants are part of the root by removing any prefixes or suffixes. The initial *vav* can be identified as a *vav* consecutive and the *yod* as an imperfect prefix, based on their pointing. (See Lesson 16A.3.) The *shureq* is a plural verb suffix, which (along with the *yod*) identifies the verb as imperfect, *qal*, *3MP*. Thus when prefixes and suffixes are removed, the remaining root consonants are בכ. Since nearly all verb roots are triconsonantal, one can assume that a root consonant has dropped out in this verb. Using the preceding list of six classifications of weak verbs that commonly lose a consonant, one can form a list of potential candidates for the weak root of this verb:

Pe-yod:	יבך
Pe-nun:	נבך
Ayin-vav:	בוך
Ayin-yod:	ביך
Double-*ayin*:	בכך
Lamed-he:	בכה

The next step is to check a lexicon to determine which of these options are extant roots; then which of the extant roots occur in imperfect, *qal* (the form in Ge 50:3); and finally which remaining option best fits the context of Ge 50:3. Such a check reveals that only two of these options are verb roots that appear in the *MT:* בוך and בכה. The first can be eliminated from consideration for two reasons. The lexicon indicates that בוך only occurs in *nifal* and only in the perfect and participle; therefore, the root does not appear in imperfect, *qal* (the form in Ge 50:3). Moreover, the meaning of בוך ("confuse") does not fit the context of the verse. By this process of elimination one arrives at בכה ("weep") as the root for the verb וַיִּבְכּוּ – a root which does occur in imperfect, *qal,* and which has a meaning that fits the context of the verse. Thus the analysis of וַיִּבְכּוּ is > בכה, *impf, qal, 3MP + vav cons* = "and they wept."

(b) While the preceding process for determining a verb root is lengthy, it can be employed effectively with most verbs. Other clues will appear in succeeding lessons that will abbreviate the procedure for uncovering a consonant that has been dropped from a weak verb.

Lesson 21: Exercises

a. From memory list three vowel classes for stative verbs and an example of a verb from each class.

b. Reproduce from memory the chart that gives the classifications of weak verbs (in terms of פ, ע, and ל), as presented in section 21B.1b.

c. Identify the classification of the following weak verbs; some may fall into more than one class.

- *Example:* עָלָה ("he went up") ⇒ *Answer: pe*-guttural and *lamed-he*

(1) עָבַד	("he worked")	(11) חָזַק	("he was strong")
(2) דָּמַם	("he stood still")	(12) תמם	("be complete")
(3) יָרַד	("he went down")	(13) יָדַע	("he knew")
(4) מָצָא	("he found")	(14) שׁוּב	("[to] turn")
(5) שִׂית	("[to] put")	(15) הָרַג	("he killed")
(6) לָקַח	("he took")	(16) נוּחַ	("[to] rest")
(7) אָהֵב	("he loved")	(17) אָסַף	("he gathered")
(8) נָתַן	("he gave")	(18) נָפַל	("he fell")
(9) בּוֹא	("[to] come")	(19) רָאָה	("he saw")
(10) בָּנָה	("he built")	(20) בִּין	("[to] understand")

d. From memory list the six classifications of weak verbs which commonly experience the disappearance of a consonant when inflected (as presented in section 21B.2b(1)).

e. Learn to recognize, pronounce, and translate the following vocabulary.

	Word	*Translation*	*Notes*
(1)	אָהֵב	he loved (*V*)	Also אָהַב
(2)	בָּבֶל	Babylon, Babel (*proper N*)	

(3)	הִנֵּה	look, behold (*particle*)	*PS:* הִנְנִי or הִנֵּנִי, הִנְּךָ, etc.
(4)	חָזַק	he was strong (*V*)	
(5)	יָטַב	he was good (*V*)	
(6)	יָכֹל	he was able, prevailed, endured (*V*)	Also יָכוֹל; *impf, qal, 3MS:* יוּכַל
(7)	יָרֵא	he was afraid, feared (*V*)	
(8)	כָּבֵד	he was heavy, honored (*V*)	
(9)	כָּבוֹד	honor, glory (*NMS*)	*Cs:* כְּבוֹד; *Ab* also כָּבֹד
(10)	מְאֹד	(a) very (*adv*) (b) power, might (*NMS*)	
(11)	מָלֵא	he was full, filled (*V*)	
(12)	קָדַשׁ	he was holy (*V*)	
(13)	קָטֹן	he was small, insignificant (*V*)	
(14)	רָבָה	he was great, became numerous (*V*)	
(15)	שֵׁשׁ (*M*), שִׁשָּׁה (*F*)	six (*NM/FS*)	*FS Cs:* שֵׁשֶׁת; *P:* שִׁשִּׁים = "sixty"; שִׁשִּׁי (*M*), שִׁשִּׁית (*F*) = "sixth"

f. Read aloud and translate Genesis 1:24-31 from the Hebrew Bible. Also provide an analysis of all verbs (finite and non-finite). If necessary, use the process described above in section 21B.2b(2) for help in locating the roots of weak verbs that have lost consonants.

Verse 24

(1) תּוֹצֵא (> יצא) One characteristic of some *pe-yod* verbs is that the *yod* usually becomes a *vav* in *nifal*, *hifil*, and *hofal*.

(2) חַיְתוֹ (> חיה) is a *NFS Cs* with a paragogic וֹ (which may be the remnant of an archaic case ending). The וֹ has no significance for translation other than emphasizing that the noun is construct.[1]

[1] See Joüon, §93r; and Kautzsch, §90k, o.

Verse 26

Interpret the significance of note "b" for this verse in the critical apparatus.

Verse 29

נָתַתִּי (> נתן) has the irregular feature that its final *nun* in this and other forms assimilates into the ת of the verb suffix – something which does not usually occur with verb roots ending in *nun*.

Lesson 22

Weak Verbs: *Pe*-Guttural, *Pe-Alef*, *Ayin*-Guttural, and *Lamed*-Guttural; Particles of Existence and Nonexistence

22A Weak Verbs: *Pe*-Guttural, *Pe-Alef*, *Ayin*-Guttural, and *Lamed*-Guttural

1. Introduction

a. Each of the classifications of weak verbs has its own characteristics. This and succeeding lessons will describe the major characteristics of the weak verb classes and provide clues for recognizing their roots and forms.

b. The present lesson focuses on the way in which the guttural consonants (א, ה, ח, and ע) and ר affect weak verbs. The unique features of these consonants, which were summarized earlier in Lesson 6C, are repeated here for convenience.

(1) The gutturals (including ר) cannot take a *dagesh-forte*, and as compensation for this weakness the vowel before a guttural (or ר) may lengthen.

(2) The gutturals (excluding ר) normally take a composite *sheva* where other consonants would have a simple *sheva.*

(3) The gutturals (including ר) prefer A-class vowels beneath and before them.

2. *Pe*-guttural verbs

a. *Pe*-guttural verbs have one of the following letters in the first consonant position: ה, ח, ע, or ר. Examples of some *pe*-guttural verbs are הָרַג ("he killed"), חָזַק ("he was strong"), and עָמַד ("he stood"). Verbs that begin with *alef* are not included in the *pe*-guttural class because they sometimes have unique characteristics. *Pe-alef* verbs are discussed in the next section.

b. The unique features of guttural consonants affect *pe*-guttural verbs in the following stems: *qal*, *nifal*, *hifil*, and *hofal.* *Pe*-guttural verbs are spelled like strong verbs in *piel*, *pual*, and *hitpael*.

c. Major characteristics of *pe*-guttural verbs

(1) *Pe*-gutturals (including ר) cannot take the *dagesh-forte* that occurs in some *nifal* forms of the strong verb – namely, in the imperfect, imperative, and infinitive construct. As compensation for the fact that *pe*-guttural verbs reject the *dagesh-forte*, the vowel before the *pe*-guttural (and under the *nifal* prefix), lengthens from *hireq* to *sere*.

✓ To summarize in symbolic form: where the strong verb has a *nifal* pattern of □□□ָּ◁ִ, a *pe*-guttural verb follows the pattern of □□□ָ◁ֵ.

The following chart illustrates this characteristic, using עמד as a model for *pe*-gutturals and giving the relevant forms of משל for comparison.

Nifal		
	משל	עמד
Impf, 3MS	יִמָּשֵׁל	יֵעָמֵד
Impv, 2MS / Inf Cs	הִמָּשֵׁל	הֵעָמֵד

✓ While the charts in this section provide selected examples to illustrate characteristics of weak verbs, Appendix 3, paradigm 3, gives the full conjugation for *pe*-guttural verbs.

(2) A number of forms of the strong verb require a simple *sheva* under the first root consonant. In these cases *pe*-gutturals (excluding ר) take a composite rather than a simple *sheva*. The most commonly occurring composite *sheva* for *pe*-gutturals is *hatef-patah*, because of the preference of gutturals for A-class vowels.

(a) In *qal* this characteristic (of the *pe*-guttural taking a composite rather than simple *sheva*) occurs a few times when there is no verb prefix.

✓ To summarize: where the pattern for the strong verb is □□□ְ, the *pe*-guttural pattern is □□□ֲ, as the following illustrate.

Qal		
	משל	עמד
Perf, 2MP	מְשַׁלְתֶּם	עֲמַדְתֶּם
Impv, 2MS / Inf Cs	מְשֹׁל	עֲמֹד

(b) *Pe*-gutturals take composite *shevas* in several stems that employ verb prefixes. In these cases the vowel before the composite *sheva* (and under the prefix) is a short vowel that corresponds to the composite *sheva*. Thus, the patterns that appear in *pe*-gutturals are □□□ֲ◁ַ, □□□ֱ◁ֶ, and □□□ֳ◁ָ. The first pattern is most common; the last occurs only in *hofal*. The following charts illustrate these *pe*-guttural patterns in the perfect, imperfect, imperative, infinitive, and participle conjugations.

Perfect		
	משל	עמד
Nif, 3MS	נִמְשַׁל	נֶעֱמַד
Hif, 3MS	הִמְשִׁיל	הֶעֱמִיד
Hof, 3MS	הָמְשַׁל	הָעֳמַד

Imperfect		
	משל	עמד
Qal, 3MS	יִמְשֹׁל	יַעֲמֹד[1]
Qal, 1CS	אֶמְשֹׁל	אֶעֱמֹד
Hif, 3MS	יַמְשִׁיל	יַעֲמִיד
Hof, 3MS	יָמְשַׁל	יָעֳמַד

✓ Note that the imperfect, *qal, 3MS* form above (יַעֲמֹד) has a prefix vowel of *patah* – a prefix vowel that serves as a clue to imperfect, *hifil* in strong verbs. The *patah* appears in יַעֲמֹד because this verb is *pe*-guttural and therefore prefers A-class vowels before and beneath the guttural. The imperfect, *hifil, 3MS* form יַעֲמִיד also has a *patah* prefix vowel; however, the *hireq-yod* marks it as *hifil* and distinguishes it from the *qal* form. When there is difficulty distinguishing between *qal* and *hifil* in imperfect *pe*-gutturals, the student should rely on a lexicon and the context in which a verb appears.

Imperative		
	משל	עמד
Hif, 2MS	הַמְשֵׁל	הַעֲמֵד

[1] *Pe*-gutturals that begin with ח prefer E-class vowels in imperfect, *qal*, where other guttural consonants prefer A-class vowels. For example, where עמד ("stand") in *impf, qal, 3MS* is יַעֲמֹד, the stative verb חזק ("be strong") is יֶחֱזַק. See Horsnell, 369.

	Infinitive			
	Construct		*Absolute*	
	משל	עמד	משל	עמד
Nif			נִמְשֹׁל	נַעֲמוֹד
Hif	הַמְשִׁיל	הַעֲמִיד	הַמְשֵׁל	הַעֲמֵד
Hof			הָמְשֵׁל	הָעֳמֵד

Participle		
	משל	עמד
Nif, MS Ab	נִמְשָׁל	נֶעֱמָד
Hif, MS Ab	מַמְשִׁיל	מַעֲמִיד
Hof, MS, Ab	מָמְשָׁל	מָעֳמָד

✓ As a rule, a simple *sheva* cannot follow a composite *sheva*. There are a few situations in the inflection of *pe*-guttural verbs where a composite *sheva* would normally appear before a simple *sheva*. For example, where the strong verb is נִמְשְׁלָה (*perf, nif, 3FS*), a *pe*-guttural would be נֶעֱמְדָה, except for the fact that such spelling places a simple *sheva* after a composite *sheva*. To correct the problem, the composite *sheva* lengthens to a short vowel, with the resulting form of נֶעֶמְדָה (*impf, nif, 3FS*). Another example is imperfect, *qal, 3MP,* where the *pe*-guttural pattern is יַעַמְדוּ (rather than יַעֲמְדוּ). Situations like these arise in *pe*-gutturals where there is a verb prefix and a vowel suffix (הָ◌, וּ, or ◌ִי) or a pronominal suffix.

3. *Pe-alef* verbs

a. Most *pe-alef* verbs are spelled in a similar fashion to *pe*-guttural verbs. However, some *pe-alefs* – such as אָבַד ("he was lost"), אָכַל ("he ate"), and אָמַר ("he said") – also have certain unique features that do not occur in other *pe*-guttural verbs. As a result, *pe-alefs* are placed in a distinct classification.

b. The unique features that some *pe-alef* verbs display occur in imperfect, *qal*, as described below.

(1) Since *alef* is a quiescent (as well as a guttural), it sometimes loses its capacity to support a vowel in imperfect, *qal*. When such occurs, *pe-alef* is preceded by a *holem* prefix vowel.

(2) In imperfect, *qal*, some *pe-alef* verbs require a *patah* for the second root consonant where strong verbs take a *holem*.

(3) In imperfect, *qal*, *1CS*, the *pe-alef* consonant drops out as the **א** verb prefix is attached.

✓ To summarize:

(a) Where the strong verb pattern is ◁ִ□ְ□ֹ□, some *pe-alef* verbs have ◁אֹ□ַ□

(b) Where the strong verb pattern is אֶ□ְ□ֹ□, some *pe-alef* verbs have אֹ□ַ□.

The following chart illustrates, using אכל as a model.

Imperfect, *Qal*		
	משל	אכל
3MS	יִמְשֹׁל	יֹאכַל
1CS	אֶמְשֹׁל	אֹכַל
3FP / 2FP	תִּמְשֹׁלְנָה	תֹּאכַלְנָה

✓ See Appendix 3, paradigm 4, for the full *qal* conjugation of *pe-alefs*.

c. אָמַר has an irregular feature in infinitive, *qal,* construct. When this form is preceded by the prefixed preposition לְ, the *alef* becomes quiescent and the vowel under the ל lengthens. To illustrate, אֱמֹר (*inf, qal, Cs*) + לְ *prep* = לֵאמֹר.

2nd

4. *Ayin*-guttural verbs

a. *Ayin*-guttural verbs have a middle root consonant that is a guttural or ר. Examples of *ayin*-gutturals are בָּחַר ("he chose") and ברך ("bless"). *Ayin*-guttural verbs follow patterns that are similar to *pe*-gutturals.

b. Major characteristics of *ayin*-guttural verbs

(1) *Ayin*-gutturals (including ר) cannot take the *dagesh-forte* that occurs in strong verbs in *piel, pual,* and *hitpael.*

(a) When the *ayin*-guttural is א, ר, and sometimes ע, the rejection of the *dagesh-forte* is compensated for by the lengthening of the preceding vowel (under the first root consonant). The lengthening follows these patterns:

Strong verb: □ִ□ּ□ ⇒ *ayin*-guttural: □ֵ□□

Strong verb: □ֻ□ּ□ ⇒ *ayin*-guttural: □ֹ□□

Strong verb: □ַ□ּ□ ⇒ *ayin*-guttural: □ָ□□

(b) When the *ayin*-guttural is ה, ח, and sometimes ע, the preceding vowel (under the first root consonant) is not lengthened. With these *ayin*-gutturals the patterns are:

Strong verb: □□ּ□ִ ⇒ *ayin*-guttural: □□□ִ

Strong verb: □□ּ□ֻ ⇒ *ayin*-guttural: □□□ֻ

Strong verb: □□ּ□ַ ⇒ *ayin*-guttural: □□□ַ

(c) The following chart illustrates these patterns using ברך and בחר as models.

	משל	ברך (With compensatory lengthening of preceding vowel)	בחר (Without compensatory lengthening of preceding vowel)
Perf, piel, 3MS	מִשֵּׁל	בֵּרֵךְ	בִּחֵר
Perf, pual, 3MS	מֻשַּׁל	בֹּרַךְ	בֻּחַר
Impf, piel, 3MS	יְמַשֵּׁל	יְבָרֵךְ	יְבַחֵר
Impf, pual, 3MS	יְמֻשַּׁל	יְבֹרַךְ	יְבֻחַר
Perf, hit, 3MS / Impv, hit, 2MS / Inf, hit, Cs	הִתְמַשֵּׁל	הִתְבָּרֵךְ	הִתְבַּחֵר
Impv, piel, 2MS / Inf, piel, Cs & Ab	מַשֵּׁל	בָּרֵךְ	בַּחֵר

(2) *Ayin*-gutturals (normally excluding ר) take a composite *sheva* where a simple *sheva* appears in a strong verb. To be more specific, where the strong verb has □□ְ□, an *ayin*-guttural has □□ֲ□. This situation arises in perfect, imperfect, and imperative where there is a vowel suffix, as the following chart illustrates.

• no dagesh
• no simple sheva
• a class preference

	משל	בחר
Perf, qal, 3FS	מָשְׁלָה	בָּחֲרָה
Impf, nif, 2FS	תִּמָּשְׁלִי	תִּבָּחֲרִי
Impv, qal, 2MP	מִשְׁלוּ	בַּחֲרוּ

✓ Note that in the *impv, qal, 2MP* form בַּחֲרוּ the *hatef-patah* is preceded by the corresponding short vowel of *patah,* rather than the *hireq* that appears in strong verbs.

(3) *Ayin*-gutturals (including ר) demonstrate a preference for A-class vowels, as the following illustrate.

	משל	בחר
Perf, qal, 3FS	מָֽשְׁלָה	בָּחֲרָה
Perf, piel, 3MS	מִשֵּׁל	בִּחַר
Impf, qal, 3MS	יִמְשֹׁל	יִבְחַר
Imv, qal, 2MS	מְשֹׁל	בְּחַר

- ✓ As noted previously, the first example illustrates the preference of *ayin*-gutturals for *hatef-patah*. The other examples show a preference for *patah* beneath the *ayin*-guttural when a strong verb has a *sere* (*perf, piel, 3MS*) or *holem* (*impf, qal, 3MS,* and *impv, qal, 2MS*).
- ✓ See Appendix 3, paradigm 8, for the full conjugation of *ayin*-gutturals.

5. *Lamed*-guttural verbs

a. *Lamed*-guttural verbs have a final consonant of הּ, ח, or ע. Verbs ending in ר are not included because they are inflected like strong verbs, and verbs with a final א or ה (without *mappiq*) are excluded because they have unique features that place them in separate classes. Examples of *lamed*-gutturals are גָּבַהּ ("he was high"), שָׁלַח ("he sent"), and שָׁמַע ("he heard").

b. The major characteristic of *lamed*-guttural verbs is that they must be preceded by an A-class vowel. In some cases this feature requires a furtive *patah* beneath the *lamed*-guttural.

(1) Often the vowel before or beneath the *lamed*-guttural is changed to an A-class vowel. The following charts illustrate, using שלח as a model.

Perfect		
	משל	שלח
Qal, 2FS	מָשַׁלְתְּ	שָׁלַחַתְּ
Piel, 3MS	מִשֵּׁל	שִׁלַּח
Hit, 3MS	הִתְמַשֵּׁל	[1]הִשְׁתַּלַּח

Imperfect		
	משל	שלח
Qal, 3MS	יִמְשֹׁל	יִשְׁלַח
Nif, 3MS	יִמָּשֵׁל	יִשָּׁלַח
Piel, 3MS	יְמַשֵּׁל	יְשַׁלַּח

[1] Because שׁ is a sibilant, it changes places with the ת of the verb prefix. See Lesson 13A.7c.

Imperative		
	משל	שלח
Impv, qal, 2MS	מְשֹׁל	שְׁלַח
Impv, nif, 2MS	הִמָּשֵׁל	הִשָּׁלַח
Impv, piel, 2MS	מַשֵּׁל	שַׁלַּח

(2) When a *lamed*-guttural appears after a naturally-long vowel and sometimes after *holem* and *sere*, those vowels do not change and the *lamed*-guttural requires a furtive *patah* beneath it.

• prefer a class
• furtive – after hl vowel

	משל	שלח
Perf, hif, 3MS	הִמְשִׁיל	הִשְׁלִיחַ
Inf, qal, Ab	מָשׁוֹל	שָׁלוֹחַ
Part, qal, pass, MS, Ab	מָשׁוּל	שָׁלוּחַ
Part, qal, act, MS, Ab	מֹשֵׁל	שֹׁלֵחַ
Impv, qal, 2MS / Inf, qal, Cs	מְשֹׁל	שְׁלַח

✓ See Appendix 3, paradigm 12, for the full conjugation of *lamed*-gutturals.

6. Summary of characteristics of *pe*-gutturals, *pe-alefs, ayin*-gutturals, and *lamed*-gutturals

a. The following is a succinct summary of the major characteristics of verbs with guttural weaknesses.

(1) A guttural or ר in a verb root rejects a *dagesh-forte* and sometimes causes the preceding vowel to lengthen.

(2) A guttural in a verb root takes a composite *sheva* where a strong consonant takes a simple *sheva*. The consonant preceding a guttural with a composite *sheva* may take the short vowel that corresponds to the composite *sheva* (as in □□□◁, □□□◁, or □□□◁).

(3) A guttural or ר in a verb root prefers an A-class vowel before it and beneath it.

(4) For some *pe-alefs* in imperfect, *qal:*

(a) The imperfect prefix causes the *pe-alef* to quiesce and the prefix to take a *holem* (as in □□א◁).

(b) The imperfect *1CS* prefix (א) causes the *pe-alef* to drop out (as in □□אֹ).

b. The following verbs with analyses illustrate the process of identifying the forms of verbs with guttural weaknesses.

(1) תֵּחָרֵשׁ (Mic 3:12) > חרשׁ, *impf, nif, 3FS,* "it will be plowed"

The *sere* under the imperfect prefix (תֵּ) and *qames* under the *pe*-guttural (חָ) are clues that the verb is imperfect, *nifal.* The guttural has the *qames* that normally appears in imperfect, *nifal;* however, it cannot take the typical *dagesh-forte.* To compensate, the vowel before the guttural has lengthened from *hireq* (which appears in strong verbs) to *sere.*

(2) יַעַזְבֵנוּ (1Ki 8:57) > עזב, *impf, qal, 3MS + PS 1CP,* "he will leave us"

The imperfect prefix has a *patah* (יַ), which is a clue to imperfect, *hifil* in strong verbs. However, in this case the verb is *qal,* and the *patah* appears because the *pe*-guttural prefers A-class vowels. (Besides this fact, the verb עזב never occurs in *hifil.*) Notice also that the *ayin* has a *patah* (עַ) instead of the expected composite *sheva* (עֲ). The *patah* occurs to prevent a composite *sheva* from appearing before a simple *sheva,* which would be an impossible vocalization.

(3) וְתֹאבְדוּ (Ps 2:12) > אבד, *impf, qal, 2MP + vav conj,* "and you will perish"

The *holem* prefix vowel and the quiescent *pe-alef* (תֹא) are clues that the form is imperfect, *qal.*

(4) וְאֹכְלֵם (Hos 13:8), > אכל, *impf, qal, 1CS + vav conj + PS 3MP,* "and I will devour them"

The *alef* with a *holem* (אֹ) is a clue that the form is imperfect, *qal, 1CS.* (The *pe-alef* of the root has dropped out.) The *holem* and the *sheva* under the second root consonant resemble the vowels of a participle, *qal,* active (when occurring with a suffix). However, the context of the verb requires an imperfect instead of a participle.

22B Particles of Existence and Nonexistence

1. Hebrew has two particles that serve to express the existence or nonexistence of someone or something: יֵשׁ (or יֶשׁ־) conveys existence; and אַיִן, or the more common construct form אֵין, conveys nonexistence.

2. The particles of existence and nonexistence can have a variety of meanings and translations.

   a. Often their translation requires the use of English state-of-being verbs. For example, יֵשׁ can mean "there is/are" or "there was/were"; and אַ֫יִן or אֵין can have such meanings as "there is/are not," "there was/were not," "there is no one/nothing." While these translations involve verbs in English, one must remember that יֵשׁ, אַ֫יִן, and אֵין are particles, not verbs.
      - יֵשׁ נָבִיא בְּיִשְׂרָאֵל = "There is (יֵשׁ) a prophet in Israel" (2Ki 5:8).
      - וַנִּרְאֶה כִּי־אַ֫יִן = "When we saw that there were none (אַ֫יִן)" (1Sa 10:14).
      - כִּי־אֵין בַּ֫יִת אֲשֶׁר אֵין־שָׁם מֵת = "For there was not (אֵין) a house in which there was no one (אֵין) dead" (Ex 12:30).

   b. The particles of existence and nonexistence can also express possession. In such a situation the particle is followed by the prefixed preposition לְ.
      - יֶשׁ־לָנוּ אָב = "There is (יֶשׁ־) to us a father," or more idiomatically, "We have a father" (Ge 44:20).
      - אֵין לָהּ וָלָד = "There was not (אֵין) to her a child," or more idiomatically, "She had no child" (Ge 11:30).

   c. The particles of existence and nonexistence can also take pronominal suffixes, in which case the pronominal suffix is subjective and the translation typically requires a state-of-being verb in English.
      - אִם־יֶשְׁנוֹ בָּאָ֫רֶץ = "If he is (יֶשְׁנוֹ) in the land" (1Sa 23:23).
      - וְאֵינְךָ עַד־עוֹלָם = "And you will be no more (וְאֵינְךָ) forever" (Eze 27:36).

Lesson 22: Exercises

a. Learn to recognize, pronounce, and translate the following vocabulary.

	Word	*Translation*	*Notes*
(1)	אָבַד	he was lost, perished (*V*)	
(2)	אוֹ	or (*conj*)	
(3)	אַ֫יִן	there is/are not, there was/were not, there is no one/nothing (*particle*)	*Cs:* אֵין; *PS:* אֵינְךָ, אֵינֶ֫נּוּ, etc.
(4)	אֵל	God, god (*NMS*)	

(5)	בָּחַר	he chose (*V*)	
(6)	יְרוּשָׁלַ͏ִם[1]	Jerusalem (*proper N*)	
(7)	יֵשׁ	there is/are, there was/ were (*particle*)	יֶשׁ־; with *PS:* יֶשְׁךָ, יֶשְׁכֶם, etc.
(8)	כְּלִי	vessel, equipment, implement (*NMS*)	*P:* כֵּלִים
(9)	לְמַעַן	(a) with regard to, for the sake of, because of (*prep*) (b) in order that, so that (*conj*)	
(10)	נָבִיא	prophet (*NMS*)	*P:* נְבִיאִים
(11)	עָבַד	he worked, served (*V*)	
(12)	עָבַר	he passed, went over (*V*)	
(13)	עָלָה	he went up, ascended (*V*)	
(14)	עֹלָה	burnt offering (*NFS*)	Also עוֹלָה
(15)	עָמַד	he stood, took a stand (*V*)	
(16)	עָנָה	he answered (*V*)	
(17)	שָׂדֶה	field(s) (*NMS*)	*Cs:* שְׂדֵה; *S* with *PS:* שָׂדִי, שָׂדְךָ, etc.; *P:* שָׂדוֹת, שְׂדוֹת or שְׂדֵי
(18)	שֶׁבַע (*M*), שִׁבְעָה (*F*)	seven (*NM/FS*)	*P:* שִׁבְעִים = "seventy"; שְׁבִיעִי (*M*), שְׁבִיעִית (*F*) = "seventh"

b. Analyze the following words, working without the help of paradigm charts or a lexicon so far as possible. When there is more than one option for analysis, consult the biblical text to determine which is appropriate in context.

---

[1] This spelling is a contraction of יְרוּשָׁלַיִם that is used in the *MT*. See the discussion of perpetual *qere* below in the translation exercise c(2) for 2Ki 4:2.

- *Example:* וַיַּעַזְבֵנִי (1Sa 30:13) ⇒ *Answer:* > עזב, *impf, qal, 3MS + vav cons + PS 1CS,* "and he left me"

(1) יִגְבַּהּ (Pr 18:12)
(2) לְהַעֲבִיד (2Ch 2:17; *Eng* 2:18)
(3) נִתְרָאֶה (2Ki 14:8)
(4) הֶחֱיָה (Jos 6:25)
(5) מְגֹאָל (Mal 1:7)
(6) תֹאבֶה (Dt 13:9; *Eng* 13:8)
(7) וְאַשְׁבִּיעֲךָ (Ge 24:3)
(8) מַעֲנֶה (Ecc 5:19; *Eng* 5:20)
(9) וּבִעַרְתָּ (Dt 13:6; *Eng* 13:5)
(10) יֵעָבֵר (Eze 47:5)
(11) יִפְעַל (Job 33:29)
(12) וַתֹּאבַדְנָה (1Sa 9:3)
(13) וְיֹדֵעַ (Nu 24:16)
(14) הִתְנַעֲרִי (Is 52:2)
(15) לַחֲטֹא (Ex 9:34)
(16) וָאֹמַר (Ge 20:13)
(17) לְבַהֲלֵנִי (2Ch 35:21)
(18) וַיַּעַצְמוּ (Ex 1:7)

c. Read aloud and translate the following texts from the Hebrew Bible. Also provide an analysis of all verbs (finite and non-finite).

(1) Genesis 2:1-6

Verse 2

Interpret the significance of note "a" for this verse in the critical apparatus.

Verse 3

לַעֲשׂוֹת (> עשׂה) *Lamed-he* verbs typically drop the ה and add an וֹת suffix in infinitive, *qal,* construct.

(2) 2 Kings 4:1-3

Verse 1

(a) יָרֵא This form can be classified either as a perfect or a participle; however, the perfect verb option does not fit the context. Another clue that the word is a participle is the principle that when a finite verb is followed by another verb that has no conjunction (as in the case of הָיָה יָרֵא), the second verb is typically non-finite.

(b) לָקַחַת (> לקח) This verb adds a ת suffix in infinitive, *qal,* construct.

Verse 2

(a) הַגִּידִי The *dagesh-forte* is a clue that the root of this verb is *pe-nun,* as discussed in the next lesson.

(b) לְכִי

[1] *Ketib* and *qere*

[a] Occasionally the *MT* indicates in the *Mp* (the Masoretic notes in the margin) an alternate reading to the consonantal text. Since the Masoretes were committed to maintaining the consonantal text unchanged, they added a marginal note when they thought a correction was required. In such cases the reading which appears in the consonantal text is called a *ketib* (כְּתִיב), which is Aramaic for "what is written." The alternate reading in the *Mp* is called a *qere* (קְרֵי), which means "what is read" in the place of what is actually written. A *ketib* maintains the consonants of the text but has the vowels that are actually used with the consonants of the related *qere*. In light of this fact, one should never attempt to read a *ketib*, since it is normally not pronounceable, having vowels that belong to the *qere* in the margin.

[b] In 2 Ki 4:2 an instance of *ketib* and *qere* occurs with לָכְי. The circle above this word directs the reader to the left margin where the note has a ק with a dot above it, which is an abbreviation for *qere*. Then on the line above the ק is the *qere* itself – that is, the consonants of the alternate which is to be read in place of the *ketib*. Besides clearly marking a *qere* with a ק and dot, the *Mp* also staggers the lines of a *qere* one-half space to call attention to it. In order to read the marginal *qere* in verse 2, one employs the consonants of the *qere* in the margin: לך, along with the vowels that appear with the *ketib* in the consonantal text: □□ְ□ָ. Thus, the alternate reading is לָךְ, which replaces לכי in the text. The *qere,* which is also discussed in the critical apparatus, is read and translated instead of the *ketib*.

[2] Perpetual *qere*[1]

A few common words in the *MT* appear as perpetual *qere*. Every time one of these words occurs in the text, its *ketib* form has the vowels of the *qere;* however, the *qere* is not specifically indicated in the *Mp*. In

[1] See Horsnell, 219-226; and Scott, 13-14.

other words, perpetual *qere* are so common that the reader is expected to recognize them without a marginal note and to pronounce the *qere* instead of the *ketib* when reading the text. A few examples of perpetual *qere* follow.

Ketib ("What is written" in the text with the vowels of the *qere*)	**Perpetual *qere*** ("What is read" in place of the *ketib*)
יְהוָה	אֲדֹנָי ("[the] Lord")
יְהוִה	אֱלֹהִים ("God")
הִוא	הִיא ("she")
יְרוּשָׁלַםִ	יְרוּשָׁלַיִם ("Jerusalem")

(c) כִּי אִם־ Conjunctions are sometimes linked with other conjunctions, adverbs, or particles to express idioms. Lexicons typically discuss these compound forms under the heading of one or both of the semantically linked words. For example, under the heading for כִּי in *BDB,* on page 474, is a section concerning the idiom כִּי אִם.

(d) אָסוּךְ is a noun formed by prefixing א to a root. This and other noun patterns are discussed in the next lesson.

Verse 3

(a) לְכִי (> הלך) This verb root is irregular in that it drops the initial ה in some forms, following the pattern of *pe-yod* verbs. (See Lesson 24A.2.) The presence of the ִ◌י suffix without a verb prefix is the clue to its form.

(b) Note the occurrence of *ketib* and *qere* in this verse, and reflect only the *qere* in the translation. The critical apparatus also addresses the *qere*.

Lesson 23

Weak Verb: *Pe-Nun*; Noun Patterns; *He* Directive

23A Weak Verb: *Pe-Nun*

1. As the name indicates, *pe-nun* verbs have an initial *nun* consonant. Examples of common *pe-nuns* are נָגַשׁ ("he approached") and נָפַל ("he fell").
2. Major characteristics of *pe-nun* verbs
   a. When the addition of a verb prefix would normally require the *pe-nun* consonant to have a *sheva*, the *nun* assimilates into the second root consonant by means of a *dagesh-forte*. To say it another way, if □□נ + ◁ would result in □□נְ◁, then the *nun* assimilates as □□◁.[1]
      (1) In the typical *pe-nun* verb the *nun* assimilates in the following:

Qal: imperfect	*Hifil:* all conjugations
Nifal: perfect and participle	*Hofal:* all conjugations

      (2) *Pe-nuns* are spelled like the strong verb in all conjugations of *piel*, *pual*, and *hitpael*.
      (3) The following charts illustrate the manner in which *pe-nuns* assimilate the initial *nun*, using נפל and נגשׁ as examples. The strong verb משׁל also appears for comparison.

Qal		
	משׁל	נפל
Impf, 3MS	יִמְשֹׁל	יִפֹּל

Nifal		
	משׁל	נגשׁ
Perf, 3MS	נִמְשַׁל	נִגַּשׁ
Part, MS, Ab	נִמְשָׁל	נִגָּשׁ

---

[1] When a *pe-nun* verb has a guttural (which cannot take a *dagesh-forte*) as the second root consonant, the *nun* normally remains in place after a prefix. Two exceptions are the roots נחם ("be sorry") and נחת ("descend") in which the *nun* drops out with the addition of a prefix.

Hifil		
	משׁל	נגשׁ
Perf, 3MS	הִמְשִׁיל	הִגִּישׁ
Impf, 3MS	יַמְשִׁיל	יַגִּישׁ
Impv, 2MS / Inf, Ab	הַמְשֵׁל	הַגֵּשׁ
Inf, Cs	הַמְשִׁיל	הַגִּישׁ
Part, MS, Ab	מַמְשִׁיל	מַגִּישׁ

Hofal		
	משׁל	נגשׁ
Perf, 3MS	הָמְשַׁל	הֻגַּשׁ
Impf, 3MS	יָמְשַׁל	יֻגַּשׁ
Inf, Cs	[none]	הֻגַּשׁ
Inf, Ab	הָמְשֵׁל	הֻגֵּשׁ
Part, MS, Ab	מָמְשָׁל	מֻגָּשׁ

✓ Note that in *hofal* the prefix vowel for *pe-nun*s is *qibbus* rather than *qames-hatuf*. As a result, these forms reflect a □□ֻ pattern that sometimes resembles perfect, *pual*.

✓ See Appendix 3, paradigm 7, for the full conjugation of *pe-nun* verbs.

b. A few *pe-nun* verbs exhibit additional differences from the strong verb. These differences can be illustrated with the verb נָגַשׁ.

(1) Most *pe-nun* verbs in imperfect, *qal* have a stem vowel of *holem* above the second root consonant, just like strong verbs do. (See יִפֹּל [*impf, qal, 3MS*] in the preceding *qal* chart.) However, a few *pe-nun* verbs have a different stem vowel (for the second root consonant) in imperfect, *qal*. For example, נגשׁ takes a stem vowel of *patah* where the strong verb (as well as נפל) has a *holem*. Thus the imperfect, *qal, 3MS* form of נגשׁ is יִגַּשׁ.

(2) Most *pe-nun* verbs in imperative, *qal* retain the initial *nun*. However, a few *pe-nun*s like נגשׁ lose the *nun* in this conjugation. For example, the imperative, *qal*, *2MS* of נגשׁ is גַּשׁ (which is equivalent to the *impf, qal, 2MS* minus the prefix).

(3) Another characteristic of *pe-nun*s like נגשׁ is that in infinitive, *qal*, construct, they drop the initial *nun* and add a ת suffix. For example, the infinitive, *qal*, construct of נגשׁ is גֶּשֶׁת. (The two *segol*s follow a pattern called *segolate*, which is discussed later in this lesson. [See section 23B.1]).

(4) To summarize, the patterns followed by נגשׁ and a few other *pe-nun*s are as follows.

נגשׁ	
Impf, qal, 3MS	יִגַּשׁ (*patah* stem vowel)
Impv, qal, 2MS	גַּשׁ (פ״נ assimilates and *patah* stem vowel)
Inf, qal, Cs	גֶּשֶׁת (פ״נ assimilates and ת suffix)

✓ See Appendix 3, paradigm 7, for more forms of נגשׁ.

3. Two irregular verbs that occur frequently are related to the paradigm of *pe-nuns*.

   a. נָתַן ("he gave")

   This *pe-nun* verb is doubly weak in that the final *nun* assimilates when a consonantal suffix is attached. It follows the pattern of נגשׁ in imperative, *qal* and infinitive, *qal*, construct. The following forms illustrate.

נתן	
Perf, qal, 2MS	נָתַתָּ (ל״נ assimilates)
Perf, nif, 2MP	נִתַּתֶּם (פ״נ and ל״נ assimilate)
Impv, qal, 2MS	תֵּן (פ״נ assimilates)
Inf, qal, Cs	תֵּת (פ״נ and ל״נ assimilate and ת suffix) (or נְתֹן)

✓ Since this verb sometimes loses two root consonants, its identification can be challenging. A helpful clue is to remember that when the only remaining root consonants is ת, the verb is likely נתן. See Appendix 3, paradigm 15, for more forms of this verb.

   b. לָקַח ("he took")

   In part of its conjugation this *lamed*-guttural verb behaves as if its root were נקח instead of לקח. The initial consonant assimilates in imperfect, *qal* and *hofal;* imperative, *qal;* and infinitive, *qal*, construct. A *dagesh-forte* often appears as a clue to assimilation. This verb also follows the pattern of נגשׁ, as the following illustrates.

לקח	
Impf, qal, 3MS	יִקַּח (initial ל assimilates)
Impf, hof, 3MS	יֻקַּח (initial ל assimilates)
Impv, qal, 2MS	קַח (initial ל assimilates)
Inf, qal, Cs	קַחַת (initial ל assimilates and ת suffix)

✓ See Appendix 3, paradigm 15, for more forms of לקח.

4. Summary of characteristics of *pe-nun* verbs

   a. The following clues aid in recognizing *pe-nun*s.

      (1) When the addition of a prefix would normally require the *pe-nun* to have a *sheva,* the *nun* assimilates into the second root consonant with a *dagesh-forte* (if the second consonant is non-guttural).

         ✓ Thus, if only two consonants of a root remain in a prefixed verb and the first consonant has a *dagesh-forte*, the root may be *pe-nun* (□⊡◁).

      (2) A few *pe-nun*s like נגשׁ also display these characteristics:

         [a] In imperfect, *qal:* the second root consonant takes a different stem vowel than the *holem* that appears in strong verbs.

         [b] In imperative, *qal:* the *pe-nun* assimilates.

            ✓ Thus, when only two root consonants remain and there is no prefix or suffix, the form may be the imperative, *qal* of a *pe-nun* root.

               (This circumstance can occur with several other weak roots, as discussed in succeeding lessons.)

         [c] In infinitive, *qal*, construct: the *pe-nun* assimilates and a ת suffix is added.

            ✓ Thus, ◌ֶ֫◌ֶת may suggest a *pe-nun* root.

               (Other classes of weak roots also display this characteristic, as discussed elsewhere.)

      (3) The irregular verb נתן loses the final *nun* when a consonantal suffix is added. In some forms both *nun*s assimilate.

      (4) The irregular verb לקח acts as if its root were נקח in part of its conjugation. As a result, in some forms the initial ל disappears or assimilates into the ק with a *dagesh-forte*.

   b. The following verbs with analyses illustrate the process of identifying *pe-nun* roots.

      (1) הִגִּיד (Ge 3:11) > נגד, *perf, hif, 3MS,* "he told"

         The *he* prefix and *hireq-yod* are clues that the form is perfect, *hifil.* Two root consonants remain, and the *dagesh-forte* in the first is a clue that the root is *pe-nun.*

(2) גַּע (Ps 144:5) > נגע, *impv, qal, 2MS,* "touch"

When a root consonant has assimilated without a prefix or suffix, the verb may be a *pe-nun* in imperative, *qal*. Other classes of weak verbs can also lose a root consonant when there is no prefix or suffix (as discussed later). However, a check of options for the weak root of this verb reveals that only נגע has a form spelled גַּע. The A-class vowel (following the pattern of נגשׁ) appears because of the guttural.

(3) שְׂאֵת (Ge 44:1) > נשׂא, *inf, qal, Cs,* "to lift"

Since שׂאת is not an extant root, one consonant of this verb must be a prefix or suffix. The *tav* is a suffix and a clue that the verb is an infinitive, *qal,* construct form of a *pe-nun* root (following the pattern of נגשׁ).

(4) נִתַּנּוּ (Ezr 9:7) > נתן, *perf, nif, 1CP,* "we have been given"

A *hireq* under the first consonant of a root and a *dagesh-forte* in the second is a clue for perfect, *piel* in strong verbs (□□̣□ִ). However, the root נתן does not occur in *piel.* Alternatively, the initial *nun* could be a prefix for perfect, *nifal* or imperfect, *1CP.* נוּ could be a perfect, *1CP* verb ending or a *1CP* pronominal suffix. The *dagesh-forte* in the *nun* of the ending suggests a doubled *nun,* the first of which is likely a final root consonant and the second of which is part of a *1CP* ending or suffix. After removing the prefix and suffix, only one root consonant remains (תַּ); its *dagesh-forte* suggests an assimilated *pe-nun* consonant. Thus, the two *dagesh*es are clues to assimilated *nun*s, indicating that the root is נתן. The context of the verb requires the conclusion that its form is perfect, *nifal, 1CP.*

(5) וַנִּקַּח (Dt 3:8) > לקח, *impf, qal, 1CP + vav cons,* "and we took"

The pointing of the *vav* indicates that it is a *vav* consecutive on an imperfect verb. The *nun* prefix indicates imperfect, *1CP.* Two root consonants remain (קַּח), and the first has a *dagesh-forte,* which can be a clue to a *pe-nun* root. However, the root is actually לקח, which behaves as if it were *pe-nun* in part of its conjugation. (There is no extant נקח root.)

23B Noun Patterns

Nouns, like verbs, are normally based on tri-consonantal roots. In fact, verbs and nouns often share a common root, as with the verb מָלַךְ ("he reigned") and the noun מֶלֶךְ ("king"). Nouns have their own patterns of formation from roots, just as verbs do. A few of the more important patterns are discussed in this section.

1. *Segolate* nouns

a. A *segolate* noun is made up of two syllables, the first of which is accented and the second of which usually has a *segol*. The vowel of the first syllable is often a *segol;* however, it may also be a *sere* or an A-class or O-class vowel.

b. The following are examples of *segolate* nouns, appearing with their plural forms.

c.

***Segolate* Nouns**	
Singular, Ab	*Plural, Ab*
אֶרֶץ ("earth" [*F*])	אֲרָצוֹת
בֹּקֶר ("morning" [*M*])	בְּקָרִים
זֶרַע ("seed" [*M*])	[none]
חֹדֶשׁ ("new moon" [*M*])	חֳדָשִׁים
חֶרֶב ("sword" [*F*])	חֲרָבוֹת
מָוֶת ("death" [*M*])	[none]
מֶלֶךְ ("king" [*M*])	מְלָכִים
נַעַר ("boy" [*M*])	נְעָרִים
סֵפֶר ("book" [*M*])	סְפָרִים
עֶבֶד ("servant" [*M*])	עֲבָדִים
רֶגֶל ("foot" [*F*])	רַגְלַיִם [*Du*]

✓ Note that a guttural in the second syllable of a *segolate* requires that syllable to have an A-class vowel rather than a *segol*.

2. Geminate nouns

a. A geminate ("doubled") noun is derived from a double-*ayin* root, which is to say that the root of a geminate has the same letter in the second and third consonant positions. Geminates tend to shorten by assimilating the doubled letter, and a *dagesh-forte* appears where possible (when the doubled letter is not a guttural and is followed by an ending or pronominal suffix [▷□□]).

b. The following are examples of geminate nouns.

	Geminate Nouns	
Root	*Singular, Ab*	*Plural, Ab*
אמם	אֵם ("mother" [*F*])	אִמּוֹת[1]
הרר	הַר ("mountain" [*M*])	הָרִים
חקק	חֻקָּה ("statute" [*F*])	חֻקּוֹת
ימם	יָם ("sea" [*M*])	יַמִּים
לבב	לֵב ("heart" [*M*])	לִבּוֹת
עמם	עַם ("people" [*M*])	עַמִּים
רעע	רָעָה ("evil" [*F*])	רָעוֹת
שׂרר	שַׂר ("ruler" [*M*])	שָׂרִים

3. Noun prefixes and suffixes

a. Some nouns are formed by attaching certain prefixes or suffixes to a root or to another word. Common noun prefixes are מ (the most frequently used), ת, and א. The following nouns illustrate.[2]

Root		**Nouns with Prefixes**
זבח	+ מ =	מִזְבֵּחַ ("altar" [*M*])
עשׂה		מַעֲשֶׂה ("deed" [*M*])
צוה		מִצְוָה ("commandment" [*F*])
קום		מָקוֹם ("place" [*M*])
שׁפט		מִשְׁפָּט ("judgment" [*M*])
בוא	+ ת =	תְּבוּאָה ("product" [*F*])
ילד		תּוֹלְדוֹת[3] ("generations of" [*F*])

[1] The plural of this noun occurs only with pronominal suffixes; this absolute form is hypothetical.

[2] See Seow, 32-4.

[3] The *pe-yod* consonant of this root (and the next one) becomes a *vav* when a prefix is added, as discussed below in section 23B.4a(2).

ירה		תּוֹרָה ("law" [*F*])
רבע	+ א =	אַרְבַּע[1] ("four" [*M*])

✓ The student must recognize when a noun has one of these prefixes in order to locate the noun under its root in *BDB*. For example, the noun מִזְבֵּחַ is located under the root זבח.

✓ The student should also remember that a *mem* can be prefixed to a root or word in two other situations: with a prefixed מִן preposition (which is spelled מִ‍ׄ___ or מֵ___) and in certain stems of the patriciple (*piel, pual, hif, hof,* and *hit*).

b. Some nouns (and adjectives) are formed by adding a noun suffix to another word. Frequently occurring noun/adjective suffixes are ן, וּת, ◌ִי, and ◌ִית.[2] (The common endings of nouns that indicate gender, number, and state [◌ִים, ◌ָה, וֹת, etc.] are not included in this category.)

(1) The suffixes ן and וּת can be used to create abstract forms from other nouns or adjectives.[3]

- עִוֵּר ("blind") + ן suffix = עִוָּרוֹן ("blindness" [*NMS*])
- מֶלֶךְ ("king") + וּת suffix = מַלְכוּת ("royalty" [*NFS*])

(2) The suffixes ◌ִי (*M*) and ◌ִית (*F*) are used to create the cardinal numbers from "second" to "tenth" and gentilic forms (such as "Israelite"). While discussed in this section on nouns, these forms are actually adjectival.

- שֵׁשׁ ("six") + ◌ִי and ◌ִית suffixes = שִׁשִּׁי (*M*) and שִׁשִּׁית (*F*) ("sixth")
- יִשְׂרָאֵל ("Israel") + ◌ִי and ◌ִית suffixes = יִשְׂרְאֵלִי (*M*) and יִשְׂרְאֵלִית (*F*) ("Israelite")

4. Nouns based on weak roots

a. The formation of nouns is also affected by the presence of a weak consonant

[1] The א prefix is dropped in the cardinal forms of this number: רְבִיעִי (*M*) and רְבִיעִית (*F*) ("fourth").

[2] See Kautzsch, §86.

[3] Abstract concepts can also be expressed in other ways. For example, the plural forms of some nouns indicate abstraction, as illustrated by חַיִּים ("life"), נְעוּרִים ("youth"), and צְדָקוֹת ("righteousness"). Ibid., §124d-e.

in a root, just as weak consonants affect the inflection of verbs. A few factors are discussed here as an aid to recognizing the patterns of nouns that are derived from weak roots.[1]

(1) *Pe-nun* root

When a noun is formed by adding a prefix to a *pe-nun* root, the initial *nun* may assimilate into the second root consonant, as it does in *pe-nun* verbs.

- נפל + מ prefix = מַפֶּ֫לֶת ("ruin" [*NFS*])

  In this form the *pe-nun* consonant assimilates into the *pe* with a *dagesh-forte*.

- נתן + מ prefix and feminine suffix ת = מַתַּת ("gift of" [*NFS*])

  In this form the *pe-nun* assimilates with a *dagesh-forte* and the final *nun* drops out because of the suffix.

(2) *Pe-yod* root

Nouns formed on *pe-yod* roots may drop the *pe-yod* consonant, or that consonant may become a *vav* when a noun prefix is added. (Similar patterns will be discussed in the section on *pe-yod* verbs [Lesson 24A.2].)

Root	**Noun**
ידע	דַּ֫עַת ("knowledge" [*F*])
ישב	מוֹשָׁב ("seat" [*M*])

(3) *Ayin-vav* and *ayin-yod* roots

(a) In some nouns formed from these roots the *vav* and *yod* become naturally-long vowels.

Root	**Noun**
אור	אוֹר ("light" [*F*])
	אוּר ("flame" [*M*])
שׁיר	שִׁיר ("song" [*M*])
	שִׁירָה ("song" [*F*])

(b) In some nouns formed from *ayin-vav* and *ayin-yod* roots the *vav* or *yod*

[1] See Seow, 25-32.

drops out because of its reduction to a shorter vowel.

Root	**Noun**
בוש	בֹּשֶׁת ("shame" [*F*])
טוח	טֻחוֹת ("inward parts" [*F*])
גור	גֵּר ("sojourner" [*M*])
דין	דָּן ("Dan" [*M*])

✓ Note the clues for the missing *vav* consonant in the first two examples above. The *holem* in בֹּשֶׁת has reduced from וֹ, and the *qibbus* in טֻחוֹת has reduced from וּ.

✓ *Ayin-vav* and *ayin-yod* patterns will be discussed more fully in connection with verbs based on these roots. (See Lesson 25A.1.)

(4) Double-*ayin* root

The manner in which nouns are formed from double-*ayin* roots was discussed earlier in connection with geminate nouns. (See section 23B.2.) To summarize, a double-*ayin* root typically assimilates one of the doubled letters, and a *dagesh-forte* appears where it can.

(5) *Lamed-he* root

(a) Nouns based on *lamed-he* roots frequently appear with a *segol* before the *he* in masculine forms (◌ֶה) and a *qames* before the *he* in feminine forms (◌ָה).

Root	**Noun**
שׂדה	שָׂדֶה ("field" [*M*])
שׁנה	שָׁנָה ("year" [*F*])
עלה	מַעֲלֶה ("ascent" [*M*])
	עֹלָה ("burnt offering" [*F*])

(b) *Lamed-he* may become *vav* or *yod* in noun forms. The reason for this change is that most roots which appear to be *lamed-he* were originally *lamed-vav* or *lamed-yod.* In some nouns the original *vav* or *yod* reappears, as the following examples illustrate.

Root	**Noun**
ברה	בְּרִית ("covenant" [*F*])
כלה	כְּלִי ("vessel" [*M*])
ענה	עָנָו ("poor" [*M*])
	עֲנָוָה ("humility" [*F*])
	עֳנִי ("affliction" [*M*])

(c) In some nouns based on *lamed-he* roots the final *he* drops out.

Root	**Noun**
אבה	אָב ("father" [*M*])
אחה	אָח ("brother" [*M*])
עצה	עֵץ ("tree" [*M*])

✓ Note that for the first two examples above, a *yod* appears in the singular, construct forms as a clue that these nouns are derived from *lamed-he* roots that were originally *lamed-yod:* אֲבִי ("father of") and אֲחִי ("brother of").

b. Summary of clues for identifying the weak roots of nouns

(1) Weak root consonants may assimilate in the formation of nouns, as they do in weak verbs. The following is a summary of clues for reconstructing the root of a noun when a weak consonant has dropped out.

(a) The weak roots on which nouns are formed, like the weak roots of verbs, often assimilate a consonant in these classes: *pe-yod*, *pe-nun*, *ayin-vav*, *ayin-yod*, double-*ayin*, and *lamed-he*. When only two root consonants remain in a noun, the student can usually discover the root by checking for one of these six weaknesses. In addition, the following clues can abbreviate the process of identifying the weak root of some nouns.

(b) If two root consonants remain in a noun and the first has a *dagesh-forte* (□□◁), then the root may be *pe-nun*. (This clue is relevant only when there is a prefix.)

(c) If two root consonants remain and the second has a *dagesh-forte* (▷⊡□), the root may be double-*ayin*. (This clue is relevant only when there is a noun ending or suffix.)

(d) If *vav* (in the form of a consonant or a vowel) appears after a prefix in the position of the first root consonant (□□ו◁), the verb may be *pe-yod*.

(e) If a *vav* or *yod* appears in the position of a third root consonant (ו□□ or י□□), the root may be *lamed-he*.

(2) The following examples of nouns with analyses illustrate the process of identifying a weak root when a consonant is missing.

(a) מַטֶּה (Ex 4:2) > נטה, *NMS*, *Ab*, "staff"

מטה is not an extant root. If one assumes the מ is a noun prefix, then טָּה are two remaining root consonants. The first has a *dagesh-forte*, which is a clue to a *pe-nun* root. (מַטֶּה can also be a *part, hif,* as it is in Dt 27:19.)

(b) שַׂקִּים (Jos 9:4) > שׂקק, *NMP, Ab*, "sacks"

When the *MP* ending ִים□ is removed, two root consonants remain. The *dagesh-forte* in the second is a clue that the root is double-*ayin*.

(c) תּוֹדָה (Lv 7:12) > ידה, *NFS*, *Ab*, "thanksgiving"

The *holem-vav* after the imperfect prefix indicates that the root is *pe-yod*.

(d) גַּאֲוָה (Ps 36:12; *Eng* 36:11) > גאה, *NFS*, *Ab*, "pride"

Removal of the *FS* ending ָה□ leaves a final *vav* consonant, which is a clue to a *lamed-he* root.

(e) פְּרִי (Hos 9:16) > פרה, *NMS*, *Ab*, "fruit"

The final *yod* is a clue that the root is *lamed-he*.

(f) רֶשֶׁת (Ps 57:7; Eng 57:6) > ירשׁ, *NFS*, *Ab*, "net"

Since רשׁת is not an extant root, ֶת□ must be a feminine, singular ending. The word provides no particular clue as to its root; consequently, a check of the six roots that commonly lose a consonant reveals these options: ירשׁ, רישׁ/רושׁ, and רשׁשׁ. The lexicon indicates that the noun רֶ֫שֶׁת is derived from the first of these roots.

(g) קָמָה (Jdg 15:5) > קום, *NFS*, *Ab*, "standing grain"

There is no root קמה; thus one can assume ◌ָה is a feminine, singular ending. A check of the weak roots that commonly lose a consonant leads to קום.

(h) רֵעַ (2Sa 13:3) > רעה, *NMS*, *Ab*, "friend"

The lexicon indicates that two roots are bases for nouns with this spelling: רוע and רעה. However, the one derived from רוע does not fit the context of 2Sa 13:3. *BDB* lists three different רעה roots, and two are the bases of nouns spelled as רֵעַ. Only one of these nouns fits the context: רֵעַ ("friend"), derived from the second רעה root.

23C *HE* DIRECTIVE

1. A few nouns and adverbs can take a unique suffix that indicates direction toward something. The suffix is called a *he* (ה) directive and is formed by attaching ◌ָה to the end of a word.
   - ✓ The *he* directive is spelled the same as the common feminine, singular, absolute ending for nouns (◌ָה). One can distinguish between the two based on context and a knowledge of which words take the common feminine ending. It is also helpful to know that the feminine noun ending occurs very frequently, while the *he* directive appears on only a few words.
2. When the *he* directive is suffixed to a word, changes in the spelling of that word may occur. The *he* directive normally is not accented.
   - הָעִיר ("the city") + *he* directive = הָעִ֫ירָה ("to the city" [Ge 44:13])
   - מִצְרַ֫יִם ("Egypt") + *he* directive = מִצְרַ֫יְמָה ("to Egypt" [Ge 12:10])
   - שָׁם ("there") + *he* directive = שָׁ֫מָּה ("to there" [Ge 19:20])
   -

Lesson 23: EXERCISES

a. Learn to recognize, pronounce, and translate the following vocabulary.

Word	*Translation*	*Notes*

(1)	אַמָּה	cubit (*NFS*)	*Du:* אַמָּתַיִם; *P:* אַמּוֹת
(2)	זָהָב	gold (*NMS*)	No *P*
(3)	חֹדֶשׁ	new moon, month (*NMS*)	*S* with *PS:* חָדְשׁוֹ, חָדְשָׁהּ, etc.; *P:* חֳדָשִׁים, חָדְשֵׁי
(4)	לָקַח	he took, seized (*V*)	Inflects like a *pe-nun* verb in part of its conjugation
(5)	מִדְבָּר	wilderness, desert (*NMS*)	
(6)	מִזְבֵּחַ	altar (*NMS*)	*P:* מִזְבְּחוֹת
(7)	מַטֶּה	staff, tribe (*NMS*)	*Cs:* מַטֵּה; *P:* מַטּוֹת
(8)	מַלְאָךְ	messenger (*NMS*)	*Cs:* מַלְאַךְ
(9)	מַעֲשֶׂה	deed, work (*NMS*)	*Cs:* מַעֲשֵׂה
(10)	מִצְרַיִם	Egypt (*proper N*)	מִצְרִי (*adj MS*) = "Egyptian"
(11)	נגד	הִגִּיד (*hif*): he told, declared; הֻגַּד (*hof*): he was told (*V*)	Usually occurs in *hif* & *hof*
(12)	נָגַשׁ	he approached, drew near (*V*)	
(13)	נָטָה	he extended, stretched out, turned, bent (*V*)	
(14)	נכה	הִכָּה (*hif*): he struck; הֻכָּה (*hof*): he was struck (*V*)	Usually occurs in *hif* & *hof*
(15)	נַעַר	boy, youth, servant (*NMS*)	P: נְעָרִים
(16)	נָפַל	he fell (*V*)	
(17)	פְּלֶשֶׁת	Philistia (*proper N*)	פְּלִשְׁתִּי (*adj MS*) = "Philistine"
(18)	רֶגֶל	foot, leg (*NFS*)	*Du:* רַגְלַיִם
(19)	רֵעַ	friend, companion (*NMS*)	

b. Analyze the following nouns and verbs. Do as much analysis as possible before consulting a lexicon. Also, check the context of the word when necessary to determine the most appropriate translation.

- *Example:* לְמַטָּרָה (1Sa 20:20) ⇒ *Answer:* > נטר, *NFS, Ab* + ל *prep,* "at a mark"
- *Example:* אֶתְּקֶנְךָּ (Jer 22:24) ⇒ *Answer:* > נתק, *impf, qal, 1CS + PS 2MS,* "I would tear you off"

(1) תִּדֹּר (Dt 12:17)
(2) בִּמְחוֹל (Jer 31:4)
(3) מֵחֳלִי (2Ki 1:2)
(4) נִחַמְתִּי (Ge 6:7)
(5) הַטֵּה (2Ki 19:16)
(6) תְּהִלָּה (Ne 12:46)
(7) הַמֻּכֶּה (Nu 25:14)
(8) יֵאָצֵר (Is 23:18)
(9) יִקָּחֶךָ (Dt 30:4)
(10) תּוֹחֶלֶת (Pr 13:12)
(11) וַיַּגֵּר (Ps 75:9; *Eng* 75:8)
(12) תֹּר (Est 2:12)
(13) הָמוֹן (Is 13:4)
(14) מֵאֵן (Ex 7:14)
(15) יֻסַּךְ (Ex 25:29)
(16) נִצָּבִים (Ex 5:20)
(17) בְּקֶשֶׁת (Hos 1:7)
(18) מִטָּה (2Ki 4:10)
(19) תְּנִי (Ge 30:14)
(20) מַשִּׁיקוֹת (Eze 3:13)
(21) לְהַדִּיחַ (Ps 62:5; *Eng* 62:4)
(22) הַחִוִּי (Ge 10:17)
(23) שֵׁנָה (Ps 90:5)
(24) לָפַּחַת (Eze 22:20)
(25) וְאֹכֵלָה (Ge 27:4)
(26) וְהִבִּיט (Nu 21:9)

c. Read aloud and translate Genesis 2:7-17 from the Hebrew Bible. Also provide an analysis of all verbs (finite and non-finite).

Verse 7

(1) Verbs of creation may be followed by a double object in which the first object is the thing made and the second the material employed in creation. Such a construction appears in this verse.

(2) Much of this lesson has focused on the weakness of *pe-nun* roots. However, a *nun* in the second or third consonants of a root can also assimilate. Such is the case with בְּאַפָּיו. The *dagesh-forte* is a clue to an assimilated *nun.*

Verse 10

לְהַשְׁקוֹת (> שׁקה) adds a ת suffix in the infinitive construct in a manner similar to certain *pe-nun* verbs.

Lesson 24

Weak Verb: *Pe-Yod*; Interrogative Clauses

24A Weak Verb: *Pe-Yod*

There are two major groups of *pe-yod* verbs. One may be called "true *pe-yod*." This group retains the initial *yod* throughout its conjugation. The other major group of *pe-yod* verbs sometimes loses the initial *yod* or exchanges it for a *vav*. The verbs in this second group are actually derived from roots that were originally *pe-vav*. Consequently, this group may be called *pe-yod/vav*.

1. True *pe-yod* verbs

a. There are only a few verbs which are true *pe-yod*s, and most of them occur infrequently, with the exception of the stative verb יָטַב ("he was good").

b. Major characteristics of true *pe-yod* verbs

(1) These verbs retain the initial *yod* in all forms.

(2) True *pe-yod*s only vary from strong verbs in certain *qal* conjugations (*impf* and *impv*) and in all *hifil* conjugations.

(a) *Qal*: In imperfect the verb prefix causes the *pe-yod* consonant to become a *hireq-yod*. Also, in imperfect and imperative the stem vowel (above the second root consonant) is *patah* instead of the *holem* that appears in strong verbs.

Qal		
	משל	יטב
Impf, 3MS	יִמְשֹׁל	יִיטַב
Impv, 2MS	מְשֹׁל	יְטַב

(b) *Hifil*: In all conjugations the verb prefix causes the *pe-yod* consonant to become a *sere-yod*.

Hifil		
	משל	יטב
Perf, 3MS	הִמְשִׁיל	הֵיטִיב
Impf, 3MS	יַמְשִׁיל	יֵיטִיב
Imv, 2MS / Inf, Ab	הַמְשֵׁל	הֵיטֵב
Inf, Cs	הַמְשִׁיל	הֵיטִיב
Part, MS, Ab	מַמְשִׁיל	מֵיטִיב

✓ See Appendix 3, paradigm 5, for the full conjugation of true *pe-yod*s.

2. *Pe-yod/vav* verbs (*pe-yod* based on *pe-vav*)

a. Most *pe-yod* verbs are not "true *pe-yod*s" – which is to say, the initial *yod* is not retained throughout their conjugations. At points in their inflections the *yod* either disappears or becomes a *vav*. The later change is due to the fact that these *pe-yod* verbs are actually based on roots that were originally *pe-vav*. To illustrate, the verb יָשַׁב ("he dwelled") is a *pe-yod* verb because it has an initial *yod* in its lexical form (*perf, qal, 3MS*). However, in certain parts of its conjugation where there is a verb prefix, the initial *yod* is replaced by a *vav*, as in הוֹשִׁיב (*perf, hif, 3MS*). In such a situation an original *pe-vav* root (ושב) reappears. Because these *pe-yod* verbs have developed from ancient *pe-vav* roots and because these old roots reappear at times, this Grammar refers to them as *pe-yod/vav*.

b. Examples of common *pe-yod/vav* verbs are יָדַע ("he knew"), יָלַד ("he brought forth"), יָצָא ("he went out"), יָרַד ("he went down"), and יָשַׁב ("he dwelled").

c. Major characteristics of *pe-yod/vav* verbs[1]

(1) *Pe-yod/vav* verbs vary from the paradigm of the strong verb in four stems: *qal*, *nifal*, *hifil*, and *hofal*. *Pe-yod/vav* verbs typically follow the pattern of the strong verb in *piel*, *pual*, and *hitpael*.[2]

---

[1] See Horsnell, 400-403; and Kelley, 338-345.

[2] An exception occurs with some *pe-yod/vav* verbs in *hitpael*, where the *pe-yod* consonant is replaced by a *vav*, as in הִתְוַדָּה (> ידה = "confess"). See Joüon, §75a.

(2) *Qal*

(a) Perfect, infinitive absolute, and participle, *qal: Pe-yod/vav* verbs follow the pattern of the strong verb. Since these *qal* conjugations require no verb prefix, the initial *yod* remains in place.

(b) Imperfect, *qal:* The imperfect prefix causes the *pe-yod* consonant to drop out and the prefix to take a *sere*. The second root consonant may have an E-class stem vowel where the strong verb has a *holem*.

- ‣ ישׁב + י (*impf, qal, 3MS* prefix) = יֵשֵׁב

(c) Imperative, *qal:* The initial *yod* drops out as it does in imperfect, *qal* (since the imperative, *qal* is like the imperfect, *qal* without the prefix).

- ‣ תֵּשֵׁב (*impf, qal, 2MS*) minus imperfect prefix = שֵׁב (*impv, qal, 2MS*)

✓ This pattern is similar to the imperative, *qal* of *pe-nun* verbs like נגשׁ. (See Lesson 23A.2b.)

(d) Infinitive, *qal*, construct: The initial *yod* drops out and a *tav* suffix is added. The two remaining root consonants take *segol*s, forming a *segolate* pattern. (See Lesson 23B.1.)

- ‣ ישׁב minus י and + ת prefix = שֶׁבֶת

✓ This pattern is similar to the infinitive, *qal,* construct of *pe-nun* verbs like נגשׁ. (See Lesson 23A.2b.)

(e) The following chart summarizes the manner in which the *pe-yod/vav* verb differs from the strong verb in *qal*.

Qal		
	משׁל	ישׁב
Impf, qal, 3MS	יִמְשֹׁל	יֵשֵׁב
Impv, qal, 2MS	מְשֹׁל	שֵׁב
Inf, qal, Cs	מְשֹׁל	שֶׁבֶת

✓ See Appendix 3, paradigm 6, for the full conjugation of *pe-yod/vav* verbs.

(3) *Nifal*

In this stem the *pe-yod* consonant becomes a *vav* with the addition of the verb prefix. The *vav* may appear either as a naturally-long vowel or a consonant.

(a) Perfect and participle, *nifal:* The initial *yod* becomes a *holem-vav,* which serves as the prefix vowel (□□נוֹ).

(b) Imperfect, imperative, and infinitive, *nifal:* The *yod* becomes a *vav* consonant with a *dagesh-forte* (□□וָּ◁).

(c) The following chart summarizes the manner in which *pe-yod/vav* verbs differ from the strong verb in *nifal.*

Nifal		
	משל	ישב
Perf, 3MS	נִמְשַׁל	נוֹשַׁב
Impf, 3MS	יִמָּשֵׁל	יִוָּשֵׁב
Impv, 2MS / Inf Cs	הִמָּשֵׁל	הִוָּשֵׁב
Inf Ab	הִמָּשֹׁל	הִוָּשֵׁב
Part, MS, Ab	נִמְשָׁל	נוֹשָׁב

(4) *Hifil*

In all conjugations of this stem the *pe-yod* consonant becomes a *holem-vav*, which serves as the prefix vowel (□□וֹ◁). The following chart illustrates the differences from the strong verb.

Hifil		
	משל	ישב
Perf, 3MS	הִמְשִׁיל	הוֹשִׁיב
Impf, 3MS	יַמְשִׁיל	יוֹשִׁיב
Impv, 2MS / Inf Ab	הַמְשֵׁל	הוֹשֵׁב
Inf Cs	הַמְשִׁיל	הוֹשִׁיב
Part, MS, Ab	מַמְשִׁיל	מוֹשִׁיב

(5) *Hofal*

In all conjugations of this stem the *pe-yod* becomes a *shureq*, which serves as the prefix vowel (□□וּ◁). The following chart illustrates the differences from the strong verb.

Hofal		
	משל	ישב
Perf, 3MS	הָמְשַׁל	הוּשַׁב
Impf, 3MS	יָמְשַׁל	יוּשַׁב
Inf, Ab	הָמְשֵׁל	הוּשֵׁב
Part, MS, Ab	מָמְשָׁל	מוּשָׁב

d. Other notes concerning *pe-yod* verbs

(1) A few verbs combine the characteristics of true *pe-yod*s and *pe-yod/vav*s. For example, יָרֵא ("he feared") and יָרַשׁ ("he possessed") retain the *pe-yod* consonant in imperfect, *qal*, like true *pe-yod*s; but in some other forms the *yod* drops out or becomes a *vav,* as with *pe-yod/vav*s. The following forms illustrate, using ירשׁ.

	משל	ירשׁ
Impf, qal, 3MS	יִמְשֹׁל	יִירַשׁ
Impf, nif, 3MS	יִמָּשֵׁל	יִוָּרֵשׁ
Perf, hif, 3MS	הִמְשִׁיל	הוֹרִישׁ
Impf, hif, 3MS	יַמְשִׁיל	יוֹרִישׁ
Impv, qal, 2MS	מְשֹׁל	רֵשׁ
Inf, qal, Cs	מְשֹׁל	רֶשֶׁת

(2) A few *pe-yod* verbs that have a sibilant as the second root consonant, like יָצַק ("he poured out"), follow the pattern of *pe-nun* verbs. Sometimes when a verb prefix is added, these verbs assimilate the *pe-yod* and the sibilant takes a *dagesh-forte* as compensation. For example, the imperfect, *qal, 3MS* form of יצק is יִצֹּק.

(3) The very common verb הָלַךְ ("he went") is irregular. In its lexical form it appears as a *pe*-guttural; however, in part of its conjugation it is inflected as if it were a *pe-yod/vav* verb. הָלַךְ acts as if its root were ילך in the *qal* stem of the imperfect, imperative, and infinitive construct, and in all conjugations of *hifil*, as the following forms illustrate.

	Qal	
	משׁל	הלך
Impf, 3MS	יִמְשֹׁל	יֵלֵךְ
Imv, 2MS	מְשֹׁל	לֵךְ
Inf, Cs	מְשֹׁל	לֶכֶת
	Hifil	
Perf, 3MS	הִמְשִׁיל	הוֹלִיךְ
Impf, 3MS	יַמְשִׁיל	יוֹלִיךְ
Impv, 2MS	הַמְשֵׁל	הוֹלֵךְ
Inf, Cs	הַמְשִׁיל	הוֹלִיךְ
Inf, Ab	הַמְשֵׁל	הוֹלֵךְ
Part, MS, Ab	מַמְשִׁיל	מוֹלִיךְ

✓ See Appendix 3, paradigm 15, for more forms of הלך.

3. Summary of characteristics of *pe-yods*

a. The following clues aid in recognizing *pe-yod* verbs.

(1) True *pe-yods*

(a) The *pe-yod* consonant remains in place in all conjugations.

(b) The *pe-yod* becomes a *hireq-yod* in imperfect, *qal*, and a *sere-yod* in all *hifil* conjugations.

✓ Thus □□יִ◁ is a clue to a true *pe-yod* in imperfect, *qal;* and □□יֵ◁ is a clue to a true *pe-yod* in imperfect, *hifil.*

(2) *Pe-yod/vavs* (*pe-yod* based on *pe-vav*)

(a) *Qal*

[1] Perfect, infinitive absolute, and participle, *qal:* the *pe-yod* remains in place.

[2] Imperfect, *qal:* the *pe-yod* drops out and the prefix vowel is *sere.*

✓ Thus □□◁ֵ is a clue to *pe-yod/vav* in imperfect, *qal.*

(A *sere* prefix vowel also appears with stative double-*ayins* in imperfect, *qal* [as discussed in the next lesson] and with *pe-gutturals* in *nifal.* [In the latter case a root consonant does not drop out.])

[3] Imperative, *qal:* the *pe-yod* drops out.

✓ A situation of two root consonants without a prefix or suffix may suggest a *pe-yod/vav* in imperative, *qal.*

(This pattern also appears with other weak roots, such as a *pe-nun* like נגשׁ.)

[4] Infinitive, *qal,* construct: the *pe-yod* disappears and a *tav* suffix is added with *segol*s for vowels.

✓ Thus ◌ֶ◌ֶת may be a clue to a *pe-yod/vav* root.

(This pattern also appears with other weak roots, such as a *pe-nun* like נגשׁ.)

(b) *Nifal*

[1] Perfect and participle, *nifal:* the *pe-yod* becomes a *holem-vav* (□□נוֹ).

[2] Imperfect, imperative, and infinitive, *nifal:* the *pe-yod* becomes a *vav* consonant (□□וָ◁).

(c) *Hifil* (all conjugations): the *pe-yod* becomes a *holem-vav* (□□וֹ◁).

(d) *Hofal* (all conjugations): the *pe-yod* becomes a *shureq* (□□וּ◁).

✓ Thus □□וֹ◁, □□וָ◁, and □□וּ◁ are clues to a *pe-yod/vav* verb in *nifal, hifil,* and *hofal.*

(3) Some *pe-yod*s like יָרַשׁ share characteristics of true *pe-yod*s and of *pe-yod/vav*s.

(4) Some *pe-yod*s with a sibilant for the second root consonant (like יָצַק) follow the pattern of *pe-nun*s in that the *yod* assimilates into the sibilant with a *dagesh-forte* when a prefix is added.

✓ Thus □⊡◁ may be a clue to a *pe-yod* root when the consonant with a *dagesh-forte* is a sibilant.

(This situation may also arise with a *pe-nun* root.)

(5) הָלַךְ is inflected as if its root were ילך in part of its conjugation.

b. The following verbs with analyses illustrate the process of identifying *pe-yod* roots.

(1) וַיִּיקַץ (Ge 28:16) > יקץ, *impf, qal, 3MS + vav cons,* "and he woke"

The *hireq-yod* prefix vowel is a clue that the verb is a true *pe-yod* in imperfect, *qal.*

(2) יֵקַד (Is 10:16) > יקד, *impf, qal, 3MS,* "it will burn"

The *sere* suggests the *yod* is an imperfect prefix; it is also a clue that the verb is *pe-yod/vav* in imperfect, *qal*.

(3) הַב (Pr 30:15) > יהב, *impv, qal, 2MS,* "give"

When two root consonants remain without a prefix or suffix, the verb may be an imperative, *qal* from a *pe-nun* root (like נגשׁ) or from a *pe-yod/vav* root. (Other options exist, but have not yet been discussed.) In this case the verb is *pe-yod/vav*.

(4) לָרֶדֶת (Ge 44:26) > ירד, *inf,qal, Cs* + ל *prep,* "to go down"

The ל preposition and the *segolate* pattern with a *tav* suffix suggest infinitive, *qal*, construct. This pattern occurs in *pe-nuns* (like נגשׁ) and in *pe-yod/vavs*. In this case the root is *pe-yod/vav*.

(5) נוֹחָלָה (Eze 19:5) > יחל, *perf, nif, 3FS,* "she waited"

The *holem-vav* in the position of the first root consonant in a clue to *pe-yod/vav* in *nifal* (*perf* and *part*) and in *hifil* (all conjugations). The *nun* prefix indicates this form is *nifal*.

(6) אִוָּעֵד (Ex 29:42) > יעד, *impf, nif, 1CS,* "I will meet"

The *vav* with a *dagesh-forte* and *qames* is a clue to *pe-yod/vav* in imperfect, *nifal*.

(7) תּוּבַל (Ps 45:15; *Eng* 45:14) > יבל, *impf, hof, 3FS,* "she is led"

The *shureq* is a clue to *pe-yod/vav* in *hofal*.

(8) יַצִּיעַ (Is 58:5) > יצע, *impf, hif, 3MS,* "he will spread out"

The pattern of a *dagesh-forte* in the first of two remaining root consonants suggests either a *pe-nun* root or a *pe-yod/vav* root in which the second consonant is a sibilant. The later is the correct option for this word.

(9) תֵּלַכְנָה (Ru 1:11) > הלך, *impf, qal, 2FP,* "you will go"

The *sere* prefix vowel suggests a *pe-yod/vav* root; however, the root is actually הלך, which acts like a *pe-yod/vav* in part of its conjugation.

24B Interrogative Clauses

1. Introduction

a. Interrogative clauses (that is, clauses which ask a question) can be expressed in several ways. Occasionally they employ no special grammatical feature, and their interrogative nature is simply determined by their context. For example, the following question has no linguistic element to indicate it is interrogative other than its context:

וַאֲנִי לֹא אָחוּס עַל־נִינְוֵה = "Shall I not have pity on Nineveh?" (Jon 4:11).[1]

b. While some questions are determined by context alone, it is more often the case that interrogative clauses employ one of three grammatical clues: a *he* (ה) interrogative, an interrogative pronoun, or an interrogative adverb.

2. *He* interrogative

a. Simple questions are usually expressed with a *he* interrogative. This interrogative is formed by prefixing the particle *he* (הֲ) to the first word of an interrogative clause. Such a clause normally expects a simple "yes" or "no" answer. For example, the following is an indicative clause:

יֵשׁ לָכֶם אָח = "You have a brother."

If the *he* interrogative is prefixed to the first word, it becomes an interrogative clause:

הֲיֵשׁ לָכֶם אָח = "Do you have a brother?" (Ge 43:7).

b. Pointing of the *he* interrogative

(1) The *he* interrogative is pointed as follows.

(a) In most cases the *he* interrogative is הֲ.

- הֲשַׂמְתָּ לִבְּךָ אֶל־עַבְדִּי אִיּוֹב = "Have you considered my servant Job?" (Job 2:3).

(b) Before a consonant with a *sheva* and before most gutturals, the *he* interrogative is הַ.

- הַבְרָכָה אַחַת הִוא־לְךָ – "Have you only one blessing?" (Ge 27:38).
- הַאֵין פֹּה נָבִיא לַיהוָה = "Is there no prophet of the LORD here?" (1Ki 22:7).

(c) Before a guttural with a *qames* or *hatef-qames*, the *he* interrogative is הֶ.

- הֶחָכָם יִהְיֶה = "Is he wise?" (Ecc 2:19).
- הֶחֳדַלְתִּי = "Shall I stop? (Jdg 9:9).

[1] For the examples of *he* interrogatives in this section and for other examples, see Joüon, §102l-o; and Kautzsch, §150a.

(2) The following clues help to distinguish the *he* interrogative from the definite article.

(a) Most of the time the *he* interrogative is pointed with a *hatef-patah*, a vowel which never occurs with the article.

(b) A *dagesh-forte* does not typically follow the *he* interrogative, while it does normally follow the article.[1]

(c) In those few situations where the pointing is the same for the *he* interrogative and the article, the context determines which form is intended.

3. Interrogative pronouns

a. Another way of forming an interrogative clause is by using one of two interrogative pronouns. Neither of these pronouns can be declined to show gender or number.

b. מִי is the personal interrogative pronoun. It typically refers to persons and may be translated in such ways as "who?, whom?, whose?" or "whoever?" Its spelling does not vary and it can occur with a prefixed preposition or a *maqqef*.

- מִי אַתָּה בְּנִי = "Who are you, my son?" (Ge 27:18).
- אֶת־מִי רַצּוֹתִי = "Whom have I oppressed?" (1Sa 12:3).
- בַּת־מִי אַתְּ = "Whose daughter are you?" (Ge 24:23).
- מִי־יָרֵא = "Whoever is afraid?" (Jdg 7:3).
- לְמִי־אַתָּה = "To whom do you belong?" (Ge 32:18; *Eng* 32:17).

c. מָה is the impersonal interrogative pronoun. It typically refers to things and is usually translated as "what?" or "how?" מָה is often followed by a *maqqef*.

(1) Unlike מִי, the pointing of the impersonal interrogative pronoun does vary, depending upon its context. Its pointing is similar to that of the definite article.

(a) In most cases the pointing is מַה־ followed by a *dagesh-forte* (placed in the following consonant).

---

[1] On rare occasions a *dagesh-forte* does follow the *he* interrogative, as in Eze 20:30:
הַבְּדֶרֶךְ אֲבוֹתֵיכֶם אַתֶּם נִטְמְאִים = "In the manner of your ancestors will you defile yourselves?"

- מַה־זֹּאת עָשִׂיתָ לִּי = "What is this you have done to me?" (Ge 12:18).

✓ In the preceding example the *dagesh-forte* in לִּי is commonly called a "euphonic" or "conjunctive" *dagesh-forte*. As the terms suggest, it appears for the sake of euphony (ease of pronunciation) or to emphasize a link with the preceding word. It serves no other grammatical purpose.[1]

(b) Before the gutturals and ר (which cannot take a *dagesh-forte*) the pointing is מָה, מַה, or מֶה with or without a *maqqef*.[2]

- מָה הָעֲבֹדָה הַזֹּאת לָכֶם = "What does this service mean to you?" (Ex 12:26)
- בֵּינִי וּבֵינְךָ מַה־הִוא = "What is that between me and you?" (Ge 23:15)
- מֶה־עָשִׂיתָ = "What have you done?" (Ge 20:9).

(2) מָה can also take prefixed prepositions.

- בַּמָּה = "in what?, by what?, how?"
- כַּמָּה = "like what?, how many/much/often/long?"
- לָמָּה = "why?, to what purpose?, for what reason?"

d. The interrogative pronouns מִי and מָה can also be used to express an indirect question, as the following illustrate.[3]

- לֹא יָדַעְתִּי מִי עָשָׂה אֶת־הַדָּבָר הַזֶּה = "I do not know who has done this thing" (Ge 21:26).
- הִגִּיד לְךָ אָדָם מַה־טּוֹב = "He has revealed to you, O mortal, what is good" (Mic 6:8).

4. Interrogative adverbs

Interrogative clauses may also be introduced by an interrogative adverb. The preceding forms of מָה with prefixed prepositions can serve this purpose (בַּמָּה,

---

[1] See Kelley, 147; and Weingreen, 16.

[2] Since מָה is rather inconsistent in its pointing before gutturals, this general rule is adequate for recognizing the impersonal interrogative pronoun. For further discussion of its pointing see Horsnell, 205-206.

[3] For these and other examples, see Gibson, §8.

כַּמָּה, and לָ֫מָּה). In addition, the following are some of the more frequently used interrogative adverbs.

אַיֵּה	=	"where?"	אָן or אָ֫נָה	=	"where?, to where?"
אֵי	=	"where?"	מֵאַ֫יִן	=	"from where?"
אֵיךְ	=	"how?"	מַדּוּעַ	=	"why?"

Lesson 24: Exercises

a. Learn to recognize, pronounce, and translate the following vocabulary.

	Word	*Translation*	*Notes*
(1)	אֶ֫בֶן	stone (*NFS*)	*P:* אֲבָנִים
(2)	אַבְרָהָם	Abraham (*proper N*)	
(3)	בָּנָה	he built (*V*)	
(4)	בָּשָׂר	flesh (*NMS*)	*Cs:* בְּשַׂר; *P:* בְּשָׂרִים
(5)	דָּוִד	David (*proper N*)	
(6)	הֲ___	(*he* interrogative)	Also הַ or הֶ; prefixed at the beginning of an interrogative clause
(7)	הָלַךְ	he went, came, walked (*V*)	Inflects like a *pe-yod/vav* verb in part of its conjugation
(8)	חֶ֫סֶד	steadfast love, kindness, loyalty (*NMS*)	*S* with *PS:* חַסְדִּי, חַסְדְּךָ, etc.; *P:* חֲסָדִים, חַסְדֵי
(9)	יְהוֹשׁוּעַ	Joshua (*proper N*)	
(10)	יוֹסֵף	Joseph (*proper N*)	
(11)	יָסַף	he added, increased (*V*)	
(12)	יָצָא	he went out (*V*)	
(13)	יָרַד	he went down, descended (*V*)	
(14)	יָרַשׁ	he took possession of, inherited, displaced (*V*)	

(15)	ישׁע	נוֹשַׁע (*nif*): he was saved; הוֹשִׁיעַ (*hif*): he saved, delivered (*V*)	Only occurs in *nif* & *hif*
(16)	מָה	what? how? (*pron*)	Also: מַה or מֶה; followed by *dagesh-forte* where possible
(17)	מִי	who?, whom?, whose?, whoever? (*pron*)	
(18)	מִלְחָמָה	battle, war (*NFS*)	*Cs:* מִלְחֶמֶת
(19)	פַּרְעֹה	Pharaoh (*NMS*)	

b. Analyze the following verbs, doing as much of the work as possible before consulting a lexicon. Also, check the context of the word when necessary to determine the most appropriate translation.

- *Example:* בְּהִוָּסְדָם (Ps 31:14; *Eng* 31:13) ⇒ *Answer:* > יסד, *inf, hif, Cs* + ב *prep* + *PS 3MP,* "in their conspiring"

(1)	וְהוֹרַדְתָּ	(1Ki 2:9)	(9)	וְאֵימְנָה	(Ge 13:9)
(2)	לֶדֶת	(Zep 2:2)	(10)	נוֹרָא	(Ex 15:11)
(3)	הוֹתֵר	(Ps 79:11)	(11)	וְהוֹלִיכוֹ	(Pr 16:29)
(4)	אֹהֲבֵם	(Hos 14:5; *Eng* 14:4)	(12)	מוּצָאוֹת	(Jer 38:22)
(5)	וְהִוָּשְׁעוּ	(Is 45:22)	(13)	וּסְעוּ	(Nu 14:25)
(6)	סְפוּ	(Is 29:1)	(14)	וְיֵדָעֵם	(Hos 14:10; *Eng* 14:9)
(7)	וְהֵילִילוּ	(Am 8:3)	(15)	תַּבַּעְנָה	(Ps 119:171)
(8)	לָטַעַת	(Ecc 3:2)	(16)	יוֹעֲצִים	(Job 12:17)

c. Read aloud and translate the following texts from the Hebrew Bible. Also provide an analysis of all verbs (finite and non-finite).

(1) Genesis 2:18-25

Verse 18

(a) הֱיוֹת In *lamed-he* verbs, as with *pe-yod/vavs* and some *pe-nuns*, a ת suffix is added in infinitive, *qal,* construct. The *vav* before the ת in this word is a clue that the root is *lamed-he*.

(b) אֶעֱשֶׂה־לּוֹ Interpret [1] the significance of note “a” in the critical apparatus relating to this verb, and [2] the reason for the *dagesh-forte* in the *lamed.*

Verse 25

יִתְבֹּשָׁשׁוּ (> בּוֹשׁ) The so-called “intensive” stems of *ayin-vav* verbs usually double the third root consonant rather than the second, as discussed in the next lesson. The stem of this word is *hitpolel,* which is equivalent in meaning to *hitpael.*

(2) 2Samuel 7:5

(3) Isaiah 6:8

(4) Exodus 18:14

Lesson 25

Weak Verbs: *Ayin-Vav, Ayin-Yod,* and Double-*Ayin*; Numbers

25A Weak Verbs: *Ayin-Vav, Ayin-Yod,* and Double-*Ayin*

1. *Ayin-vav* and *ayin-yod* verbs

a. *Ayin-vav* and *ayin-yod* verbs are treated together in this section because they follow very similar patterns. These verbs have either a *vav* or *yod* as the middle root consonant, as in קום ("rise") and שׂים ("set"). The middle *vav* or *yod* typically disappears or becomes a naturally-long vowel as they are inflected. Consequently, these weak verbs are also called "middle vowel" or "hollow" verbs.

b. The lexical form of *ayin-vav* and *ayin-yod* verbs is the infinitive, *qal,* construct, because this form retains the middle *vav* or *yod*. Other verbs employ perfect, *qal, 3MS* as the lexical form; however, this form in *ayin-vav* and *ayin-yod* verbs typically loses the middle consonant. For example, the lexical form for the root קום is the infinitive, *qal,* construct: קוּם, rather than the perfect, *qal, 3MS,* which is קָם.

c. Some verbs have both an *ayin-vav* and an *ayin-yod* root, as with the verb שִׂים, שׂוּם ("[to] set").

d. Most *ayin-vav* verbs follow the pattern of the very common verb קוּם ("[to] rise" or "stand"). Some exceptions do occur, as with two common *ayin-vav* stative verbs: בּוֹשׁ ("[to] be ashamed") and מוּת ("[to] die").

e. *Ayin-yod* verbs also follow the pattern of קום in all conjugations and stems except in the *qal* stem in imperfect, imperative, and infinitive construct.

f. Major characteristics of *ayin-vav* and *ayin-yod* verbs in *qal, nifal, hifil,* and *hofal*

(1) Disappearance of the middle *vav* or *yod*

(a) *Qal* in perfect and active participle

[1] The middle *vav* or *yod* typically disappears in perfect, *qal,* and in

participle, *qal,* active. When the middle *vav* or *yod* disappears in these forms, the first root consonant normally takes an A-class vowel (either *qames* or *patah*). The following charts illustrate, using קוּם and שִׂים as models.

Perfect, *Qal*		
3MS	קָם	שָׂם
3FS	קָ֫מָה	שָׂ֫מָה
2MP	קַמְתֶּם	שַׂמְתֶּם
1CP	קַ֫מְנוּ	שַׂ֫מְנוּ

Participle, *Qal,* Active		
MS, Ab	קָם	שָׂם
FS, Ab	קָמָה	שָׂמָה
MP, Ab	קָמִים	שָׂמִים
FP, Ab	קָמוֹת	שָׂמוֹת

✓ Note the similar forms:

- *Perf, qal, 3MS* and *part, qal, act, MS, Ab* are identical.
- *Perf, qal, 3FS* and *part, qal, act, FS, Ab* differ only in the accent.

✓ See Appendix 3, paradigm 9, for the full conjugation of קוּם, and paradigm 10 for the *qal* conjugation of other *ayin-vav/ayin-yod* verbs.

[2] *Ayin-vav* and *ayin-yod* stative verbs may take different vowels for the first consonant than the A-class vowels that appear with קוּם.

- בּוֹשׁ (*inf, qal, Cs*) is also בּוֹשׁ in *perf, qal, 3MS,* and in *part, qal, act, MS, Ab* (in contrast with קָם).
- מוּת (*inf, qal, Cs*) is מֵת in *perf, qal, 3MS,* and in *part, qal, act, MS, Ab* (in contrast with קָם).

✓ See Appendix 3, paradigm 10, for the full *qal* conjugation of these stative verbs.

(b) *Hifil* and *hofal* in all conjugations

The middle consonant of *ayin-vav* and *ayin-yod* verbs also disappears in all conjugations of *hifil* and *hofal.* The following chart illustrates, using קוּם.

Perfect					
	Hifil	*Hofal*		*Hifil*	*Hofal*
3MS	הֵקִים	הוּקַם	*3CP*	הֵקִ֫ימוּ	הוּקְמוּ
3FS	הֵקִ֫ימָה	הוּקְמָה			
2MS	הֲקִימ֫וֹתָ	הוּקַ֫מְתָ	*2MP*	הֲקִימוֹתֶם	הוּקַמְתֶּם
2FS	הֲקִימוֹת	הוּקַמְתְּ	*2FP*	הֲקִימוֹתֶן	הוּקַמְתֶּן
1CS	הֲקִימ֫וֹתִי	הוּקַ֫מְתִּי	*1CP*	הֲקִימ֫וֹנוּ	הוּקַ֫מְנוּ

✓ Note that in perfect, *hifil* a *holem-vav* appears as a connecting vowel before verb endings that begin with a consonant.

Imperfect		
	Hifil	*Hofal*
3MS	יָקִים	יוּקַם
3MP	יָקִ֫ימוּ	יוּקְמוּ
3FP/2FP	תָּקֵ֫מְנָה	תּוּקַ֫מְנָה

Imperative	
	Hifil
2MS	הָקֵם
2MP	הָקִ֫ימוּ
2FP	הָקֵ֫מְנָה

Infinitive		
	Hifil	*Hofal*
Cs	הָקִים	הוּקַם
Ab	הָקֵם	הוּקֵם

Participle		
	Hifil	*Hofal*
MS, Ab	מֵקִים	מוּקָם
MP, Ab	מְקִימִים	מוּקָמִים

(2) Sometimes the middle *vav* or *yod* becomes a naturally-long vowel, namely *holem-vav*, *shureq*, or *hireq-yod*. This shift to a naturally-long vowel occurs in the *nifal* stem in all conjugations and the *qal* stem in imperfect, imperative, and infinitive. The following charts illustrate, using קוּם as a model. שִׂים also appears as a model at points where *ayin-yod* verbs differ from *ayin-vav* verbs.

Perfect, *Nifal*				
3MS	נָקוֹם		*3CP*	נָקוֹמוּ
3FS	נָקוֹמָה			
2MS	נְקוּמוֹתָ		*2MP*	נְקֹמוֹתֶם
2FS	נְקוּמוֹת		*2FP*	נְקֹמוֹתֶן
1CS	נְקוּמוֹתִי		*1CP*	נְקוּמוֹנוּ

✓ Note that in perfect, *nifal* (as in perfect, *hifil*) a *holem-vav* appears as a connecting vowel before verb endings that begin with a consonant.

Imperfect				
	Qal	*Nifal*		*Qal*
3MS	יָקוּם	יִקּוֹם		יָשִׂים
3MP	יָקוּמוּ	יִקּוֹמוּ		יָשִׂימוּ
3FP/2FP	תְּקוּמֶינָה	תִּקּוֹמְנָה		תְּשִׂימֶינָה

✓ Note that in imperfect, *qal*, *3FP/2FP, segol yod* (◌ֶי) appears before a consonantal verb ending.

Imperative				
	Qal	*Nifal*		*Qal*
2MS	קוּם	הִקּוֹם		שִׂים
2MP	קוּמוּ	הִקּוֹמוּ		שִׂימוּ
Infinitive				
	Qal	*Nifal*		*Qal*
Cs	קוּם	הִקּוֹם		שִׂים
Ab	קוֹם	הִקּוֹם		שׂוֹם

Participle, *Nifal*	
MS, Ab	נָקוֹם
MP, Ab	נְקוֹמִים

(3) The vowel employed with verb prefixes can be a clue to the stem of *ayin-vavs* and *ayin-yods* in *qal, nifal, hifil,* and *hofal,* as indicated in the following chart.

<table>
<tr><th colspan="2">Verb Prefix Vowels</th></tr>
<tr><td rowspan="3">◌ָ (qames)
(reducing to ◌ְ in some forms)</td><td>Qal in impf [1]</td></tr>
<tr><td>Nifal in perf & part</td></tr>
<tr><td>Hifil in impf, impv & inf</td></tr>
<tr><td>◌ֵ (sere)
(reducing to ◌ְ or ◌ֲ)</td><td>Hifil in perf & part</td></tr>
<tr><td>◌ִ (hireq) or ◌ֶ (segol)</td><td>Nifal in impf, impv & inf</td></tr>
<tr><td>וּ◌ (shureq)</td><td>Hofal in all conjugations</td></tr>
</table>

g. Major characteristics of *ayin-vav* and *ayin-yod* verbs in the "intensive" stems

(1) *Ayin-vav* and *ayin-yod* verbs usually form the so-called "intensive" stems in a different manner than the strong verb does. Whereas the "intensive" stems of the strong verb require a doubling of the second root consonant (in *piel, pual,* and *hitpael*), *ayin-vav* and *ayin-yod* verbs typically double the final root consonant, creating stems that are called *polel, polal,* and *hitpolel.* In meaning *polel* = *piel; polal* = *pual;* and *hitpolel* = *hitpael.* The following chart illustrates the forms.

	Polel	*Polal*	*Hitpolel*
Perf, 3MS	קוֹמֵם	קוֹמַם	הִתְקוֹמֵם
Impf, 3MS	יְקוֹמֵם	יְקוֹמַם	יִתְקוֹמֵם
Impv, 2MS	קוֹמֵם	[none]	הִתְקוֹמֵם
Inf, Cs/Ab	קוֹמֵם	קוֹמַם	הִתְקוֹמֵם
Part, MS, Ab	מְקוֹמֵם	מְקוֹמָם	מִתְקוֹמֵם

✓ See Appendix 3, paradigm 9, for the full conjugation of these stems.

(2) A few *ayin-vav* verbs employ another rare "intensive" stem pattern in which both the first and the third root consonants are doubled, creating stems known as *pilpel, polpal* (or *pulpal*), and *hitpalpel.* For example, the root כול ("contain") hypothetically can appear in these stems in perfect, *3MS:* כִּלְכֵּל is *pilpel* (= *piel*); כָּלְכַּל is *polpal* (= *pual*); and הִתְכַּלְכֵּל is *hitpalpel* (= *hitpael*).

[1] The stative verb בוֹשׁ takes a *sere* prefix vowel in *impf, qal,* as in יֵבוֹשׁ (*3MS*).

(3) Occasionally *ayin-vav* and *ayin-yod* verbs also have "intensive" forms which follow the pattern of *piel, pual,* and *hitpael* in the strong verb.

h. Some *ayin-vav* and *ayin-yod* verbs that have a guttural for the third consonant retain the middle *vav* or *yod* as a consonant throughout their conjugations. Common verbs in this category are הָיָה ("he was"), חָיָה ("he lived"), and צוה ("command").[1] These verbs behave like other *lamed-he* verbs, which are discussed in the next lesson.

2. Double-*ayin* verbs

a. Double-*ayin* verbs are ones in which the second and third consonants of the root are the same, as with the roots סבב ("surround") and קלל ("be light"). Double-*ayin* verbs are also called "geminates."

b. Major characteristics of double-*ayin* verbs in *qal, nifal, hifil,* and *hofal*

(1) In *qal, nifal, hifil,* and *hofal,* the final (doubled) consonant tends to assimilate. However, some *double-ayin*s inflect like the strong verb, retaining the doubled consonant in all or part of these stems. A few double-*ayin*s have two sets of forms: one in which the doubled consonant is retained and another in which it assimilates.

(2) When the doubled root consonant assimilates, the patterns are as follows.

(a) The assimilation of the doubled consonant requires a *dagesh-forte* where possible – that is, when the last root consonant is followed by an ending or suffix. For example, סבב becomes סַב (*perf, qal, 3MS*) where there is no ending. With an ending it becomes סַ֫בָּה (*perf, qal, 3FS*).

(b) When the doubled root consonant assimilates, the first root consonant tends to take the vowel that would normally appear with the second root consonant in the strong verb. For example, where the strong verb would have מָשַׁל, a double-*ayin* has סַב (*perf, qal, 3MS*).

✓ An exception to this tendency occurs in *hifil,* where the first root consonant takes a *sere*. For example, where the strong verb in *hifil* has הִמְשִׁיל (*perf*) or יַמְשִׁיל (*impf*), a double-*ayin* has הֵסֵב (*perf, hif, 3MS*) or יָסֵב (*impf, hif, 3MS*).

(c) The following charts illustrate the patterns of most double-*ayin* verbs

[1] See Horsnell, 409.

when assimilation occurs, using סבב as a model. Stative double-*ayins* exhibit some distinctive features, as illustrated in the charts by קלל.

Perfect				
	Qal[1]	*Nifal*	*Hifil*	*Hofal*
3MS	סַב	נָסַב	הֵסֵב	הוּסַב
3FS	סַבָּה	נָסַבָּה	הֵסַבָּה	הוּסַבָּה
2MS	סַבּוֹתָ	נְסַבּוֹתָ	הֲסִבּוֹתָ	הוּסַבּוֹתָ
3CP	סַבּוּ	נָסַבּוּ	הֵסַבּוּ	הוּסַבּוּ
1CP	סַבּוֹנוּ	נְסַבּוֹנוּ	הֲסִבּוֹנוּ	הוּסַבּוֹנוּ

- ✓ Note that in the perfect a *holem-vav* appears before a consonantal suffix and that vowel suffixes are not accented. The rejection of the accent with a vowel suffix also occurs in imperfect and imperative.
- ✓ See Appendix 3, paradigm 11, for the full conjugation of double-*ayin* verbs.

Imperfect					
	Qal	*Nifal*	*Hifil*	*Hofal*	*Qal*
3MS	יָסֹב	יִסַּב	יָסֵב	יוּסַב	יֵקַל
3MP	יָסֹבּוּ	יִסַּבּוּ	יָסֵבּוּ	יוּסַבּוּ	יֵקַלּוּ
3FP/2FP	תְּסֻבֶּינָה	תִּסַּבֶּינָה	תְּסִבֶּינָה	תּוּסַבֶּינָה	תְּקַלֶּינָה

Imperative			
	Qal	*Nifal*	*Hifil*
2MS	סֹב	הִסַּב	הָסֵב
2MP	סֹבּוּ	הִסַּבּוּ	הָסֵבּוּ
2FP	סֻבֶּינָה	הִסַּבֶּינָה	הֲסִבֶּינָה

- ✓ Note that in the imperfect and imperative *segol yod* (◌ֶי) appears before the consonantal suffix in feminine plural forms and that the vowel suffixes reject the accent.

[1] סבב has some alternate forms that retain the doubled consonant: סָבַב (*3MS*), סָבְבָה (*3FS*), and סָבְבוּ (*3CP*).

Infinitive				
	Qal	*Nifal*	*Hifil*	*Hofal*
Cs	סֹב	הִסֵּב	הָסֵב	הוּסַב
Ab	סָבוֹב	הִסּוֹב	הָסֵב	הוּסֵב

Participle						
	Qal, Act	*Nifal*	*Hifil*	*Hofal*		*Qal*
MS, Ab	סֹבֵב	נָסָב	מֵסֵב	מוּסָב		קַל
MP, Ab	סֹבְבִים	נְסַבִּים	מְסִבִּים	מוּסָבִּים		קַלִּים

(3) The vowel employed with verb prefixes can be a clue to the stem for double-*ayin* verbs in *qal, nifal, hifil,* and *hofal*. These prefix vowels parallel those used with most *ayin-vav* and *ayin-yod* verbs.

Verb Prefix Vowels	
◌ָ (*qames*) (reducing to ◌ְ or ◌ֲin some forms)	*Qal* in *impf*
	Nifal in *perf* & *part*
	Hifil in *impf, impv* & *inf*
◌ֵ (*sere*) (reducing to ◌ְ or ◌ֲ)	*Hifil* in *perf* & *part*
◌ִ(*hireq*) or ◌ֶ (*segol*)	*Nifal* in *impf, impv* & *inf*
◌וּ (*shureq*)	*Hofal* in all conjugations

(4) Sometimes double-*ayin* verbs form the imperfect, *qal* like *pe-nun* verbs, which is to say that one of the doubled consonants assimilates with a *dagesh-forte* into the first root consonant, rather than the last consonant. For example, the root סבב can be inflected in imperfect, *qal* according to the pattern of יִסֹּב (*3MS*), תִּסֹּב (*3FS/2MS*), תִּסֹּבִּי (*2FS*), etc.

(5) Stative verbs may take alternate vowels to the pattern of סבב given in the preceding charts. For example, the stative קלל ("be light") in imperfect, *qal* takes an E-class prefix vowel where סבב has an A-class. For example, the imperfect, *qal, 3MS* form of קלל is יֵקַל (in contrast with יָסֹב). Also, the

participle, *qal,* active form of קלל is קַל (*MS, Ab*) (in contrast with סֹבֵב).

c. Major characteristics of double-*ayin* verbs in "intensive" stems

(1) In the so-called "intensive" stems double-*ayin* verbs usually follow the pattern of the strong verb in forming *piel, pual,* and *hitpael* conjugations. Occasionally, double-*ayins* instead follow a pattern similar to *ayin-vavs* and *ayin-yods* in forming the "intensives" as *poel* (= *piel*), *poal* (= *pual*), and *hitpoel* (= *hitpael*).

	Poel	*Poal*	*Hitpoel*
Perf, 3MS	סוֹבֵב	סוֹבַב	הִסְתּוֹבֵב
Impf, 3MS	יְסוֹבֵב	יְסוֹבַב	יִסְתּוֹבֵב
Impv, 2MS	סוֹבֵב	[none]	הִסְתּוֹבֵב
Inf, Cs/Ab	סוֹבֵב	סוֹבַב	הִסְתּוֹבֵב
Part, MS, Ab	מְסוֹבֵב	מְסוֹבָב	מִסְתּוֹבֵב

✓ Note that the sibilant consonant *samek* exchanges places with the *pe* in *hitpoel,* as is common with sibilants in *hitpael*.

(2) Double-*ayin* verbs in rare instances imitate the pattern of *ayin-vavs* and *ayin-yods* in forming *pilpel* and *hitpalpel* stems. For example, the root גלל ("roll") hypothetically can appear in these stems in perfect, *3MS:* גִּלְגֵּל is *pilpel* (= *piel*) and הִתְגַּלְגֵּל is *hitpalpel* (= *hitpael*).

3. Summary of characteristics of *ayin-vavs*, *ayin-yods*, and double-*ayins*

a. The following is a succinct summary of the major characteristics of these *ayin* weakness verbs

(1) *Ayin-vavs* and *ayin-yods* in *qal, nifal, hifil,* and *hofal*

(a) The lexical form is infinitive, *qal,* construct.

(b) The *vav* or *yod* may disappear.

[1] Such occurs in the *qal* stem in perfect and active participle. In these two conjugations the first root consonant is usually A-class (□□ָ or ◁□□ַ).

✓ Thus, when only two root consonants remain, the verb may be double-*ayin* in perfect, *qal* or participle, *qal,* active.

(□□ or ◁□□ [with various vowels] also occurs with *pe-nuns* [like נגשׁ] and *pe-yod/vavs* in imperative, *qal,* as discussed previously.)

[2] The *vav* or *yod* also disappears in all conjugations of *hifil* and *hofal.*

(c) The *vav* or *yod* may become a naturally-long vowel: *holem-vav, shureq,* or *hireq-yod.*

✓ Thus, □וֹ□, □וּ□, or □י□ִ (with or without prefixes and suffixes) may indicate an *ayin-vav* or *ayin-yod* root.

(□י□ִ◁ can also occur with other weak verbs in *hifil.*)

(2) Double-*ayins* in *qal, nifal, hifil,* and *hofal*

(a) Double-*ayins* may inflect like the strong verb.

(b) They may also assimilate the last (doubled) consonant, in which case a *dagesh-forte* appears in the second root consonant where possible.

✓ Thus, when only two root consonants remain and the second has a *dagesh-forte,* the root may be double-*ayin.* This clue is relevant only when there is an ending or suffix: ▷□ּ□.

(c) Occasionally the first of the doubled consonants may assimilate into the first root consonant with a *dagesh-forte* (following the pattern of *pe-nuns*).

✓ Thus, when only two root consonants remain and the first has a *dagesh-forte,* the root may be double-*ayin.* This clue is relevant only when there is a prefix: □□ּ◁.

(This situation commonly occurs with a *pe-nun* root.)

(3) The prefix vowels for *ayin-vavs, ayin-yods,* and double-*ayins* provide clues to the conjugations and stems (in *qal, nif, hif,* and *hof*).

Verb Prefix Vowels	
◁ָ (*qames*) (reducing to ◁ְ or ◁ֲ)	*Qal* in *impf*[1]
	Nifal in *perf & part*
	Hifil in *impf, impv & inf*
◁ֵ (*sere*) (reducing to ◁ְ or ◁ֲ)	*Hifil* in *perf & part*
◁ִ(*hireq*) or ◁ֶ (*segol*)	*Nifal* in *impf, impv & inf*
וּ◁ (*shureq*)	*Hofal* in all conjugations

[1] Stative verbs with *ayin* weaknesses may take a *sere* prefix vowel in imperfect, *qal.*

(4) *Ayin-vav*s, *ayin-yod*s, and double-*ayin*s in "intensive" stems

(a) Verbs with *ayin* weaknesses may follow the pattern of the strong verb in *piel, pual,* and *hitpael.*

(b) They may also form "intensives" in the patterns of *polel/poel, polal/poal,* and *hitpolel/hitpoel;* or *pilpel, polpal* (*pulpal*), and *hitpalpel.*

b. The following verbs with analyses illustrate the process of identifying the forms of verbs with *ayin-vav, ayin-yod,* and double-*ayin* weaknesses.

(1) רוּם (Dt 17:20) > רום, *inf, qal, Cs,* "exalting"

The naturally-long vowel in the place of the second root consonant suggests an *ayin-vav* or *ayin-yod* verb. The absence of a prefix and suffix suggests infinitive or imperative in *qal;* the context calls for an infinitive.

(2) בָּ֫אָה (Ge 15:17) > בוא, *perf, qal, 3FS,* "it went"

This word cannot be from a root באה, since no such root exists. (Also, the accent indicates that the form cannot be perfect, *qal, 3MS* from such a root.) The ◌ָה is a perfect, *qal, 3FS* verb ending. The presence of only two root consonants and an A-class vowel for the first suggests an *ayin-vav* or *ayin-yod* root.

(3) וָרָב (Is 19:20) > ריב, *part, qal, act, MS, Ab + vav,* "and a defender"

The two root consonants with an A-class vowel suggests an *ayin-vav* or *ayin-yod* root in perfect, *qal* or participle, *qal,* active. The context requires the latter.

(4) יִנּוֹעַ (Am 9:9) > נוע, *impf, nif, 3MS,* "it is shaken"

The *hireq* prefix vowel and *dagesh-forte* in the first root consonant suggest imperfect, *nifal.* The naturally-long vowel in the place of the middle consonant suggests an *ayin-vav* or *ayin-yod* verb.

(5) הֵנִיס (Ex 9:20) > נוס, *perf, hif, 3MS,* "he caused to flee"

The *he* prefix and *hireq-yod* suggest perfect, *hifil.* The *sere* prefix vowel suggests a *hifil* form of an *ayin* weakness.

(6) וַיָּמֹ֫דּוּ (Ex 16:18) > מדד, *impf, qal, 3MP + vav cons,* "and they measured"

The *dagesh-forte* in the second root consonant suggests a double-*ayin* root.

(7) תּוּשַּׁד (Is 33:1) > שדד, *impf, hof, 2MS,* "you will be destroyed"

The *shureq* prefix vowel suggests *hofal* in either *pe-yod, ayin-vav, ayin-*

yod, or double-*ayin*. The *dagesh-forte* in the first of two remaining root consonants can be a clue to *pe-nun*, *pe-yod* (when the consonant is a sibilant), or double-*ayin*. The *shureq* rules out *pe-nun;* there is no extant ישׁד root. Thus, the root is double-*ayin*.

(8) מִתְגּוֹרֵר (1Ki 17:20) > גור, *part, hitpolel, MS, Ab,* "staying"

The prefix together with a root that has doubled consonants and "o-e" vowels suggest a *hitpolel* form of an *ayin* weakness. The lexicon indicates that the form in *ayin-vav*.

25B Numbers[1]

1. Numbers from "one/first" to "ten/tenth"

   a. Hebrew numbers, like those in English, appear in the forms of both ordinals ("one," "two," "three," etc.) and cardinals ("first," "second," "third," etc.). Both sets of forms occur in masculine and feminine, and the ordinals appear in absolute and construct states. The following charts illustrate.

Ordinal Numbers				
	Masculine		*Feminine*	
	Ab	*Cs*	*Ab*	*Cs*
One	אֶחָד	אַחַד	אַחַת	אַחַת
Two	שְׁנַיִם	שְׁנֵי	שְׁתַּיִם	שְׁתֵּי
Three	שָׁלוֹשׁ	שְׁלֹשׁ	שְׁלֹשָׁה	שְׁלֹשֶׁת
Four	אַרְבַּע	אַרְבַּע	אַרְבָּעָה	אַרְבַּעַת
Five	חָמֵשׁ	חֲמֵשׁ	חֲמִשָּׁה	חֲמֵשֶׁת
Six	שֵׁשׁ	שֵׁשׁ	שִׁשָּׁה	שֵׁשֶׁת
Seven	שֶׁבַע	שְׁבַע	שִׁבְעָה	שִׁבְעַת
Eight	שְׁמֹנֶה	שְׁמֹנֶה	שְׁמֹנָה	שְׁמֹנַת
Nine	תֵּשַׁע	תְּשַׁע	תִּשְׁעָה	תִּשְׁעַת
Ten	עֶשֶׂר	עֶשֶׂר	עֲשָׂרָה	עֲשֶׂרֶת

Cardinal Numbers		
	Masculine	*Feminine*
First	רִאשׁוֹן	רִאשׁוֹנָה
Second	שֵׁנִי	שֵׁנִית
Third	שְׁלִישִׁי	שְׁלִישִׁית
Fourth	רְבִיעִי	רְבִיעִית
Fifth	חֲמִישִׁי	חֲמִישִׁית
Sixth	שִׁשִּׁי	שִׁשִּׁית
Seventh	שְׁבִיעִי	שְׁבִיעִית
Eighth	שְׁמִינִי	שְׁמִינִית
Ninth	תְּשִׁיעִי	תְּשִׁיעִית
Tenth	עֲשִׂירִי	עֲשִׂירִית

[1] See Horsnell, 227-31; Kelley, 96-100; Seow, 268-72; and Christo H.J. van der Merwe, Jackie A. Naudé, and Jan H. Kroeze, *A Biblical Hebrew Reference Grammar* (Sheffield, Eng: Sheffield Academic Press, 2000), 263-70.

b. Notes concerning the ordinals from "one" to "ten"

(1) The number for "one" – אֶחָד (*M*), אַחַת (*F*) – is an adjective that follows the noun it modifies and agrees with it in gender and number.

- יוֹם אֶחָד = "one day" (Ge 27:45)

(2) The numbers from "two" to "ten" are nouns.

[a] The absolute forms may appear before or after the related noun; the construct forms (which have the same meaning as the absolute) can only appear before the noun.

- חָמֵשׁ שָׁנִים = "five years" (Ge 5:6)
- וְאַדְנֵיהֶם אַרְבָּעָה = "and their four bases" (Ex 27:16)
- שֵׁשֶׁת־יָמִים = "six days" (Ex 20:11)

[b] The number "two" – שְׁנַיִם (*M*), שְׁתַּיִם (*F*) – agrees in gender with the noun to which it relates.

- שְׁנַיִם חֳדָשִׁים = "two months" (Jdg 11:37)
- שְׁתַּיִם מַעֲרָכוֹת = "two rows" (Lv 24:6)

[c] The numbers from "three" to "ten" appear in the opposite gender of the nouns to which they relate. In other words, a masculine noun takes the feminine form of these numbers, while a feminine noun takes the masculine numbers.

- שְׁלֹשָׁה בָנִים = "three sons" (Ge 6:10)
- שֶׁבַע כְּבָשֹׂת = "seven ewe lambs" (Ge 21:29)

(3) The numbers can take pronominal suffixes.

- שְׁלָשְׁתָּם = "three of them" (Nu 12:4)

c. Notes concerning the cardinals from "first" to "tenth"

(1) The cardinal "first" (רִאשׁוֹן [*M*], רִאשׁוֹנָה [*F*]) is derived from the noun רֹאשׁ ("head"). The cardinals from "second" to "tenth" are formed by placing the endings ◌ִי (*M*) or ◌ִית (*F*) on the ordinals.

(2) The cardinals function as adjectives; they follow nouns and agree with them in gender.

- הַפָּר הָרִאשׁוֹן = "the first bull" (Lv 4:21).

2. Ordinals from "eleven" to "nineteen"

a. The ordinal numbers from "eleven" to "nineteen" are formed by the numbers for “one” to “nine” followed by the number “ten,” which is spelled as עָשָׂר (*M*) or עֶשְׂרֵה (*F*). The following chart illustrates.

	Masculine (Used with masculine nouns)	*Feminine* (Used with feminine nouns)
Eleven	אַחַד עָשָׂר[1]	אַחַת עֶשְׂרֵה
Twelve	שְׁנֵים עָשָׂר[2]	שְׁתֵּים עֶשְׂרֵה
Thirteen	שְׁלֹשָׁה עָשָׂר	שְׁלֹשׁ עֶשְׂרֵה
Fourteen, etc.	אַרְבָּעָה עָשָׂר	אַרְבַּע עֶשְׂרֵה

b. The two words that form the numbers “eleven” and “twelve” agree in gender with one another and with nouns to which they relate.

- אַחַד עָשָׂר יְלָדָיו = “his eleven children” (Ge 32:23; *Eng* 32:22)
- שְׁתֵּים עֶשְׂרֵה שָׁנָה = “twelve years” (Ge 14:4)

For the numbers from “thirteen” to “nineteen,” the number designation “ten” (עָשָׂר [*M*] or עֶשְׂרֵה [*F*]) agrees in gender with the noun to which it relates. However, the accompanying number designation for the unit (from “three” to “nine”) appears in the opposite gender from עָשָׂר or עֶשְׂרֵה and also the opposite gender from the related noun.

- שְׁלֹשָׁה עָשָׂר אֵילִם = “thirteen young bulls” (Nu 29:13)
- נָשִׁים אַרְבַּע עֶשְׂרֵה = “fourteen wives” (2Ch 13:21)

3. Ordinals for “twenty” and above

a. Multiples of “ten” are formed with the masculine, plural ending.

(1) The number “twenty” is the plural of the number “ten”: עֶשְׂרִים.

(2) Multiples of “ten” beginning with “thirty” are created by adding the plural ending to the numbers from “three” to “nine.”

שְׁלֹשִׁים = “thirty”
אַרְבָּעִים = “forty”
חֲמִשִּׁים = “fifty,” etc.

[1] Alternate forms for “eleven” are עַשְׁתֵּי עָשָׂר (*M*), עַשְׁתֵּי עֶשְׂרֵה (*F*).

[2] Alternate forms for “twelve” are שְׁנֵי עָשָׂר (*M*), שְׁתֵּי עֶשְׂרֵה (*F*).

b. Units beginning with "one" may be added to the multiples of ten, using a *vav* conjunction. The units may appear before or after the other numbers.

עֶשְׂרִים וְאֶחָד = "twenty-one" (*M*)

שְׁתַּ֫יִם וּשְׁלֹשִׁים = "thirty-two" (*F*), etc.

c. "100" and the multiples of "100" employ the feminine noun מֵאָה according to the following pattern.

מֵאָה = "100"

מָאתַ֫יִם = "200" (*Du*)

שְׁלֹשׁ מֵאוֹת = "300," etc.[1]

d. "1000" and the multiples of "1000" employ the masculine noun אֶ֫לֶף according to the following pattern.

אֶ֫לֶף = "1000"

אַלְפַּ֫יִם = "2000" (*Du*)

שְׁלֹ֫שֶׁת אֲלָפִים = "3000," etc.[2]

Lesson 25: Exercises

a. Learn to recognize, pronounce, and translate the following vocabulary.

	Word	*Translation*	*Notes*
(1)	אֶ֫לֶף	thousand (*NMS*)	*Du:* אַלְפַּ֫יִם = "2000"; *P:* אַלְפֵי, אֲלָפִים = "thousands"
(2)	בּוֹא	(to) come, go, enter (*V*)	Appears in Lesson 5 vocabulary as בָּא (*perf, qal, 3MS*)
(3)	בּוֹשׁ	(to) be ashamed (*V*)	
(4)	גַּם	also, likewise, again (*adv*)	
(5)	יְהוּדָה	Judah (*proper N*)	יְהוּדִי (*adj MS*) = "Jewish, Jew"
(6)	כּוּן	נָכוֹן (*nif*): he was fixed, firm, established; הֵכִין (*hif*): he made firm, established (*V*)	Does not occur in *qal*

[1] Note the pattern of the feminine noun מֵאוֹת requiring a coordinate masculine noun שְׁלֹשׁ.

[2] Note the pattern of the masculine noun אֲלָפִים requiring a coordinate feminine noun שְׁלֹ֫שֶׁת.

(7)	כֶּ֫סֶף	silver (*NMS*)	No *P*
(8)	מֵאָה	hundred (*NFS*)	*Cs:* מְאַת; *Du:* מָאתַ֫יִם = “200”; *P:* מֵאוֹת = “hundreds”
(9)	מוּת	(to) die (*V*)	
(10)	מִנְחָה	gift, offering (*NFS*)	
(11)	סָבַב[1]	he surrounded, went around, turned around (*V*)	
(12)	סוּר	(to) turn aside (*V*)	
(13)	עֶ֫שֶׂר (*M*), עֲשָׂרָה (*F*)	ten (*NM/FS*)	*P:* עֶשְׂרִים = “twenty”; עֲשִׂירִי (*M*), עֲשִׂירִית (*F*) = “tenth”; spelled עָשָׂר (*M*) and עֶשְׂרֵה (*F*) when combined with units to form numbers “11” to “19”
(14)	פָּקַד	he took care of, sought, missed, appointed (*V*)	
(15)	קוּם	(to) rise, stand (*V*)	
(16)	קלל[2]	קַל (*qal*): he was light, despised (*V*)	
(17)	שִׂים	(to) set, place (*V*)	Root also spelled as שׂוּם
(18)	שׁוּב	(to) turn, return (*V*)	
(19)	שְׁמֹנֶה (*M*), שְׁמֹנָה (*F*)	eight (*NM/FS*)	*P:* שְׁמֹנִים = “eighty”; שְׁמִינִי (*M*), שְׁמִינִית (*F*) = “eighth”
(20)	תֵּ֫שַׁע (*M*), תִּשְׁעָה (*F*)	nine (*NM/FS*)	*P:* תִּשְׁעִים: “ninety”; תְּשִׁיעִי (*M*), תְּשִׁיעִית (*F*) = “ninth”

[1] For this verb *perf, qal, 3MS* may also be spelled as סַב, as indicated earlier in this lesson.

[2] The root is employed as the lexical form for this word since the *perf, qal, 3MS* form (קַל) loses a root consonant.

b. Analyze the following verbs, doing as much of the work as possible before consulting a lexicon. Also, check the context of the word when necessary to determine the most appropriate translation.

- *Example:* כְּרֻבָּם (Hos 4:7) ⇒ *Answer:* > רבב, *inf, qal, Cs* + כּ *prep* + *PS 3MP*, "as they were increasing"

(1) לָעוּף (Pr 26:2)
(2) יוּאָר (Nu 22:6)
(3) וְגַלְתִּי (Is 65:19)
(4) יָסִירוּ (Is 5:23)
(5) עִוֵּר (2Ki 25:7)
(6) יָדִין (Ge 49:16)
(7) וַיִּתְמֹדֵד (1Ki 17:21)
(8) צוֹר (Is 8:16)
(9) הִוָּדְעִי (Jer 31:19)
(10) שָׂרִים (2Sa 19:36; *Eng* 19:35)
(11) קִלְקַל (Eze 21:26; *Eng* 21:21)
(12) יְכוֹנֵן (Is 62:7)
(13) לְהָנִיחַ (Eze 44:30)
(14) מֵבִישׁ (Pr 10:5)
(15) וְחַתּוּ (Is 20:5)
(16) תֹּם (Lv 25:29)
(17) תְּשֹׁבֶינָה (Eze 16:55)
(18) הָרִיעוּ (Jos 6:10)
(19) תְחָנֵּם (Dt 7:2)
(20) וְיֻדַּד (Job 20:8)
(21) מֵתָה (Ge 35:18)
(22) נָבוֹן (Ge 41:33)
(23) שֶׁבֶת (1Sa 7:2)
(24) הֲשִׁמּוֹתָ (Job 16:7)
(25) תִּדֹּם (La 2:18)
(26) שִׂמִי (Jer 31:21)

c. Read aloud and translate the following texts from the Hebrew Bible. Also provide an analysis of all verbs (finite and non-finite).

(1) Genesis 3:1-12

Verse 9

אַיֶּכָּה has a *PS 2MS* with a long spelling that adds a final *he*.

(2) Numbers 1:27

(3) Leviticus 23:39

Lesson 26

Weak Verbs: *Lamed-Alef* and *Lamed-He*; Identification of Weak Verb Roots

26A Weak Verbs: *Lamed-Alef* and *Lamed-He*

As discussed previously, verb roots that end in *alef* or *he* are not included in the classification of *lamed*-gutturals, since they display certain unique characteristics. This section considers the particular features of *lamed-alef* and *lamed-he* verbs.

1. ***Lamed-alef* verbs**
   a. *Lamed-alef* verbs have a final *alef,* as in the verb מָצָא ("he found"). The inflection of *lamed-alefs* is affected by the fact that they end with a consonant that is both a guttural and a quiescent.
   b. Major characteristics of *lamed-alef* verbs
      (1) The *lamed-alef* quiesces in certain situations.
         (a) When the *lamed-alef* ends a syllable, it quiesces in the sense of losing its consonantal capacity to close a syllable, meaning that it must be preceded by a long vowel. The result is that a *lamed-alef* at the end of a word is preceded by a *qames* where the strong verb has a *patah.* In other words, where the strong verb has □□ַ□, a *lamed-alef* has □□ָא. The following chart illustrates, using מצא as a model.

Perfect		
	משל	מצא
Qal, 3MS	מָשַׁל	מָצָא
Nif, 3MS	נִמְשַׁל	נִמְצָא
Pual, 3MS	מֻשַּׁל	מֻצָּא
Hof, 3MS	הָמְשַׁל	הֻמְצָא

         (b) Before a consonantal verb ending, the *lamed-alef* quiesces in the sense of losing its consonantal capacity to support a vowel, as illustrated by these perfect, *qal* forms: מָצָ֫אתָ (*2MS*), מָצָאת (*2FS*), מָצָ֫אתִי (*1CS*), etc.

(2) The *lamed-alef* requires certain other vowel alterations. One is mentioned here: *lamed-alef* is preceded by *qames* where the strong verb has a *holem* in imperfect and imperative, *qal*.

	משל	מצא
Impf, qal, 3MS	יִמְשֹׁל	יִמְצָא
Impv, qal, 2MS	מְשֹׁל	מְצָא

✓ See Appendix 3, paradigm 13, for other vowel changes from the strong verb and for the full *lamed-alef* conjugation.

(3) Several *lamed-alefs* are E-class stative verbs, such as יָרֵא ("he was afraid") and מָלֵא ("he was full"). As their lexical forms indicate, they require a *sere* before the *alef* in perfect, *qal,* where other *lamed-alefs* have a *qames* (as illustrated by comparing יָרֵא and מָלֵא with מָצָא). In participle, *qal,* active, stative *lamed-alefs* follow the pattern of מָלֵא (*MS*), מְלֵאָה (*FS*), etc.

2. *Lamed-he* verbs

a. *Lamed-he* verbs have a final *he,* like the verb גָּלָה ("he uncovered"). At one time Hebrew had some roots that were *lamed-vav* (ו◌◌) and *lamed-yod* (י◌◌); however, they all evolved into *lamed-he* roots. At certain points in the conjugation of *lamed-hes*, the original *lamed-vav* or *lamed-yod* reappears.

b. Major characteristics of *lamed-he* verbs

(1) When a *lamed-he* verb has no ending, the vowel before the final *he* is a clue to its conjugation and stem.

Vowel before Final *Lamed-He*	
◌ָה	*Perf* in all stems
◌ֶה	*Impf* in all stems
	Part, MS, Ab in all stems except *qal, pass*
◌ֵה	*Impv* in all stems
	Inf, Ab in *piel* (sometimes), *hif,* & *hof*
◌ֹה	*Inf, Ab* in *qal, nif, piel* (sometimes), *pual,* & *hit*

(2) The *lamed-he* sometimes drops out and sometimes becomes a *yod* or *tav* with the addition of verb endings.

(a) When vowel endings are added:

[1] The *lamed-he* becomes *tav* with the perfect, *3FS* ending (◌ָה).

	משל	גלה
Perf, qal, 3FS	מָשְׁלָה	גָּלְתָה

[2] The *lamed-he* drops out with other vowel endings.

	משל	גלה
Perf, qal, 3CP	מָשְׁלוּ	גָּלוּ
Impf, qal, 2FS	תִּמְשְׁלִי	תִּגְלִי

(b) When consonantal endings are added, the *lamed-he* becomes a *yod* in the form of ◌ִי (*hireq-yod*), ◌ֵי (*sere-yod*), or ◌ֶי (*segol yod*).

	משל	גלה
Perf, qal, 2MS	מָשַׁלְתָּ	גָּלִיתָ
Perf, nif, 2FS	נִמְשַׁלְתְּ	נִגְלֵית
Impf, piel, 3FP	תְּמַשֵּׁלְנָה	תְּגַלֶּינָה

(3) In all infinitive, construct forms the *lamed-he* is replaced with וֹת.

	משל	גלה
Inf, qal, Cs	מְשֹׁל	גְּלוֹת
Inf, nif, Cs	הִמָּשֵׁל	הִגָּלוֹת
Inf, piel, Cs	מַשֵּׁל	גַּלּוֹת

(4) In participle, *qal,* passive, the *lamed-he* becomes a *yod.*

	משל	גלה
Part, qal, pass, MS, Ab	מָשׁוּל	גָּלוּי
Part, qal, pass, MP, Ab	מְשׁוּלִים	גְּלוּיִים

✓ See Appendix 3, paradigm 14, for the full *lamed-he* conjugation. For the *qal* conjugation of the irregular *lamed-he* verb הָיָה, see Appendix 3, paradigm 15.

(5) *Lamed-he* verbs employ a shortened imperfect form in all stems in the jussive and when there is a *vav* consecutive. This shortened form involves dropping the *lamed-he*. Examples are given for three *lamed-he* verbs, two of which have more than one weak consonant.

	משל	גלה	היה	ראה
Impf, qal, 3MS, jussive	יִמְשֹׁל	יִ֫גֶל	יְהִי	יֵ֫רֶא
Impf, hif, 3MS, jussive	יַמְשֵׁל	יֶ֫גֶל	[none]	[none]
Impf, qal, 3MS + vav cons	וַיִּמְשֹׁל	וַיִּ֫גֶל	וַיְהִי	וַיַּ֫רְא
Impf, hif, 3MS + vav cons	וַיַּמְשֵׁל	וַיֶּ֫גֶל	[none]	וַיַּ֫רְא

3. Summary of characteristics of *lamed-alef*s and *lamed-he*s

a. The following is a succinct summary of the major characteristics of *lamed-alef* and *lamed-he* verbs.

(1) *Lamed-alef* verbs typically do not lose the *alef;* however, that consonant sometimes quiesces and sometimes requires certain changes in vowels from the strong verb. Two of those vowel changes are as follows.

(a) Where the strong verb has a *patah* stem vowel (◌◌ַ◌), a *lamed-alef* has a *qames* (◌◌ָ◌).

(b) Where the strong verb has a *holem* stem vowel in imperfect and imperative (◌◌ֹ◌), a *lamed-alef* has a *qames* (◌◌ָ◌).

(2) *Lamed-he* verbs

(a) The stem vowel (before the final *he*) is a clue to the conjugation and stem.

Vowel before Final *Lamed-He*	
◌ָה	*Perf* in all stems
◌ֶה	*Impf* in all stems
	Part, MS, Ab in all stems except *qal, pass*
◌ֵה	*Impv* in all stems
	Inf, Ab in *piel* (sometimes), *hif,* & *hof*
◌ֹה	*Inf, Ab* in *qal, nif, piel* (sometimes), *pual,* & *hit*

(b) The *lamed-he* may drop out or become a *yod* or *tav*.

[1] *Lamed-he* drops out before some vowel verb endings (□□וּ, ◁□□ִי, and ◁□□וּ) and in two imperfect forms without an ending: jussive and *vav* consecutive (◁□□ and ו◁□□).

[2] *Lamed-he* becomes *yod* before a consonantal verb ending (□□יתָ, □□ית, and □□ינָה) and in participle, *qal,* passive (□□וּי).

[3] *Lamed-he* becomes *tav* before a הָ ending (□□תָה).

(c) In infinitive, construct the *lamed-he* is replaced with an וֹת ending (□□וֹת).

(A *tav* suffix also appears in infinitive, construct in some *pe-nuns* [like נגשׁ] and *pe-yod/vavs.*)

b. The following verbs with analyses illustrate the process of identifying the forms of verbs with *lamed-alef* and *lamed-he* weaknesses.

(1) נַעֲנֶה (Is 53:7) > ענה, *part, nif, MS, Ab,* "being afflicted"

The *segol* before the *he* is a clue to a *lamed-he* verb in imperfect or participle. The context calls for a participle, *nifal,* rather than an imperfect in *1CP*.

(2) שְׁתֵה (Ge 24:14) > שׁתה, *impv, qal, 2MS,* "drink"

The *sere* before the he is a clue to a *lamed-he* verb in imperative or certain stems of infinitive, absolute. The *sheva* under the first consonant is also a clue that the verb is imperative, *qal.*

(3) יִבְכּוּ (Nu 11:13) > בכה, *impf, qal, 3MP,* "they will weep"

When the imperfect prefix and suffix are removed, two root consonants remain. Several options for the missing consonant can be eliminated. If it were *pe-nun,* there would likely be a *dagesh-forte* in the first remaining root consonant. If it were double-*ayin,* the second remaining root consonant would probably have a *dagesh-forte*. (The *kaf* has a *dagesh-lene,* not a *dagesh-forte*.) When a consonant is lost in an *ayin* weaknesses, the imperfect, *qal* prefix vowel is normally *qames,* instead of the *hireq* which appears. There is only one other classification of weak verb which commonly loses a consonant: *lamed-he*.

(4) וְכִלֵּיתִי (Eze 6:12) > כלה, *perf, piel, 1CS* + *vav* cons, "I will accomplish"

Lamed-he becomes a *yod* with a consonantal verb suffix.

(5) לִפְדוֹת (2Sa 7:23) > פדה, *inf, qal, Cs* + לְ *prep,* "to redeem"

The ending וֹת can be a feminine, plural ending on a participle; however, the rest of the spelling is inconsistent with a participle. This ending also occurs with *lamed-he* verbs in infinitive, construct. The prefixed preposition is also a common feature with infinitive constructs.

(6) וַיִּפֶן (Ex 2:12) > פנה, *impf, qal, 3MS* + *vav* cons, "and he turned"

The root is likely not a *pe-nun,* since no *dagesh-forte* appears in the first remaining root consonant. It is unlikely that the root is *pe-yod,* since that weak verb class usually takes a *sere* prefix vowel in imperfect, *qal.* Similarly, when *ayin* weaknesses have lost a consonant, they usually take a *qames* prefix vowel. By process of elimination, the root is *lamed-he,* which loses its final *he* in jussive and *vav* consecutive forms.

26B Identification of Weak Verb Roots

1. In the lessons on weak verbs several clues have been provided for identifying a verb's root when it has lost a weak root consonant. This section summaries some of those clues in a succinct format.
2. Clues to identification of weak verb roots
   a. Six classifications of weak verbs commonly lose a root consonant in the course of inflection: *pe-yod/vav, pe-nun, ayin-vav, ayin-yod,* double-*ayin,* and *lamed-he*.
   b. Clues with regard to the presence of a *dagesh-forte* (which is not required by a particular stem)
      (1) When two root consonants remain in a prefixed verb and the first has a *dagesh-forte,* it is likely *pe-nun* (□⊡◁).
         ✓ However, □⊡◁ also occurs in a *pe-yod/vav* with a sibilant for its second root consonant and occasionally in a double-*ayin*.
      (2) When two root consonants remain in a suffixed verb and the second has a *dagesh-forte,* it is likely double-*ayin* (▷⊡□).
   c. When two root consonants remain without any prefix or suffix, the verb may be one of the following:
      (1) *Pe-yod/vav* or *pe-nun* in imperative, *qal*

(2) *Ayin-vav, ayin-yod,* or double-*ayin* in perfect, *qal* or in participle, *qal,* active. (In this situation the first root consonant usually has an A-class vowel.)

d. When two root consonants remain with a naturally-long vowel between them (□ִי□, □וֹ□, □וּ□ with or without a prefix or suffix), the root may be *ayin-vav, ayin-yod,* or double-*ayin.*

✓ However, ◁□ִי□ occurs in some other weak verbs in *hifil.*

e. A *yod* or *tav* in the third root consonant position followed by a suffix (□□י▷ or □□תָה) is a clue to a *lamed-he* root.

f. Clues with regard to prefix vowels

(1) When a root consonant has dropped out in imperfect, *qal,* the prefix vowel can be a clue to the weak verb root.

Prefix Vowel in *Impf, Qal*	Options for Weak Verb
◁ָ (*qames*)	*Ayin-vav, ayin-yod,* double-*ayin*
◁ֵ (*sere*)	*Pe-yod/vav,* double-*ayin*[1]
◁ִ (*hireq*)	*Pe-nun, lamed-he,* double-*ayin*

(2) When a root consonant has dropped out and a *holem-vav* or *shureq* appears as a prefix vowel, it can be a clue to the root and stem.

<table>
<tr><th>Prefix Vowel</th><th colspan="2">Options for Weak Verb</th></tr>
<tr><td rowspan="2">◁וֹ (holem-vav)</td><td rowspan="2">Pe-yod/vav</td><td>In nif (perf and part)</td></tr>
<tr><td>In hif (all conjugations)</td></tr>
<tr><td rowspan="2">◁וּ (shureq)</td><td>Pe-yod/vav</td><td rowspan="2">In hof (all conjugations)</td></tr>
<tr><td>Ayin-vav, ayin-yod, double-ayin</td></tr>
</table>

g. Clues regarding a *tav* suffix in infinitive, construct:

(1) When two root consonants remain with a *tav* suffix, the form may be infinitive, *qal,* construct in *pe-yod/vav, pe-nun,* or *lamed-he.*

✓ In *pe-yod/vav* and *pe-nun* the infinitive, *qal,* construct may become a

[1] *Qames* is the typical prefix vowel for double-*ayin*s in imperfect, *qal*. However, stative double-*ayin*s can take a *sere,* and some double-*ayin*s (that have forms following the *pe-nun* pattern) can take *hireq*.

segolate form (◌ֶ֫◌ֶת).

(2) In *lamed-he* the infinitive, construct ends with וֹת in all stems.

3. The final lessons of this Grammar have focused on the major classes of weak verbs. Some verbs fall into more than one class and are therefore doubly or even triply weak; therefore, they may incorporate patterns of inflection from more than one class or inflect in a unique manner. Still other verbs are irregular in their conjugations. The student should consult a lexicon for help in their analysis.

Lesson 26: Exercises

a. Learn to recognize, pronounce, and translate the following vocabulary.

	Word	*Translation*	*Notes*
(1)	אָרוֹן	ark, chest (*NMS*)	With *art:* הָאָרוֹן
(2)	בֶּ֫גֶד	garment, cloth (*NMS*)	*P:* בְּגָדִים, בִּגְדֵי
(3)	גְּבוּל	border, boundary, territory (*NMS*)	
(4)	דֶּ֫רֶךְ	way, road, path, journey, manner (*NMS*)	*P:* דְּרָכִים, דַּרְכֵי
(5)	חַ֫יִל	strength, wealth, army (*NMS*)	*Cs:* חֵיל; *P:* חֲיָלִים
(6)	יַעֲקֹב	Jacob (*proper N*)	
(7)	כָּלָה	he completed, finished (*V*)	
(8)	לֵוִי	(a) Levi (*proper N*) (b) Levite (*adj MS*)	*P:* לְוִיִּם = "Levites"
(9)	מָצָא	he found, met (*V*)	
(10)	מִשְׁפָּחָה	clan (*NFS*)	
(11)	נַחֲלָה	inheritance, heritage, possession (*NFS*)	*P:* נְחָלוֹת
(12)	עָוֹן	sin, guilt, punishment (*NMS*)	*Cs:* עֲוֹן; *S* also עָווֹן, עֲווֹן; *P:* עֲוֹנוֹת or עֲוֹנֹת
(13)	עֵת	time (*NM/FS*)	*Cs:* עֵת, עֶת־; *S* with *PS:* עִתּוֹ, עִתָּהּ, etc.; *P:* עִתִּים

(14)	צֹאן	small cattle, sheep, goats, flock(s) (*NFS*)	
(15)	קֶ֫רֶב	inward part, midst (*NMS*)	*S* with *PS:* קִרְבִּי, קִרְבְּךָ, etc.; *P* with *PS:* קְרָבַי
(16)	רָשָׁע	guilty, wicked (*adj MS*)	*FS:* רְשָׁעָה; *MP:* רְשָׁעִים, רִשְׁעֵי
(17)	שָׁאוּל	Saul (*proper N*)	
(18)	שָׁם	there (*adv*)	
(19)	שַׁ֫עַר	gate (*NMS*)	*P:* שְׁעָרִים, שַׁעֲרֵי
(20)	שָׁתָה	he drank (*V*)	*Pual* and *hif* for this verb use the root שׁקה ("drink, water")

b. Analyze the following verbs, doing as much of the work as possible before consulting a lexicon. Also, check the context of the word when necessary to determine the most appropriate translation.

- *Example:* רִפֵּאתֶם (Eze 34:4) ⇒ *Answer:* > רפא, *perf, piel, 2MP,* "you healed "

(1)	קָנִ֑יתָ	(Ex 15:16)	(13)	אֹבִים	(Eze 3:7)
(2)	עֹלֶה	(Ge 38:13)	(14)	לָגֶ֫שֶׁת	(Jdg 20:23)
(3)	יֶחֱטָא	(Lv 4:3)	(15)	וְהוּכַח	(Job 33:19)
(4)	מָל	(Jos 5:4)	(16)	שְׂנֹאת	(Pr 8:13)
(5)	תֻּכַל	(Ex 18:18)	(17)	וְחָיְתָה	(Ge 12:13)
(6)	לְהִבָּנ֑וֹת	(Hag 1:2)	(18)	כְּסוּי	(Ps 32:1)
(7)	צֵא	(Ge 8:16)	(19)	תְּחוֹלֶלְכֶ֑ם	(Is 51:2)
(8)	יִרְצֶ֫ךָ	(2Sa 24:23)	(20)	גֹּ֫לּוּ	(Jos 10:18)
(9)	כִּמְתַעְתֵּעַ	(Ge 27:12)	(21)	הִרְבֵּ֫יתִי	(Hos 2:10; *Eng* 2:8)
(10)	וְהֵפִיץ	(Dt 4:27)	(22)	וְתֵלַ֫דְנָה	(Jer 29:6)
(11)	חָרֹה	(1Sa 20:7)	(23)	מִבָּנִים	(Jer 49:7)
(12)	תְּצַפֶּה	(Ex 26:29)	(24)	יוּדָק	(Is 28:28)

(25) וּרְעִי (SS 1:8)

(26) וַיָּ֫שָׁב (Ge 26:18)

(27) הוֹאַ֫לְתָּ (1Ch 17:27)

(28) וּתְחִי (Ge 19:20)

(29) הַזְנֵה (Hos 4:18)

(30) שָׂא (Ge 13:14)

(31) וַיִּסֹּב (Ge 42:24)

(32) וְנִבֵּ֫אתִי (Eze 37:7)

(33) תֵּאָפֶ֫ינָה (Lv 23:17)

(34) יִֽכְלוּ (Is 1:28)

c. Read aloud and translate Genesis 3:13-24 from the Hebrew Bible. Also provide an analysis of all verbs (finite and non-finite).

Appendix 1

Grammatical Summary

1. Consonants

a. Consonantal chart

Name		Hebrew Form	Trans-literation	Pronunciation	
English	Hebrew			Modern	Traditional
Alef [*Aleph*]	אָלֶף	א	ʾ	{silent}	
Bet	בֵּית	בּ ב	b ḇ [bh, v]	*b* as in *boy* *v* as in *vine*	
Gimel	גִּמֶל	גּ ג	g ḡ [gh]	*g* as in *girl*	*g* as in *girl* *g* as in *leg*
Dalet	דָּלֶת	דּ ד	d ḏ [dh]	*d* as in *door*	*d* as in *door* *th* as in *thin*
He	הֵא	ה	h	*h* as in *hat*	
Vav [*Waw*]	וָו	ו	v [w]	*v* as in *vine*	*w* as in *well*
Zayin	זַיִן	ז	z	*z* as in *zeal*	
Het	חֵית	ח	ḥ [ch]	*ch* as in *Bach*	
Tet	טֵית	ט	ṭ	*t* as in *time*	*t* as in *cut*
Yod	יוֹד	י	y	*y* as in *yes*	
Kaf [*Kaph*]	כַּף	כּ ך כ	k ḵ [kh]	*k* as in *king* *ch* as in *Bach*	
Lamed	לָמֶד	ל	l	*l* as in *let*	
Mem	מֵם	ם מ	m	*m* as in *met*	
Nun	נוּן	ן נ	n	*n* as in *net*	
Samek	סָמֶךְ	ס	s	*s* as in *set*	
Ayin	עַיִן	ע	ʿ	{silent}	
Pe	פֵּא	פּ ף פ	p p̄ [ph, f]	*p* as in *pet* *f* as in *fun*	
Sade	צָדֵי	ץ צ	ṣ	*ts* as in *nets*	
Qof [*Qoph*]	קוֹף	ק	q [ḳ]	*k* as in *king*	*k* as in *bark*
Resh	רֵישׁ	ר	r	*r* as in *rich*	

Sin	שִׂין	שׂ	ś	*s* as in *set*	
Shin	שִׁין	שׁ	š [sh]	*sh* as in *shoe*	
Tav [*Taw*]	תָּו	תּ ת	t ṯ [th]	*t* as in *time*	*t* as in *time* *th* as in *thin*

b. Consonantal groups

(1) Final forms: ך, ם, ן, ף, and ץ. These forms appear at the end of a word.

(2) *Begadkefats*: בּ, גּ, דּ, כּ, פּ, and תּ. These consonants can take a *dagesh-lene*.

(3) Gutturals: א, ה, ח, and ע

(a) These consonants:

[1] Prefer composite *sheva*s, which are always vocal

[2] Prefer A class vowels before and after them

[3] Cannot take a *dagesh-forte.*

(b) In some situations ר behaves like a guttural.

(4) Labials: בּ, מ, and פּ. These consonants take a *vav* conjunction pointed as וּ.

(5) Quiescents: א, ה, ו, and י

(a) These consonants may lose consonantal properties, such as the capacity to support a vowel or close a syllable. (A *mappiq* strengthens a final ה [as הּ], so that it retains its full consonantal character.)

(b) ו and י may become naturally-long vowels.

(6) Sibilants: ז, ס, צ, שׂ, and שׁ

These consonants exchange positions with the ת of the *Hitpael* prefix הִתְ.

2. Vowels

a. Vowel chart

(1) Full Vowels

(a) Short

Name		Form	Trans-literation	Pronunciation	
English	Hebrew			Modern	Traditional
Patah	פַּתַח	◌ַ	a	*a* as in *father*	*a* as in *had*
Segol	סֶגוֹל	◌ֶ	e	*e* as in *bed*	
Hireq	חִירֶק	◌ִ	i	*i* as in *machine*	*i* as in *hit*

Qames-hatuf	קָמֶץ חָטוּף	◌ָ	o	*o* as in *row*	*o* as in *top*
Qibbus	קִבּוּץ	◌ֻ	u	*u* as in *rule*	*u* as in *nut*

(b) Long

Qames	קָמֶץ	◌ָ	ā	*a* as in *father*	
Sere	צֵרֵי	◌ֵ	ē	*e* as in *bed*	*e* as in *they*
Holem	חוֹלֶם	◌ֹ	ō	*o* as in *row*	

(c) Naturally-long

Sere-yod	צֵרֵי יוֹד	◌ֵי	ê	*e* as in *they*	
Hireq-yod	חִירֶק יוֹד	◌ִי	î	*i* as in *machine*	
Holem-vav [*-waw*]	חוֹלֶם וָו	◌וֹ	ô	*o* as in *row*	
Shureq	שׁוּרֶק	◌וּ	û	*u* as in *rule*	

(2) Half vowels

(a) Simple *sheva*

Sheva [*Shewa*]	שְׁוָא	◌ְ	e[1]	*e* as in *below* (or silent)	

(b) Composite *shevas*

Hatef-patah	חָטֵף פַּתַח	◌ֲ	ă	*a* as in *father*	*a* as in *had*
Hatef-segol	חָטֵף סֶגוֹל	◌ֱ	ĕ	*e* as in *bed*	
Hatef-qames	חָטֵף קָמֶץ	◌ֳ	ŏ	*o* as in *row*	*o* as in *top*

b. The characteristics of the furtive *patah*, *qames-hatuf*, and half vowels are described in section 4 of this Appendix.

3. Accenting

a. Most words are accented on the final syllable, but may be accented on the next to the last (penultimate) syllable.

b. A *meteg* is a secondary accent which causes one to pause in pronunciation.

c. The *MT* has numerous disjunctive and conjunctive accents. Two key disjunctive

[1] The transliteration for each of the half vowels is a superscript letter.

accents are *silluq* (□ֽ), which appears at the end of a verse, and *atnah* (□֑), which marks the mid-point of a verse. Words with these accents are pausal (or "in pause"), and syllables with these accents may have lengthened vowels.

4. Syllables and Transliteration

The following points are general guidelines for recognizing and transliterating syllables. Some exceptions do occur; however, these guidelines are valuable for the transliteration exercises in this Grammar.

a. Syllable
   - (1) A syllable always begins with a consonant, not a vowel.[1]
   - (2) A syllable always has one, and only one, full vowel (except in the case of a furtive *patah*).
   - (3) A consonant with a half vowel cannot form a syllable.

b. Open syllable
   - (1) An open syllable ends with a full vowel [CV].
   - (2) An open syllable usually has a long vowel, unless accented, in which case the vowel may be short.
     - ✓ Exceptions can occur. For example, a short vowel may appear in an unaccented, open syllable before a composite *sheva*. (In □ַ□ֲ, □ֶ□ֱ, or □ָ□ֳ the composite *shevas* are preceded by corresponding short vowels in open, unaccented syllables).[2]
   - (3) An open syllable may begin with two consonants, the first of which has a half vowel [CCV].
   - (4) A *meteg* creates an open syllable, whose vowel may be long or short.
   - (5) א cannot close a syllable, leaving it open [CVʾ].
   - (6) ה cannot close a final syllable (that is, the last syllable in a word), leaving it open [cvh]

[1] An exception occurs when the prefixed *vav* conjunction appears as a *shureq* (וּ). See Lesson 6B.2b(2).

[2] See Lesson 6A.2b(4) and 6B.2b(4). These exceptions do not occur in the transliteration exercises of this Grammar.

c. Closed syllables

(1) A closed syllable ends with a consonant [CVC].

(2) A closed syllable has a short vowel, unless accented, in which case the vowel may be long.

(3) A closed syllable may begin with two consonants, the first of which has a half vowel [CCVC].

(4) A closed syllable may also have a quiescent א after the vowel [CVʾC].

d. A furtive *patah* may occur under ה, ח, or ע at the end of a word, in which case the *patah* is transliterated and pronounced before the final consonant.

e. A composite *sheva* is always vocal, appearing only with the gutturals at the beginning of a syllable.

f. Simple *sheva*

(1) A simple *sheva* is vocal when it occurs at the beginning of a syllable.

(2) A simple *sheva* is silent at the end (under the final consonant) of a closed syllable. A silent *sheva* occurs after a short vowel and serves as a syllable divider.

(3) In the case of two simple *shevas* (under successive consonants) in the middle of a word, the first is silent and the second is vocal.

(4) A simple *sheva* after an open syllable (or after a long vowel) is vocal.

g. *Qames-hatuf*

(1) A *qames-hatuf* occurs in a closed and unaccented syllable.

✓ An exception is that a *qames-hatuf* appears in an open syllable before a *hatef-qames*. (In ◌ָ◌ֳ or ◌ָֽ◌ֳ the first vowel is *qames-hatuf*.)[1]

(2) If an unaccented ◌ָ is followed by a silent *sheva*, it is a *qames-hatuf*. If ◌ָ is followed by a vocal *sheva*, it is a *qames*.

✓ In this Grammar a *meteg* helps to make this distinction. ◌ָ◌ְ indicates a *qames-hatuf* followed by a silent *sheva*, while ◌ָֽ◌ְ is a *qames* followed by a vocal *sheva*.

(3) The vowel ◌ָ is a *qames* when it is accented, when it forms an open syllable, or when it stands beside a *meteg* (noting the exception above regarding a *qames-hatuf* preceding a *hatef-qames*).

[1] See Lesson 6A.2b(4) and 6B.2b(4).

h. See the next section for a description of how *dagesh*es impact syllabification and transliteration.

5. *Dageshes*

a. A *dagesh-lene*, which theoretically strengthens the pronunciation of a consonant, can only appear in the *begadkefat* consonants (בּ, גּ, דּ, כּ, פּ, תּ) when they begin a syllable that is not preceded by a full vowel. A *dagesh-lene* may not occur at the beginning of a word if the preceding word ends with a full vowel or with a full vowel followed by א or ה.

b. A dagesh-forte, which doubles a letter, can appear in any consonant except the gutturals (א, ה, ח, ע) and ר. It cannot occur in the first letter of a word and is always preceded by a full vowel.

c. The following guidelines help distinguish between *dagesh-lene* and *dagesh-forte*.

   (1) A *dagesh* which appears in the interior of a word in any consonant other than a *begadkefat* consonant is a *dagesh-forte*.

   (2) A *dagesh* in a *begadkefat* consonant which is not preceded by a full vowel is a *dagesh-lene*.

   (3) A *dagesh* in a *begadkefat* consonant which is preceded by a full vowel is a *dagesh-forte*.

6. Definite Article

a. The definite article is a prefixed ה which is pointed as follows:

   (1) Before any consonant except the gutturals and ר = הַ◌ּ

   (2) Before ה and ח = הַ◌

   (3) Before א, ע, and ר = הָ◌

   (4) Before an accented הָ or עָ = הָ◌

   (5) Before every חָ and before an unaccented הָ or עָ = הֶ◌

7. Prefixed Prepositions

a. The rules for pointing the prefixed prepositions בְּ, כְּ, and לְ (using בְּ as an example):

(1) In most situations = בְּ___

(2) Before ___ְ = בִּ___ְ

(3) Before יְ___ = בִּי___

(4) Before a guttural with a composite *sheva* it takes the corresponding short vowel (בַּ___ֲ, בֶּ___ֱ, בָּ___ֳ).

✓ Special cases where א with a composite *sheva* loses its vowel (using לְ as an example):

- Before אֲדֹנָי = לַאדֹנָי ("to [the] Lord")
- Before אֱלֹהִים = לֵאלֹהִים ("to God")
- Before אֱמֹר = לֵאמֹר ("to say")

(5) Before יְהוָה = בַּיהוָה ("to [the] LORD")

(6) Before ___́ frequently = בָּ___́

(7) Before a definite article the ה drops out and the preposition takes the pointing of the article (as in הַ___ּ + בְּ = בַּ___ּ).

b. The rules for pointing the prefixed מִן:

(1) In most situations = מִ___ּ

(2) Before a guttural or ר = מֵ___

(3) Before יְ = מִי___

(4) Before a definite article the ה remains in place (הַ___ּ + מִן = מֵהַ___ּ).

8. *Vav* Conjunction

a. In most situations = וְ___

b. Before ___ְ and before the labials (בּ, מ, פּ) = וּ___ (that is, וּ___ְ, וּב___, וּמ___, וּפ___)

c. Before יְ = וִי___

d. Before a guttural with a composite *sheva* it takes the corresponding short vowel (וַ___ֲ, וֶ___ֱ, וָ___ֳ).

✓ Special cases where א with a composite *sheva* loses its vowel:

- Before אֲדֹנָי = וַאדֹנָי ("and [the] Lord")
- Before אֱלֹהִים = וֵאלֹהִים ("and God")

e. Before יְהוָה = וַיהוָה ("and [the] LORD")

f. Before ___́ frequently = וָ___́

g. When attached to a definite article or a prefixed preposition, the article or preposition remains intact and unchanged by וְ.

9. Nouns and Adjectives

a. The common endings for nouns and adjectives:

	Singular		Plural	
	Absolute	*Construct*	*Absolute*	*Construct*
M	[none]	[none]	◌ִים	◌ֵי
F	◌ָה	◌ַת	וֹת	וֹת

b. The dual endings for nouns:

	Dual	
	Absolute	*Construct*
M or *F*	◌ַ֫יִם	◌ֵי

c. Common nouns that are irregular:

Singular		Plural		
Ab	*Cs*	*Ab*	*Cs*	
אָב	אֲבִי	אָבוֹת	אֲבוֹת	("father" [*M*])
אָח	אֲחִי	אַחִים	אֲחֵי	("brother" [*M*])
אִישׁ	אִישׁ	אֲנָשִׁים	אַנְשֵׁי	("man" [*M*])
אִשָּׁה	אֵ֫שֶׁת	נָשִׁים	נְשֵׁי	("woman" [*F*])
בַּ֫יִת	בֵּית	בָּתִּים	בָּתֵּי	("house" [*M*])
בֵּן	בֶּן־ בֵּן	בָּנִים	בְּנֵי	("son" [*M*])
בַּת	בַּת	בָּנוֹת	בְּנוֹת	("daughter" [*F*])
יוֹם	יוֹם	יָמִים	יְמֵי	("day" [*M*])
כְּלִי	כְּלִי	כֵּלִים	כְּלֵי	("vessel" [*M*])
פֶּה	פִּי	פִּיּוֹת פֵּיוֹת	—	("mouth" [*M*])
רֹאשׁ	רֹאשׁ	רָאשִׁים	רָאשֵׁי	("head" [*M*])

d. Function of nouns

(1) Nouns usually function substantively (for example, as the subject or object of a verb, as a predicate nominative, or as the object of a preposition).

(2) However, nouns may also function adjectivally in a construct relationship, in which case the absolute noun modifies the construct noun.

e. Function of adjectives

(1) An attributive adjective describes an attribute of a noun. It normally follows the noun it modifies, and it agrees with the noun in gender, number, and definiteness.

(2) A predicate adjective appears in a verbless sentence. It usually occurs before the noun it modifies and agrees with that noun in gender and number. A predicate adjective cannot take a definite article.

(3) A substantival adjective functions like a noun; it may or may not have an article.

f. Adjectives expressing degrees of comparison

(1) The comparative degree can be expressed by the adjective followed by מִן (usually prefixed), in which case מִן means "than."

(2) The superlative degree can be expressed by:

(a) An articular adjective, often followed by the prefixed preposition בְּ

(b) A construct adjective, often followed by a definite noun.

10. Pronominal Suffixes

a. Pronominal suffixes may be placed on nouns, substantival adjectives, finite verbs (*perf, impf,* and *impv*), infinitive constructs, participles, prepositions, adverbs, and particles.

b. Pronominal suffixes for singular nouns. (Also used on adjectives, infinitive constructs, participles, prepositions, adverbs, and particles.)

1CS	□ִי	*1CP*	□ֵ֫נוּ
2MS	□ְךָ	*2MP*	□ְכֶם
2FS	□ֵךְ	*2FP*	□ְכֶן
3MS	וֹ [הוּ, ו]	*3MP*	□ָם [הֶם]
3FS	□ָהּ [הָ]	*3FP*	□ָן [הֶן]

c. Pronominal suffixes for plural nouns. (Also used with adjectives, participles, and prepositions.)

1CS	□ַי
2MS	□ֶיךָ
2FS	□ַיִךְ
3MS	□ָיו
3FS	□ֶיהָ

1CP	□ֵינוּ
2MP	□ֵיכֶם
2FP	□ֵיכֶן
3MP	□ֵיהֶם [□ָם]
3FP	□ֵיהֶן [□ָן]

✓ Clues for recognizing pronominal suffixes on plural nouns:

(1) The *1CS* pronominal suffix on plural nouns is □ַי.

(2) The other pronominal suffixes for plural nouns also have a *yod* (□ֶיךָ, □ַיִךְ, □ָיו, □ֶיהָ, □ֵינוּ, □ֵיכֶם, □ֵיכֶן, □ֵיהֶם, and □ֵיהֶן).

(3) An exception can occur with nouns that have the plural ending of וֹת or □ֹת. Such nouns may take the pronominal suffixes of □ָם (*3MP*) and □ָן (*3FP*), in which case the suffixes have no *yod* (as in שְׁמוֹתָם or שְׁמוֹתָן = "their names").

d. Pronominal suffixes for finite verbs (perfect, imperfect, and imperative):

	On finite verbs ending with vowels	**On finite verbs ending with consonants**	
		Perfects verbs[1]	*Imperfect and imperative verbs*
1CS	נִי[2]	□ַנִי	□ֶנִּי, □ֵנִי
2MS	ךָ	□ְךָ	□ֶךָּ, □ְךָ
2FS	ךְ	□ָךְ, □ֵךְ	□ֵךְ
3MS	הוּ, ו	□ָהוּ, וֹ	□ֶנּוּ, □ֵהוּ
3FS	הָ	□ָהּ	□ֶנָּה, □ָהּ, □ֶהָ
1CP	נוּ	□ָנוּ	□ֶנּוּ, □ֵנוּ
2MP	כֶם	□ְכֶם	□ְכֶם
2FP	כֶן	□ְכֶן	□ְכֶן
3MP	ם	□ַם, □ָם	□ֵם
3FP	ן	□ַן, □ָן	□ֵן

[1] A silent *sheva* may also appear before the first consonant of the suffixes in *1CS, 3MS,* and *1CP*.

[2] While infinitive constructs and participles usually take the pronominal suffixes for nouns, they occasionally employ this form which is typically used with finite verbs.

e. Function of pronominal suffixes:

(1) Pronominal suffixes can function subjectively with some infinitive constructs, particles, and adverbs.

(2) Pronominal suffixes function genitivally with nouns and substantival adjectives, usually serving the role of possessive pronouns in English. Substantival participles can also have pronominal suffixes that are genitival.

(3) Pronominal suffixes have an accusative or objective function with finite verbs and prepositions, and with some infinitive constructs, participles, particles, and adverbs.

(4) Pronominal suffixes do not occur with infinitive absolutes.

f. The pronominal suffixes on the sign of the object function like objective personal pronouns in English:

	Form	*Translation*
1CS	אֹתִי	"me"
2MS	אֹתְךָ	"you"
2FS	אֹתָךְ	"you"
3MS	אֹתוֹ	"him, it"
3FS	אֹתָהּ	"her, it"

	Form	*Translation*
1CP	אֹתָ֫נוּ	"us"
2MP	אֶתְכֶם	"you"
2FP	אֶתְכֶן	"you"
3MP	אֹתָם or אֶתְהֶם	"them"
3FP	אֹתָן or אֶתְהֶן	"them"

11. Personal Pronouns

a. The personal pronouns express subjective pronominal ideas:

	Form	*Translation*
1CS	אֲנִי or אָנֹכִי	"I"
2MS	אַתָּה	"you"
2FS	אַתְּ	"you"
3MS	הוּא	"he, it"
3FS	הִיא	"she, it"

	Form	*Translation*
1CP	אֲנַ֫חְנוּ	"we"
2MP	אַתֶּם	"you"
2FP	אַתֵּ֫נָה or אַתֵּן	"you"
3MP	הֵ֫מָּה or הֵם	"they"
3FP	הֵ֫נָּה	"they"

b. Function of personal pronouns

(1) They can function like nouns in the nominative case, most often serving as

subjects in verbless clauses.

(2) They can appear with a verb in order to emphasize the pronominal aspect of a verb.

12. Demonstrative Adjectives

a. The demonstrative adjectives are classified as near and remote.

	Near Demonstratives		Remote Demonstratives	
	Form	*Translation*	*Form*	*Translation*
MS	זֶה	"this"	הוּא	"that"
FS	זֹאת	"this"	הִיא	"that"
MP	אֵלֶּה	"these"	הֵם or הֵמָּה	"those"
FP	אֵלֶּה	"these"	הֵנָּה	"those"

b. The demonstrative adjectives can function like other adjectives in an attributive, predicative, or substantival manner.

13. Verbs in General

a. Verbs may be generally categorized in the following ways.

(1) Strong and weak verbs

Strong verbs follow fixed, regular patterns of inflection; weak verbs inflect irregularly due to the appearance or a weak consonant or a doubled consonant in the verb root. (See Appendix 3 for paradigms of strong and weak verbs.)

(2) Finite and non-finite verbs

Perfect, imperfect, and imperative verbs are finite because they are limited by their inflections to particular persons, genders, and numbers. Infinitives and participles are non-finite verbs since they lack the inflectional limitations characteristic of finite verbs.

(3) Fientive and stative verbs

Fientive verbs express action or motion; stative verbs describe a state of existence rather than an activity. (See Appendix 3 for paradigms of feintive and stative verbs.)

(4) Volitional verbs

Volition (or the will of someone) may be expressed in the following manners:

(a) The imperative expresses direct, positive commands. A prohibition is usually expressed by the imperfect with לֹא or by the jussive with אַל.

(b) The jussive is a form of the imperfect that expresses such ideas as desire, wish, request, etc. It usually occurs in the third person, singular or plural, and typically is spelled the same as a non-jussive, although it sometimes employs a shortened form, especially with weak roots. A jussive verb can often be translated with the help of auxiliary verbs like "let" or "may."

(c) The cohortative is a form of the imperfect that expresses such ideas as desire, intention, request, etc. It occurs only in the first person, singular or plural, and requires the addition of a ◌ָה suffix. A cohortative verb can often be translated with the help of auxiliary verbs like "let" or "may."

b. Tenses

(1) The indicative mood in Hebrew appears in the perfect and imperfect tenses of finite verbs.

(2) The perfect conveys an action or state that is completed in the past, present or future (although it most often expresses the notion of a simple past tense verb in English). The imperfect conveys an action or state that is incomplete in the past, present, or future (although it most often expresses the idea of a simple English future tense verb).

c. Stems

Some of the connotations of the major verb stems are as follows.

(1) *Qal:* simple action in the active voice

(2) *Nifal*

(a) Passive or reflexive of *qal*

(b) With a few verbs:

[1] Reciprocal action

[2] Passive or reflexive of non-*qal* stems

[3] Simple action in the active voice

(3) *Piel*

(a) Intensification of *qal* in the active voice

(b) Causation in the active voice

(c) With a few verbs:

[1] Notion of deprivation in the active voice

[2] Simple action in the active voice

(4) *Pual*

(a) Passive of *piel*

(b) With a few verbs: passive of *qal*

(5) *Hifil*

(a) Causative of *qal* in the active voice

(b) With some verbs: simple action in the active voice

(6) *Hofal:* passive of *hifil*

(7) *Hitpael*

(a) Reflexive of *qal*, *piel*, or *hifil*

(b) With a few verbs:

[1] Reciprocal action

[2] Passive of an active stem

[3] Intensified action

[4] Simple action in the active voice

14. Clues for Strong Verbs

The following clues are helpful for identifying the forms of strong verbs. Some clues in the various conjugations are identical. In these cases the context of a verb or verbal is the clue for recognizing its conjugation.

Perfect Conjugation

a. Clues for recognizing the person, gender, and number of any perfect stem:

3MS	□□□	*3CP*	□□□וּ
3FS	□□□ָה		
2MS	□□□תָּ	*2MP*	□□□תֶּם
2FS	□□□תְּ	*2FP*	□□□תֶּן
1CS	□□□תִּי	*1CP*	□□□נוּ

b. Clues for recognizing the stems of the perfect:

Qal	*Nifal*	*Piel*	*Pual*	*Hifil*	*Hofal*	*Hitpael*
[1]□ָ□□	נִ□ְ□□	□ִ□ּ□	□ֻ□ּ□	הִ□ְ□□	הָ□ְ□□	הִתְ□ַ□ּ□

c. The *vav* consecutive on the perfect is spelled the same as the *vav* conjunction.

Imperfect Conjugation

a. Clues for recognizing the person, gender, and number of any imperfect stem:

3MS	י□□□	*3MP*	י□□□וּ
3FS	ת□□□	*3FP*	ת□□□נָה
2MS	ת□□□	*2MP*	ת□□□וּ
2FS	ת□□□ִי	*2FP*	ת□□□נָה
1CS	א□□□	*1CP*	נ□□□

b. Clues for recognizing the stems of the imperfect:

Qal	*Nifal*	*Piel*	*Pual*	*Hifil*	*Hofal*	*Hitpael*
◁ִ□ְ□□	◁ִ□ָּ□□	◁ְ□ַ□ּ□	◁ְ□ֻ□ּ□	◁ַ□ְ□□	◁ָ□ְ□□	◁ִתְ□ַ□ּ□
or	or	or	or			or
◁ֶ□ְ□□	◁ֶ□ָּ□□	◁ֲ□ַ□ּ□	◁ֲ□ֻ□ּ□			◁ֶתְ□ַ□ּ□

c. The *vav* consecutive on the imperfect is typically spelled as וַ__ּ__, וָא__, or וַיְ__, and may cause the imperfect to shorten and its accent to move to the penultimate.

Imperative Conjugation

a. Clues for recognizing the person, gender, and number of any imperative stem:

2MS	□□□	*2MP*	□□□וּ
2FS	□□□ִי	*2FP*	□□□נָה

[1] A *qames* does not appear in every form (in particular, not in *2MP* or *2FP*). Another clue for the recognition of the perfect, *qal* is the absence of the clues for the other stems.

b. Clues for recognizing the stems of the imperative:

Qal	*Nifal*	*Piel*	*Pual*	*Hifil*	*Hofal*	*Hitpael*
□ְ□ֹ□ or □ִ□ְ□[1]	הִ□ָּ□□	□ַ□ּ□		הַ□ְ□□		הִתְ□ַ□ּ□

c. The *2MS* imperative sometimes appears in a longer form that employs a □ָה suffix.

Infinitive Conjugation

Clues for recognizing the stems of the infinitive:

Construct						
Qal	*Nifal*	*Piel*	*Pual*	*Hifil*	*Hofal*	*Hitpael*
□ְ□ֹ□	הִ□ָּ□ֵ□	□ַ□ֵּ□		הַ□ְ□ִי□		הִתְ□ַ□ֵּ□
Absolute						
□ָ□וֹ□	נִ□ְ□ֹ□ or הִ□ָּ□ֹ□	□ַ□ֹּ□ or □ַ□ֵּ□	□ֻ□ֹּ□	הַ□ְ□ֵ□	הָ□ְ□ֵ□	הִתְ□ַ□ֵּ□

Participle Conjugation

a. Clues for recognizing gender and number in any participle stem:

	Singular		**Plural**	
	Absolute	*Construct*	*Absolute*	*Construct*
M	□□□	□□□	□□□ִים	□□□ֵי
F	□□□ֶת or □□□ָה	□□□ֶת or □□□ַת	□□□וֹת	□□□וֹת

[1] The first form is relevant for *2MS* and *2FP,* the second for *2FS* and *2MP*.

b. Clues for recognizing the stems of the participle:

Qal	*Nifal*	*Piel*	*Pual*	*Hifil*	*Hofal*	*Hitpael*
			Active			
□ֹ□□		מְ□ַ□ּ□		מַ□ְ□□		מִתְ□ַ□ּ□
			Passive			
□□וּ□	נִ□ְ□ָ□[1]		מְ□ֻ□ּ□		מָ□ְ□□	

15. Weak Verbs

a. The following chart lists the classifications of weak verbs – for example, *pe*-guttural, *pe-alef, pe-yod, pe-nun, ayin*-guttural, etc.

ל (*3rd root consonant position*)	ע (*2nd root consonant position*)	פ (*1st root consonant position*)
Guttural	Guttural (including ר)	Guttural (including ר)
א	ו (middle vowel)	א
ה	י (middle vowel)	י
	עע[2] (double-*ayin*)	נ

b. For summaries of the characteristics of weak verb classes see Lesson 22A.6 (*pe*-gutturals, *pe-alefs*, *ayin*-gutturals, and *lamed*-gutturals); Lesson 23A.4 (*pe-nuns*); Lesson 24A.3 (*pe-yods*); Lesson 25A.3 (*ayin-vavs*, *ayin-yods*, and double-*ayins*); and Lesson 26A.3 (*lamed-alefs* and *lamed-hes*).

c. Six classifications of weak verbs commonly lose a root consonant in the course of inflection: *pe-yod/vav, pe-nun, ayin-vav, ayin-yod,* double-*ayin,* and *lamed-he*. Other clues for identifying weak roots appear in Lesson 26B and the Lessons mentioned in the preceding paragraph.

---

[1] When the construct endings are added, the *qames* reduces.

[2] עע represents a doubling of any consonant (not necessarily ע), so that the consonant that appears in the ע (second consonant) position also appears in the ל (third consonant) position.

Appendix 2

Analysis of Words

Any word can be analyzed ("parsed" or "located") in terms of its grammatical status. This appendix provides a scheme for the analysis of the major words in a sentence.

1. Analysis of Finite Verbs

a. The elements in analyzing finite verbs (perfects, imperfects, or imperatives) are as follows:

(1) Root (triconsonantal root of a verb)

(2) Conjugation (*perf, impf,* or *impv*)

(3) Stem (*qal, nif, piel*, etc.)

(4) Person (*1, 2,* or *3*), gender (*M* or *F*), and number (*S* or *P*)

(5) Additional features (such as a prefixed *conj* or *PS*)

(6) Translation (of the verb form, not the root)

b. The chart below illustrates the analysis of finite verbs.

Word	Root	Conjugation	Stem	P/G/N	Additional Features	Translation
נִשְׁמָ֑ר (Hos 12:14; *Eng* 12:13)	> שׁמר	*perf*	*nif*	*3MS*		"he was guarded"
וַיִּֽמְשְׁלוּ (Ps 106:41)	> משׁל	*impf*	*qal*	*3MP*	+ *vav cons*	"and they ruled"
וְהִשְׁמַ֫עְתִּי (Is 43:12)	> שׁמע	*perf*	*hif*	*1CS*	+ *vav conj*	"and I caused to hear"
בָּֽרְכֵ֫נִי (Ge 27:34)	> ברך	*impv*	*piel*	*2MS*	+ *PS 1CS*	"bless me"

2. Analysis of Non-Finite Verbs

a. The elements in analyzing non-finite verbs (infinitives or participles) are as follows:

(1) Root (triconsonantal root of a verb)

(2) Conjugation (*inf* or *part*)

(3) Stem (*qal, nif, piel*, etc.)

(4) In the case of a participle, *qal* also indicate voice (*act* or *pass*)

(5) In the case of any participle indicate gender (*M* or *F*) and number (*S* or *P*) – not applicable to infintives

(6) State (*Ab* or *Cs*)

(7) Additional features (such as a prefixed *prep* or *PS*)

(8) Translation (of the verb form, not the root)

b. The chart below illustrates the analysis of non-finite verbs.

Word	Root	Conju-gation	Stem[1]	G/N	State	Additional Features	Translation
לְחַזֵּק (Jos 11:20)	> חזק	*inf*	*piel*	--	*Cs*	+ *prep* לְ	"to harden"
הִפָּקֵד (1Ki 20:39)	> פקד	*inf*	*nif*	--	*Ab*		"being missed"
הַהֹלְכִים (Ex 10:8)	> הלך	*part*	*qal act*	*MP*	*Ab*	+ *art*	"the ones going"
מַאֲכִילָם (Jer 9:14; *Eng* 9:15)	> אכל	*part*	*hif*	*MS*	*Cs*	+ *PS 3MP*	"one caus-ing them to eat"

3. Analysis of Nouns and Adjectives

a. The elements in analyzing nouns and adjectives are as follows:

(1) Root (not the lexical form, but the triconsonantal root from which a noun or adjective is derived, if one can be determined)

(2) Part of speech (*N* or *adj*)

(3) Gender (*M* or *F*) and number (*S, P*, or *Du*)

[1] When a participle is in the *qal* stem, also indicate in this column whether it is active or passive.

(4) State (*Ab* or *Cs*)

(5) Any additional features (such as an *art* or *PS*)

(6) Translation of the word (not the lexical form)

b. The chart below illustrates the analysis of nouns and adjectives.

Word	Root	Part of Speech	G/N	State	Additional Features	Translation
חַכְמוֹת (Jdg 5:29)	> חכם	*adj*	*FP*	*Cs*		"wise women of"
יָדַיִם (Jos 8:20)	– [2]	*N*	*FDu*	*Ab*		"hands"
הַטּוֹבָה (Dt 1:35)	> טוב	*adj*	*FS*	*Ab*	+ *art*	"the good"
וּמִמִּקְדָּשִׁי (Eze 9:6)	> קדשׁ	*N*	*MS*	*Cs*	+ *prep* מִן, *vav conj*, & *PS 1CS*	"and from my sanctuary"

4. Analysis Chart

The chart on the next page provides a model for use by the student in analyzing words. The student has permission to duplicate the page.

[2] Sometimes no triconsonantal root can be identified for a noun.

Word	**Root**	**Identification**[3]	**Additional Features**	**Translation**

[3] The elements required in the "Identification" section are as follows:

For finite verbs: conjugation (*perf, impf,* or *impv*), stem (*qal, nif,* etc.), and *P/G/N*

For non-finite verbs: conjugation (*inf* or *part*), stem (for *part, qal* also give voice [*act* or *pass*]), *G/N* for *part* only, and state (*Ab* or *Cs*)

For nouns and adjectives: part of speech (*N* or *adj*), *G/N*, and state.

Appendix 3

Strong and Weak Verb Paradigms

This appendix contains paradigms for regular and weak verbs, as indicated in the following list. Some hypothetical forms (that is, forms that are not extant in the Hebrew Bible) appear for the sake of illustration. The verb roots that are employed in the paradigms appear in parentheses.

1. Strong Verb (מָשַׁל)
2. Strong Stative Verb (קָטֹן, קָדַשׁ, כָּבֵד)
3. Weak Verb: *Pe*-Guttural (חָזַק, עָמַד)
4. Weak Verb: *Pe-Alef* (אָכַל)
5. Weak Verb: True *Pe-Yod* (יָטַב)
6. Weak Verb: *Pe-Yod/Vav* (*Pe-Yod* based on *Pe-Vav*) (יָרַשׁ, יָשַׁב)
7. Weak Verb: *Pe-Nun* (נָגַשׁ, נָפַל)
8. Weak Verb: *Ayin*-Guttural (ברך, בָּחַר)
9. Weak Verb: *Ayin-Vav* (קוּם)
10. Weak Verb: *Ayin-Vav* and *Ayin-Yod* (מוּת, בּוֹשׁ, שִׂים, בּוֹא)
11. Weak Verb: Double-*Ayin* (סבב)
12. Weak Verb: *Lamed*-Guttural (שָׁלַח)
13. Weak Verb: *Lamed-Alef* (מָצָא)
14. Weak Verb: *Lamed-He* (גָּלָה)
15. Weak Verb: Irregular (הָיָה, הָלַךְ, לָקַח, נָתַן)
16. Practice Chart for Strong Verb (משׁל)[1]

[1] The practice chart provides a structure for the student to practice the forms of the strong verb using משׁל as a model. The student has the author's permission to reproduce the chart.

1. Strong Verb Paradigm (מָשַׁל)

	Perfect						
	Qal	*Nifal*	*Piel*	*Pual*	*Hifil*	*Hofal*	*Hitpael*
3MS	מָשַׁל	נִמְשַׁל	מִשֵּׁל	מֻשַּׁל	הִמְשִׁיל	הָמְשַׁל	הִתְמַשֵּׁל
3FS	מָֽשְׁלָה	נִמְשְׁלָה	מִשְּׁלָה	מֻשְּׁלָה	הִמְשִׁילָה	הָמְשְׁלָה	הִתְמַשְּׁלָה
2MS	מָשַׁלְתָּ	נִמְשַׁלְתָּ	מִשַּׁלְתָּ	מֻשַּׁלְתָּ	הִמְשַׁלְתָּ	הָמְשַׁלְתָּ	הִתְמַשַּׁלְתָּ
2FS	מָשַׁלְתְּ	נִמְשַׁלְתְּ	מִשַּׁלְתְּ	מֻשַּׁלְתְּ	הִמְשַׁלְתְּ	הָמְשַׁלְתְּ	הִתְמַשַּׁלְתְּ
1CS	מָשַׁלְתִּי	נִמְשַׁלְתִּי	מִשַּׁלְתִּי	מֻשַּׁלְתִּי	הִמְשַׁלְתִּי	הָמְשַׁלְתִּי	הִתְמַשַּׁלְתִּי
3CP	מָֽשְׁלוּ	נִמְשְׁלוּ	מִשְּׁלוּ	מֻשְּׁלוּ	הִמְשִׁילוּ	הָמְשְׁלוּ	הִתְמַשְּׁלוּ
2MP	מְשַׁלְתֶּם	נִמְשַׁלְתֶּם	מִשַּׁלְתֶּם	מֻשַּׁלְתֶּם	הִמְשַׁלְתֶּם	הָמְשַׁלְתֶּם	הִתְמַשַּׁלְתֶּם
2FP	מְשַׁלְתֶּן	נִמְשַׁלְתֶּן	מִשַּׁלְתֶּן	מֻשַּׁלְתֶּן	הִמְשַׁלְתֶּן	הָמְשַׁלְתֶּן	הִתְמַשַּׁלְתֶּן
1CP	מָשַׁלְנוּ	נִמְשַׁלְנוּ	מִשַּׁלְנוּ	מֻשַּׁלְנוּ	הִמְשַׁלְנוּ	הָמְשַׁלְנוּ	הִתְמַשַּׁלְנוּ

	Imperfect						
	Qal	*Nifal*	*Piel*	*Pual*	*Hifil*	*Hofal*	*Hitpael*
3MS	יִמְשֹׁל	יִמָּשֵׁל	יְמַשֵּׁל	יְמֻשַּׁל	יַמְשִׁיל	יָמְשַׁל	יִתְמַשֵּׁל
3FS	תִּמְשֹׁל	תִּמָּשֵׁל	תְּמַשֵּׁל	תְּמֻשַּׁל	תַּמְשִׁיל	תָּמְשַׁל	תִּתְמַשֵּׁל
2MS	תִּמְשֹׁל	תִּמָּשֵׁל	תְּמַשֵּׁל	תְּמֻשַּׁל	תַּמְשִׁיל	תָּמְשַׁל	תִּתְמַשֵּׁל
2FS	תִּמְשְׁלִי	תִּמָּֽשְׁלִי	תְּמַשְּׁלִי	תְּמֻשְּׁלִי	תַּמְשִׁילִי	תָּמְשְׁלִי	תִּתְמַשְּׁלִי
1CS	אֶמְשֹׁל	אֶמָּשֵׁל	אֲמַשֵּׁל	אֲמֻשַּׁל	אַמְשִׁיל	אָמְשַׁל	אֶתְמַשֵּׁל
3MP	יִמְשְׁלוּ	יִמָּֽשְׁלוּ	יְמַשְּׁלוּ	יְמֻשְּׁלוּ	יַמְשִׁילוּ	יָמְשְׁלוּ	יִתְמַשְּׁלוּ
3FP	תִּמְשֹׁלְנָה	תִּמָּשַׁלְנָה	תְּמַשֵּׁלְנָה	תְּמֻשַּׁלְנָה	תַּמְשֵׁלְנָה	תָּמְשַׁלְנָה	תִּתְמַשַּׁלְנָה
2MP	תִּמְשְׁלוּ	תִּמָּֽשְׁלוּ	תְּמַשְּׁלוּ	תְּמֻשְּׁלוּ	תַּמְשִׁילוּ	תָּמְשְׁלוּ	תִּתְמַשְּׁלוּ
2FP	תִּמְשֹׁלְנָה	תִּמָּשַׁלְנָה	תְּמַשֵּׁלְנָה	תְּמֻשַּׁלְנָה	תַּמְשֵׁלְנָה	תָּמְשַׁלְנָה	תִּתְמַשַּׁלְנָה
1CP	נִמְשֹׁל	נִמָּשֵׁל	נְמַשֵּׁל	נְמֻשַּׁל	נַמְשִׁיל	נָמְשַׁל	נִתְמַשֵּׁל

1. Strong Verb Paradigm (מָשַׁל)

	Imperative						
	Qal	*Nifal*	*Piel*		*Hifil*		*Hitpael*
2MS	מְשֹׁל [2]	הִמָּשֵׁל	מַשֵּׁל		הַמְשֵׁל		הִתְמַשֵּׁל
2FS	מִשְׁלִי	הִמָּשְׁלִי	מַשְּׁלִי		הַמְשִׁילִי		הִתְמַשְּׁלִי
2MP	מִשְׁלוּ	הִמָּשְׁלוּ	מַשְּׁלוּ		הַמְשִׁילוּ		הִתְמַשְּׁלוּ
2FP	מְשֹׁלְנָה	הִמָּשַׁלְנָה	מַשֵּׁלְנָה		הַמְשֵׁלְנָה		הִתְמַשֵּׁלְנָה

Infinitive						
Construct						
Qal	*Nifal*	*Piel*	*Pual*	*Hifil*	*Hofal*	*Hitpael*
מְשֹׁל	הִמָּשֵׁל	מַשֵּׁל		הַמְשִׁיל		הִתְמַשֵּׁל
Absolute						
מָשׁוֹל	נִמְשֹׁל or הִמָּשֹׁל	מַשֹּׁל or מַשֵּׁל	מֻשֹּׁל	הַמְשֵׁל	הָמְשֵׁל	הִתְמַשֵּׁל

	Participle						
	Active						
	Qal	*Nifal*	*Piel*	*Pual*	*Hifil*	*Hofal*	*Hitpael*
MS, Ab[3]	מֹשֵׁל		מְמַשֵּׁל		מַמְשִׁיל		מִתְמַשֵּׁל
FS, Ab	מֹשֶׁלֶת or מֹשְׁלָה		מְמַשְּׁלָה		מַמְשִׁילָה		מִתְמַשְּׁלָה
MP, Ab	מֹשְׁלִים		מְמַשְּׁלִים		מַמְשִׁילִים		מִתְמַשְּׁלִים
FP, Ab	מֹשְׁלוֹת		מְמַשְּׁלוֹת		מַמְשִׁילוֹת		מִתְמַשְּׁלוֹת
	Passive						
MS, Ab	מָשׁוּל	נִמְשָׁל		מְמֻשָּׁל		מָמְשָׁל	
FS, Ab	מְשׁוּלָה	נִמְשָׁלָה		מְמֻשָּׁלָה		מָמְשָׁלָה	
MP, Ab	מְשׁוּלִים	נִמְשָׁלִים		מְמֻשָּׁלִים		מָמְשָׁלִים	
FP, Ab	מְשׁוּלוֹת	נִמְשָׁלוֹת		מְמֻשָּׁלוֹת		מָמְשָׁלוֹת	

---

[2] *2MS impv* can appear in a long form, as in מָשְׁלָה (*impv, qal, 2MS* + ה suffix). See Lesson 17B.3.

[3] Participles can also appear in construct, as in מֹשְׁלֵי (*qal, act, MP, Cs*).

2. Strong Stative Verb Paradigm (כָּבֵד, קָדַשׁ, קָטֹן)

	Perfect, *Qal*		
	E-class	*A-class*	*O-class*
3MS	כָּבֵד	קָדַשׁ	קָטֹן
3FS	כָּֽבְדָה	קָֽדְשָׁה	קָֽטְנָה
2MS	כָּבַדְתָּ	קָדַשְׁתָּ	קָטֹנְתָּ
2FS	כָּבַדְתְּ	קָדַשְׁתְּ	קָטֹנְתְּ
1CS	כָּבַדְתִּי	קָדַשְׁתִּי	קָטֹנְתִּי
3CP	כָּֽבְדוּ	קָֽדְשׁוּ	קָֽטְנוּ
2MP	כְּבַדְתֶּם	קְדַשְׁתֶּם	קְטָנְתֶּם
2FP	כְּבַדְתֶּן	קְדַשְׁתֶּן	קְטָנְתֶּן
1CP	כָּבַדְנוּ	קָדַשְׁנוּ	קָטֹנּוּ[4]

	Imperfect, *Qal*		
	E-class	*A-class*	*O-class*
3MS	יִכְבַּד	יִקְדַּשׁ	יִקְטַן
3FS	תִּכְבַּד	תִּקְדַּשׁ	תִּקְטַן
2MS	תִּכְבַּד	תִּקְדַּשׁ	תִּקְטַן
2FS	תִּכְבְּדִי	תִּקְדְּשִׁי	תִּקְטְנִי
1CS	אֶכְבַּד	אֶקְדַּשׁ	אֶקְטַן
3MP	יִכְבְּדוּ	יִקְדְּשׁוּ	יִקְטְנוּ
3FP	תִּכְבַּדְנָה	תִּקְדַּשְׁנָה	תִּקְטַנָּה
2MP	תִּכְבְּדוּ	תִּקְדְּשׁוּ	תִּקְטְנוּ
2FP	תִּכְבַּדְנָה	תִּקְדַּשְׁנָה	תִּקְטַנָּה
1CP	נִכְבַּד	נִקְדַּשׁ	נִקְטַן

[4] The final *nun* of the verb root has assimilated into the *nun* of the verb suffix by means of a *dagesh-forte*. The same situation occurs at other places in the conjugations of this verb.

2. Strong Stative Verb Paradigm (קָטֹן, קָדַשׁ, כָּבֵד)

	Imperative, *Qal*		
	E-class	*A-class*	*O-class*
2MS	כְּבַד	קְדַשׁ	קְטַן
2FS	כִּבְדִי	קִדְשִׁי	קִטְנִי
2MP	כִּבְדוּ	קִדְשׁוּ	קִטְנוּ
2FP	כְּבַ֫דְנָה	קְדַ֫שְׁנָה	קְטַ֫נָּה

Infinitive, *Qal*		
E-class	*A-class*	*O-class*
Construct		
כְּבַד	קְדֹשׁ	קְטֹן
Absolute		
כָּבוֹד	קָדוֹשׁ	קָטוֹן

	Participle, *Qal*, Active		
	E-class	*A-class*	*O-class*
MS, Ab	כָּבֵד	קָדֵשׁ	קָטֹן

3. Weak Verb Paradigm: *Pe*-Guttural (עָמַד, חָזַק[5])

	Perfect					
	Qal	*Nifal*	*Hifil*	*Hofal*		*Qal*
3MS	עָמַד	נֶעֱמַד	הֶעֱמִיד	הָעֳמַד		חָזַק
3FS	עָֽמְדָה	נֶעֶמְדָה	הֶעֱמִידָה	הָעָמְדָה		חָֽזְקָה
2MS	עָמַדְתָּ	נֶעֱמַדְתָּ	הֶעֱמַדְתָּ	הָעֳמַדְתָּ		חָזַקְתָּ
2FS	עָמַדְתְּ	נֶעֱמַדְתְּ	הֶעֱמַדְתְּ	הָעֳמַדְתְּ		חָזַקְתְּ
1CS	עָמַדְתִּי	נֶעֱמַדְתִּי	הֶעֱמַדְתִּי	הָעֳמַדְתִּי		חָזַקְתִּי
3CP	עָֽמְדוּ	נֶעֶמְדוּ	הֶעֱמִידוּ	הָעָמְדוּ		חָֽזְקוּ
2MP	עֲמַדְתֶּם	נֶעֱמַדְתֶּם	הֶעֱמַדְתֶּם	הָעֳמַדְתֶּם		חֲזַקְתֶּם
2FP	עֲמַדְתֶּן	נֶעֱמַדְתֶּן	הֶעֱמַדְתֶּן	הָעֳמַדְתֶּן		חֲזַקְתֶּן
1CP	עָמַדְנוּ	נֶעֱמַדְנוּ	הֶעֱמַדְנוּ	הָעֳמַדְנוּ		חָזַקְנוּ

	Imperfect					
	Qal	*Nifal*	*Hifil*	*Hofal*		*Qal*
3MS	יַעֲמֹד	יֵעָמֵד	יַעֲמִיד	יָעֳמַד		יֶחֱזַק
3FS	תַּעֲמֹד	תֵּעָמֵד	תַּעֲמִיד	תָּעֳמַד		תֶּחֱזַק
2MS	תַּעֲמֹד	תֵּעָמֵד	תַּעֲמִיד	תָּעֳמַד		תֶּחֱזַק
2FS	תַּעַמְדִי	תֵּעָֽמְדִי	תַּעֲמִידִי	תָּעָמְדִי		תֶּחֶזְקִי
1CS	אֶעֱמֹד	אֵעָמֵד	אַעֲמִיד	אָעֳמַד		אֶחֱזַק
3MP	יַעַמְדוּ	יֵעָֽמְדוּ	יַעֲמִידוּ	יָעָמְדוּ		יֶחֶזְקוּ
3FP	תַּעֲמֹדְנָה	תֵּעָמַדְנָה	תַּעֲמֵדְנָה	תָּעֳמַדְנָה		תֶּחֱזַקְנָה
2MP	תַּעַמְדוּ	תֵּעָֽמְדוּ	תַּעֲמִידוּ	תָּעָמְדוּ		תֶּחֶזְקוּ
2FP	תַּעֲמֹדְנָה	תֵּעָמַדְנָה	תַּעֲמֵדְנָה	תָּעֳמַדְנָה		תֶּחֱזַקְנָה
1CP	נַעֲמֹד	נֵעָמֵד	נַעֲמִיד	נָעֳמַד		נֶחֱזַק

[5] חָזַק is a stative verb.

3. Weak Verb Paradigm: *Pe*-Guttural (עָמַד, חָזַק)

	Imperative				
	Qal	*Nifal*	*Hifil*		*Qal*
2MS	עֲמֹד	הֵעָמֵד	הַעֲמֵד		חֲזַק
2FS	עִמְדִי	הֵעָמְדִי	הַעֲמִידִי		חִזְקִי
2MP	עִמְדוּ	הֵעָמְדוּ	הַעֲמִידוּ		חִזְקוּ
2FP	עֲמֹדְנָה	הֵעָמַדְנָה	הַעֲמֵדְנָה		חֲזַקְנָה

Infinitive			
Construct			
Qal	*Nifal*	*Hifil*	*Hofal*
עֲמֹד	הֵעָמֵד	הַעֲמִיד	
Absolute			
עָמוֹד	נַעֲמוֹד	הַעֲמֵד	הָעֳמֵד

	Participle			
	Active			
	Qal	*Nifal*	*Hifil*	*Hofal*
MS, Ab	עֹמֵד		מַעֲמִיד	
FS, Ab	עֹמֶדֶת		מַעֲמִידָה	
MP, Ab	עֹמְדִים		מַעֲמִידִים	
FP, Ab	עֹמְדוֹת		מַעֲמִידוֹת	
	Passive			
MS, Ab	עָמוּד	נֶעֱמָד		מָעֳמָד
FS, Ab	עֲמוּדָה	נֶעֱמָדָה		מָעֳמָדָה
MP, Ab	עֲמוּדִים	נֶעֱמָדִים		מָעֳמָדִים
FP, Ab	עֲמוּדוֹת	נֶעֱמָדוֹת		מָעֳמָדוֹת

4. Weak Verb Paradigm: *Pe-Alef* (אָכַל)

	Perfect *Qal*
3MS	אָכַל
3FS	אָֽכְלָה
2MS	אָכַ֫לְתָּ
2FS	אָכַלְתְּ
1CS	אָכַ֫לְתִּי
3CP	אָֽכְלוּ
2MP	אֲכַלְתֶּם
2FP	אֲכַלְתֶּן
1CP	אָכַ֫לְנוּ

	Imperfect *Qal*
3MS	יֹאכַל
3FS	תֹּאכַל
2MS	תֹּאכַל
2FS	תֹּאכְלִי
1CS	אֹכַל
3MP	יֹאכְלוּ
3FP	תֹּאכַ֫לְנָה
2MP	תֹּאכְלוּ
2FP	תֹּאכַ֫לְנָה
1CP	נֹאכַל

	Imperative *Qal*
2MS	אֱכֹל
2FS	אִכְלִי
2MP	אִכְלוּ
2FP	אֱכֹ֫לְנָה

Infinitive *Qal*
Construct
אֱכֹל
Absolute
אָכוֹל

	Participle *Qal*		
	Active		**Passive**
MS, Ab	אֹכֵל		אָכוּל
FS, Ab	אֹכְלָה		אֲכוּלָה
MP, Ab	אֹכְלִים		אֲכוּלִים
FP, Ab	אֹכְלוֹת		אֲכוּלוֹת

5. Weak Verb Paradigm: True *Pe-Yod* (יָטַב)

	Perfect	
	Qal	*Hifil*
3MS	יָטַב	הֵיטִיב
3FS	יָֽטְבָה	הֵיטִיבָה
2MS	יָטַבְתָּ	הֵיטַבְתָּ
2FS	יָטַבְתְּ	הֵיטַבְתְּ
1CS	יָטַבְתִּי	הֵיטַבְתִּי
3CP	יָֽטְבוּ	הֵיטִיבוּ
2MP	יְטַבְתֶּם	הֵיטַבְתֶּם
2FP	יְטַבְתֶּן	הֵיטַבְתֶּן
1CP	יָטַבְנוּ	הֵיטַבְנוּ

	Imperfect	
	Qal	*Hifil*
3MS	יִיטַב	יֵיטִיב
3FS	תִּיטַב	תֵּיטִיב
2MS	תִּיטַב	תֵּיטִיב
2FS	תִּיטְבִי	תֵּיטִיבִי
1CS	אִיטַב	אֵיטִיב
3MP	יִיטְבוּ	יֵיטִיבוּ
3FP	תִּיטַבְנָה	תֵּיטַבְנָה
2MP	תִּיטְבוּ	תֵּיטִיבוּ
2FP	תִּיטַבְנָה	תֵּיטַבְנָה
1CP	נִיטַב	נֵיטִיב

	Imperative	
	Qal	*Hifil*
2MS	יְטַב	הֵיטֵב
2FS	יִטְבִי	הֵיטִיבִי
2MP	יִטְבוּ	הֵיטִיבוּ
2FP	יְטַבְנָה	הֵיטֵבְנָה

Infinitive	
Qal	*Hifil*
Construct	
יְטֹב	הֵיטִיב
Absolute	
יָטוֹב	הֵיטֵב

	Participle	
	Active	
	Qal	*Hifil*
MS, Ab	יֹטֵב	מֵיטִיב
FS, Ab	יֹטְבָה	מֵיטִיבָה
MP, Ab	יֹטְבִים	מֵיטִיבִים
FP, Ab	יֹטְבוֹת	מֵיטִיבוֹת

6. Weak Verb Paradigm: *Pe-Yod/Vav* (*Pe-Yod* Based on *Pe-Vav*)

(יָרַשׁ, יָשַׁב)

	Perfect					
	Qal	*Nifal*	*Hifil*	*Hofal*		*Qal*
3MS	יָשַׁב	נוֹשַׁב	הוֹשִׁיב	הוּשַׁב		יָרַשׁ[6]
3FS	יָֽשְׁבָה	נוֹשְׁבָה	הוֹשִׁיבָה	הוּשְׁבָה		יָֽרְשָׁה
2MS	יָשַׁבְתָּ	נוֹשַׁבְתָּ	הוֹשַׁבְתָּ	הוּשַׁבְתָּ		יָרַשְׁתָּ
2FS	יָשַׁבְתְּ	נוֹשַׁבְתְּ	הוֹשַׁבְתְּ	הוּשַׁבְתְּ		יָרַשְׁתְּ
1CS	יָשַׁבְתִּי	נוֹשַׁבְתִּי	הוֹשַׁבְתִּי	הוּשַׁבְתִּי		יָרַשְׁתִּי
3CP	יָֽשְׁבוּ	נוֹשְׁבוּ	הוֹשִׁיבוּ	הוּשְׁבוּ		יָֽרְשׁוּ
2MP	יְשַׁבְתֶּם	נוֹשַׁבְתֶּם	הוֹשַׁבְתֶּם	הוּשַׁבְתֶּם		יְרַשְׁתֶּם
2FP	יְשַׁבְתֶּן	נוֹשַׁבְתֶּן	הוֹשַׁבְתֶּן	הוּשַׁבְתֶּן		יְרַשְׁתֶּן
1CP	יָשַׁבְנוּ	נוֹשַׁבְנוּ	הוֹשַׁבְנוּ	הוּשַׁבְנוּ		יָרַשְׁנוּ

	Imperfect					
	Qal	*Nifal*	*Hifil*	*Hofal*		*Qal*
3MS	יֵשֵׁב	יִוָּשֵׁב	יוֹשִׁיב	יוּשַׁב		יִירַשׁ
3FS	תֵּשֵׁב	תִּוָּשֵׁב	תּוֹשִׁיב	תּוּשַׁב		תִּירַשׁ
2MS	תֵּשֵׁב	תִּוָּשֵׁב	תּוֹשִׁיב	תּוּשַׁב		תִּירַשׁ
2FS	תֵּשְׁבִי	תִּוָּֽשְׁבִי	תּוֹשִׁיבִי	תּוּשְׁבִי		תִּירְשִׁי
1CS	אֵשֵׁב	אִוָּשֵׁב	אוֹשִׁיב	אוּשַׁב		אִירַשׁ
3MP	יֵשְׁבוּ	יִוָּֽשְׁבוּ	יוֹשִׁיבוּ	יוּשְׁבוּ		יִירְשׁוּ
3FP	תֵּשַׁבְנָה	תִּוָּשַׁבְנָה	תּוֹשֵׁבְנָה	תּוּשַׁבְנָה		תִּירַשְׁנָה
2MP	תֵּשְׁבוּ	תִּוָּֽשְׁבוּ	תּוֹשִׁיבוּ	תּוּשְׁבוּ		תִּירְשׁוּ
2FP	תֵּשַׁבְנָה	תִּוָּשַׁבְנָה	תּוֹשֵׁבְנָה	תּוּשַׁבְנָה		תִּירַשְׁנָה
1CP	נֵשֵׁב	נִוָּשֵׁב	נוֹשִׁיב	נוּשַׁב		נִירַשׁ

[6] יָרַשׁ and a few other verbs like it combine characteristics of true *pe-yod* and *pe-yod/vav* verbs.

6. Weak Verb Paradigm: *Pe-Yod/Vav* (*Pe-Yod* Based on *Pe-Vav*)

(יָרַשׁ, יָשַׁב)

	Imperative				
	Qal	*Nifal*	*Hifil*		*Qal*
2MS	שֵׁב	הִוָּשֵׁב	הוֹשֵׁב		רַשׁ
2FS	שְׁבִי	הִוָּשְׁבִי	הוֹשִׁיבִי		רְשִׁי
2MP	שְׁבוּ	הִוָּשְׁבוּ	הוֹשִׁיבוּ		רְשׁוּ
2FP	שֵׁבְנָה	הִוָּשַׁבְנָה	הוֹשֵׁבְנָה		רַשְׁנָה

Infinitive					
Construct					
Qal	*Nifal*	*Hifil*	*Hofal*		*Qal*
שֶׁבֶת	הִוָּשֵׁב	הוֹשִׁיב	הוּשַׁב		רֶשֶׁת
Absolute					
יָשׁוֹב	הִוָּשֵׁב	הוֹשֵׁב	הוּשֵׁב		יָרוֹשׁ

	Participle					
	Active					
	Qal	*Nifal*	*Hifil*	*Hofal*		*Qal*
MS, Ab	יֹשֵׁב		מוֹשִׁיב			יוֹרֵשׁ
FS, Ab	יֹשְׁבָה		מוֹשִׁיבָה			יֹרְשָׁה
MP, Ab	יֹשְׁבִים		מוֹשִׁיבִים			יֹרְשִׁים
FP, Ab	יֹשְׁבוֹת		מוֹשִׁיבוֹת			יֹרְשׁוֹת
	Passive					
MS, Ab		נוֹשָׁב		מוּשָׁב		
FS, Ab		נוֹשָׁבָה		מוּשָׁבָה		
MP, Ab		נוֹשָׁבִים		מוּשָׁבִים		
FP, Ab		נוֹשָׁבוֹת		מוּשָׁבוֹת		

7. WEAK VERB PARADIGM: *PE-NUN* (נָגַשׁ, נָפַל)

	Perfect					
	Qal		*Qal*	*Nifal*	*Hifil*	*Hofal*
3MS	נָפַל		נָגַשׁ	נִגַּשׁ	הִגִּישׁ	הֻגַּשׁ
3FS	נָֽפְלָה		נָֽגְשָׁה	נִגְּשָׁה	הִגִּישָׁה	הֻגְּשָׁה
2MS	נָפַלְתָּ		נָגַשְׁתָּ	נִגַּשְׁתָּ	הִגַּשְׁתָּ	הֻגַּשְׁתָּ
2FS	נָפַלְתְּ		נָגַשְׁתְּ	נִגַּשְׁתְּ	הִגַּשְׁתְּ	הֻגַּשְׁתְּ
1CS	נָפַלְתִּי		נָגַשְׁתִּי	נִגַּשְׁתִּי	הִגַּשְׁתִּי	הֻגַּשְׁתִּי
3CP	נָֽפְלוּ		נָֽגְשׁוּ	נִגְּשׁוּ	הִגִּישׁוּ	הֻגְּשׁוּ
2MP	נְפַלְתֶּם		נְגַשְׁתֶּם	נִגַּשְׁתֶּם	הִגַּשְׁתֶּם	הֻגַּשְׁתֶּם
2FP	נְפַלְתֶּן		נְגַשְׁתֶּן	נִגַּשְׁתֶּן	הִגַּשְׁתֶּן	הֻגַּשְׁתֶּן
1CP	נָפַלְנוּ		נָגַשְׁנוּ	נִגַּשְׁנוּ	הִגַּשְׁנוּ	הֻגַּשְׁנוּ

	Imperfect					
	Qal		*Qal*	*Nifal*	*Hifil*	*Hofal*
3MS	יִפֹּל		יִגַּשׁ	יִנָּגֵשׁ	יַגִּישׁ	יֻגַּשׁ
3FS	תִּפֹּל		תִּגַּשׁ	תִּנָּגֵשׁ	תַּגִּישׁ	תֻּגַּשׁ
2MS	תִּפֹּל		תִּגַּשׁ	תִּנָּגֵשׁ	תַּגִּישׁ	תֻּגַּשׁ
2FS	תִּפְּלִי		תִּגְּשִׁי	תִּנָּֽגְשִׁי	תַּגִּישִׁי	תֻּגְּשִׁי
1CS	אֶפֹּל		אֶגַּשׁ	אֶנָּגֵשׁ	אַגִּישׁ	אֻגַּשׁ
3MP	יִפְּלוּ		יִגְּשׁוּ	יִנָּֽגְשׁוּ	יַגִּישׁוּ	יֻגְּשׁוּ
3FP	תִּפֹּלְנָה		תִּגַּשְׁנָה	תִּנָּגַשְׁנָה	תַּגֵּשְׁנָה	תֻּגַּשְׁנָה
2MP	תִּפְּלוּ		תִּגְּשׁוּ	תִּנָּֽגְשׁוּ	תַּגִּישׁוּ	תֻּגְּשׁוּ
2FP	תִּפֹּלְנָה		תִּגַּשְׁנָה	תִּנָּגַשְׁנָה	תַּגֵּשְׁנָה	תֻּגַּשְׁנָה
1CP	נִפֹּל		נִגַּשׁ	נִנָּגֵשׁ	נַגִּישׁ	נֻגַּשׁ

7. Weak Verb Paradigm: *Pe-Nun* (נָפַל, נָגַשׁ)

	Imperative				
	Qal		*Qal*	*Nifal*	*Hifil*
2MS	נְפֹל		גַּשׁ	הִנָּגֵשׁ	הַגֵּשׁ
2FS	נִפְלִי		גְּשִׁי	הִנָּגְשִׁי	הַגִּ֫ישִׁי
2MP	נִפְלוּ		גְּשׁוּ	הִנָּגְשׁוּ	הַגִּ֫ישׁוּ
2FP	נְפֹ֫לְנָה		גַּ֫שְׁנָה	הִנָּגַ֫שְׁנָה	הַגֵּ֫שְׁנָה

Infinitive					
Construct					
Qal		*Qal*	*Nifal*	*Hifil*	*Hofal*
נְפֹל		גֶּ֫שֶׁת	הִנָּגֵשׁ	הַגִּישׁ	הֻגַּשׁ
Absolute					
נָפוֹל		נָגוֹשׁ	הִנָּגֵשׁ	הַגֵּשׁ	הֻגֵּשׁ

	Participle					
	Active					
	Qal		*Qal*	*Nifal*	*Hifil*	*Hofal*
MS, Ab	נֹפֵל		נֹגֵשׁ		מַגִּישׁ	
FS, Ab	נֹפֶ֫לֶת		נֹגְשָׁה		מַגִּישָׁה	
MP, Ab	נֹפְלִים		נֹגְשִׁים		מַגִּישִׁים	
FP, Ab	נֹפְלוֹת		נֹגְשׁוֹת		מַגִּישׁוֹת	
	Passive					
MS, Ab			נָגוּשׁ	נִגָּשׁ		מֻגָּשׁ
FS, Ab			נְגוּשָׁה	נִגָּשָׁה		מֻגָּשָׁה
MP, Ab			נְגוּשִׁים	נִגָּשִׁים		מֻגָּשִׁים
FP, Ab			נְגוּשׁוֹת	נִגָּשׁוֹת		מֻגָּשׁוֹת

8. Weak Verb Paradigm: *Ayin*-Guttural (בָּחַר, ברך)

	Perfect					
	Qal	*Nifal*		*Piel*	*Pual*	*Hitpael*
3MS	בָּחַר	נִבְחַר		בֵּרַךְ	בֹּרַךְ	הִתְבָּרֵךְ
3FS	בָּחֲרָה	נִבְחֲרָה		בֵּרְכָה	בֹּרְכָה	הִתְבָּרֲכָה
2MS	בָּחַרְתָּ	נִבְחַרְתָּ		בֵּרַכְתָּ	בֹּרַכְתָּ	הִתְבָּרַכְתָּ
2FS	בָּחַרְתְּ	נִבְחַרְתְּ		בֵּרַכְתְּ	בֹּרַכְתְּ	הִתְבָּרַכְתְּ
1CS	בָּחַרְתִּי	נִבְחַרְתִּי		בֵּרַכְתִּי	בֹּרַכְתִּי	הִתְבָּרַכְתִּי
3CP	בָּחֲרוּ	נִבְחֲרוּ		בֵּרְכוּ	בֹּרְכוּ	הִתְבָּרֲכוּ
2MP	בְּחַרְתֶּם	נִבְחַרְתֶּם		בֵּרַכְתֶּם	בֹּרַכְתֶּם	הִתְבָּרַכְתֶּם
2FP	בְּחַרְתֶּן	נִבְחַרְתֶּן		בֵּרַכְתֶּן	בֹּרַכְתֶּן	הִתְבָּרַכְתֶּן
1CP	בָּחַרְנוּ	נִבְחַרְנוּ		בֵּרַכְנוּ	בֹּרַכְנוּ	הִתְבָּרַכְנוּ

	Imperfect					
	Qal	*Nifal*		*Piel*	*Pual*	*Hitpael*
3MS	יִבְחַר	יִבָּחֵר		יְבָרֵךְ	יְבֹרַךְ	יִתְבָּרֵךְ
3FS	תִּבְחַר	תִּבָּחֵר		תְּבָרֵךְ	תְּבֹרַךְ	תִּתְבָּרֵךְ
2MS	תִּבְחַר	תִּבָּחֵר		תְּבָרֵךְ	תְּבֹרַךְ	תִּתְבָּרֵךְ
2FS	תִּבְחֲרִי	תִּבָּהֲרִי		תְּבָרֲכִי	תְּבֹרְכִי	תִּתְבָּרֲכִי
1CS	אֶבְחַר	אֶבָּחֵר		אֲבָרֵךְ	אֲבֹרַךְ	אֶתְבָּרֵךְ
3MP	יִבְחֲרוּ	יִבָּחֲרוּ		יְבָרֲכוּ	יְבֹרְכוּ	יִתְבָּרֲכוּ
3FP	תִּבְחַרְנָה	תִּבָּחַרְנָה		תְּבָרֵכְנָה	תְּבֹרַכְנָה	תִּתְבָּרֵכְנָה
2MP	תִּבְחֲרוּ	תִּבָּחֲרוּ		תְּבָרֲכוּ	תְּבֹרְכוּ	תִּתְבָּרֲכוּ
2FP	תִּבְחַרְנָה	תִּבָּחַרְנָה		תְּבָרֵכְנָה	תְּבֹרַכְנָה	תִּתְבָּרֵכְנָה
1CP	נִבְחַר	נִבָּחֵר		נְבָרֵךְ	נְבֹרַךְ	נִתְבָּרֵךְ

8. Weak Verb Paradigm: *Ayin*-Guttural (בָּחַר, ברך)

	Imperative					
	Qal	*Nifal*		*Piel*		*Hitpael*
2MS	בְּחַר	הִבָּחֵר		בָּרֵךְ		הִתְבָּרֵךְ
2FS	בַּחֲרִי	הִבָּחֲרִי		בָּרְכִי		הִתְבָּרְכִי
2MP	בַּחֲרוּ	הִבָּחֲרוּ		בָּרְכוּ		הִתְבָּרְכוּ
2FP	בְּחַ֫רְנָה	הִבָּחַ֫רְנָה		בָּרֵ֫כְנָה		הִתְבָּרֵ֫כְנָה

Infinitive					
Construct					
Qal	*Nifal*		*Piel*	*Pual*	*Hitpael*
בְּחֹר	הִבָּחֵר		בָּרֵךְ	בֹּרַךְ	הִתְבָּרֵךְ
Absolute					
בָּחוֹר	נִבְחֹר		בָּרֵךְ		הִתְבָּרֵךְ

	Participle					
	Active					
	Qal	*Nifal*		*Piel*	*Pual*	*Hitpael*
MS, Ab	בֹּחֵר			מְבָרֵךְ		מִתְבָּרֵךְ
FS, Ab	בֹּחֲרָה			מְבָרְכָה		מִתְבָּרְכָה
MP, Ab	בֹּחֲרִים			מְבָרְכִים		מִתְבָּרְכִים
FP, Ab	בֹּחֲרוֹת			מְבָרְכוֹת		מִתְבָּרְכוֹת
	Passive					
MS, Ab	בָּחוּר	נִבְחָר			מְבֹרָךְ	
FS, Ab	בְּחוּרָה	נִבְחָרָה			מְבֹרָכָה	
MP, Ab	בְּחוּרִים	נִבְחָרִים			מְבֹרָכִים	
FP, Ab	בְּחוּרוֹת	נִבְחָרוֹת			מְבֹרָכוֹת	

9. Weak Verb Paradigm: *Ayin-Vav* (קוּם)

	Perfect						
	Qal	*Nifal*	*Polel*	*Polal*	*Hifil*	*Hofal*	*Hitpolel*
3MS	קָם	נָקוֹם	קוֹמֵם	קוֹמַם	הֵקִים	הוּקַם	הִתְקוֹמֵם
3FS	קָמָה	נָקוֹמָה	קוֹמְמָה	קוֹמְמָה	הֵקִימָה	הוּקְמָה	הִתְקוֹמְמָה
2MS	קַמְתָּ	נְקוּמוֹתָ	קוֹמַמְתָּ	קוֹמַמְתָּ	הֲקִימוֹתָ	הוּקַמְתָּ	הִתְקוֹמַמְתָּ
2FS	קַמְתְּ	נְקוּמוֹת	קוֹמַמְתְּ	קוֹמַמְתְּ	הֲקִימוֹת	הוּקַמְתְּ	הִתְקוֹמַמְתְּ
1CS	קַמְתִּי	נְקוּמוֹתִי	קוֹמַמְתִּי	קוֹמַמְתִּי	הֲקִימוֹתִי	הוּקַמְתִּי	הִתְקוֹמַמְתִּי
3CP	קָמוּ	נָקוֹמוּ	קוֹמְמוּ	קוֹמְמוּ	הֵקִימוּ	הוּקְמוּ	הִתְקוֹמְמוּ
2MP	קַמְתֶּם	נְקֻמוֹתֶם	קוֹמַמְתֶּם	קוֹמַמְתֶּם	הֲקִימוֹתֶם	הוּקַמְתֶּם	הִתְקוֹמַמְתֶּם
2FP	קַמְתֶּן	נְקֻמוֹתֶן	קוֹמַמְתֶּן	קוֹמַמְתֶּן	הֲקִימוֹתֶן	הוּקַמְתֶּן	הִתְקוֹמַמְתֶּן
1CP	קַמְנוּ	נְקוּמוֹנוּ	קוֹמַמְנוּ	קוֹמַמְנוּ	הֲקִימוֹנוּ	הוּקַמְנוּ	הִתְקוֹמַמְנוּ

	Imperfect						
	Qal	*Nifal*	*Polel*	*Polal*	*Hifil*	*Hofal*	*Hitpolel*
3MS	יָקוּם	יִקּוֹם	יְקוֹמֵם	יְקוֹמַם	יָקִים	יוּקַם	יִתְקוֹמֵם
3FS	תָּקוּם	תִּקּוֹם	תְּקוֹמֵם	תְּקוֹמַם	תָּקִים	תּוּקַם	תִּתְקוֹמֵם
2MS	תָּקוּם	תִּקּוֹם	תְּקוֹמֵם	תְּקוֹמַם	תָּקִים	תּוּקַם	תִּתְקוֹמֵם
2FS	תָּקוּמִי	תִּקּוֹמִי	תְּקוֹמְמִי	תְּקוֹמְמִי	תָּקִימִי	תּוּקְמִי	תִּתְקוֹמְמִי
1CS	אָקוּם	אֶקּוֹם	אֲקוֹמֵם	אֲקוֹמַם	אָקִים	אוּקַם	אֶתְקוֹמֵם
3MP	יָקוּמוּ	יִקּוֹמוּ	יְקוֹמְמוּ	יְקוֹמְמוּ	יָקִימוּ	יוּקְמוּ	יִתְקוֹמְמוּ
3FP	תְּקוּמֶינָה	תִּקּוֹמְנָה	תְּקוֹמֵמְנָה	תְּקוֹמַמְנָה	תָּקֵמְנָה	תּוּקַמְנָה	תִּתְקוֹמֵמְנָה
2MP	תָּקוּמוּ	תִּקּוֹמוּ	תְּקוֹמְמוּ	תְּקוֹמְמוּ	תָּקִימוּ	תּוּקְמוּ	תִּתְקוֹמְמוּ
2FP	תְּקוּמֶינָה	תִּקּוֹמְנָה	תְּקוֹמֵמְנָה	תְּקוֹמַמְנָה	תָּקֵמְנָה	תּוּקַמְנָה	תִּתְקוֹמֵמְנָה
1CP	נָקוּם	נִקּוֹם	נְקוֹמֵם	נְקוֹמַם	נָקִים	נוּקַם	נִתְקוֹמֵם

9. Weak Verb Paradigm: *Ayin-Vav* (קוּם)

	Imperative						
	Qal	*Nifal*	*Polel*		*Hifil*		*Hitpolel*
2MS	קוּם	הִקוֹם	קוֹמֵם		הָקֵם		הִתְקוֹמֵם
2FS	קוּמִי	הִקוֹמִי	קוֹמְמִי		הָקִימִי		הִתְקוֹמְמִי
2MP	קוּמוּ	הִקוֹמוּ	קוֹמְמוּ		הָקִימוּ		הִתְקוֹמְמוּ
2FP	קֹמְנָה	הִקוֹמְנָה	קוֹמֵמְנָה		הָקֵמְנָה		הִתְקוֹמֵמְנָה

Infinitive						
Construct						
Qal	*Nifal*	*Polel*		*Hifil*	*Hofal*	*Hitpolel*
קוּם	הִקוֹם	קוֹמֵם		הָקִים	הוּקַם	הִתְקוֹמֵם
Absolute						
קוֹם	הִקוֹם			הָקֵם	הוּקֵם	הִתְקוֹמֵם

	Participle						
	Active						
	Qal	*Nifal*	*Polel*	*Polal*	*Hifil*	*Hofal*	*Hitpolel*
MS, Ab	קָם		מְקוֹמֵם		מֵקִים		מִתְקוֹמֵם
FS, Ab	קָמָה		מְקוֹמְמָה		מְקִימָה		מִתְקוֹמְמָה
MP, Ab	קָמִים		מְקוֹמְמִים		מְקִימִים		מִתְקוֹמְמִים
FP, Ab	קָמוֹת		מְקוֹמְמוֹת		מְקִימוֹת		מִתְקוֹמְמוֹת
	Passive						
MS, Ab		נָקוֹם		מְקוֹמָם		מוּקָם	
FS, Ab		נְקוֹמָה		מְקוֹמָמָה		מוּקָמָה	
MP, Ab		נְקוֹמִים		מְקוֹמָמִים		מוּקָמִים	
FP, Ab		נְקוֹמוֹת		מְקוֹמָמוֹת		מוּקָמוֹת	

10. Weak Verb Paradigm: *Ayin-Vav* and *Ayin-Yod*

(בּוֹא, שִׂים, בּוֹשׁ, מוּת[7])

	Perfect			
	בּוֹא	שִׂים	בּוֹשׁ	מוּת
	Qal	*Qal*	*Qal*	*Qal*
3MS	בָּא	שָׂם	בּוֹשׁ	מֵת
3FS	בָּאָה	שָׂמָה	בּוֹשָׁה	מֵתָה
2MS	בָּאתָ	שַׂמְתָּ	בֹּשְׁתָּ	מַתָּה
2FS	בָּאת	שַׂמְתְּ	בֹּשְׁתְּ	מַתְּ
1CS	בָּאתִי	שַׂמְתִּי	בֹּשְׁתִּי	מַתִּי
3CP	בָּאוּ	שָׂמוּ	בּוֹשׁוּ	מֵתוּ
2MP	בָּאתֶם	שַׂמְתֶּם	בָּשְׁתֶּם	מַתֶּם
2FP	בָּאתֶן	שַׂמְתֶּן	בָּשְׁתֶּן	מַתֶּן
1CP	בָּאנוּ	שַׂמְנוּ	בֹּשְׁנוּ	מַתְנוּ

	Imperfect			
	בּוֹא	שִׂים	בּוֹשׁ	מוּת
	Qal	*Qal*	*Qal*	*Qal*
3MS	יָבוֹא	יָשִׂים	יֵבוֹשׁ	יָמוּת
3FS	תָּבוֹא	תָּשִׂים	תֵּבוֹשׁ	תָּמוּת
2MS	תָּבוֹא	תָּשִׂים	תֵּבוֹשׁ	תָּמוּת
2FS	תָּבוֹאִי	תָּשִׂימִי	תֵּבוֹשִׁי	תָּמוּתִי
1CS	אָבוֹא	אָשִׂים	אֵבוֹשׁ	אָמוּת
3MP	יָבוֹאוּ	יָשִׂימוּ	יֵבוֹשׁוּ	יָמוּתוּ
3FP	תָּבוֹאנָה	תְּשִׂימֶינָה	תֵּבוֹשְׁנָה	תְּמוּתֶינָה
2MP	תָּבוֹאוּ	תָּשִׂימוּ	תֵּבוֹשׁוּ	תָּמוּתוּ
2FP	תָּבוֹאנָה	תְּשִׂימֶינָה	תֵּבוֹשְׁנָה	תְּמוּתֶינָה
1CP	נָבוֹא	נָשִׂים	נֵבוֹשׁ	נָמוּת

---

[7] בּוֹשׁ and מוּת are stative verbs.

10. Weak Verb Paradigm: *Ayin-Vav* and *Ayin-Yod*

(מוּת, בּוֹשׁ, שִׂים, בּוֹא)

	Imperative						
	בּוֹא		שִׂים		בּוֹשׁ		מוּת
	Qal		*Qal*		*Qal*		*Qal*
2MS	בּוֹא		שִׂים		בּוֹשׁ		מוּת
2FS	בּ֫וֹאִי		שִׂ֫ימִי		בּ֫וֹשִׁי		מ֫וּתִי
2MP	בּ֫וֹאוּ		שִׂ֫ימוּ		בּוֹשׁוּ		מ֫וּתוּ
2FP	בּ֫וֹאנָה		שֵׂ֫מְנָה		בּ֫וֹשְׁנָה		מֹ֫תְנָה

Infinitive						
Construct						
Qal		*Qal*		*Qal*		*Qal*
בּוֹא		שִׂים		בּוֹשׁ		מוּת
Absolute						
בּוֹא		שׂוֹם		בּוֹשׁ		מוֹת

	Participle						
	Active						
	Qal		*Qal*		*Qal*		*Qal*
MS, Ab	בָּא		שָׂם		בּוֹשׁ		מֵת
FS, Ab	בָּאָה		שָׂמָה		בּוֹשָׁה		מֵתָה
MP, Ab	בָּאִים		שָׂמִים		בּוֹשִׁים		מֵתִים
FP, Ab	בָּאוֹת		שָׂמוֹת		בּוֹשׁוֹת		מֵתוֹת

11. Weak Verb Paradigm: Double-*Ayin* (סבב)

	Perfect						
	Qal	*Nifal*	*Poel* [8]	*Poal*	*Hifil*	*Hofal*	*Hitpoel*
3MS	סַב[9]	נָסַב	סוֹבֵב	סוֹבַב	הֵסֵב	הוּסַב	הִסְתּוֹבֵב
3FS	סַבָּה	נָסַבָּה	סוֹבְבָה	סוֹבְבָה	הֵסֵבָּה	הוּסַבָּה	הִסְתּוֹבְבָה
2MS	סַבּוֹתָ	נְסַבּוֹתָ	סוֹבַבְתָּ	סוֹבַבְתָּ	הֲסִבּוֹתָ	הוּסַבּוֹתָ	הִסְתּוֹבַבְתָּ
2FS	סַבּוֹת	נְסַבּוֹת	סוֹבַבְתְּ	סוֹבַבְתְּ	הֲסִבּוֹת	הוּסַבּוֹת	הִסְתּוֹבַבְתְּ
1CS	סַבּוֹתִי	נְסַבּוֹתִי	סוֹבַבְתִּי	סוֹבַבְתִּי	הֲסִבּוֹתִי	הוּסַבּוֹתִי	הִסְתּוֹבַבְתִּי
3CP	סַבּוּ	נָסַבּוּ	סוֹבְבוּ	סוֹבְבוּ	הֵסֵבּוּ	הוּסַבּוּ	הִסְתּוֹבְבוּ
2MP	סַבּוֹתֶם	נְסַבּוֹתֶם	סוֹבַבְתֶּם	סוֹבַבְתֶּם	הֲסִבּוֹתֶם	הוּסַבּוֹתֶם	הִסְתּוֹבַבְתֶּם
2FP	סַבּוֹתֶן	נְסַבּוֹתֶן	סוֹבַבְתֶּן	סוֹבַבְתֶּן	הֲסִבּוֹתֶן	הוּסַבּוֹתֶן	הִסְתּוֹבַבְתֶּן
1CP	סַבּוֹנוּ	נְסַבּוֹנוּ	סוֹבַבְנוּ	סוֹבַבְנוּ	הֲסִבּוֹנוּ	הוּסַבּוֹנוּ	הִסְתּוֹבַבְנוּ

	Imperfect						
	Qal[10]	*Nifal*	*Poel*	*Poal*	*Hifil*	*Hofal*	*Hitpoel*
3MS	יָסֹב	יִסַּב	יְסוֹבֵב	יְסוֹבַב	יָסֵב	יוּסַב	יִסְתּוֹבֵב
3FS	תָּסֹב	תִּסַּב	תְּסוֹבֵב	תְּסוֹבַב	תָּסֵב	תּוּסַב	תִּסְתּוֹבֵב
2MS	תָּסֹב	תִּסַּב	תְּסוֹבֵב	תְּסוֹבַב	תָּסֵב	תּוּסַב	תִּסְתּוֹבֵב
2FS	תָּסֹבִּי	תִּסַּבִּי	תְּסוֹבְבִי	תְּסוֹבְבִי	תָּסֵבִּי	תּוּסַבִּי	תִּסְתּוֹבְבִי
1CS	אָסֹב	אֶסַּב	אֲסוֹבֵב	אֲסוֹבַב	אָסֵב	אוּסַב	אֶסְתּוֹבֵב
3MP	יָסֹבּוּ	יִסַּבּוּ	יְסוֹבְבוּ	יְסוֹבְבוּ	יָסֵבּוּ	יוּסַבּוּ	יִסְתּוֹבְבוּ
3FP	תְּסֱבֶּינָה	תִּסַּבֶּינָה	תְּסוֹבֵבְנָה	תְּסוֹבַבְנָה	תְּסִבֶּינָה	תּוּסַבֶּינָה	תִּסְתּוֹבֵבְנָה
2MP	תָּסֹבּוּ	תִּסַּבּוּ	תְּסוֹבְבוּ	תְּסוֹבְבוּ	תָּסֵבּוּ	תּוּסַבּוּ	תִּסְתּוֹבְבוּ
2FP	תְּסֱבֶּינָה	תִּסַּבֶּינָה	תְּסוֹבֵבְנָה	תְּסוֹבַבְנָה	תְּסִבֶּינָה	תּוּסַבֶּינָה	תִּסְתּוֹבֵבְנָה
1CP	נָסֹב	נִסַּב	נְסוֹבֵב	נְסוֹבַב	נָסֵב	תּוּסַב	נִסְתּוֹבֵב

---

[8] Double-*ayin* verbs usually follow the strong verb pattern in *piel, pual,* and *hitpael*; however, they may also use the alternate forms of *poel, poal,* and *hitpoel,* as illustrated in this chart. In *hitpoel* the sibilant consonant of סבב changes places with the ת of the prefix. (See Lesson 13A.7c and Lesson 15A.7c.)

[9] In *perf, qal,* סבב has these alternate forms: *3MS:* סָבַב; *3FS:* סָבְבָה; and *3CP:* סָבְבוּ.

[10] Some double-*ayins* display variations from this paradigm in the prefix vowel for *impf, qal.* For example, סבב can also be inflected as יִסֹּב, תִּסֹּב, תִּסֹּב, תִּסֹּבִּי, etc.; and the stative verb קלל in *impf, qal* follows the pattern of יֵקַל, תֵּקַל, תֵּקַל, תֵּקַלִּי, etc.

11. Weak Verb Paradigm: Double-*Ayin* (סבב)

	Imperative						
	Qal	*Nifal*	*Poel*		*Hifil*		*Hitpoel*
2MS	סֹב	הִסַּב	סוֹבֵב		הָסֵב		הִסְתּוֹבֵב
2FS	סֹ֫בִּי	הִסַּ֫בִּי	סוֹבְבִי		הָסֵ֫בִּי		הִסְתּוֹבְבִי
2MP	סֹ֫בּוּ	הִסַּ֫בּוּ	סוֹבְבוּ		הָסֵ֫בּוּ		הִסְתּוֹבְבוּ
2FP	סֻבֶּ֫ינָה	הִסַּבֶּ֫ינָה	סוֹבֵ֫בְנָה		הֲסִבֶּ֫ינָה		הִסְתּוֹבֵ֫בְנָה

Infinitive						
Construct						
Qal	*Nifal*	*Poel*	*Poal*	*Hifil*	*Hofal*	*Hitpoel*
סֹב	הִסֵּב	סוֹבֵב	סוֹבַב	הָסֵב	הוּסַב	הִסְתּוֹבֵב
Absolute						
סָבוֹב	הִסּוֹב	סוֹבֵב	סוֹבַב	הָסֵב	הוּסֵב	הִסְתּוֹבֵב

	Participle						
	Active						
	Qal [11]	*Nifal*	*Poel*	*Poal*	*Hifil*	*Hofal*	*Hitpoel*
MS, Ab	סֹבֵב		מְסוֹבֵב		מֵסֵב		מִסְתּוֹבֵב
FS, Ab	סֹבְבָה		מְסוֹבְבָה		מְסִבָּה		מִסְתּוֹבְבָה
MP, Ab	סֹבְבִים		מְסוֹבְבִים		מְסִבִּים		מִסְתּוֹבְבִים
FP, Ab	סֹבְבוֹת		מְסוֹבְבוֹת		מְסִבּוֹת		מִסְתּוֹבְבוֹת
	Passive						
MS, Ab		נָסָב		מְסוֹבָב		מוּסָב	
FS, Ab		נְסַבָּה		מְסוֹבָבָה		מוּסָבָה	
MP, Ab		נְסַבִּים		מְסוֹבָבִים		מוּסָבִים	
FP, Ab		נְסַבּוֹת		מְסוֹבָבוֹת		מוּסָבוֹת	

[11] The stative verb קלל in *part, qal, act* is inflected as קַל, קַלָּה, קַלִּים, and קַלּוֹת.

12. Weak Verb Paradigm: *Lamed*-Guttural (שָׁלַח)

	Perfect						
	Qal	*Nifal*	*Piel*	*Pual*	*Hifil*	*Hofal*	*Hitpael*
3MS	שָׁלַח	נִשְׁלַח	שִׁלַּח	שֻׁלַּח	הִשְׁלִיחַ	הָשְׁלַח	הִשְׁתַּלַּח[12]
3FS	שָֽׁלְחָה	נִשְׁלְחָה	שִׁלְּחָה	שֻׁלְּחָה	הִשְׁלִיחָה	הָשְׁלְחָה	הִשְׁתַּלְּחָה
2MS	שָׁלַחְתָּ	נִשְׁלַחְתָּ	שִׁלַּחְתָּ	שֻׁלַּחְתָּ	הִשְׁלַחְתָּ	הָשְׁלַחְתָּ	הִשְׁתַּלַּחְתָּ
2FS	שָׁלַחַתְּ	נִשְׁלַחַתְּ	שִׁלַּחַתְּ	שֻׁלַּחַתְּ	הִשְׁלַחַתְּ	הָשְׁלַחַתְּ	הִשְׁתַּלַּחַתְּ
1CS	שָׁלַחְתִּי	נִשְׁלַחְתִּי	שִׁלַּחְתִּי	שֻׁלַּחְתִּי	הִשְׁלַחְתִּי	הָשְׁלַחְתִּי	הִשְׁתַּלַּחְתִּי
3CP	שָֽׁלְחוּ	נִשְׁלְחוּ	שִׁלְּחוּ	שֻׁלְּחוּ	הִשְׁלִיחוּ	הָשְׁלְחוּ	הִשְׁתַּלְּחוּ
2MP	שְׁלַחְתֶּם	נִשְׁלַחְתֶּם	שִׁלַּחְתֶּם	שֻׁלַּחְתֶּם	הִשְׁלַחְתֶּם	הָשְׁלַחְתֶּם	הִשְׁתַּלַּחְתֶּם
2FP	שְׁלַחְתֶּן	נִשְׁלַחְתֶּן	שִׁלַּחְתֶּן	שֻׁלַּחְתֶּן	הִשְׁלַחְתֶּן	הָשְׁלַחְתֶּן	הִשְׁתַּלַּחְתֶּן
1CP	שָׁלַחְנוּ	נִשְׁלַחְנוּ	שִׁלַּחְנוּ	שֻׁלַּחְנוּ	הִשְׁלַחְנוּ	הָשְׁלַחְנוּ	הִשְׁתַּלַּחְנוּ

	Imperfect						
	Qal	*Nifal*	*Piel*	*Pual*	*Hifil*	*Hofal*	*Hitpael*
3MS	יִשְׁלַח	יִשָּׁלַח	יְשַׁלַּח	יְשֻׁלַּח	יַשְׁלִיחַ	יָשְׁלַח	יִשְׁתַּלַּח
3FS	תִּשְׁלַח	תִּשָּׁלַח	תְּשַׁלַּח	תְּשֻׁלַּח	תַּשְׁלִיחַ	תָּשְׁלַח	תִּשְׁתַּלַּח
2MS	תִּשְׁלַח	תִּשָּׁלַח	תְּשַׁלַּח	תְּשֻׁלַּח	תַּשְׁלִיחַ	תָּשְׁלַח	תִּשְׁתַּלַּח
2FS	תִּשְׁלְחִי	תִּשָּֽׁלְחִי	תְּשַׁלְּחִי	תְּשֻׁלְּחִי	תַּשְׁלִיחִי	תָּשְׁלְחִי	תִּשְׁתַּלְּחִי
1CS	אֶשְׁלַח	אֶשָּׁלַח	אֲשַׁלַּח	אֲשֻׁלַּח	אַשְׁלִיחַ	אָשְׁלַח	אֶשְׁתַּלַּח
3MP	יִשְׁלְחוּ	יִשָּֽׁלְחוּ	יְשַׁלְּחוּ	יְשֻׁלְּחוּ	יַשְׁלִיחוּ	יָשְׁלְחוּ	יִשְׁתַּלְּחוּ
3FP	תִּשְׁלַחְנָה	תִּשָּׁלַחְנָה	תְּשַׁלַּחְנָה	תְּשֻׁלַּחְנָה	תַּשְׁלַחְנָה	תָּשְׁלַחְנָה	תִּשְׁתַּלַּחְנָה
2MP	תִּשְׁלְחוּ	תִּשָּֽׁלְחוּ	תְּשַׁלְּחוּ	תְּשֻׁלְּחוּ	תַּשְׁלִיחוּ	תָּשְׁלְחוּ	תִּשְׁתַּלְּחוּ
2FP	תִּשְׁלַחְנָה	תִּשָּׁלַחְנָה	תְּשַׁלַּחְנָה	תְּשֻׁלַּחְנָה	תַּשְׁלַחְנָה	תָּשְׁלַחְנָה	תִּשְׁתַּלַּחְנָה
1CP	נִשְׁלַח	נִשָּׁלַח	נְשַׁלַּח	נְשֻׁלַּח	נַשְׁלִיחַ	נָשְׁלַח	נִשְׁתַּלַּח

[12] In *hitpael* the sibilant consonant of שלח changes places with the ת of the prefix. (See Lesson 13A.7c and Lesson 15A.7c.)

12. Weak Verb Paradigm: *Lamed*-Guttural (שָׁלַח)

	Imperative						
	Qal	*Nifal*	*Piel*		*Hifil*		*Hitpael*
2MS	שְׁלַח	הִשָּׁלַח	שַׁלַּח		הַשְׁלַח		הִשְׁתַּלַּח
2FS	שִׁלְחִי	הִשָּֽׁלְחִי	שַׁלְּחִי		הַשְׁלִ֫יחִי		הִשְׁתַּלְּחִי
2MP	שִׁלְחוּ	הִשָּֽׁלְחוּ	שַׁלְּחוּ		הַשְׁלִ֫יחוּ		הִשְׁתַּלְּחוּ
2FP	שְׁלַ֫חְנָה	הִשָּׁלַ֫חְנָה	שַׁלַּ֫חְנָה		הַשְׁלַ֫חְנָה		הִשְׁתַּלַּ֫חְנָה

Infinitive						
Construct						
Qal	*Nifal*	*Piel*		*Hifil*	*Hofal*	*Hitpael*
שְׁלֹחַ	הִשָּׁלַח	שַׁלַּח		הַשְׁלִיחַ		הִשְׁתַּלַּח
Absolute						
שָׁלוֹחַ	נִשְׁלוֹחַ or הִשָּׁלֵחַ	שַׁלֵּחַ		הַשְׁלֵחַ	הָשְׁלֵחַ	

	Participle						
	Active						
	Qal	*Nifal*	*Piel*	*Pual*	*Hifil*	*Hofal*	*Hitpael*
MS, Ab	שֹׁלֵחַ		מְשַׁלֵּחַ		מַשְׁלִיחַ		מִשְׁתַּלֵּחַ
FS, Ab	שֹׁלְחָה		מְשַׁלְּחָה		מַשְׁלִיחָה		מִשְׁתַּלְּחָה
MP, Ab	שֹׁלְחִים		מְשַׁלְּחִים		מַשְׁלִיחִים		מִשְׁתַּלְּחִים
FP, Ab	שֹׁלְחוֹת		מְשַׁלְּחוֹת		מַשְׁלִיחוֹת		מִשְׁתַּלְּחוֹת
	Passive						
MS, Ab	שָׁלוּחַ	נִשְׁלָח		מְשֻׁלָּח		מָשְׁלָח	
FS, Ab	שְׁלוּחָה	נִשְׁלָחָה		מְשֻׁלָּחָה		מָשְׁלָחָה	
MP, Ab	שְׁלוּחִים	נִשְׁלָחִים		מְשֻׁלָּחִים		מָשְׁלָחִים	
FP, Ab	שְׁלוּחוֹת	נִשְׁלָחוֹת		מְשֻׁלָּחוֹת		מָשְׁלָחוֹת	

13. Weak Verb Paradigm: *Lamed-Alef* (מָצָא)

	Perfect						
	Qal[13]	*Nifal*	*Piel*	*Pual*	*Hifil*	*Hofal*	*Hitpael*
3MS	מָצָא	נִמְצָא	מִצֵּא	מֻצָּא	הִמְצִיא	הֻמְצָא	הִתְמַצֵּא
3FS	מָצְאָה	נִמְצְאָה	מִצְּאָה	מֻצְּאָה	הִמְצִ֫יאָה	הֻמְצְאָה	הִתְמַצְּאָה
2MS	מָצָ֫אתָ	נִמְצֵ֫אתָ	מִצֵּ֫אתָ	מֻצֵּ֫אתָ	הִמְצֵ֫אתָ	הֻמְצֵ֫אתָ	הִתְמַצֵּ֫אתָ
2FS	מָצָאת	נִמְצֵאת	מִצֵּאת	מֻצֵּאת	הִמְצֵאת	הֻמְצֵאת	הִתְמַצֵּאת
1CS	מָצָ֫אתִי	נִמְצֵ֫אתִי	מִצֵּ֫אתִי	מֻצֵּ֫אתִי	הִמְצֵ֫אתִי	הֻמְצֵ֫אתִי	הִתְמַצֵּ֫אתִי
3CP	מָצְאוּ	נִמְצְאוּ	מִצְּאוּ	מֻצְּאוּ	הִמְצִ֫יאוּ	הֻמְצְאוּ	הִתְמַצְּאוּ
2MP	מְצָאתֶם	נִמְצֵאתֶם	מִצֵּאתֶם	מֻצֵּאתֶם	הִמְצֵאתֶם	הֻמְצֵאתֶם	הִתְמַצֵּאתֶם
2FP	מְצָאתֶן	נִמְצֵאתֶן	מִצֵּאתֶן	מֻצֵּאתֶן	הִמְצֵאתֶן	הֻמְצֵאתֶן	הִתְמַצֵּאתֶן
1CP	מָצָ֫אנוּ	נִמְצֵ֫אנוּ	מִצֵּ֫אנוּ	מֻצֵּ֫אנוּ	הִמְצֵ֫אנוּ	הֻמְצֵ֫אנוּ	הִתְמַצֵּ֫אנוּ

	Imperfect						
	Qal	*Nifal*	*Piel*	*Pual*	*Hifil*	*Hofal*	*Hitpael*
3MS	יִמְצָא	יִמָּצֵא	יְמַצֵּא	יְמֻצָּא	יַמְצִיא	יֻמְצָא	יִתְמַצֵּא
3FS	תִּמְצָא	תִּמָּצֵא	תְּמַצֵּא	תְּמֻצָּא	תַּמְצִיא	תֻּמְצָא	תִּתְמַצֵּא
2MS	תִּמְצָא	תִּמָּצֵא	תְּמַצֵּא	תְּמֻצָּא	תַּמְצִיא	תֻּמְצָא	תִּתְמַצֵּא
2FS	תִּמְצְאִי	תִּמָּצְאִי	תְּמַצְּאִי	תְּמֻצְּאִי	תַּמְצִ֫יאִי	תֻּמְצְאִי	תִּתְמַצְּאִי
1CS	אֶמְצָא	אֶמָּצֵא	אֲמַצֵּא	אֲמֻצָּא	אַמְצִיא	אֻמְצָא	אֶתְמַצֵּא
3MP	יִמְצְאוּ	יִמָּצְאוּ	יְמַצְּאוּ	יְמֻצְּאוּ	יַמְצִ֫יאוּ	יֻמְצְאוּ	יִתְמַצְּאוּ
3FP	תִּמְצֶ֫אנָה	תִּמָּצֶ֫אנָה	תְּמַצֶּ֫אנָה	תְּמֻצֶּ֫אנָה	תַּמְצֶ֫אנָה	תֻּמְצֶ֫אנָה	תִּתְמַצֶּ֫אנָה
2MP	תִּמְצְאוּ	תִּמָּצְאוּ	תְּמַצְּאוּ	תְּמֻצְּאוּ	תַּמְצִ֫יאוּ	תֻּמְצְאוּ	תִּתְמַצְּאוּ
2FP	תִּמְצֶ֫אנָה	תִּמָּצֶ֫אנָה	תְּמַצֶּ֫אנָה	תְּמֻצֶּ֫אנָה	תַּמְצֶ֫אנָה	תֻּמְצֶ֫אנָה	תִּתְמַצֶּ֫אנָה
1CP	נִמְצָא	נִמָּצֵא	נְמַצֵּא	נְמֻצָּא	נַמְצִיא	נֻמְצָא	נִתְמַצֵּא

[13] Stative *lamed-alefs* follow a variant pattern of inflection in *perf, qal,* as illustrated by מָלֵא, מָֽלְאָה, מָלֵ֫אתָ, מָלֵאת, מָלֵ֫אתִי, etc.

13. Weak Verb Paradigm: *Lamed-Alef* (מָצָא)

	Imperative						
	Qal	*Nifal*	*Piel*		*Hifil*		*Hitpael*
2MS	מְצָא	הִמָּצֵא	מַצֵּא		הַמְצֵא		הִתְמַצֵּא
2FS	מִצְאִי	הִמָּצְאִי	מַצְּאִי		הַמְצִיאִי		הִתְמַצְּאִי
2MP	מִצְאוּ	הִמָּצְאוּ	מַצְּאוּ		הַמְצִיאוּ		הִתְמַצְּאוּ
2FP	מְצֶאנָה	הִמָּצֶאנָה	מַצֶּאנָה		הַמְצֶאנָה		הִתְמַצֶּאנָה

Infinitive						
Construct						
Qal	*Nifal*	*Piel*	*Pual*	*Hifil*	*Hofal*	*Hitpael*
מְצֹא	הִמָּצֵא	מַצֵּא	מֻצָּא	הַמְצִיא	הֻמְצָה	הִתְמַצֵּא
Absolute						
מָצוֹא	נִמְצֹא	מַצֹּא	מֻצֹּא	הַמְצֵא	הֻמְצֵא	הִתְמַצֵּא

	Participle						
	Active						
	Qal [14]	*Nifal*	*Piel*	*Pual*	*Hifil*	*Hofal*	*Hitpael*
MS, Ab	מֹצֵא		מְמַצֵּא		מַמְצִיא		מִתְמַצֵּא
FS, Ab	מֹצֵאת		מְמַצְּאָה		מַמְצִיאָה		מִתְמַצְּאָה
MP, Ab	מֹצְאִים		מְמַצְּאִים		מַמְצִיאִים		מִתְמַצְּאִים
FP, Ab	מֹצְאוֹת		מְמַצְּאוֹת		מַמְצִיאוֹת		מִתְמַצְּאוֹת
	Passive						
MS, Ab	מָצוּא	נִמְצָא		מְמֻצָּא		מֻמְצָא	
FS, Ab	מְצוּאָה	נִמְצָאָה		מְמֻצָּאָה		מֻמְצָאָה	
MP, Ab	מְצוּאִים	נִמְצָאִים		מְמֻצָּאִים		מֻמְצָאִים	
FP, Ab	מְצוּאוֹת	נִמְצָאוֹת		מְמֻצָּאוֹת		מֻמְצָאוֹת	

[14] Stative *lamed-alefs* follow a variant pattern of inflection in *part, qal, act,* as illustrated by מָלֵא, מְלֵאָה, מְלֵאִים, מְלֵאוֹת.

14. Weak Verb Paradigm: *Lamed-He* (גָּלָה)

	Perfect						
	Qal	*Nifal*	*Piel*	*Pual*	*Hifil*	*Hofal*	*Hitpael*
3MS	גָּלָה	נִגְלָה	גִּלָּה	גֻּלָּה	הִגְלָה	הָגְלָה	הִתְגַּלָּה
3FS	גָּלְתָה	נִגְלְתָה	גִּלְּתָה	גֻּלְּתָה	הִגְלְתָה	הָגְלְתָה	הִתְגַּלְּתָה
2MS	גָּלִיתָ	נִגְלֵיתָ	גִּלִּיתָ	גֻּלֵּיתָ	הִגְלִיתָ	הָגְלֵיתָ	הִתְגַּלִּיתָ
2FS	גָּלִית	נִגְלֵית	גִּלִּית	גֻּלֵּית	הִגְלִית	הָגְלֵית	הִתְגַּלִּית
1CS	גָּלִיתִי	נִגְלֵיתִי	גִּלִּיתִי	גֻּלֵּיתִי	הִגְלִיתִי	הָגְלֵיתִי	הִתְגַּלִּיתִי
3CP	גָּלוּ	נִגְלוּ	גִּלּוּ	גֻּלּוּ	הִגְלוּ	הָגְלוּ	הִתְגַּלּוּ
2MP	גְּלִיתֶם	נִגְלֵיתֶם	גִּלִּיתֶם	גֻּלֵּיתֶם	הִגְלִיתֶם	הָגְלֵיתֶם	הִתְגַּלִּיתֶם
2FP	גְּלִיתֶן	נִגְלֵיתֶן	גִּלִּיתֶן	גֻּלֵּיתֶן	הִגְלִיתֶן	הָגְלֵיתֶן	הִתְגַּלִּיתֶן
1CP	גָּלִינוּ	נִגְלֵינוּ	גִּלִּינוּ	גֻּלֵּינוּ	הִגְלִינוּ	הָגְלֵינוּ	הִתְגַּלִּינוּ

	Imperfect						
	Qal	*Nifal*	*Piel*	*Pual*	*Hifil*	*Hofal*	*Hitpael*
3MS	יִגְלֶה	יִגָּלֶה	יְגַלֶּה	יְגֻלֶּה	יַגְלֶה	יָגְלֶה	יִתְגַּלֶּה
3FS	תִּגְלֶה	תִּגָּלֶה	תְּגַלֶּה	תְּגֻלֶּה	תַּגְלֶה	תָּגְלֶה	תִּתְגַּלֶּה
2MS	תִּגְלֶה	תִּגָּלֶה	תְּגַלֶּה	תְּגֻלֶּה	תַּגְלֶה	תָּגְלֶה	תִּתְגַּלֶּה
2FS	תִּגְלִי	תִּגָּלִי	תְּגַלִּי	תְּגֻלִּי	תַּגְלִי	תָּגְלִי	תִּתְגַּלִּי
1CS	אֶגְלֶה	אֶגָּלֶה	אֲגַלֶּה	אֲגֻלֶּה	אַגְלֶה	אָגְלֶה	אֶתְגַּלֶּה
3MP	יִגְלוּ	יִגָּלוּ	יְגַלּוּ	יְגֻלּוּ	יַגְלוּ	יָגְלוּ	יִתְגַּלּוּ
3FP	תִּגְלֶינָה	תִּגָּלֶינָה	תְּגַלֶּינָה	תְּגֻלֶּינָה	תַּגְלֶינָה	תָּגְלֶינָה	תִּתְגַּלֶּינָה
2MP	תִּגְלוּ	תִּגָּלוּ	תְּגַלּוּ	תְּגֻלּוּ	תַּגְלוּ	תָּגְלוּ	תִּתְגַּלּוּ
2FP	תִּגְלֶינָה	תִּגָּלֶינָה	תְּגַלֶּינָה	תְּגֻלֶּינָה	תַּגְלֶינָה	תָּגְלֶינָה	תִּתְגַּלֶּינָה
1CP	נִגְלֶה	נִגָּלֶה	נְגַלֶּה	נְגֻלֶּה	נַגְלֶה	נָגְלֶה	נִתְגַּלֶּה

14. Weak Verb Paradigm: *Lamed-He* (גָלָה)

Imperative

	Qal	*Nifal*	*Piel*	*Pual*	*Hifil*	*Hofal*	*Hitpael*
2MS	גְלֵה	הִגָּלֵה	גַּלֵּה		הַגְלֵה		הִתְגַּלֵּה
2FS	גְלִי	הִגָּלִי	גַּלִּי		הַגְלִי		הִתְגַּלִּי
2MP	גְלוּ	הִגָּלוּ	גַּלּוּ		הַגְלוּ		הִתְגַּלּוּ
2FP	גְלֶינָה	הִגָּלֶינָה	גַּלֶּינָה		הַגְלֶינָה		הִתְגַּלֶּינָה

Infinitive

	Qal	*Nifal*	*Piel*	*Pual*	*Hifil*	*Hofal*	*Hitpael*
Construct	גְלוֹת	הִגָּלוֹת	גַּלּוֹת	גֻּלּוֹת	הַגְלוֹת	הָגְלוֹת	הִתְגַּלּוֹת
Absolute	גָלֹה	נִגְלֹה	גַּלֹּה	גֻּלֹּה	הַגְלֵה	הָגְלֵה	הִתְגַּלֵּה

Participle

	Qal	*Nifal*	*Piel*	*Pual*	*Hifil*	*Hofal*	*Hitpael*
Active							
MS, Ab	גֹלֶה		מְגַלֶּה		מַגְלֶה		מִתְגַּלֶּה
FS, Ab	גֹלָה		מְגַלָּה		מַגְלָה		מִתְגַּלָּה
MP, Ab	גֹלִים		מְגַלִּים		מַגְלִים		מִתְגַּלִּים
FP, Ab	גֹלוֹת		מְגַלּוֹת		מַגְלוֹת		מִתְגַּלּוֹת
Passive							
MS, Ab	גָלוּי	נִגְלֶה		מְגֻלֶּה		מָגְלֶה	
FS, Ab	גְלוּיָה	נִגְלָה		מְגֻלָּה		מָגְלָה	
MP, Ab	גְלוּיִם	נִגְלִים		מְגֻלִּים		מָגְלִים	
FP, Ab	גְלוּיוֹת	נִגְלוֹת		מְגֻלּוֹת		מָגְלוֹת	

15. Weak Verb Paradigm: Irregular Verbs (נָתַן, לָקַח[15], הָלַךְ[16], הָיָה)

	Perfect									
	Qal	*Nifal*		*Qal*	*Nifal*		*Qal*	*Hifil*		*Qal*
3MS	נָתַן	נִתַּן		לָקַח	נִלְקַח		הָלַךְ	הוֹלִיךְ		הָיָה
3FS	נָתְנָה	נִתְּנָה		לָקְחָה	נִלְקְחָה		הָלְכָה			הָיְתָה
2MS	נָתַ֫תָּ[17]	נִתַּ֫תָּ		לָקַ֫חְתָּ			הָלַ֫כְתָּ			הָיִ֫יתָ
2FS	נָתַתְּ			לָקַ֫חַתְּ			הָלַכְתְּ			הָיִית
1CS	נָתַ֫תִּי			לָקַ֫חְתִּי			הָלַ֫כְתִּי	הוֹלַ֫כְתִּי		הָיִ֫יתִי
3CP	נָתְנוּ			לָקְחוּ			הָלְכוּ			הָיוּ
2MP	נְתַתֶּם	נִתַּתֶּם		לְקַחְתֶּם			הֲלַכְתֶּם			הֱיִיתֶם
2FP	נְתַתֶּן			לְקַחְתֶּן			הֲלַכְתֶּן			הֱיִיתֶן
1CP	נָתַ֫נּוּ	נִתַּ֫נּוּ		לָקַ֫חְנוּ			הָלַ֫כְנוּ			הָיִ֫ינוּ

	Imperfect									
	Qal	*Nifal*		*Qal*	*Nifal*		*Qal*	*Hifil*		*Qal*
3MS	יִתֵּן	יִנָּתֵן		יִקַּח	יִלָּקַח		יֵלֵךְ	יוֹלִיךְ		יִהְיֶה
3FS	תִּתֵּן	תִּנָּתֵן		תִּקַּח	תִּלָּקַח		תֵּלֵךְ			תִּהְיֶה
2MS	תִּתֵּן	תִּנָּתֵן		תִּקַּח			תֵּלֵךְ			תִּהְיֶה
2FS	תִּתְּנִי			תִּקְּחִי			תֵּלְכִי			תִּהְיִי
1CS	אֶתֵּן			אֶקַּח	אֶלָּקַח		אֵלֵךְ	אוֹלִיךְ		אֶהְיֶה
3MP	יִתְּנוּ	יִנָּתְנוּ		יִקְּחוּ			יֵלְכוּ	יוֹלִ֫יכוּ		יִהְיוּ
3FP	תִּתֵּ֫נָּה			תִּקַּ֫חְנָה			תֵּלַ֫כְנָה			תִּהְיֶ֫ינָה
2MP	תִּתְּנוּ			תִּקְּחוּ			תֵּלְכוּ			תִּהְיוּ
2FP	תִּתֵּ֫נָּה			תִּקַּ֫חְנָה			תֵּלַ֫כְנָה			תִּהְיֶ֫ינָה
1CP	נִתֵּן			נִקַּח			נֵלֵךְ			נִהְיֶה

[15] לָקַח is inflected as if its root were *pe-nun* in part of its conjugation – namely, in imperfect, *qal* and *hofal;* imperative, *qal;* and infinitive, *qal,* construct.

[16] הָלַךְ is inflected as if its root were *pe-yod/vav* in part of its conjugation – namely, in the *qal* stem of the imperfect, imperative, and infinitive, construct; and in all conjugations of *hifil.*

[17] In some forms of נָתַן the final nun assimilates into the first consonant of the suffix.

15. Weak Verb Paradigm: Irregular Verbs (הָיָה, הָלַךְ, לָקַח, נָתַן)

	Imperative									
	Qal	*Nifal*		*Qal*	*Nifal*		*Qal*	*Hifil*		*Qal*
2MS	תֵּן			קַח			לֵךְ	הוֹלֵךְ		הֱיֵה
2FS	תְּנִי			קְחִי			לְכִי	הֵילִ֫יכִי		הֲיִי
2MP	תְּנוּ			קְחוּ			לְכוּ	הֹלִ֫יכוּ		הֱיוּ
2FP							לֵ֫כְנָה			

Infinitive									
Construct									
Qal	*Nifal*		*Qal*	*Nifal*		*Qal*	*Hifil*		*Qal*
נְתֹן or תֵּת	הִנָּתֵן		קַ֫חַת	הִלָּקַח		לֶ֫כֶת	הוֹלִיךְ		הֱיוֹת
Absolute									
נָתוֹן	הִנָּתֹן		לָקוֹחַ			הָלֹךְ			הָיֹה

	Participle									
	Active									
	Qal	*Nifal*		*Qal*	*Nifal*		*Qal*	*Hifil*		*Qal*
MS, Ab	נֹתֵן			לֹקֵחַ			הֹלֵךְ	מוֹלִיךְ		הוֹיָה
FS, Ab							הֹלֶ֫כֶת			
MP, Ab	נֹתְנִים			לֹקְחִים			הֹלְכִים			
FP, Ab							הֹלְכוֹת	מוֹלִכוֹת		
	Passive									
MS, Ab	נָתוּן	נִתָּן			נִלְקָה					
FS, Ab										
MP, Ab	נְתֻנִים			לְקֻחִים						
FP, Ab	נְתֻנוֹת									

16. Practice Chart for Strong Verb (משל)

Perfect

	Qal	*Nifal*	*Piel*	*Pual*	*Hifil*	*Hofal*	*Hitpael*
3MS	משל	משל	משל	משל	משל	משל	משל
3FS	משל	משל	משל	משל	משל	משל	משל
2MS	משל	משל	משל	משל	משל	משל	משל
2FS	משל	משל	משל	משל	משל	משל	משל
1CS	משל	משל	משל	משל	משל	משל	משל
3CP	משל	משל	משל	משל	משל	משל	משל
2MP	משל	משל	משל	משל	משל	משל	משל
2FP	משל	משל	משל	משל	משל	משל	משל
1CP	משל	משל	משל	משל	משל	משל	משל

Imperfect

	Qal	*Nifal*	*Piel*	*Pual*	*Hifil*	*Hofal*	*Hitpael*
3MS	משל	משל	משל	משל	משל	משל	משל
3FS	משל	משל	משל	משל	משל	משל	משל
2MS	משל	משל	משל	משל	משל	משל	משל
2FS	משל	משל	משל	משל	משל	משל	משל
1CS	משל	משל	משל	משל	משל	משל	משל
3MP	משל	משל	משל	משל	משל	משל	משל
3FP	משל	משל	משל	משל	משל	משל	משל
2MP	משל	משל	משל	משל	משל	משל	משל
2FP	משל	משל	משל	משל	משל	משל	משל
1CP	משל	משל	משל	משל	משל	משל	משל

16. Practice Chart for Strong Verb (משל)

Imperative

	Qal	*Nifal*	*Piel*	*Hifil*	*Hitpael*
2MS	משל	משל	משל	משל	משל
2FS	משל	משל	משל	משל	משל
2MP	משל	משל	משל	משל	משל
2FP	משל	משל	משל	משל	משל

Infinitive

Construct

Qal	*Nifal*	*Piel*	*Pual*	*Hifil*	*Hofal*	*Hitpael*
משל	משל	משל		משל		משל

Absolute

Qal	*Nifal*	*Piel*	*Pual*	*Hifil*	*Hofal*	*Hitpael*
משל	משל or	משל or	משל	משל	משל	משל
	משל	משל				

Participle

Active

	Qal	*Nifal*	*Piel*	*Pual*	*Hifil*	*Hofal*	*Hitpael*
MS, Ab	משל		משל		משל		משל
FS, Ab	משל or		משל		משל		משל
	משל		משל		משל		משל
MP, Ab	משל		משל		משל		משל
FP, Ab	משל		משל		משל		משל

Passive

	Qal	*Nifal*	*Pual*	*Hofal*
MS, Ab	משל	משל	משל	משל
FS, Ab	משל	משל	משל	משל
MP, Ab	משל	משל	משל	משל
FP, Ab	משל	משל	משל	משל

Appendix 4

Vocabulary

The following is an alphabetical list of the words which appear 200 or more times in the Hebrew Bible.[1] These words also appear in the vocabulary lists of the lessons in this Grammar. The lesson number in which a vocabulary word was introduced appears in brackets after the word. A few words that occur less than 200 times are included in this vocabulary because of their grammatical importance or their use in paradigms; they are marked with an asterisk. Mastering this list will give beginning students a good working vocabulary for reading biblical Hebrew.

	Word		*Translation*	*Notes*[2]
			ALEF א	
	אָב	[14]	father (*NMS*)	*Cs:* אֲבִי, אַב; *S* with *PS:* אָבִי, אָבִיךָ, etc.; *P:* אָבוֹת, אֲבוֹת;[3] *P* with *PS:* אֲבוֹתַי or אֲבֹתַי, אֲבוֹתָם or אֲבוֹתֵיהֶם, etc.
*	אָבַד[4]	[22]	he was lost, perished (*V*)	
	אֶבֶן	[24]	stone (*NFS*)	*P:* אֲבָנִים
	אַבְרָהָם	[24]	Abraham (*proper N*)	
	אָדוֹן	[19]	lord, master (*NMS*)	אֲדֹנָי (literally "my lord") usually means "Lord"; substitute for יהוה
	אָדָם	[6]	man, mortal, humankind (*NMS*)	

[1] In the case of some words that have similar noun and adjective forms, it is difficult to distinguish between the frequency of usage as noun and as adjective. Two such words are חַי and רָעָה. The former is listed in this vocabulary in its adjective form and the latter in its noun form.

[2] Forms that are irregular, unique, or may otherwise be difficult for the student are given in the *Notes.*

[3] When two forms follow *P* (plural) or *Du* (dual), the first is absolute and the second is construct.

[4] Verbs appear in their lexical forms; that form is usually *perf, qal, 3MS*, as with this verb.

	Word		Translation	Notes
	אֲדָמָה	[16]	land, ground, earth (*NFS*)	*Cs:* אַדְמַת
	אָהֵב	[21]	he loved (*V*)	Also אָהַב
	אֹהֶל	[16]	tent (*NMS*)	*P:* אֹהָלִים
	אַהֲרֹן	[20]	Aaron (*proper N*)	
	אוֹ	[22]	or (*conj*)	
	אָח	[13]	brother (*NMS*)	*Cs:* אֲחִי; *S* with *PS:* אָחִי, אָחִיךָ, etc.; *P:* אַחִים, אֲחֵי; *P* with *PS:* אַחַי, אַחֶיךָ, etc.
	אֶחָד	[12]	one (*adj. MS*)	*Cs:* אַחַד; *FS, Ab* & *Cs:* אַחַת
	אַחַר	[19]	after, behind (*prep, adv,* or *conj*)	*PS* on *prep:* אַחֲרָיו, אַחֲרֶיךָ, etc.
	אָיַב	[20]	he was an enemy (*V*)	
	אַיִן	[22]	there is/are not, there was/were not, there is no one/nothing (*particle*)	*Cs:* אֵין; *PS:* אֵינֶנּוּ, אֵינְךָ, etc.
	אִישׁ	[7]	man, husband (*NMS*)	*P:* אֲנָשִׁים, אַנְשֵׁי
	אָכַל	[19]	he ate (*V*)	
	אַל	[17]	no, not (*particle*)	
	אֵל	[22]	God, god (*NMS*)	
	אֶל	[5]	to, into, toward (*prep*)	*PS:* אֵלֶיךָ, אֵלַי, etc.
	אֵלֶּה	[11]	these (*dem adj M/FP*)	
	אֱלֹהִים	[5]	God, gods (*NMP*)	
	אֶלֶף	[25]	thousand *(NMS)*	*Du:* אַלְפַּיִם = "2000"; *P:* אֲלָפִים, אַלְפֵי = "thousands"
	אֵם	[20]	mother (*NFS*)	*S* with *PS:* אִמְּךָ, אִמִּי, etc.; *P* with *PS:* אִמֹּתֵנוּ, אִמֹּתָם, etc.
	אִם	[15]	if (*particle*)	
	אַמָּה	[23]	cubit (*NFS*)	*Du:* אַמָּתַיִם; *P:* אַמּוֹת
	אָמַר	[14]	he said (*V*)	
*	אֲנַחְנוּ	[11]	we (*pron 1CP*)	
	אָנֹכִי, אֲנִי	[11]	I (*pron 1CS*)	
	אָסַף	[16]	he gathered, removed (*V*)	

	Word		Translation	Notes
	אַף	[19]	anger, nose, nostril (*NFS*)	*S* with *PS:* אַפִּי, אַפְּךָ, etc.; *Du:* אַפַּיִם = "face"; *Du* with *PS:* אַפֶּיךָ, אַפָּיו, etc.
	אַרְבַּע (*M*), אַרְבָּעָה (*F*)[5]	[19]	four (*N M/F S*)	*P:* אַרְבָּעִים = "forty"; רְבִיעִי (*M*), רְבִיעִית (*F*) = "fourth"
	אֲרוֹן	[26]	ark, chest (*NMS*)	With *art:* הָאָרוֹן
	אֶרֶץ	[5]	earth, land (*NFS*)	With *art:* הָאָרֶץ; *P:* אֲרָצוֹת, אַרְצוֹת
	אֵשׁ	[19]	fire *(NFS)*	No *P*
	אִשָּׁה	[7]	woman, wife (*NFS*)	*Cs:* אֵשֶׁת; *S* with *PS:* אִשְׁתִּי, אִשְׁתְּךָ, etc.; *P:* נָשִׁים, נְשֵׁי
	אֲשֶׁר	[11]	who, whom, whose, which, where, when (*particle*)	כַּאֲשֶׁר functions as *conj* = "as"
	אֵת	[8]	(a) [sign of the object – no translation] (*particle*)	*Cs:* אֵת, אֶת־; *PS:* אֹתִי, אֹתְךָ, etc.
		[10]	(b) with (*prep*)	*Cs:* אֵת אֶת־; *PS:* אִתִּי, אִתְּךָ, etc.
*	אַתְּ	[11]	you (*pron 2FS*)	
	אַתָּה	[11]	you (*pron 2MS*)	
*	אַתֶּם	[11]	you (*pron 2MP*)	
*	אַתֵּן, אַתֵּנָה	[11]	you (*pron 2FP*)	

B ET ב

	Word		Translation	Notes
	בְּ___	[6]	in, by, with (*prep*)	Prefixed; *PS:* בִּי, בְּךָ, etc.
	בָּא	[5]	[See בּוֹא]	
	בָּבֶל	[21]	Babylon, Babel (*proper N*)	
	בֶּגֶד	[26]	garment, cloth (*NMS*)	*P:* בְּגָדִים, בִּגְדֵי
	בּוֹא[6]	[25]	(to) come, go, enter (*V*)	Appears in Lesson 5 vocabulary as בָּא (*perf, qal 3MS*)
*	בּוֹשׁ	[25]	(to) be ashamed (*V*)	

[5] The numbers from two to ten appear as nouns with both *M* and *F* forms.

[6] *Ayin-vav* and *ayin-yod* verbs typically employ the *inf, qal, Cs* as the lexical form, as with this word.

	Word		*Translation*	*Notes*
*	בָּחַר	[22]	he chose (*V*)	
	בֵּין	[13]	between (*prep*)	*PS:* בֵּינִי, בֵּינְךָ, etc.; or בֵּינֵינוּ, בֵּינֵיכֶם, etc.
	בַּיִת	[14]	house (*NMS*)	*Cs:* בֵּית; *P:* בָּתִּים, בָּתֵּי
	בֵּן	[7]	son, child (*NMS*)	*Cs:* בֶּן־, בִּן־; *S* with *PS:* בְּנִי, בִּנְךָ, etc.; *P:* בָּנִים, בְּנֵי; *P* with *PS:* בָּנַי, בָּנֶיךָ, etc.
	בָּנָה	[24]	he built (*V*)	
	בֹּקֶר	[16]	morning (*NMS*)	*P:* בְּקָרִים
	בקשׁ[7]	[19]	בִּקֵּשׁ (*piel*): he sought, asked (*V*)	Never occurs in *qal*
	בְּרִית	[16]	covenant (*NFS*)	
*	ברך	[19]	בֵּרַךְ (*piel*): he blessed (*V*)	Usually occurs in *piel*
	בָּשָׂר	[24]	flesh (*NMS*)	*Cs:* בְּשַׂר; *P:* בְּשָׂרִים
	בַּת	[7]	daughter (*NFS*)	*S* with *PS:* בִּתִּי, בִּתְּךָ, etc.; *P:* בָּנוֹת, בְּנוֹת; *P* with *PS:* בְּנוֹתַי, בְּנוֹתֶיךָ, etc.

Gimel ג

	גְּבוּל	[26]	border, boundary, territory (*NMS*)	
	גָּדוֹל	[8]	great (*adj MS*)	*MS Cs:* גְּדוֹל; *MP:* גְּדוֹלִים, גְּדֹלֵי; *FS:* גְּדוֹלָה; *FP:* גְּדֹלוֹת
	גּוֹי	[5]	nation (*NMS*)	*P:* גּוֹיִם, גּוֹיֵי or גּוֹיֵ
*	גָּלָה	[17]	he uncovered, revealed, went into exile (*V*)	
	גַּם	[25]	also, likewise, again (*adv*)	

Dalet ד

	דָּבָר	[9]	word, speech, thing (*NMS*)	*Cs:* דְּבַר; *P:* דְּבָרִים, דִּבְרֵי
	דבר	[18]	דִּבֶּר (*piel*): he spoke (*V*)	Usually *piel;* in *qal* only as *inf* and *part*

---

[7] A verb's root (without vowel pointing) appears as its lexical form in the case of a verb that does not occur in *perf, qal, 3MS* (as with this verb), and in some cases where a verb's *perf, qal, 3MS* form omits a root consonant.

Word		*Translation*	*Notes*
דָּוִד	[24]	David (*proper N*)	
דָּם	[19]	blood (*NMS*)	*Cs:* דַּם
דֶּ֫רֶךְ	[26]	way, road, path, journey, manner (*NMS*)	*P:* דְּרָכִים, דַּרְכֵי

H E ה

---הַ	[5]	the (*art*)	Also: הָ or הֶ; prefixed and followed by *dagesh-forte* where possible
---הֲ	[24]	(*he* interrogative)	Also הַ or הֶ; prefixed at the beginning of an interrogative clause
הוּא	[11]	(a) he (*pron 3MS*) (b) that (*dem adj MS*)	
הִיא	[11]	(a) she (*pron 3FS*), (b) that (*dem adj FS*)	Sometimes הִוא in *MT*
הָיָה	[8]	he was, became, existed (*V*)	With an impersonal subject = "it/there was, happened, occurred"
הָלַךְ	[24]	he went, came, walked (*V*)	Inflects like a *pe-yod/vav* verb in part of its conjugation
הֵם, הֵ֫מָּה	[11]	(a) they (*pron 3MP*) (b) those (*dem adj MP*)	
* הֵ֫נָּה	[11]	(a) they (*pron 3FP*), (b) those (*dem adj FP*)	
הִנֵּה	[21]	look, behold (*particle*)	*PS:* הִנְנִי or הִנֵּ֫נִי, הִנְּךָ, etc.
הַר	[5]	mountain (*NMS*)	With *art*: הָהָר; *P:* הָרִים

V A V ו

---וְ	[6]	and (*conj*)[8]	Prefixed; may link words, phrases, or clauses

[8] The *vav* conjunction can convey a number of other meanings, depending upon its context, such as, "or, but, also, then, when, since, therefore."

	Word		*Translation*	*Notes*
			ZAYIN ז	
	זֹאת	[11]	this (*dem adj FS*)	
	זֶה	[11]	this (*dem adj MS*)	
	זָהָב	[23]	gold (*NMS*)	No *P*
	זָכַר	[16]	he remembered (*V*)	
	זֶרַע	[18]	seed, offspring, sowing (*NMS*)	*S* with *PS:* זַרְעִי, זַרְעֲךָ, etc.
			HET ח	
	חֹדֶשׁ	[23]	new moon, month (*NMS*)	*S* with *PS:* חָדְשׁוֹ, חָדְשָׁהּ, etc.; *P:* חֳדָשִׁים, חָדְשֵׁי
*	חָזַק	[21]	he was strong (*V*)	
	חָטָא	[20]	he sinned, missed (*V*)	
	חַטָּאת	[20]	sin, sin offering (*NFS*)	*Cs:* חַטַּאת; *P:* חַטָּאוֹת
	חַי	[20]	alive, living (*adj MS*)	*FS:* חַיָּה; *P:* חַיִּים; חַיָּה is also *NFS* = "living thing, animal"; חַיִּים is also *NMP* = "life"
	חָיָה	[17]	he lived, revived (*V*)	
	חַיִל	[26]	strength, wealth, army (*NMS*)	*Cs:* חֵיל; *P:* חֲיָלִים
	חָמֵשׁ (*M*), חֲמִשָּׁה (*F*)	[20]	five (*NM/FS*)	*P:* חֲמִשִּׁים = "fifty"; חֲמִישִׁי (*M*), חֲמִישִׁית (*F*) = "fifth"
	חֶסֶד	[24]	steadfast love, kindness, loyalty (*NMS*)	*S* with *PS:* חַסְדִּי, חַסְדְּךָ, etc.; *P:* חֲסָדִים, חַסְדֵי
	חֶרֶב	[14]	sword, dagger (*NFS*)	*P:* חֲרָבוֹת, חַרְבוֹת
			TET ט	
	טוֹב	[8]	good (*adj MS*)	
			YOD י	
	יָד	[7]	hand (*NFS*)	*Cs:* יַד; *Du:* יָדַיִם, יְדֵי; *P:* יָדוֹת, יְדוֹת
	יָדַע	[8]	he knew (*V*)	
	יְהוּדָה	[25]	Judah (*proper N*)	יְהוּדִי (*adj MS*) = "Jewish, Jew"

	Word		*Translation*	*Notes*
	יְהוָה	[6]	LORD, the LORD (*proper N*)	Pointing of יְהוָה indicates the word is to be read as אֲדֹנָי; sometimes pointed as יְהוִה and read as אֱלֹהִים
	יְהוֹשׁוּעַ	[24]	Joshua (*proper N*)	
	יוֹם	[7]	day (*NMS*)	*Du:* יוֹמַ֫יִם; *P:* יָמִים, יְמֵי
	יוֹסֵף	[24]	Joseph (*proper N*)	
*	יָטַב	[21]	he was good (*V*)	
	יָכֹל	[21]	he was able, prevailed, endured (*V*)	Also יָכוֹל; *impf, qal, 3MS:* יוּכַל
	יָלַד	[20]	he brought forth, gave birth (*V*)	
	יָם	[18]	sea (*NMS*)	*P:* יַמִּים
	יָסַף	[24]	he added, increased (*V*)	
	יַעֲקֹב	[26]	Jacob (*proper N*)	
	יָצָא	[24]	he went out (*V*)	
	יָרֵא	[21]	he was afraid, feared (*V*)	
	יָרַד	[24]	he went down, descended (*V*)	
	יְרוּשָׁלַ֫ם	[22]	Jerusalem (*proper N*)	This *MT* spelling is a contraction of יְרוּשָׁלַ֫יִם
	יָרַשׁ	[24]	he took possession of, inherited, displaced (*V*)	
	יִשְׂרָאֵל	[5]	Israel (*proper N*)	יִשְׂרְאֵלִי (*adj MS*) = "Israelite"
*	יֵשׁ	[22]	there is/are, there was/were (*particle*)	יֶשׁ־; with *PS:* יֶשְׁךָ, יֶשְׁכֶם, etc.
	יָשַׁב	[6]	he dwelled, sat (*V*)	
	ישׁע	[24]	נוֹשַׁע (*nif*): he was saved; הוֹשִׁיעַ (*hif*): he saved, delivered (*V*)	Only occurs in *nif* & *hif*

Kaf כ

כְּ___	[6]	like, as (*prep*)	Prefixed; *PS:* כָּמוֹנִי, כָּמוֹךָ, etc., & כָּכֶם, כָּהֶם, etc.

Word		*Translation*	*Notes*
* כָּבֵד	[21]	he was heavy, honored (*V*)	
כָּבוֹד	[21]	honor, glory (*NMS*)	*Cs:* כְּבוֹד; *Ab* also כָּבֹד
כֹּה	[19]	thus (*adv*)	
כֹּהֵן	[6]	priest (*NMS*)	
כון	[25]	נָכוֹן (*nif*): he was fixed, firm, established; הֵכִין (*hif*): he made firm, established (*V*)	Does not occur in *qal*
כִּי	[6]	that, for, when, because (*conj*)	Introduces a subordinate clause
כֹּל	[10]	all, every (*NMS*)	*Cs:* כֹּל, כָּל־, *PS:* כֻּלּוֹ, כֻּלָּהּ, etc.
כָּלָה	[26]	he completed, finished (*V*)	
כְּלִי	[22]	vessel, equipment, implement (*NMS*)	*P:* כֵּלִים
כֵּן	[15]	thus, so (*adv*)	With ל *prep:* לָכֵן = "therefore"
כֶּסֶף	[25]	silver (*NMS*)	No *P*
כָּרַת	[16]	he cut off, cut down (*V*)	
כָּתַב	[20]	he wrote (*V*)	

LAMED ל

___לְ	[6]	to, for, according to (*prep*)	Prefixed; *PS:* לִי, לְךָ, etc.
לֹא	[13]	no, not (*particle*)	Also spelled לוֹא
לֵב	[8]	heart, will, mind (*NMS*)	*Cs:* לֵב, לֶב־; *S* with *PS:* לִבִּי, לִבְּךָ, etc.; *P:* לִבּוֹת; *NMS* also לֵבָב (*Cs:* לְבַב; *P:* לְבָבוֹת)
לֵוִי	[26]	(a) Levi (*proper N*) (b) Levite (*adj MS*)	 *P:* לְוִיִּם = "Levites"
לֶחֶם	[20]	bread, food (*NMS*)	*S* with *PS:* לַחְמִי, לַחְמְךָ, etc.
לַיְלָה	[19]	night (*NMS*)	*Ab* also לַיִל; *Cs:* לֵיל
לְמַעַן	[22]	(a) with regard to, for the sake of, because of (*prep*) (b) in order that, so that (*conj*)	
לָקַח	[23]	he took, seized (*V*)	Inflects like a *pe-nun* verb in part of its conjugation
* לָקַט	[12]	he picked up, gathered (*V*)	

Word		*Translation*	*Notes*

Mem מ

מְאֹד	[21]	(a) very (*adv*) (b) power, might (*NMS*)	
מֵאָה	[25]	hundred (*NFS*)	*Cs:* מְאַת; *Du:* מָאתַ֫יִם = "200"; *P:* מֵאוֹת = "hundreds"
מִדְבָּר	[23]	wilderness, desert (*NMS*)	
מָה	[24]	what? how? (*pron*)	Also: מַה or מֶה; followed by *dagesh-forte* where possible
מוֹעֵד	[19]	meeting place, meeting, appointed time (*NMS*)	
מוּת	[25]	(to) die (*V*)	
מִזְבֵּחַ	[23]	altar (*NMS*)	*P:* מִזְבְּחוֹת
מַחֲנֶה	[16]	camp, army (*NM/FS*)	*Cs:* מַחֲנֵה; *MP:* מַחֲנִים; *FP:* מַחֲנוֹת
מַטֶּה	[23]	staff, tribe (*NMS*)	*Cs:* מַטֵּה; *P:* מַטּוֹת
מִי	[24]	who?, whom?, whose?, whoever? (*pron*)	
מַ֫יִם	[16]	water, waters (*NMDu*)	Occurs only in *Du*
מָלֵא	[21]	he was full, filled (*V*)	
מַלְאָךְ	[23]	messenger (*NMS*)	*Cs:* מַלְאַךְ
מִלְחָמָה	[24]	battle, war (*NFS*)	*Cs:* מִלְחֶ֫מֶת
מָלַךְ	[18]	he reigned, was/became king (or *F:* she was/ became queen) (*V*)	
מֶ֫לֶךְ	[5]	king (*NMS*)	
מִן	[6]	from, out of (*prep*)	May stand independently or be prefixed; with comparative *adj* = "than"; *PS:* מִמֶּ֫נִּי, מִמְּךָ, etc., & מִכֶּם, מֵהֶם, etc.
מִנְחָה	[25]	gift, offering (*NFS*)	
מַעֲשֶׂה	[23]	deed, work (*NMS*)	*Cs:* מַעֲשֵׂה
מָצָא	[26]	he found, met (*V*)	
מִצְרַ֫יִם	[23]	Egypt (*proper N*)	מִצְרִי (*adj MS*) = "Egyptian"
מָקוֹם	[18]	place (*NMS*)	*P:* מְקֹמוֹת

	Word		Translation	Notes
	מֹשֶׁה	[18]	Moses (*proper N*)	
*	מָשַׁל	[12]	he ruled, reigned (*V*)	When followed by ב prep, ב = "over"
	מִשְׁפָּחָה	[26]	clan (*NFS*)	
	מִשְׁפָּט	[10]	judgment, justice (*NMS*)	*Cs:* מִשְׁפַּט

Nun נ

	Word		Translation	Notes
	נָא	[17]	please, now, I pray (*particle*)	Usually employed with *cohort, juss*, or *impv*
	נְאֻם	[20]	utterance, oracle (*NMS Cs*)	Occurs only in *S Cs*
	נָבִיא	[22]	prophet (*NMS*)	*P:* נְבִיאִים
	נגד	[23]	הִגִּיד (*hif*): he told, declared; הֻגַּד (*hof*): he was told (*V*)	Usually occurs in *hif* & *hof*
*	נָגַשׁ	[23]	he approached, drew near (*V*)	
	נַחֲלָה	[26]	inheritance, heritage, possession (*NFS*)	*P:* נְחָלוֹת
	נָטָה	[23]	he extended, stretched out, turned, bent (*V*)	
	נכה	[23]	הִכָּה (*hif*): he struck; הֻכָּה (*hof*): he was struck (*V*)	Usually occurs in *hif* & *hof*
	נַ֫עַר	[23]	boy, youth, servant (*NMS*)	P: נְעָרִים
	נָפַל	[23]	he fell (*V*)	
	נֶ֫פֶשׁ	[20]	living being, soul, person, self (*NFS*)	*P:* נַפְשׁוֹת, נְפָשׁוֹת
	נָשָׂא	[9]	he lifted, lifted up, carried (*V*)	
	נָתַן	[10]	he gave, put, set (*V*)	

Samek ס

	Word		Translation	Notes
*	סָבַב	[25]	he surrounded, went around, turned around (*V*)	
	סָבִיב	[16]	(a) around, all around (*adv* or *prep*) (b) circuit, neighborhood (*NM/FS*)	*Cs:* סְבִיב; *MP:* סְבִיבִים; *FP:* סְבִיבוֹת; *P* with *PS:* סְבִיבֶ֫יהָ, סְבִיבוֹתַי, etc.

Word		Translation	Notes
סוּר	[25]	(to) turn aside (*V*)	

AYIN ע

Word		Translation	Notes
עָבַד	[22]	he worked, served (*V*)	
עֶ֫בֶד	[17]	servant, slave (*NMS*)	*PS:* עַבְדִּי, עַבְדְּךָ, etc.; *P:* עֲבָדִים, עַבְדֵי
עָבַר	[22]	he passed, went over (*V*)	
עַד	[13]	(a) until (*prep*) (b) perpetuity (*NMS*)	*Prep* with *PS:* עָדַי, עָדֶ֫יךָ, etc.
עוֹד	[18]	yet, still, again, besides (*adv*)	
עוֹלָם	[15]	eternity, antiquity, forever, a long time (*NMS*)	
עָוֹן	[26]	sin, guilt, punishment (*NMS*)	*Cs:* עֲוֹן; *S* also עָווֹן, עֲווֹן; *P:* עֲוֹנוֹת or עֲוֹנֹת
עַ֫יִן	[17]	eye (*NFS*)	*Du:* עֵינַ֫יִם
עִיר	[9]	city, town (*NFS*)	*P:* עָרִים, עָרֵי
עַל	[10]	on, upon, over (*prep*)	*PS:* עָלַי, עָלֶ֫יךָ, etc.
עָלָה	[22]	he went up, ascended (*V*)	
עֹלָה	[22]	burnt offering (*NFS*)	Also עוֹלָה
עַם	[5]	people (*NMS*)	With *art*: הָעָם; *PS:* עַמִּי, עַמְּךָ, etc.; *P:* עַמִּים
עִם	[10]	with (*prep*)	*PS:* עִמִּי or עִמָּדִי, עִמְּךָ, etc.
עָמַד	[22]	he stood, took a stand (*V*)	
עָנָה	[22]	he answered (*V*)	
עֵץ	[18]	tree, trees, wood (*NMS*)	
עָשָׂה	[10]	he did, made (*V*)	
עֶ֫שֶׂר (*M*), עֲשָׂרָה (*F*)	[25]	ten (*NM/FS*)	*P:* עֶשְׂרִים = "twenty"; עֲשִׂירִי(*M*), עֲשִׂירִית (*F*) = "tenth"; spelled עָשָׂר (*M*) and עֶשְׂרֵה (*F*) when combined with units to form numbers "11" to "19"
עֵת	[26]	time (*NM/FS*)	*Cs:* עֵת, עֶת־; *S* with *PS:* עִתּוֹ, עִתָּהּ, etc.; *P:* עִתִּים

	Word		Translation	Notes
	עַתָּה	[19]	now (*adv*)	

Pe פ

	Word		Translation	Notes
	פֶּה	[19]	mouth (*NMS*)	*Cs:* פִּי; *P:* פִּיּוֹת
	פְּלֶשֶׁת	[23]	Philistia (*proper N*)	פְּלִשְׁתִּי (*adj MS*) = "Philistine"
	פָּנִים	[15]	face, faces, presence (*NMP*)	No *S; P* can mean "face"; with ל *prep:* לִפְנֵי = "before"
	פָּקַד	[25]	he took care of, sought, missed, appointed (*V*)	
	פַּרְעֹה	[24]	Pharaoh (*NMS*)	

Sade צ

	Word		Translation	Notes
	צֹאן	[26]	small cattle, sheep, goats, flock(s) (*NFS*)	
	צָבָא	[20]	army, host, war, warfare (*NMS*)	*P:* צְבָאוֹת
	צַדִּיק	[16]	righteous, just (*adj MS*)	
	צוה	[17]	צִוָּה (*piel*): he commanded, ordered (*V*)	Only occurs in *piel* and *pual*

Qof ק

	Word		Translation	Notes
*	קָדַשׁ	[21]	he was holy (*V*)	
	קֹדֶשׁ	[7]	holiness (*NMS*)	*P:* קֳדָשִׁים, קָדְשֵׁי
	קוֹל	[9]	voice, sound (*NMS*)	*P:* קוֹלוֹת or קֹלֹת
	קוּם	[25]	(to) rise, stand (*V*)	
*	קָטַל	[12]	he killed (*V*)	
*	קָטֹן	[21]	he was small, insignificant (*V*)	
*	קלל	[25]	קַל (*qal*): he was light, despised (*V*)	
	קָרָא	[9]	he called, met (*V*)	
	קֶרֶב	[26]	inward part, midst (*NMS*)	*S* with *PS:* קִרְבִּי, קִרְבְּךָ, etc.; *P* with *PS:* קְרָבַי

Resh ר

	Word		Translation	Notes
	רָאָה	[5]	he saw (*V*)	
	רֹאשׁ	[5]	head, top (*NMS*)	P: רָאשִׁים, רָאשֵׁי

Word		*Translation*	*Notes*
רַב	[8]	many, much, great *(adj MS)*	*MP:* רַבִּים, רַבֵּי; *FS:* רַבָּה, רַבַּת; *FP:* רַבּוֹת
רָבָה	[21]	he was great, became numerous (*V*)	
רֶ֫גֶל	[23]	foot, leg (*NFS*)	*Du:* רַגְלַ֫יִם
רוּחַ	[7]	spirit, breath, wind (*NFS*)	
רֵעַ	[23]	friend, companion (*NMS*)	
רָעָה	[10]	evil (*NFS*)	
רָשָׁע	[26]	guilty, wicked (*adj MS*)	*FS:* רְשָׁעָה; *MP:* רְשָׁעִים, רִשְׁעֵי
		Sin שׂ	
שָׂדֶה	[22]	field(s) (*NMS*)	*Cs:* שְׂדֵה; *S* with *PS:* שָׂדִי, שָׂדְךָ, etc.; *P:* שָׂדוֹת, שְׂדוֹת or שְׂדֵי
שִׂים	[25]	(to) set, place (*V*)	Root also spelled as שׂוּם
שַׂר	[13]	ruler, prince, official (*NMS*)	*P:* שָׂרִים
		Shin שׁ	
שָׁאוּל	[26]	Saul (*proper N*)	
שֶׁ֫בַע (*M*), שִׁבְעָה (*F*)	[22]	seven (*NM/FS*)	*P:* שִׁבְעִים = "seventy"; שְׁבִיעִי (*M*), שְׁבִיעִית (*F*) = "seventh"
שׁוּב	[25]	(to) turn, return (*V*)	
שָׁלוֹם	[20]	wholeness, well-being, prosperity, peace (*NMS*)	*Cs:* שְׁלוֹם ; *P:* שְׁלוֹמִים
שָׁלַח	[10]	he sent (*V*)	
שְׁלֹמֹה	[20]	Solomon (*proper N*)	
שָׁלֹשׁ or שָׁלוֹשׁ (*M*), שְׁלֹשָׁה (*F*)	[18]	three (*NM/FS*)	*MS Cs:* שְׁלֹשׁ; *FS Cs:* שְׁלֹשֶׁת; *P:* שְׁלֹשִׁים = "thirty"; שְׁלִישִׁי (*M*), שְׁלִישִׁית (*F*) = "third"
שָׁם	[26]	there (*adv*)	
שֵׁם	[8]	name (*NMS*)	*Cs:* שֵׁם, שֶׁם־; *P:* שֵׁמוֹת; שְׁמוֹת
שָׁמַ֫יִם	[14]	heavens, sky (*NMDu*)	Occurs only in dual

	Word		*Translation*	*Notes*
*	שְׁמֹנֶה (*M*), שְׁמֹנָה (*F*)	[25]	eight (*NM/FS*)	*P:* שְׁמֹנִים = "eighty"; שְׁמִינִי (*M*), שְׁמִינִית (*F*) = "eighth"
	שָׁמַע	[10]	he heard, listened (*V*)	When followed by ל or ב (as in שָׁמַע לְקוֹל or שָׁמַע בְּקוֹל), can have the sense of "he listened to" or "he obeyed."
	שָׁמַר	[12]	he kept, watched, guarded (*V*)	
	שָׁנָה	[7]	year (*NFS*)	*Du:* שְׁנָתַיִם; *MP:* שָׁנִים, שְׁנֵי; *FP:* שְׁנוֹת
	שְׁנַיִם (*M*), שְׁתַּיִם (*F*)	[17]	two (*NM/FDu*)	Occurs only in *Du; Cs:* שְׁנֵי (*M*), שְׁתֵּי (*F*); שֵׁנִי (*M*), שֵׁנִית (*F*) = "second"
	שַׁעַר	[26]	gate (*NMS*)	*P:* שְׁעָרִים, שַׁעֲרֵי
	שֵׁשׁ (*M*), שִׁשָּׁה (*F*)	[21]	six (*NM/FS*)	*FS Cs:* שֵׁשֶׁת; *P:* שִׁשִּׁים = "sixty"; שִׁשִּׁי (*M*), שִׁשִּׁית (*F*) = "sixth"
	שָׁתָה	[26]	he drank (*V*)	*Pual* and *hif* for this verb use the root שקה ("drink, water")

TAV ת

	תָּוֶךְ	[17]	midst, middle (*NMS*)	*Cs:* תּוֹךְ
	תּוֹרָה	[16]	instruction, direction, law (*NFS*)	
	תַּחַת	[15]	beneath, under, instead of (*prep*)	*PS:* תַּחְתַּי, תַּחְתֶּיךָ, etc.
*	תֵּשַׁע (*M*), תִּשְׁעָה (*F*)	[25]	nine (*NM/FS*)	*P:* תִּשְׁעִים = "ninety"; תְּשִׁיעִי (*M*), תְּשִׁיעִית (*F*) = "ninth"

Index